# ANTHROPOPOLIS
## City for Human Development

# ANTHROPOPOLIS
## City for Human Development

by C. A. DOXIADIS
and
a symposion with:

RENE DUBOS
ERIK H. ERIKSON
DENNIS GABOR
REGINALD S. LOURIE
MARGARET MEAD
C. H. WADDINGTON
THOMAS A. DOXIADIS
SPYROS A. DOXIADIS

W · W · NORTON & COMPANY · INC · New York

Published simultaneously in Canada
by George J. McLeod Limited, Toronto

Library of Congress Cataloging in Publication Data
Main entry under title:
Anthropopolis: city for human development.

  City for human development by C. A. Doxiadis with
the proceedings of a symposium organized by the
Athens Center of Ekistics and the Doxiadis family
and held July 6-8, 1972, in Athens.

  Bibliography: p.
  Includes index.
  1. Sociology, Urban—Congresses. 2. Cities and
towns—Planning—Congresses, I. Doxiadis,
Kōnstantinos Apostolou, 1913-    City for human
development. 1975. II. Athens Center of Ekistics.
HT107.A65 1975                301.36                75-15881
ISBN 0-393-08721-2

Printed in the United States of America
1   2   3   4   5   6   7   8   9

This book is dedicated to the memory of
Apostolos Th. Doxiadis and Evanthia Ap. Doxiadis
who led their descendants towards human development.

I believe, however, that the Office of Public Health should also include a Social Welfare Department whose objective will be not the healing and the prevention of disease, but the creation of a future generation of robust and vigorous young people capable of carrying on victoriously the civilizing struggle for peace.

Apostolos Th. Doxiadis, 1920

This book is dedicated to the memory of
Apostolos Th. Doxiadis and Evanthia Ap. Doxiadis
who led their descendants towards human development.

I believe, however, that the Office of Public Health should also include a Social Welfare Department whose objective will be not the healing and the prevention of disease, but the creation of a future generation of robust and vigorous young people capable of carrying on victoriously the civilizing struggle for peace.

Apostolos Th. Doxiadis, 1920

# Preface

This is the first of four books which try to transmit the message of the City for Human Development or in a broader sense the human city that we need (*Anthropopolis*), of the inevitable changes of scale from the small polis (town or city of the past) to the present-day megalopolis and to the City of the Future (*Ecumenopolis*), of the realistic way in which we can turn Ecumenopolis into Anthropopolis in order to avoid disasters ( *Building Entopia*), and of the ways in which we can move from theories towards action (*Action for Human Settlements*).

In 1970 it was decided by the Athens Center of Ekistics and by the Doxiadis family to organize a symposion on the City for Human Development to be dedicated to the memory of Apostolos Th. Doxiadis and Evanthia Ap. Doxiadis who brought up five boys, lost one and have helped the others to be developed and to find their roads at the expense of great personal sacrifices.

The symposion was organized in July 1972, and here we present everything that was done or said for a double purpose.

*First*, in order to collect all statements of the participants and learn from the experiences of nine persons with different professional and national backgrounds on such a difficult subject.

*Second*, in order to learn how far such a cross-disciplinary approach in a three-day symposion can lead, as we all badly need to learn how to make the connections which are missing between so many disciplines and sciences.

In attempting to achieve both goals we witnessed successes and failures in answering difficult questions and filling gaps. Although we did fill some of these gaps later, we do not present them here, not only because it was not always easy, but also because it is by the location of such gaps that we learn more. As experts on creativity say, to pose the question is a very big step towards proper creation. This is why no editing in substance of the symposion was done. The only changes we have made are in some terms of my own address (Part One) because I decided later to use simpler and more universal terms such as "Anthropos" instead of "Man"[1], such as "hustreet" (human street), and "eperopolis" (urbanized continent) which are all explained in the glossary.

The road we followed for this whole effort was:

1. I wrote my report on the City for Human Development and distributed it to the other participants in May 1972.
2. Several of them responded by issuing their papers.
3. All of us came together from 6-8 July 1972 in a symposion in Athens at the Athens Center of Ekistics with Margaret Mead as chairman.
4. The audience did not really participate in the discussion but posed questions which were distributed for eventual comments.
5. All reports were then given to the audience and sent to many people, and many parts were published in EKISTICS, April 1973 as edited by Jaqueline Tyrwhitt.

In this whole effort we owe our thanks to all participants, to Kyrkos Doxiadis who organized the meetings, to Jaqueline Tyrwhitt and to Anthy Tripp who acted as Rapporteurs and to my assistants who helped in the long effort from research to printing, J. Zachariou, E. Kaliata, L. Kyriakopoulou, K. Pertsemlidou and M. Maltezou.

C.A. Doxiadis<br>
Athens, May 1974

# Table of contents

## Part One - Anthropopolis: City for Human Development

# Part Two - Symposion on the City for Human Development

# List of illustrations

# Part one

# Anthropopolis:
# City for Human Development

# 1. Introduction

## The subject of the study

The subject of this study is to conceive, define, specify and give shape to the realization of the humane city that we need.  Today we do exist in human cities, but it is doubtful whether we can call them humane.

Even ten years ago such a statement would have been considered an exaggeration, as most people did not consciously realize or admit that our cities are not humane.  Today we have at last gone a step further and have started to realize that the city is not humane.  During this step, unfortunately, we slipped and fell down and we are crying now more than is warranted.  Thus we miss this opportunity to conceive our problem correctly and to face it objectively.  Proof of this is given by all sorts of movements, like "zero growth", which try to lead us to a great change without being fully justified either from a desirable or feasible point of view.  Doomsday is definitely not coming tomorrow and, instead of crying, we would do better to help ourselves constructively to overcome this era of confusion and distress.

Since we now know that our city is not humane, we are obliged to be perfectly clear about what humane means.  We can only be sure that the city as it is now does not serve us as much as we expect.  This failure of the city to serve Anthropos (Man) leads to a need for its re-examination.  We should not take cities as they are now for granted.  Indeed, we should not take anything related to them for granted.  We must start our thinking process by defining how, ideally, we would like them to be.  We should use the occasion of their failure for a thorough re-examination of the kind of city we now have, why and where we want to go, and how we can direct ourselves to go there.

We should not remain merely negative about what happens the wrong way and only protest and cry about what we do not want.  We need to re-examine our attitude when we look at the city; to evaluate its efficiency and to conceive, plan and build the new city according to our new observations.  Our attitude should be the attitude of an active, creative participant. It is time that we turned to normative action. We thus need to define what we mean by the humane city or, in a broader way, what the goal is of the human city. But this is still not enough. When we set a goal we must also define the time we set to establish it: our goal for tomorrow morning differs from our goal for a century from now.

So the next steps must be an attempt to define the goal of the city and to establish a time-concept for its realization that correctly reflects our notion of the future.

## The goal of the city

Today we do not have any common goal for our city, at least not any goal that has been agreed upon between us, and it is very doubtful whether we even have clear, personal goals for the city. The fact that some people have dreams which are expressed as utopias, from heavenly cities to technological monstrosities — or nightmares which are expressed like George Orwell's *1984* dystopia — does not mean that we have common, specific or realistic goals; we have some good and bad dreams from which we can learn but these are not the real goals to serve all human beings.

We are, therefore, letting our city just happen. In a society of free human beings this is all right as we can thus see the natural tendencies of each individual but this does not mean that our city is successful; the sum total of individual efforts does not correspond to the satisfaction of the sum total of all our needs. Our actions are really the result of necessity and chance[2] as is the evolution of biological processes according to many biologists. The big questions are:

*One:* Should we let every need be satisfied by individual efforts, thus creating a system of life by chance as it occurs, having as a result the city serve the needs of the powerful and lucky; or should we conceive and express the needs of mankind as a system?

*Two:* Should we allow such a large percentage of action to come by chance and individual necessity as today; or should we stress the importance of action by the community to build now and serve the needs of all human beings?

There is no doubt about the correct answer to these questions, at least for a large society. Thus we have to define our common goals and try to serve them through common efforts.

Out of all definitions of the goal of the city which we have inherited, I think that there is only one which is valid for all human societies and this is the Aristotelian one: to make the citizens happy and safe. When I used this definition years ago people smiled at the term "happy" and laughed at the term "safe".

4

They said that this could only be achieved when there are no more wars, otherwise we would not survive anyway but they overlooked the internal problems of the city. This is no longer the case and today everybody agrees in substance with this definition.

However, I have gradually learned that this definition is not complete as it corresponds to the condition of the static city of the past when people managed to reach a balance between Nature, Anthropos (Man) and Society and built the walled cities that we so much admire today. What we must recognize now is that our cities are no longer static in any way and we certainly have no balance between what we have inherited and what we build. Everything is changing around us and by our actions when building Shells and Networks we eliminated the last balances that once existed[3].

We now see the results with despair, especially in the protest of the young. The reason is quite clear: we lost the balances that had been created (Fig. 1) and thus we have a constant conflict for Anthropos (Man), who has to adapt to the city continuously changing through chance and necessity. His only other alternative is to adapt the city to his needs which he tries to do but in an unsystematic way and thus he loses the battle and suffers from the results.

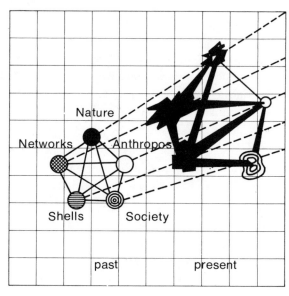

Anthropos is losing more than any other element — Nature is next — the Networks are the big winners — but for whose sake?

# 1. the loss of balance within the city

So we are confronted with a new goal: within a city or system that changes dynamically, that is within dynapolis[4], we cannot accept that the element of our direct personal concern, Anthropos (Man) himself, should only follow the trends and obey them; he must certainly be able to develop further until he reaches a new balance within his system. Then someday his city will stop being dynamic and become static again. He then may decide to stop further development but at present all signs indicate that he needs and wants to develop. In this phase of our life therefore, we must add a third goal: the City for Human Development, which I will call Anthropopolis, from the Greek words meaning "human being" and "city", that is the human or humane city. As this is a new goal which has not been thoroughly investigated before, I used it as the title of this study although the goal of the city in our era is a more complete one connecting past and present experiences: to make the citizens happy and safe and help them in their human development.

## The notion of the future

When we set a goal we can either define a time schedule or not. We will always be confused if we do not give any direction to our thinking and we will never become specific. If we speak of human development as a goal, we can think of it in terms of achieving biological changes or not; depending on this the time schedule changes immensely as does the human role for attaining this goal.

As we are not concerned with theories but with action for human development, we are speaking of goal-oriented efforts and therefore we must define the notion of the future. This needs the clarification of three points.

The first point is that we must define our era in terms of time. I do believe that for our present efforts this time should include tomorrow through to the end of the next century, that is no more than four to five generations. The reasons are many but the most important ones are: first that we cannot know whether major — and completely unpredictable — changes may perhaps happen beyond this time and; second that by then — if not earlier — humanity will have reached another levelling point at which many concepts may change. It may move again towards the notion of the static city which will require another type of human development like the paideia[5] of classical Athens.

The second point to be clarified is that the future is not being created now, as many people tend to believe, but is mostly a continuation of the past. This is why we should not continue to follow the modern trend of looking at the future only and turn our backs on the past. This is very dangerous, as dangerous perhaps as the Homeric notion of Anthropos (Man) looking to the past and turning his back on the future. The correct way is to look at time as a two-headed eagle[6] to understand the continuity of our system of life.

The third point is that we do not deal with one future, but with four (Fig. 2). Therefore in every effort we make we must think of all four futures which have completely different meanings. Thus, if we speak of tomorrow it does not have the same relation between its four ingredients as next year or a generation from now. We must realize that the time concept defines and is defined by them.

The four futures are: *First*, the constant one, such as the dimensions of our earth; *Second*, the declining past, the people who are living today; *Third*, the continuing past, the people who will be born and conditioned by the traditions of their ancestors; *Fourth*, the created future. In this way we must also look at the degree to which every part is inevitable or not, inhuman or human, and depending on this last, whether it should be changed or not (Fig. 3).

## From ideas to action

Any serious person reading these statements and agreeing will state that we need decades and generations in order to define exactly and responsibly how the Anthropopolis should be conceived and built and be sure that this is right.

To such a statement I have only one possible reply: we are not talking about theories as for example, how far the universe goes and how it expands, but about a reality that effects our daily life and our real future. If we could sit back and theorize and wait it would be all right, but this is not the case — every morning we start new buildings, new towers, new highways and thus we make changes and commit the city for generations to come. Here speaks the bricklayer and builder who feels that the needed long-term research should not be used as an escape from the changes that we need now and can implement tomorrow.

In order to reconcile these two views I think that the builder who does make decisions every morning ought to take the initiative and proceed with the development of new approaches and, since he does build the city daily, why not build with an attempt to achieve broader goals? The scholars and experts on Anthropos (Man) and development must then be as critical as possible in order not to allow the builder to follow wrong or unjustified paths.

I started this effort many years ago by trying to ameliorate gradually the city that we were building, by fighting for fences around the houses to protect the children, by refusing to build multi-level fortresses for families with children and several other ways as our projects[7] can demonstrate.

In the process I was made more and more aware of how many mistakes Anthropos (Man) makes today and how big our social responsibility really is.

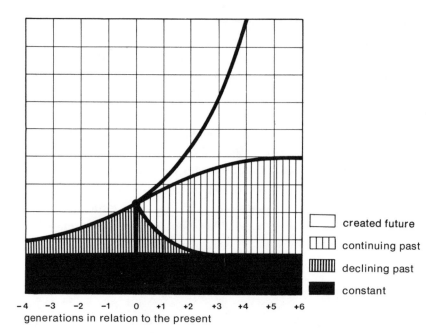

created future

continuing past

declining past

constant

-4  -3  -2  -1  0  +1  +2  +3  +4  +5  +6
generations in relation to the present

2.     the four futures of human settlements

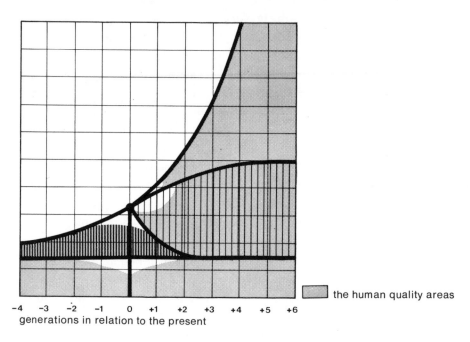

the human quality areas

-4  -3  -2  -1  0  +1  +2  +3  +4  +5  +6
generations in relation to the present

3.     the human future of human settlements

I thus came to the conclusion that to simply try to build what we think is better is not enough, we have to mobilize many resources in order to be sure what is really best, and then try to achieve it everywhere. Then I started presenting these views to several groups ranging from medical to technical in all disciplines, in order to get the correct responses[8]. What I received was great encouragement, but nothing very specific and nothing very systematic for an overall approach. Thus I thought it was my responsibility to present a whole approach in a systematic way and to challenge those who know best about Anthropos (Man).

I therefore take a strong position on many issues where I sometimes cannot prove everything, hoping to have them rejected or accepted, at least they will be debated; the value is the same if we can prove that my opinions are wrong or right because through these debates we will eventually find the truth and truth is the only thing that matters.

This position will be the challenge to our group of experts ranging from physics and development to biology and anthropology, to medicine and psychiatry. The special symposion on this subject will open our eyes on several of the points brought up here as questions or statements and when published will, hopefully, challenge many others to continue the effort of opposing or accepting our findings. In this way our personal efforts will find a broader basis and can be more useful to Anthropos (Man).

## The method

In order to achieve our goals I follow a process that can help us avoid losing too much time going in directions which cannot lead anywhere or are of no interest to Anthropos (Man). For this I always try to define what is feasible; I do not talk about a city on the moon, which was unfortunately the subject for seminars for children in schools and for students, as this can only be an experiment for a few high level scientists. I also try to define what is desirable. The measure is Anthropos (Man), the master, and not any special individuals, as these are matters for each person's own builder. Everyone of us has his needs and ideas but all of us have some common characteristics which are our subject in this study.

To achieve this end, since we do not know enough, we must start by making hypotheses (2. Hypotheses). Some can be justified and some not, but they must be made so as to be rejected, approved or left open to challenge others.

We will then continue with specific elements. We start with the city as a whole (3. The inevitable city) in order to understand the frame that Anthropos (Man) is building for his life and any of his laws which are influencing it.

We continue by studying the great client, Anthropos (Man) himself, and his requirements in all phases of his life (4. Anthropos within his city). Only then can we move to specific proposals related to what we build every morning in every unit of space (5. Specifications for the City of Anthropos).

We conclude by speaking of what we, as the instigators of this program, badly need more than anything else; this is courage, moral and intellectual courage. With this we propose a plan of action (6. Time for action).

# 2.  Hypotheses

## Basic hypothesis

We do not know where we are, we do not even know quite who we are as Alexis Carrel explained in *Man the Unknown* [9]. We are, therefore, uncertain about where we are going or even how to select the road that we must take. We have to develop systematic methods and use scientific knowledge as our basis since the witch doctor approach that we have been following is not very helpful.

Hypothesis, as already stated by others, is the soul of science. We must have the courage to develop the best possible hypotheses and then to put them to the test. Only by doing this can we provide the best possible answers to the questions posed in this system of ideas. Only in this way can we evaluate those answers which have already been tentatively presented; ameliorate them and derive justifiable conclusions. Some of the following series of hypotheses are not new at all to those who know my work[10], nor very difficult to make, but we need to repeat them in order to follow a systematic approach.

*Hypothesis one:* We are dealing with a very complex, dynamic system of life on the surface of the earth, where every part has an influence on the others. These influences follow certain principles and laws, some of which we know and some we do not because of their complexity. But the whole is a dynamically changing system that has positive or negative effects on its parts depending on the criteria we use.

This is not a situation created for the first time by Anthropos (Man) the scientist and technologist; it has always existed. When, for example, the first "metazoa" appeared seven hundred million years ago this was one step beyond the single cells, and a new system was created with new positive and negative effects depending on the criteria that were used. We do not know whether the single cells protested against the changes of their environment.

It is our task to understand as much as we can of our present system in order to achieve our goal of Anthropopolis: a City for Human Development. To achieve this we must be as specific as possible and concentrate on phenomena that we can see and, if possible, measure: Anthropos (Man) and Nature. These are only parts of our system, the other elements of it are Society, Shells and the Networks created by Anthropos (Man) [11]. Each element exercises an influence on the others and every part can react or adapt and adjust to the new influences. We cannot say that the reactions to influences or adaptations to them will be good or bad as they may be either one, depending on each specific case, the relationship that exists between them, the time it happens, the conditions, the speed, and the many other criteria that we may use. Any generalization and oversimplification is very dangerous and can lead to wrong conclusions.

From history we learn that Anthropos (Man) has always adapted to his environment in order to survive, but he has also adjusted the environment to his own needs, thus leading to a balance corresponding to the conditions (static and dynamic) of Anthropos (Man) and Nature at a certain locality and time.

Some people say that at a certain moment Anthropos (Man) ceased to adapt to his environment and began to change it. Personally, I have been unable to find any instance where Anthropos (Man) has not changed the natural environment, in some way at least. When the Paleolithic hunters killed animals and their women pulled out roots or inhabited caves they changed fauna, flora and physical conditions. What has changed with time is the scale of the impact of Anthropos (Man) on Nature (Fig. 4).

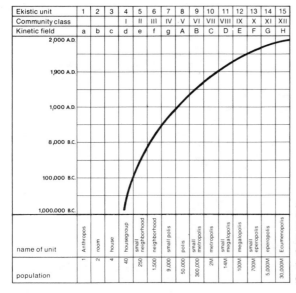

| Ekistic unit | 1 | 2 | 3 | 4 | 5 | 6 | 7 | 8 | 9 | 10 | 11 | 12 | 13 | 14 | 15 |
|---|---|---|---|---|---|---|---|---|---|---|---|---|---|---|---|
| Community class | | | | I | II | III | IV | V | VI | VII | VIII | IX | X | XI | XII |
| Kinetic field | a | b | c | d | e | f | g | A | B | C | D | E | F | G | H |
| name of unit | Anthropos | room | house | housegroup | small neighborhood | neighborhood | small polis | polis | small metropolis | metropolis | small megalopolis | megalopolis | small eperopolis | eperopolis | Ecumenopolis |
| population | 1 | 2 | 4 | 40 | 250 | 1,500 | 9,000 | 50,000 | 300,000 | 2M | 14M | 100M | 700M | 5,000M | 30,000M |

Anthropos started by influencing only the situation in his cave or hut; with the passing of time he influenced small settlements like villages or small towns; today he tends to influence the whole globe in certain ways.

## 4.  the evolution of Anthropos' impact on Nature

## Human needs

As our subject is the human city, we must start our effort to understand the complexity of the system we live in by dealing with human needs.  We are thus led to the study of human evolution and its relationship to the human city.  Such a study led me to the following conclusions.

*Hypothesis two:* Throughout human history Anthropos (Man) has been guided by the same five principles in every attempt he makes to live normally and survive by creating a settlement which is the physical expression of his system of life.

Anthropos (Man) needs to be safe and to feel safe and satisfied from all his relationships, for example with the soil (which must not yield to his weight) and with the air (which must contain enough oxygen and have a temperature corresponding to the biological needs of the human organism).  He also needs to have choices;  the ability and the occasion to select everything in all cases such as his location in space, his food and his contacts.  At times he is guided by desires for a maximum, a minimum or an optimum.  It seems that on all these occasions Anthropos (Man) has been guided by the following five principles.

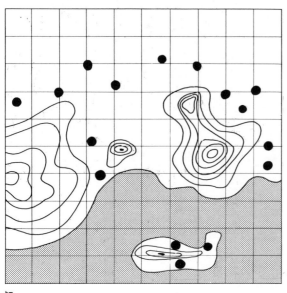

given certain conditions in a certain area

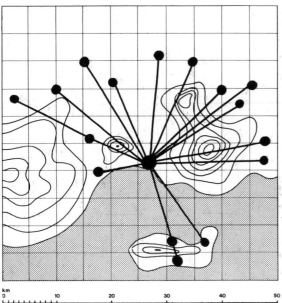

Anthropos will select the location which allows a maximum of potential contacts

5.      first principle: maximization of potential contacts

      example: selection of a new location

The first principle is the maximization of potential contacts. Anthropos (Man) tries from the position he selects to be in contact with other people around him and other elements — like water, food, trees, houses, facilities. He tries to connect. He wants to learn more and to contact more bits of knowledge. Anthropos (Man) has always attempted to increase his contacts with other social groups and their settlements, as for example by climbing the hill to see what is on the other side (Fig. 5). This, after all, amounts to an operational definition of personal human freedom. In accordance with this principle Anthropos (Man) abandoned the garden of Eden and is today attempting to conquer the cosmos.

The second principle is the minimization of effort (Fig. 6) and this can be measured in terms of energy, time and cost. In his attempt to maximize his potential contacts, Anthropos (Man) tries to bring everything close to him. To achieve this in the best possible way he always selects the course requiring his minimum effort.

The third principle is the optimization of Anthropos' (Man's) protective space

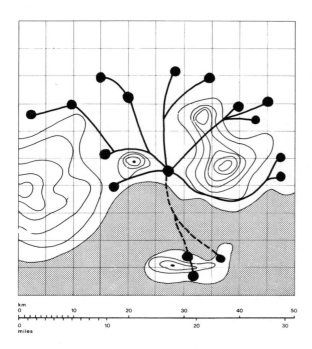

km
0            10            20            30            40            50

0                    10                    20                    30
miles

6.    second principle: minimization of effort in terms of
      energy, time and cost

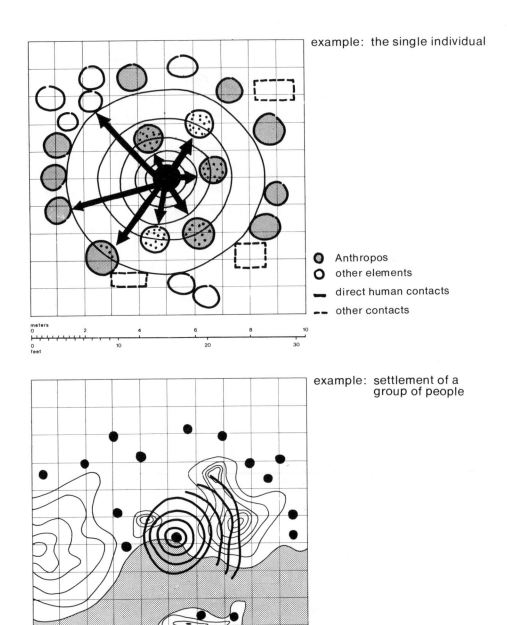

example: the single individual

○ Anthropos
○ other elements
— direct human contacts
-- other contacts

meters
0    2    4    6    8    10

0    10    20    30
feet

example: settlement of a
group of people

km
0    10    20    30    40    50

0    10    20    30
miles

7.    third principle:
       optimization of Anthropos' protective space

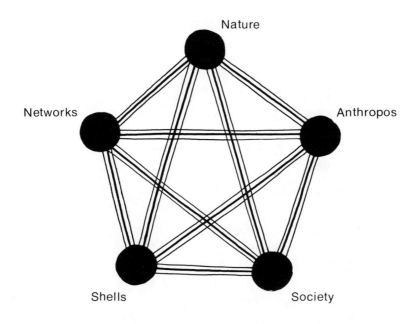

Nature

Networks

Anthropos

Shells

Society

## 8. fourth principle: optimization of the quality of Anthropos' relationship with his system of life

at every moment and in every locality, whether he deals with temporary or permanent situations, whether he is alone or part of a group (Fig. 7). In accordance with the second principle he either pulls the other elements close to him, if he can, or goes close to them. And then the moment comes when he feels crowded and reacts by trying to increase his distance. Anthropos (Man) also needs a protective space which will give him protection from noise, protection from the heat and the energy of others, and protection from his enemies.

The fourth principle is the optimization of Anthropos' (Man's) relationship with the other elements of his system of life, which consists of Nature, Society, Shells (buildings and houses of all sorts) and Networks (from roads to telecommunications) (Fig. 8). It is this system that has lost its balance in our times as we have seen (Fig. 1).

The fifth principle is that of an optimum synthesis of the previous four principles and this depends on time and space, actual conditions, and Anthropos'

(Man's) ability to create his synthesis (Fig. 9 ).  A simple expression can be seen in a room which allows Anthropos (Man) to maximize his contacts with family and friends by minimizing his effort (open a door);  to optimize his protective space (close the door), to optimize his contacts with Nature (open-close doors and windows to control view, temperature, air, etc.), with Society (open-close doors and windows to the street), and with Shells and Networks (in similar ways).

## Human balances

The most confusing question that arises when we deal with the whole system of life on the surface of the earth is which criteria we can use in order to understand the attempts of Anthropos (Man) to adapt himself to Nature and, even more, his attempts to adapt Nature to himself.  Is his action justified or not?  The answer is quite clear when we study human evolution and leads to the following conclusions.

*Hypothesis three:* The most important and most difficult to apply of the five principles serving human needs is the fifth one, guiding Anthropos (Man) to achieve the proper balance between the other four principles.  Anthropos' (Man's) attention to the whole system of life is an indirect one, his main direct

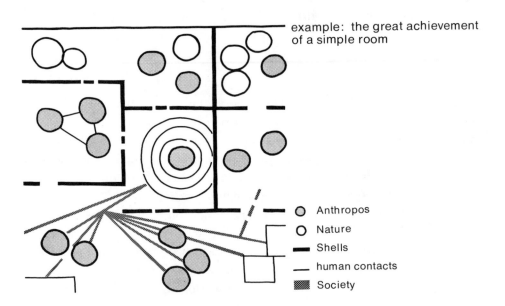

example: the great achievement of a simple room

○ Anthropos
○ Nature
▬ Shells
— human contacts
▨ Society

9.　　fifth principle:
　　optimization in the synthesis of all principles

18

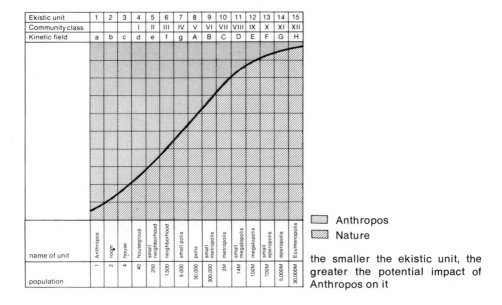

| Ekistic unit | 1 | 2 | 3 | 4 | 5 | 6 | 7 | 8 | 9 | 10 | 11 | 12 | 13 | 14 | 15 |
|---|---|---|---|---|---|---|---|---|---|---|---|---|---|---|---|
| Community class | | | | I | II | III | IV | V | VI | VII | VIII | IX | X | XI | XII |
| Kinetic field | a | b | c | d | e | f | g | A | B | C | D | E | F | G | H |
| name of unit | Anthropos | room | house | housegroup | small neighborhood | neighborhood | small polis | polis | small metropolis | metropolis | small megalopolis | megalopolis | small eperopolis | eperopolis | Ecumenopolis |
| population | 1 | 2 | 4 | 40 | 250 | 1,500 | 9,000 | 50,000 | 300,000 | 2M | 14M | 100M | 700M | 5,000M | 30,000M |

▢ Anthropos
▨ Nature

the smaller the ekistic unit, the greater the potential impact of Anthropos on it

## 10.    relationship of Anthropos and Nature by ekistic units

interest is his own safety and happiness and at times development.  Balance, on the basis of human satisfaction, is Anthropos' (Man's) ultimate goal when dealing with his system of life.  Our goal should be to reach a new balance between Anthropos (Man) and Nature corresponding to the many changes which have occurred as a result of Anthropos' (Man's) exploding forces and needs and his development;  a balance that will no longer be expressed at the village scale (this was the goal ten thousand years ago) or up to the city scale (this became the goal later), but at all scales from Anthropos (Man) to the whole earth.  This means that the system of Anthropos (Man), Nature and the other elements will have to change direction with all of them moving towards the same goal.

To achieve a new balance we must recognize that in small scales Nature has to and can be adapted more to Anthropos (Man) and in big scales Anthropos (Man) and his city have to be adapted more and more to Nature (Fig. 10 ).  A room takes the shape or a street is paved according to Anthropos' (Man's) needs, but the Trans-Asian highway follows the great plains and valleys determined by Nature and the big cities cannot grow in small plains but must adjust to geographic and topographic conditions.

This notion of achieving balance is not simple at all as it depends upon the demands of Nature, Anthropos (Man) and Society and their actions as well as upon the requirements of the Shells and Networks.  Such a balance has to be

19

achieved in many ways such as satisfying the biological needs of all its parts (those of Anthropos (Man) for space, air, etc.) or satisfying the economic, social, political, technological or cultural requirements of Anthropos (Man). Every element of the system should not be considered and evaluated by using one criterion only because different satisfactions can be required by the body of Anthropos (Man) or each of his senses, his mind and soul.

## Human settlements

The use of the term "city" is a simplified and symbolic one as our real subject and concern are the human settlements ranging from nomadic (whether with animals in the desert or trailers on the highways) to the very big cities, from their overbuilt and overcrowded central parts to their farthermost outskirts. Anthropos (Man) lives and will continue to live in human settlements and studying them leads to the following.

*Hypothesis four:* Human settlements have been created by Anthropos (Man) guided by the five principles and have been more successful, made their inhabitants happier and live longer when the fifth principle of a balance between the other four has been better applied.

As we live in an era when the old settlements like villages and cities (as they were structured in the past) begin to disappear and new ones like daily urban systems[12] and megalopolises[13] begin to appear, we can see very clearly that human settlements follow some evolutionary trends. I do not believe that we know enough yet to be completely sure of their evolution but we can clearly see the evolutionary trends. Anthropos (Man) always started his settlements in many different ways, which could perhaps be called initial coincidental efforts which were used really as experiments as Anthropos (Man) learned from them which one served him best and then he continued with many mutations until he eventually found the right direction. What is certain is that when a more satisfactory solution appeared it was the only one that survived.

We can see the truth of this statement in all types of units and at all scales of settlements. The most convincing one is the example of the room for two reasons: first it is the oldest form of ekistic unit conceived by Anthropos (Man), if we disregard pieces of furniture, and second it is the unit which appeared in the greatest numbers. This example confirms the above statements about processes and helps us to understand what is best for Anthropos (Man) from the evolutionary trends that we see.

We can try to follow the morphogenesis of the room. We do not know how and when the formation of a room started. It probably started in many parts of the world, and probably the first rooms had many forms and sizes. We have reason to believe that the first rooms were of moderate size (according to today's standards), but they may have been very small one-person, one-night huts similar, in a way, to those built and used by the apes [14]. In any case the moment came when some primitive people had round huts and others had orthogonal ones, and when there were different types of roofs or, in some cases, no roofs at all. In at least one instance which survives to our time — that of the Bushmen of the Kalahari Desert in southwest Africa — there is no door to the hut; the Bushmen jump into it over the wall [15].

Of great interest for us is the fact, that, no matter how the first room started or how it was developed, the room always ends up, given enough time for the development of a composite settlement, with a flat floor, a flat roof, and vertical orthogonal walls. We can see the reasons for this. Anthropos (Man) probably first builds the horizontal floor, so that he can lie down and rest, and walk without great effort or pain (the second principle). He then tends to build vertical orthogonal walls. The reasons for making the walls vertical and orthogonal are many: when he is in the room he feels at ease with, and likes to see, surfaces that are vertical relative to his line of sight (Fig. 11); he makes the walls vertical also in conformity with the law of gravity; and by making them vertical and orthogonal he accommodates his furniture best and saves space when he builds two rooms side by side (Fig. 12 ). For similar reasons he needs a flat roof: a horizontal surface above his head makes him feel at ease when he is inside the room, and this construction enables him to use larger pieces of natural building materials and to fit one room on top of another without any waste of space, materials, and energy. In this way the form of the room is an extension of Anthropos (Man) in space (in terms of his physical dimensions and senses) and follows biological and structural laws.

Thinking in these terms, we reach the conclusion that the morphogenesis of the room is due to several forces derived either from Anthropos (Man) or directly from Nature. When we move on to the house, the neighborhood, the city, and the metropolis we discover that several forces enter into the game, but their relationships change from case to case. The unit of the metropolis, for example, is too large to be influenced directly by the unit Anthropos (Man) (again, in terms of his physical dimensions and senses) whereas it is influenced by the natural forces of gravity and geographic formation, by modes of transportation, and by organization and growth of the system.

Thinking in this way for all 15 ekistic units, we reach the following conclusion: the changing forces of synthesis which cause morphogenesis within every type of ekistic unit follow a certain pattern which, in terms of percentages, shows a

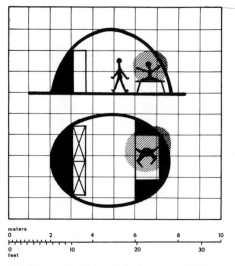

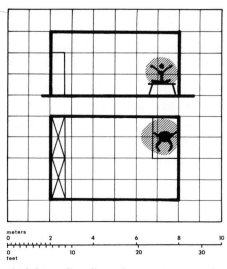

the human bubble of Anthropos whether walking or sleeping enters in conflict with curved walls which lead to waste in the synthesis of furniture to rooms

straight walls allow the most economic synthesis of furniture to rooms

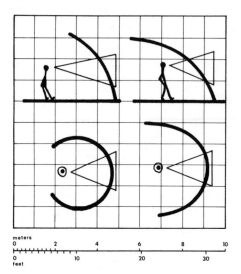

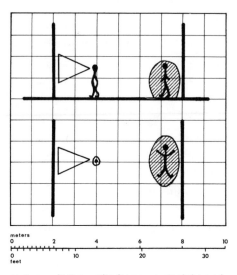

physiological forces like sight strengthen the need of straight vertical walls

as a result the walls become straight and vertical

## 11.   formation of the walls

walls have to fit the body and senses of Anthropos

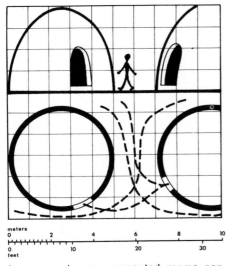

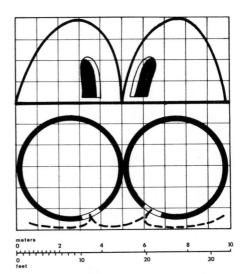

two separate, non-connected rooms can remain independent units but people tend to bring them together in order to save energy

two separate, connected rooms cannot remain independent units: they create many problem-surfaces and are very expensive

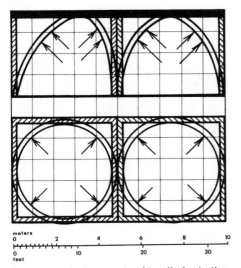

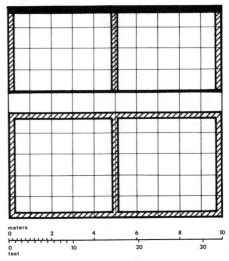

two connected rooms tend to eliminate the problem-surfaces: they tend to a minimum total area and a maximum economy

two connected rooms are united into one structure

## 12.     formation of the walls

decline of the forces derived from Anthropos' (Man's) physical dimensions and personal energy and a growth of those derived directly from Nature itself as a developing and operating system [16].

## Human future

The purpose of this study is not to learn only about the past but to use our experience and knowledge from the past in order to understand our march into the future. Such a study and a great exposure to actual trends in forty years of professional life have completely convinced me of the next hypothesis which is the key one for the development of systematic approaches and proposals.

*Hypothesis five:* Human settlements will be created in the future by Anthropos (Man) guided by his own five principles which should not and cannot be changed. It is therefore our task to learn about them and prepare ourselves for the application of the most difficult and complex of all, the fifth principle: achievement of the best balance between the other four principles for the sake of Anthropos (Man).

If we know the basic principles which guided Anthropos (Man) over perhaps millions of years, and which may have been created by him or before him (I cannot take a position on this aspect) we can see where human settlements are going. Experience shows that human settlements will find the correct road after many coincidental efforts or in special cases conscious goal-oriented efforts. Experience also shows that this effort will take time, leading to many more mistakes and making people suffer over longer periods of time than is necessary.

Our challenge is now the following: either let mistakes continue to happen and let Anthropos (Man) find his road after a long and arduous effort, or take the initiative and open the right road now and create a goal-oriented effort. This latter road is really the dream of many people, some of whom write about utopias, but this is not what we need. Such proposals have lately always existed, have at times been useful, but they do not represent the total traditional trends as they propose the theoretical or practical solution of only one individual for a single case related really only to his own life and theoretical dreams.

Our challenge now is to put aside all our personal dreams and ideas and create a goal-oriented effort representing the desires of Anthropos (Man), our great master. For this we must discover what the inevitable future is which has been decided by Nature and Anthropos (Man); what can be controlled by us; what the most desirable city for Anthropos (Man) is and finally how we can write the specifications for it, lay its foundations and build it.

This is our great task: to help Anthropos (Man) find his own road.

# 3. The inevitable city

## The changing city

Because of science and technology the city changes in a very natural way, but we are still confused and talk about improbable things such as the desirability of the small city, although we know that human kind will always abandon it and run to the big city.

*Hypothesis six:* The big city is inevitable; it is already growing and it is going to grow even more since it is now a multi-speed city. Our task is to discover and understand why the city is changing at present and where this continuous change will lead.

A simple study of this phenomenon reveals that the change came because Anthropos (Man) decided to use machines for transportation [17]. The interconnection of cities to form urban systems is, for the person who uses machines, as natural as was the small, romantic city for the pedestrian. Many small, isolated cities are gradually being interconnected. Their people can now move at higher speeds and in this way their commuting fields, which are parts of their fields of movement (kinetic fields), grow to form systems of cities which give birth to new ones where these kinetic fields overlap (Fig. 13 ). The old, static city is turning into a dynamic city, the polis into dynapolis [18], and finally into an urban system (Fig. 14 ).

Such a change does not happen now for the first time, but has occurred many

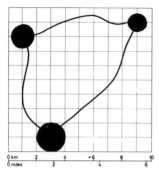

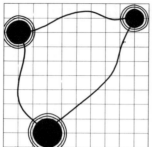

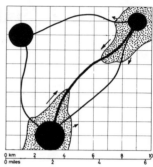

- inhabited built-up areas within a radius of less than ten minutes

- inhabited built-up areas growing because of increase of population

- inhabited built-up areas
- paved road
→ directions of easier traffic and therefore increased number of choices
- ten-minute kinetic field by machines

phase A: pedestrian kinetic fields only

phase B: pedestrian kinetic fields only

phase C: pedestrian and mechanical kinetic fields

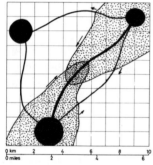

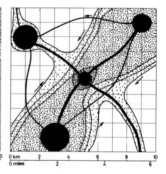

- inhabited built-up areas
- paved road
→ directions of easier traffic and therefore increased number of choices
- number of choices increases much more with overlapping kinetic fields

- inhabited built-up areas
- paved road
→ directions of easier traffic and therefore increased number of choices
- a new center is created in the area of increased choices

- inhabited built-up areas
- paved road
→ directions of easier traffic and therefore increased number of choices
- a new center grows in the area of increased choices

phase D: pedestrian and mechanical kinetic fields

phase E: pedestrian and mechanical kinetic fields

phase F: pedestrian and mechanical kinetic fields

13.    growth of a system

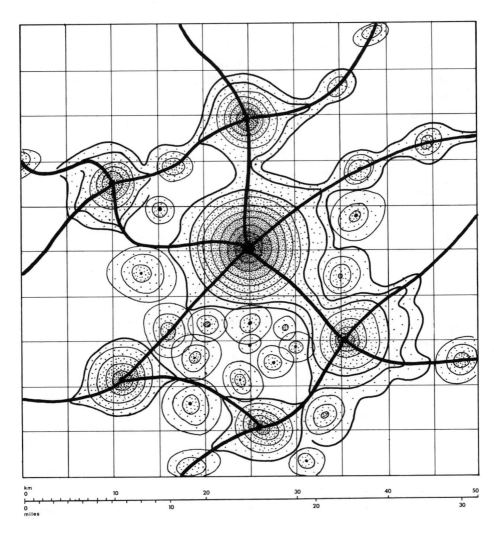

km
0            10            20            30            40            50

0            10            20            30
miles

—— basic structure because of historical development
▬ basic transportation networks

## 14.     the city becomes an urban system

all settlements, towns and villages surrounding the city and new ones
created between and beyond them have now become a part of the
system

27

times in the past. When several villages interconnected into a federation in ancient Greece in the social and economic sense this opened roads between them forming a system and a city or polis was created as their natural center and, probably because of the confusion this caused, Aristotle was forced to explain this phenomenon:

> "The partnership finally composed of several villages is the city-state; it has at last attained the limit of virtually complete self-sufficiency, and thus, while it comes into existence for the sake of life, it exists for the good life. Hence every city-state exists by nature, inasmuch as the first partnerships so exist. . . ".[19]

The cause of the change in those days was not science and technology but the ability for collaboration in larger groups and forming new social structures. The fact is that this change was as revolutionary then as today.

Since the big city is now natural and inevitable, we have to be realistic and define first which characteristics are inevitable and which ones can be changed and second, which ones are desirable and which ones are not (Fig. 15 ). In such a way we can easily decide where we should not worry, as no action is needed, and where we should worry very much and make changes. To achieve this we have to define sectors A, B, C and D as clearly as possible, then maintain the present status of sectors AC, BC and take immediate action in sector BD, like fighting pollution, even though a good solution may take time. The difficulty which we overlook today, as we concentrate on BD, is the sector AD where the situation is inevitable but creates undesirable conditions for Anthropos (Man). This is the sector on which we must concentrate and mobilize all our resources, not to avoid the inevitable, but to create within its framework new conditions which are desirable for Anthropos (Man).

In simpler terms, it is here that we pose the question of how we can create a high quality of life within the inevitable, big City of Anthropos (Man) which is now changing and frightening us.

## Inevitable structure

To achieve these goals we have to understand the inevitable changes in order to be certain of the new framework that is being created now. The first change to be understood is the completely new structure of human settlements. Experience has already shown that we are proceeding towards new shapes which means new structures.

*Hypothesis seven:* The future city will be much more complex in every respect for many reasons, from new technology and new dimensions (as we have

| | realistic prospects | A | B |
|---|---|---|---|
| | realistic evaluations | inevitable development | change is possible |
| C | desirable for Anthropos | no need for new type of action | no need for new type of action |
| D | not desirable for Anthropos | need for action for new concepts and basic changes | need for action for change |

## 15.    the changing city

already seen) to the three spatial forces which condition its shape.   All these factors taken together lead to a very high degree of complexity.

The three spatial forces which increase the complexity beyond those that the multi-speed systems create, are the attraction of:  existing urban systems, the existing and new lines of transportation and the esthetic forces.   Through these the complexity will increase as human settlements spread over wide areas and embrace new human settlements.   There is, therefore, no way of designing the shape of any one of them unless we analyze it very carefully.

In such a way we can see how several isolated settlements of the past (which we still think are isolated) are gradually becoming parts of one system (Fig. 16 ) and how the inevitable structure will be very confusing because of the many forces that will cause it.

Within such a structure we must expect a very wide range of densities of population from very high to very low. A correct study of the evolution of human settlements shows that their density increased or decreased with civilization until it reached an optimum of 200 persons per hectare (80 persons per acre) inside the city. The density occasionally increased beyond this because of danger or need but was reduced again when possible to the level of 200 persons per hectare. When mechanical means of transportation were added, then the density of the whole system was lowered although we are not able to say how much of this was due to the desire for a lower density and how much to a need for escape from the bad conditions of cities. It is my experience that many people still need to live in the optimum historical density of 200 persons per hectare (80 persons per acre) which was higher than present ones in many cities but now we do not give them the chance to do so because of *too much mishandled energy* (from air and space pollution to noise, etc.).

The reasonable forecast on the basis of the existing trends is to foresee the continuation of the trend for a lower total density than at present for the immediate future of suffering cities, although certain of their parts will have an unprecedented high density, as the present trends will continue and cannot change until we provide better solutions. Thus the total complexity will also increase because of too many density variations.


## Inevitable dimensions

The big city which spreads and increases its complexity is not a phenomenon that can be stopped, at least not overnight, as it is the result of too many forces which are not under the control of Anthropos (Man). Here we must remember that we are speaking of the future in terms of a few generations (see page 6 ).

*Hypothesis eight:* The future city will grow much more than the city of the present because of the growth of population, which will take time to be slowed down, because of the growth of income and energy which is needed and demanded by all and because of the growth of Anthropos' (Man's) mobility. The levelling off of the population of the earth will be achieved in a few generations and that of cities some time later.

The probable evolution of the population, in terms of numbers, tends towards a levelling-off point, but how this could and should be achieved is still debatable. We are not yet sure how many people the earth can sustain. We can assume

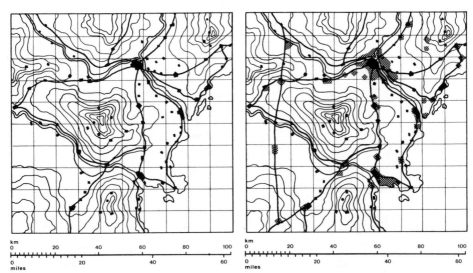

km
0    20    40    60    80    100
0         20         40         60
miles

beginning of the urban era: cities (polis)

early dynapolis: expansion as the static city becomes the center of larger political units

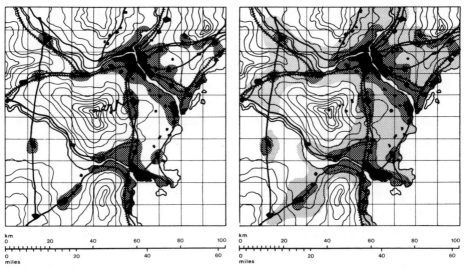

km
0    20    40    60    80    100
0         20         40         60
miles

dynapolis: expansion in the industrial and railroad era

dynametropolis: expansion in the automobile era

## 16.    the changing structure of human settlements

that, as in every similar situation, there is a natural phase of levelling-off and that we will reach it some day, but nobody can tell yet which day this will be.   On the basis of our calculations and assumptions we have arrived at a conclusion; that the population will level off in the next three to five generations, and that such an evolution will lead to a population of several billions more than at present.[20]

Even if we assume that we could do the impossible and effect an immediate levelling-off of the earth's population, the urban population would still increase to three times its present size, first because of the operation of principles one and two, and second because of the greater energy which will be available to Anthropos (Man), allowing him to inhabit larger urban settlements and to commute to his fields of endeavor.

The probable evolution of energy available to Anthropos (Man) is going to be such that even if the size of the urban population were to be immediately stabilized — which is out of the question — the total area of human settlements will still continue to grow in terms of activity and interaction of people which will require a much larger area.   The end result will be a greater total potential of the city.   We are not yet ready to measure this evolution accurately but the very fact that the energy consumed per capita today in the U.S.A. is 200,000 Cal. versus 4,000 Cal. in India shows what kind of development we must expect.

On the basis of these assumptions, we must expect the human settlements to continue to grow and to attain overwhelming dimensions.   Even without any growth of the total population of the earth, the urban settlements will have three times their present population, cover six times their present area, earn income and expend many times more energy than the present settlements.   If the population of the earth only doubles, and this is an unrealistically conservative and very improbable assumption, then the urban settlements will have 6 times the population, at least 12 times the area, 18 times the income and much more energy.

Such a growth can be understood if we take the case of the average city of the United States which was conceived by a congressional committee in Thomas Jefferson's time as corresponding to a 6 × 6 miles (10 × 10 km) square because of the notion of one hour's maximum distance for any citizen walking from the center.   This figure has become in 1960 a city 300 times larger in area (Fig. 17 ), growing at the rate of 2% to 3% per year.

Such growth leads to a crisis which is going to be intensified within each city and influence the whole globe more and more.   Our attention must be turned to the urban systems which are now under formation not only because Nature becomes a victim within and around them, but also because we spend the greatest part of our lives in them and because the problems already described are not the only ones which we have to face.

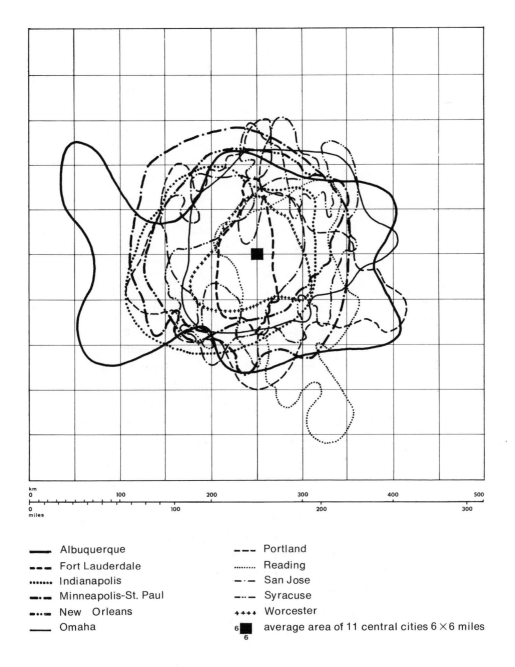

km
0          100          200          300          400          500
0                    100                    200                    300
miles

——— Albuquerque          ——— Portland
—■—■ Fort Lauderdale      ......... Reading
•••••••• Indianapolis     —·— San Jose
—■·■ Minneapolis-St. Paul —··— Syracuse
—■··■ New   Orleans       ++++ Worcester
——— Omaha                 average area of 11 central cities 6 × 6 miles

17.      commuting fields of 11 cities of the United States in
         1960

33

If we look at the dimensions of the urban systems which, more than anything else, define the conditions of life within them, we will see that their population will increase much more than the present one (Fig. 18). No matter how success-ful we can be in controlling the global population's growth we should not, and in any case cannot, control the influx of rural people to the urban systems. Throughout human history, Anthropos (Man) needs to maximize his potential contacts (first principle), he wants to live in larger systems and present-day tech-nology helps to bring him to the urban systems. We can turn to China, which still tries today to keep people by force on the farms, and we learn what happens if we attempt to stop people from coming to the city: they will enter it anyway, even without permits, and the young ones, deprived of the right to work, may stay and turn into revolutionaries or thieves.

Growth of the population of the earth will lead to much greater growth in the areas of the urban systems and even greater growth of energy within them. In the past, the growth of cities increased when their area of influence increased, but then the citizens were closer together. We could say that the bigger the city the higher the density. Now, the transportation networks help people to move farther and farther out and the areas can grow together with population and energy with the exception of complexity which is increasing the most. The trends up to now show that the area does not increase so much (Fig. 19 )but this is the case of one city in the older sense of the word only and not of the total urban system within which people are really living. If we consider this system as in Fig. 17, we do find that the area also increases enormously.

## The increasing problems

Increasing dimensions lead necessarily to a new type of city with changing prob-lems some of which have been solved, like directing waste water through sew-ers, while others are increasing in intensity, like noise and much more com-plexity. The five elements of human settlements which were at times in balance (Fig. 8 ) are now changing (Fig. 1 ) and thus even if we see them as static ones they lose any balance (Fig. 20 ). In a different way we can see a simplified type of eval-uation of the quality of terrestrial space (Fig. 21) and relate the feasible evolution either to individuals or to Anthropos (Man) as a whole.

*Hypothesis nine:* Our city is in a crisis which is due to the lack of balance between its five elements; there are certainly many reasons for this, but the basic one is the increase in all its dimensions (people, area, energy, economy, com-plexity, etc.) and the change in its physical structure all leading to an increase of problems. I think that as we have learned from psychiatry that anatomy is desti-

## Top table

| | feasible evolution in relation to present situation | | | | |
|---|---|---|---|---|---|
| **desirable evolution in relation to present situation** | **- -** | **-** | **=** | **+** | **+ +** |
| **- -** | -2 / -2 → -4 | -2 / -2 → -4 | -2 / -2 → -4 | +1 / -2 → -1 | +2 / -2 → 0 |
| **-** | -2 / -2 → -4 | -2 / -2 → -4 | -2 / -2 → -4 | +1 / -2 → -1 | +2 / -2 → 0 |
| **=** | -2 / -2 → -4 | -2 / -2 → -4 | -2 / -2 → -4 | +1 / -2 → -1 | +2 / -2 → 0 |
| **+** | -2 / +1 → -1 | -2 / +1 → -1 | -2 / +1 → -1 | +1 / +1 → +2 | +2 / +1 → +3 |
| **+ +** | -2 / +2 → 0 | -2 / +2 → 0 | -2 / +2 → 0 | +1 / +2 → +3 | +2 / +2 → +4 |

the figures in every small triangle correspond to the *degree of probability* of every feasible or desirable type of evolution and range from −2 (very improbable) to +2 (very probable)

the figures in every large triangle correspond to the *attention* that must be given to it and range from the highest degree of +4 to the lowest of −4

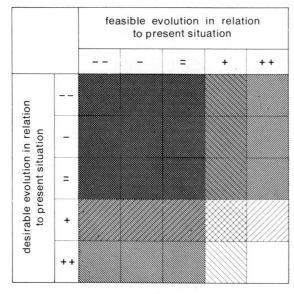

the shades in every square correspond to the attention that must be given to it and range from the highest degree of +4 □ to the lowest of −4 ▓

18.     probability of population trends of the urban systems by 2000 A.D.

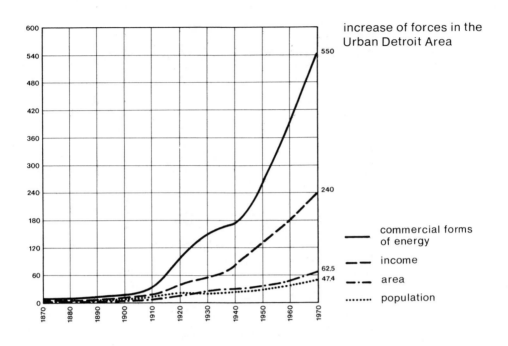

increase of forces in the
Urban Detroit Area

——— commercial forms
of energy

– – income

–·– area

········ population

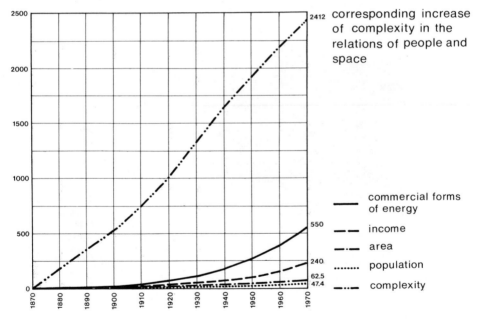

corresponding increase
of complexity in the
relations of people and
space

——— commercial forms
of energy

– – income

–·– area

········ population

–·–·– complexity

19.    growth of an urban area

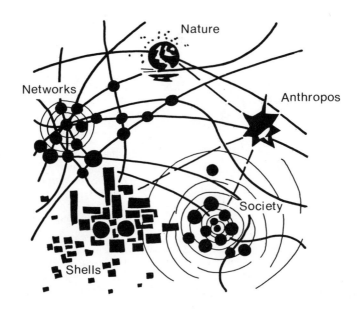

## 20. the five elements of human settlements are now out of balance

ny for Anthropos (Man), this is also valid for the city: its anatomy is destiny.

There are many questions depending upon whether we refer to Anthropos (Man) who is changing, or Society, or culture and they are all justified as such but very difficult to answer. But the questions of changing dimensions can be faced most easily as dimensions are measurable. We can take an example of a confusing social phenomenon, the case of the "blue people" who are considered new types of people and lead many to distress, but their case could well be due only to changing dimensions.

If we assume that one out of 500 persons of this earth is "different" from the others, let us call him a blue person, this means that in the era of villages with green people (farmers and peasants) there would be one blue person per village (Fig. 22) who was sometimes called "crazy" by the others. Even if he was the genius of the era, he was isolated and could decline and be lost. In the big city of red people (urban dwellers) the same blue people are many, although they remain one in 500, they can unite and express a certain new movement which for the majority can be good or bad, right or wrong. In the same way we can understand that an urban system of ten million people has 20,000 blue people who can create

## Feasible evolution in relation to present situation for individuals

| (Anthropos ↓ / individuals →) | – – | – | = | + | + + |
|---|---|---|---|---|---|
| **– –** | +2 +2 / +4 | +2 +2 / +4 | 0 +2 / +2 | –1 +2 / +1 | –2 +2 / 0. |
| **–** | +2 +2 / +4 | +2 +2 / +4 | 0 +2 / +2 | –1 +2 / +1 | –2 +2 / 0 |
| **=** | +2 –1 / +1 | +2 –1 / +1 | 0 –1 / –1 | –1 –1 / –2 | –2 –1 / –3 |
| **+** | +2 –2 / 0 | +2 –2 / 0 | 0 –2 / –2 | –1 –2 / –3 | –2 –2 / –4 |
| **+ +** | +2 –2 / 0 | +2 –2 / 0 | 0 –2 / –2 | –1 –2 / –3 | –2 –2 / –4 |

(row labels = feasible evolution in relation to present situation for Anthropos all over the world)

the figures in every small triangle correspond to the *degree of probability* of every feasible or desirable type of evolution and range from −2 (very improbable) to +2 (very probable)

the figures in every large triangle correspond to the *attention* that must be given to it and range from the highest degree of +4 to the lowest of −4

## Feasible evolution in relation to present situation for individuals

(shaded grid; rows = feasible evolution in relation to present situation for Anthropos all over the world: – –, –, =, +, + +; columns for individuals: – –, –, =, +, + +)

the shades in every square correspond to the attention that must be given to it and range from the highest degree of +4 ☐ to the lowest of −4 ▓

21.  quality of terrestrial space for individuals and for Anthropos as a whole on the basis of present trends

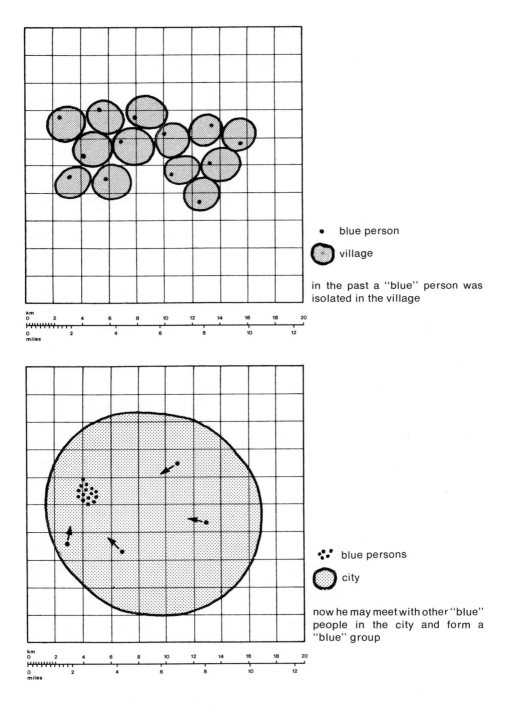

· blue person

⬤ village

in the past a "blue" person was isolated in the village

∴· blue persons

◯ city

now he may meet with other "blue" people in the city and form a "blue" group

22.  new formations of social groups

many groups with new movements and that a country with 200 million can easily assemble 400,000 for any movement, be it blue, or yellow. The Woodstock pheno-menon, where about 400,000 young people met for a few days to express them-selves in their own way, is therefore a very normal movement and there will be many such expressions, from liberation movements to political parties like the "dwarfs" of Holland [21] some of which will have greater influence than others. If we remember that we not only have blue people but also yellow, orange and violet and many other colors we will better understand the formations that come into being in an urban area.

From such a case we can see that it is probably not Anthropos (Man) who is changing as we often think, but the system. The case of increasing crime may well be similar. It could be due not to the change of Anthropos (Man), but to the change of the system and the degree of exposure of one person to the other. We do have more crimes reported in the big cities, but authorities on crime agree that this may well be because the reporting of crimes has increased with urbaniza-tion. We cannot use crime statistics for any comparison of one type of human settlements with another. Let us look at two areas of ten million people, one New York City and the other in open country (Fig. 23). Can we really say that the situa-tions are similar, when in one instance all criminals among the ten million people live not more than one hour distant from the other citizens, and in the other they may live days away? We do not know the correlation between crime and cities, except in the cases of crimes related to illegal distribution of drugs: it is in the more central and densely built areas (provided the inhabitants have low incomes and the structures are of low quality) that illegal drugs are distributed most widely. This is an immense social problem related in one way to the physical structure of the city.

Because we do not understand the changing situation and its real causes we turn into a crisis-oriented society and always complain about specific problems like housing (which is not new at all) or the natural environment which we think we are now spoiling when we forget the sewers in London and Paris a century ago. We really forget two things; first that there are many other problems, like the child lost in the big city, and second: that our real problem is the sum total of all these problems and only if we look at them as a system can we understand their relative importance and decide on priorities and solutions.

The result is a very great confusion and our inability to face the situation. We get more confused and we mix up problems which we do not need to do; for example when we relate the problems of our present-day city with the global pollution of the oceans or the decreasing global resources. These problems will affect all human beings and very indirectly the city, but they are not the problems

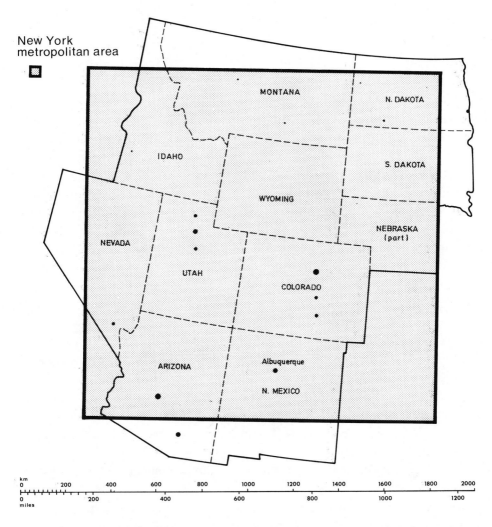

New York
metropolitan area

MONTANA · · N. DAKOTA

IDAHO · S. DAKOTA

WYOMING

NEBRASKA
(part)

NEVADA

UTAH

COLORADO

ARIZONA Albuquerque

N. MEXICO

| km | | | | | | | | | | |
|---|---|---|---|---|---|---|---|---|---|---|
| 0 | 200 | 400 | 600 | 800 | 1000 | 1200 | 1400 | 1600 | 1800 | 2000 |

| 0 | 200 | 400 | 600 | 800 | 1000 | 1200 |
|---|---|---|---|---|---|---|
| miles | | | | | | |

in metropolitan New York ten million people live in an area of 3,127 sq. km. or 1,208 sq.
miles
in the north of the U.S.A. we have to cover almost eleven states in an area of 2,731,000
sq. km. or 1,055,000 sq. miles to find ten million people
this is the reason we hear so much about crime in the one area and not in the other

23.     comparison of two areas of ten million people
         shown  on the same scale

of cities, and therefore we should learn the real scale of our phenomena and their relationships.

## Ecumenopolis

Dimensions increase and will continue increasing for a few generations and thus the most probable future in definable terms will mean a very large increase of population and energy in the City of Anthropos (Man) (Fig. 24).

*Hypothesis ten:* The inevitable evolution in the structure and the dimensions of the city will lead to a universal city, Ecumenopolis, which once again will be a static city like the ancient ones and therefore it will inevitably reach a balance of its elements.

This evolution will occur by stages in the next few generations. First with the spread of the present-day urban systems, this will lead them to interconnect as has already happened to smaller cities (Figs. 13 and 14) but this time over wider areas and the resulting settlements will be the first megalopolises, then will come the urbanized continent or eperopolis, and finally the universal City of Anthropos (Man), Ecumenopolis (Fig. 25).

These systems are inevitable and their foundation stone was laid in 1825 when the first railway ran with passengers in northern England. They are already 147 years old and they are going to become much larger. The trouble is that we do not understand these facts of life, we close our eyes in fear and we let our systems remain without proper structure, leading more and more towards bad conditions and bad qualities of life.

This change of dimensions is the inevitable future of human settlements in the next few generations and we can well foresee, assuming that we avoid any major catastrophe, that we will have to deal with a universal city whose population will tend to be stable in numbers but increasingly more developed intellectually and socially, which will dispose of much greater quantities of energy and achieve greater social interaction.

This is the kind of city where the whole of mankind will live or tend to live. This is the inevitable, natural City of Anthropos (Man) which we cannot abandon any longer. More now than at any time in the past, the poet was right in his predictions even though he wrote them for a smaller city of the past:

"You will not find new lands, not find another sea.

The city will follow you. You'll wander down

these very streets, age in these same quarters of the town,

among the same houses finally turn grey.

You'll reach this city always".[22]

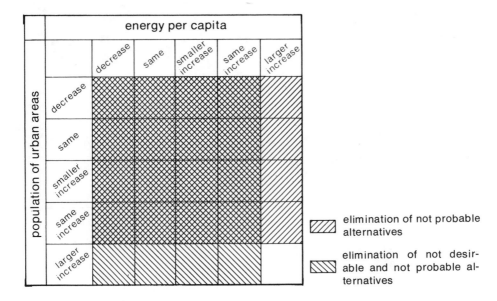

24.    the most probable future defined by the Isolation of
       Dimensions and Elimination of Alternatives
       (IDEA method)

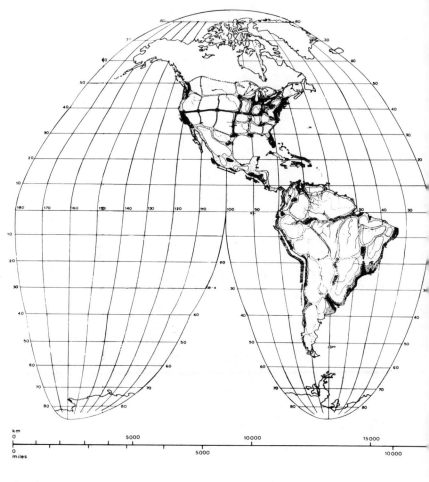

densities

■ high
▨ medium
▢ low
≋ deep ocean waters

25.     Ecumenopolis on a global scale

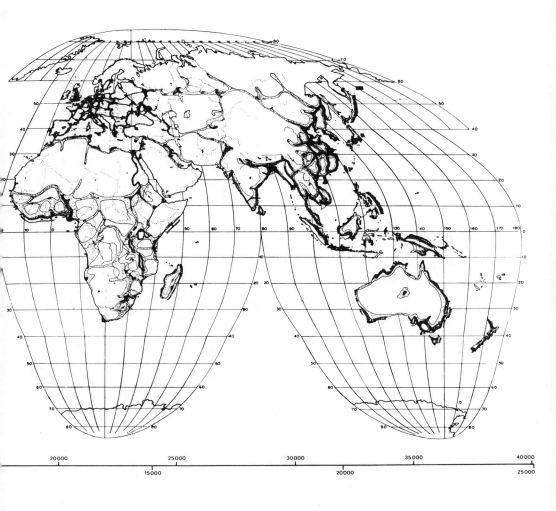

# 4.  Anthropos (Man) within his city

## Human development

We have seen that we must reach a balance between the five elements of our system of life (hypothesis ten) but we have also seen that some day the whole system will reach a balance which could again be called a static city.  Does this mean that we tend towards a phase when Anthropos (Man) will not develop more than before?  I do not believe that this needs to happen, but it may well have to happen.  The fact is that such a phase of a static city is generations ahead and this question is not a basic one neither for the subject of this study nor for the capacity of its author.

Our goal is to direct the whole system to find as early as possible a balance that will help Anthropos (Man) to be happy and safe, so that he may develop further in a positive and creative way without adjusting himself to any change of the system that is not desirable for him.  We must not put him in a position where he must over-adjust himself even to personally desirable changes as such action may be disastrous for him, lead him to decline, depression, etc.  Even a generation ago, Alexis Carrel warned us about this:

> "Civilization has created new stimuli against which we have no defense.  Our organism tries in vain to adapt itself to the noises of the large cities and factories, to the agitation of modern life, the worries and the crowding of our days.  We do not get used to lack of sleep.  We are incapable of resisting hypnotic poisons, such as opium or cocaine.  Strange to say, we adjust ourselves without suffering to most of these conditions.  But such adjustment is far from being a victorious

adaptation. It brings about organic and mental changes which are equivalent to a degradation of civilized Man". [23]

And again:

"We utilize our adaptive functions much less than our ancestors did. For a quarter of a century, especially, we have accommodated ourselves to our environment through mechanisms created by our intelligence, and no longer through physiological mechanisms. Science has supplied us with means for keeping our intraorganic equilibrium, which are more agreeable and less laborious than the natural processes. We have mentioned how the physical conditions of our daily life are prevented from varying; how muscular exercise, food, and sleep are standardized; how modern civilization has done away with effort and moral responsibility, and transformed the modes of activity of our muscular, nervous, circulatory, and glandular systems". [24]

At this stage we must clarify that we always speak of Anthropos (Man) with a capital "A" and therefore use the case of an average person in the broadest sense of the word, because only by defining him in such a way can we conceive *the city*, where people live together with their common desires and characteristics. But, at the same time, we must recognize that people, as individuals, tend to be different and insure that this will be *the city of free human beings* and not of bees or ants.

Since I am speaking of common desires and characteristics, we must recall the established and unchanging human constants several of which are now overlooked. This can be proved by the fact that we forget completely what the human scale is, a scale defined by Anthropos (Man) as an organism, his body, his senses, his mind and probably his soul; this composite, total Anthropos (Man) has not changed at all for at least ten thousand years. If we dispute this truth, we should try to cross a street without observing the red light or try to enjoy a modern avenue as people did in the old cities. A study of the ancient Greek city[25] demonstrates the existence of human scale at all levels from the room, to the agora, to the stadium, to the city-state. Anthropos (Man) needed space corresponding to his own dimensions and he managed to form it, but contemporary Anthropos (Man) has now forgotten it.

How do we want Anthropos (Man) to develop? Here we must again recognize that we speak of the average Anthropos (Man) and Society as a whole and the goals he has set. We have certainly had societies such as that of ancient Sparta where the goal in life was attack and defense, or the great Mongols where a man had to be developed as a soldier able to attack and conquer, or the British in the colonial era where their goal was to develop some of their people to govern other nations of "lower" standard. Our goal cannot be a repetition of these efforts of such societies, but that of what we could call average societies, trying to develop Anthropos (Man) to be happy and safe, both for his own sake and for the benefit of society as a whole.

The question then arises, what kind of a person and which process is the ideal for creating such a situation? I must certainly admit that this requires a very difficult answer. We have so many theories that I cannot, being no expert, take any position on such questions as, for example, to what extent B.F. Skinner was correct in his theories presented in *Walden Two* or in *Beyond Freedom and Dignity*[26]. I can only depend upon the notion that Anthropos (Man) himself needs to be happy, safe and free to develop. The needs of Society require him to be humane and he therefore believes in humane development.

If we speak, though, of the average person and his development, the question then arises: What should be the method to encourage and help a few to reach very high and thus to lift the average or, to help all (Fig. 26)? How do we reach our goals — by interfering genetically with few or many — or by taking care of overall social development?

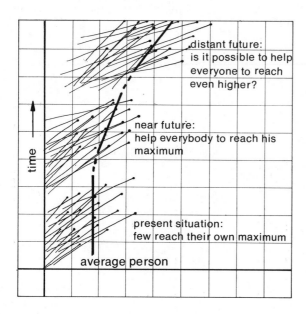

26. human development

*Hypothesis eleven:* Human development must have as a goal first: to help the average person develop to the maximum of his potential (as we do now for longevity) and second: to gradually increase the level of this potential to its maximum in order to help humanity develop further.

This second goal certainly is reminiscent of the statement of Teilhard de Chardin: "Man the ascending arrow of the great biological synthesis". [27] But how quickly this ascending arrow can now ascend I do not know.

On this goal and its feasibility I cannot take a position, but I am prepared to present it as a dream even if it is a very distant one, beyond the time-frame already set by us. In any case, we can hope that, although the genetical evolution of Anthropos (Man) is already preconditioned, we may have the possibility of intervention to avoid some genetic defects and gradually, at some unknown date, reach higher levels.

In this way we can dream of a future which will help Anthropos (Man) develop his body fully (achieve proper health, food and biological environment) and elevate further his total system in terms of his senses, mind and soul because we have no sign that these aspects have reached their maximum, at least not in our era. In any case, since the numbers of people will increase, the total potential of Anthropos (Man) will be much greater than at present (Fig. 27).

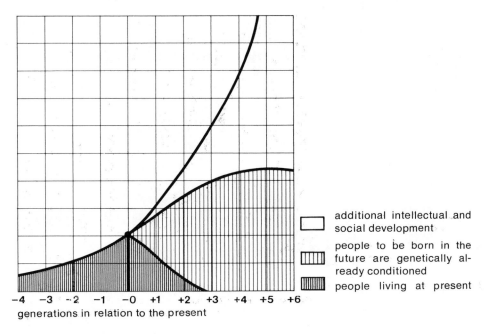

additional intellectual and social development

people to be born in the future are genetically already conditioned

people living at present

generations in relation to the present

27.    the total potential of Anthropos in the future

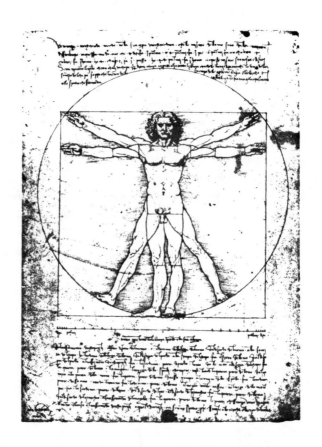

28.    the human bubble as drawn by Leonardo da Vinci:
       the body defines the bubble

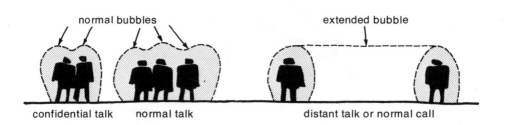

normal bubbles

extended bubble

confidential talk    normal talk

distant talk or normal call

29.    the human bubbles as conceived by E.T. Hall

## The developing human system

We must now look at Anthropos (Man) as a system; he consists of many parts and can be viewed in many ways, this presents many possible single or combined aspects like body, senses, mind and soul. To understand total Anthropos (Man) in space we can proceed as follows: If we consider only his body we can present him as Leonardo da Vinci did by showing the limits of his body alone (Fig. 28). But Anthropos (Man) needs more space than that occupied by his body. Anthropos (Man) really occupies a "human bubble" as Edward T. Hall [28] called it. Such bubbles define the relationships of several people in space (Fig. 29). [29] If next we attempt to present not only Anthropos'(Man's) body, but also the four aspects of Anthropos (Man) as a sequence of spheres, we can see his real relation to space (Fig. 30). Anthropos' (Man's) body occupies the smallest sphere; then comes the sphere of his senses; then the sphere of his mind (whether of one person or of all of us — the "noosphere" as Teilhard de Chardin[30] has called it); then the unknown sphere of his soul which reaches perhaps beyond the one of the mind.

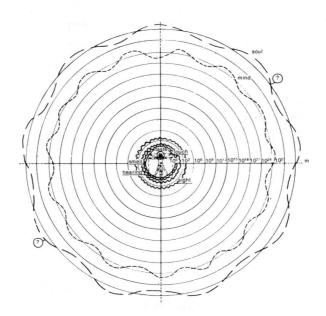

30.     total Anthropos is the center of a system of spheres
        defined by his body, senses, mind and soul

Our goal is to lead this whole system to a balanced development, as in ancient Athens, and not to lay a special emphasis on a single aspect like the intellectual one as, for example, in ancient Rome where even a philosopher like Seneca attacked the notion of athletic training. To achieve this we must understand all aspects of Anthropos (Man) and all his capacities to find the "causal relationships", as C.H. Waddington [31] called them, between all of these and the other elements of human settlements. Otherwise, there is no hope of understanding the system in relation to all Anthropos'(Man's) aspects as anyone sees them, whether from a rational or an esthetic view.

To understand the system and the causal relationships within it we must understand all of its parts and first of all Anthropos (Man) himself. The question then arises which type of Anthropos (Man) shall we study out of the three and a half billion people who are alive today, or the many more who have lived and those who are going to be born. There is no question that there are as many types of people as the total number of individuals and that they can be grouped in all possible ways, ethnic, racial, etc. We can find different characteristics and habits everywhere (Fig. 31). Margaret Mead stated recently "that even the Chinese in America are different in two cities like in New York and in San Francisco". [32] There is no doubt, too, that all these people are constantly changing and do not accept today everything that they accepted yesterday. We cannot take any single individual or case. It is impossible to speak about any special type of person and so, as we have already said, we must speak of all human beings with all their common characteristics.

How can we study the relations of Anthropos (Man) with his settlements in such a general way? The answer is that once we speak of balanced human development, Anthropos' (Man's) relationship to the whole system must be examined by the phases of his life: as in this respect we do witness similar phenomena all over the world. This, I think, is the single most important classification for our goals and can be followed later by many others.

*Hypothesis twelve:* The greatest difference which exists in the relationship of Anthropos (Man) and his settlements is the difference between people in varying phases of their life. Any grown-up can walk in the street with cars; even if he has not seen one before he can adjust to them, but not so a one-year-old child. This certainly would be much more difficult for an adult living in a primitive cultural phase but still, he could more easily save himself from such a great danger than the child can.

We have to study Anthropos (Man) as a developing system on the basis of "life cycles" as Erik Erikson[33] has so clearly stated and to remember that old successful cultures found solutions for balances throughout the life cycle. At present

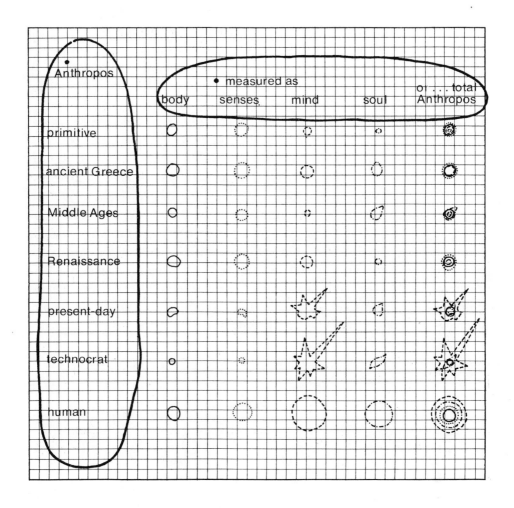

| Anthropos | measured as | | | | or ... total Anthropos |
|---|---|---|---|---|---|
| | body | senses | mind | soul | |
| primitive | ○ | ○ | ○ | ○ | ◎ |
| ancient Greece | ○ | ○ | ○ | ○ | ○ |
| Middle Ages | ○ | ○ | ○ | ○ | ○ |
| Renaissance | ○ | ○ | ○ | ○ | ◎ |
| present-day | ○ | ○ | ✲ | ○ | ✲ |
| technocrat | ○ | ○ | ✲ | ○ | ✲ |
| human | ○ | ○ | ○ | ○ | ◎ |

31.  a symbolic presentation of some types of people in accordance to their culture and phase of development

we have lost this balance because we are in the middle of a great explosion [34], We therefore must find the truth about all periods during the life cycle and make all the necessary connections. This has been done already in many ways as I found out by reading several related studies, some of which are admirable for their great details. The problem is that there are so many studies covering endless details that the total picture is missing and several aspects of the system are not known at all, although many sciences now may be dealing with them.

When this problem came up during previous discussions, Robert Aldrich used the "watermelon" diagram (Fig. 32) [35] showing the many phases of life from birth to death.  At these discussions all participants agreed that we know little about how each curve changes.  I cannot add anything more now about how these changes occur but, as we have to build the foundations for understanding the whole system, I can only suggest that we give this structure certain new dimensions (even more if we add colors) in order to transmit and emphasize the very different situation in every phase of human development (Fig. 33).

When we utilize such an approach we will be able to follow the life cycle in every phase and eventually some day will understand the rhythms of the human system which are so important for every individual's development.  Today we are too inclined towards a uniformity which is very dangerous for all human beings, especially in organized societies — either because of new methods of production and style of living or because of autocratic political systems.  Such statements must make us realize how important it is to act for human development and to start our study as early as possible in the life cycle, even before birth, because a big part of a human being's potential for the future has already been decided before his birth and before the age of five.

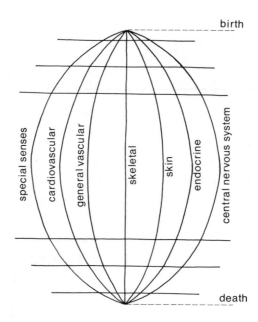

32.      the watermelon diagram of human life

54

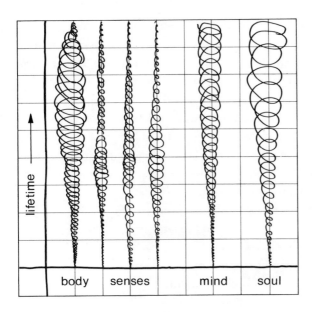

lifetime

body  senses  mind  soul

33.  a schematic presentation of human development
     with different aspects of Anthropos
     which need to be in balance in every phase

## Phases of human development

Looking at the developing human system we must remember the following:

1. When Anthropos (Man) is born he is only partially developed in body, senses, mind and soul.  Unlike machines, which are ready to move as soon as they are out of the factory, Anthropos (Man) is not ready to move;  he is simply ready to develop.

2. In comparison to other animals, Anthropos (Man) needs a longer period of development in proportion to the length of his life.  Up to a certain point this development is positive;  beyond it it becomes negative because some of his capacities, as Anthropos (Man) gradually grows old, his forces, of body, senses, mind and perhaps soul, begin to diminish.

3. There is an optimum rhythm of growth and development for Anthropos (Man);  such rhythm should define the speed at which growth and development take place and the balance which should exist at each phase of development between the different aspects of Anthropos (Man).

To follow this developing human system we need to understand the numerous phases of its development;  here we can concentrate on the basic ones.

Biological sciences have not yet agreed on the same phases of human development although they use several of them corresponding to the sector of their concern; be it medicine or psychiatry, etc. Several cultures, like Sanskrit, and authors like Shakespeare have also invented and used their own. On the other hand Confucius says about himself: "At fifteen I set my heart upon learning. At thirty, I had planted my·feet firm upon the ground. At forty, I no longer suffered from perplexities. At fifty, I knew what were the biddings of Heaven. At sixty, I heard them with docile ear. At seventy, I could follow the dictates of my own heart; for what I desired no longer overstepped the boundaries of right". Related to this is a Song of a Life which starts:

"Man's life from of old has rarely reached seventy;
Take away the early childhood years and the late years of old age;
Between these a man's time is not long.
And even so there is heat and frost, trouble and vexation.
Once past Mid-autumn the moon is less bright;
Once past April the flowers are less beautiful".[36]

It is interesting that these older opinions do not go into details about early phases of our life cycle and this, shows that only lately has Anthropos (Man) learned how important the first years are.

As there is no generally accepted scale for the phases of human development, I felt the need to propose a scale of phases corresponding to basic findings of different sciences which seem to correspond to the needs of this spatial relationship of Anthropos (Man) with his city.

To achieve this I used the scales proposed, or used by several experts or groups of them [37] as well as the old Sanskrit, the Incas [38], Confucius, and Shakespeare's opinion [39] (Fig. 34) and with this combined information I adopted the twelve following phases:

1. prenatal or fetal
2. breast dependence (0-6 months)
3. infant (7-15 months)
4. toddler (16-30 months)
5. preschool (play age, strider, early childhood) (2.5-5 years)
6. school age (6-12 years)
7. adolescence (13-18 years)
8. young adulthood (19-25 years)
9. middle adulthood (26-40 years)
10. real adulthood (41-60 years)
11. early old age (61-75 years)
12. old age (76-100 years)

| Sanskrit | Incas of Peru | Confucius | Shakespeare | Chandler, Lourie & Peters | Stone & Church | Erikson | World Health Organization | Author's suggestion |
|---|---|---|---|---|---|---|---|---|
| 5. retiring stage | 10. old man sleeping | 6. desires no longer overstepped boundaries of right | 7. second childishness | | | 8. old age | 7. senescence | 12. old age |
| 4. monastic stage | | 5. hears biddings of heaven with docile ear | 6. old | | | | | 11. early old age |
| 3. forest dweller's stage | 9. half old: doing light work | 4. knows biddings of heaven | | | | 7. adulthood | | 10. real adulthood |
| | | 3. no longer perplexed | | | | | | |
| 2. householder stage | 8. able-bodied: tribute payer and head of family | 2. feet planted firm | 5. justice | | | | 6. age of production and reproduction | 9. middle adulthood |
| | 7. almost a youth worker | | 4. soldier | | | 6. young adulthood | | 8. young adulthood |
| | 6. coca picker: worker | | 3. lover | | 7. adolescence | 5. adolescence | 5. adolescence | 7. adolescence |
| 1. student stage | 5. light worker | 1. desires to learn | 2. schoolboy | | 6. school child | 4. school age | 4. school age | 6. school age |
| | 4. bread receiver | | | | | | | |
| | 3. under six years | | | 3. strider | 5. preschool | 3. play age | | 5. preschool age |
| | | | 1. infant | 2. toddler | 4. toddler | 2. early childhood | 3. preschool age | 4. toddler |
| | 2. able to stand | | | 1. infant | | | | 3. infant |
| | | | | | 3. infant | | | |
| | 1. baby in arms | | | | 2. neonatal | 1. infancy | 2. breast dependence | 2. breast dependence |
| | | | | | 1. prenatal | | 1. fetal life | 1. prenatal or fetal |

34.    several concepts of human development phases

To reach this conclusion I did not use some phases like the neonatal phase used by some pediatricians as it does not mean anything different from the breast dependence phase in relation to our problem. This neonatal phase can be seen (where necessary) as a subphase of the breast dependence stage. I also added two phases, first in adulthood because this is the longest main phase, and it is useful to break it into parts which do not contain a span of more than 20 years. Secondly I extended the old age span as I think that with health conditions getting better many more people are very productive up to age 75 and only begin to retire after that year.

| development phases | name of phases | ages |
|---|---|---|
| 12 | old age | 76-100 |
| 11 | early old age | 61-75 |
| 10 | real adulthood | 41-60 |
| 9 | middle adulthood | 26-40 |
| 8 | young adulthood | 19-25 |
| 7 | adolescence | 13-18 |
| 6 | school age | 6-12 |
| 5 | preschool (play age, strider, early childhood) | 2.5-5 |
| 4 | toddler | 16-30 months |
| 3 | infant | 7-15 months |
| 2 | breast dependence | 0-6 months |
| 1 | prenatal or fetal | -9 months-0 |

35.    tentative scale for human development measurements

In order to facilitate the reading of this scale I have redrawn it logarithmically (Fig. 35) to transmit better the meaning of phases of equal or related importance.

Every phase can be now subdivided but this effort meets the same difficulties as every aspect of human development leads to its own scale.  If we take the second and third phase only we see (Fig. 36) that the manual for COLR research form and the Bayley scales of mental development only coincide with the Stone and Church scale at two points.  I therefore had to propose a scale which represents all these sub-phases only as an indication of how we can proceed, for an overall scale.

| months | Bayley scale of motor development | Bayley scale of mental development | Stone and Church | author's suggestion |
|---|---|---|---|---|
| 16 | | | | 25 |
| 15 | | 11 | | 24 |
| 14 | | | | 23 |
| 13 | | 10 | | 22 |
| 12 | 8 | | | 21 |
| 11 | | 9 | | 20 |
| 10 | 7 | | | 19 |
| 9 | 6 | 8 | 3 | 18 |
| 8 | 5 | | | 17 |
| 7 | 4 | 7 | | 16 |
| 6 | | 6 | | 15 |
| 5 | 3 | 5 | | 14 |
| 4 | | 4 | | 13 |
| 3 | 2 | 3 | | 12 |
| 2 | | 2 | | 11 |
| 1 | 1 | 1 | 2 | 10 |
| | | | | 9 |
| | | | | 8 |
| | | | | 7 |
| | | | | 6 |
| | | | 1 | 5 |
| | | | | 4 |
| | | | | 3 |
| | | | | 2 |
| | | | | 1 |

36.    sub-division of phases 2 and 3 of human development

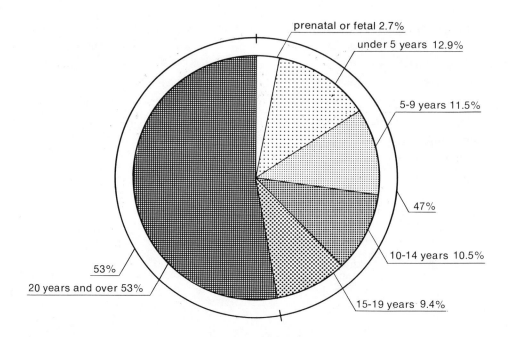

prenatal or fetal 2.7%

under 5 years 12.9%

5-9 years 11.5%

47%

10-14 years 10.5%

15-19 years 9.4%

53%

20 years and over 53%

37.     analysis of the world population by age-groups

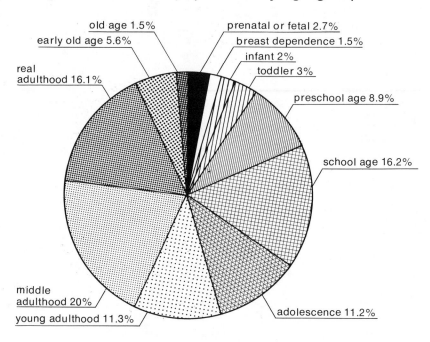

old age 1.5%

early old age 5.6%

real
adulthood 16.1%

prenatal or fetal 2.7%

breast dependence 1.5%

infant 2%

toddler 3%

preschool age 8.9%

school age 16.2%

middle
adulthood 20%

young adulthood 11.3%

adolescence 11.2%

38.     analysis of the world population
by development phases

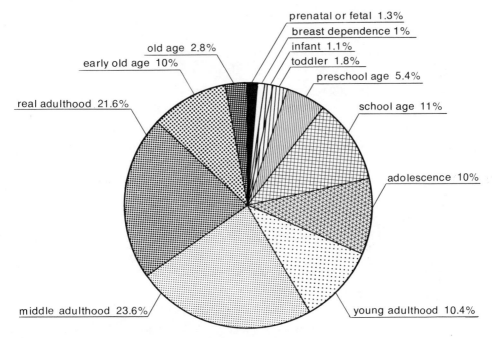

prenatal or fetal 1.3%
breast dependence 1%
infant 1.1%
toddler 1.8%
preschool age 5.4%
school age 11%
old age 2.8%
early old age 10%
real adulthood 21.6%
adolescence 10%
middle adulthood 23.6%
young adulthood 10.4%

39.    analysis of the Greek population
       by development phases

We now can proceed and attempt to find out about what happens during every phase and, where possible, sub-phase; decide what we do know about human needs, and what we can ask about the sectors we do not know. Only then can we make propositions for the human settlements used by Anthropos (Man) in each single phase.

We also can calculate the numbers of people by age-groups in every phase and find out the dimensions of the problem we are dealing with (Figs. 37, 38 and 39).

## Freedom to move

We can now ask, what does Anthropos (Man) demand in his city? His first desire is freedom to move; otherwise he is in a prison and we have no instances where people like this. Such a demand corresponds to the first principle of maximization of potential contacts, which means a maximum of choices for everyone no matter what his color, religion, race, sex or sexual habit may be. This is proper and easy to state; the difficulty arises when we think of the specific aspects of how far we want and can go, how we go and how we can be safe in the process of all this and do it for better development.

As we state our belief in equal people, we have to clarify that anyone should be allowed to go out as far he wants. Of course this is not true of children or those who are not mentally and physically fit to do so. We therefore have to define the limits of the kinetic fields for all age-groups and be aware that these are valid for those people who correspond to normal development.

*Hypothesis thirteen:* Anthropos (Man) should be given the opportunity to move out as far and to as many places as he needs in every phase of his development. This, for the average person, means to start from the minimum distance — the body of his mother — and to expand until he reaches the whole earth or even go beyond it and then, gradually, reduce his movement to the smaller areas corresponding to his actual needs and interests. This is an ultimate goal facilitated by modern science and technology.

The real issue probably is not this hypothesis, but how we translate it in space. The way I present it (Fig. 40) shows that the child starts from inside the mother, stays close to her and gradually conquers the whole earth from the age of 19 on. Is this right? Or should it happen later, perhaps after college? What we know from history is that the great conquerors were in their twenties as are today the great conquerors of space in terms of speed. We also know that the astronauts are more than 25 years old, which makes sense in this curve. The last question is whether old people should step back in their latter phases. I personally consider that this would be natural although many leaders in art and science may disagree because of their own achievements.

There is no question from the technological point of view [40] or from the economic one that mobility will be facilitated more and more. Therefore, the big question is whether — once we can go far out in an easier way — we should also allow or help children to do so or not. Isn't this going to be very dangerous? Does the fact, for example, that some people proved a two-year-old child can do anything in a pool [41] mean that we should give this opportunity for additional mobility to all children of this age-group? This kind of question is very difficult to answer as Anthropos (Man) is probably the first element of Nature which is so free to move far out, but at the same time certainly depends on his mother and family for quite a long phase of his lifetime.

Such a goal leads to the idea of special measures and new concepts of mobility even for the units beyond the large city which should also be reached as easily as possible. This leads to the goal of an ultimate terrestrial city within which the mobility theoretically should be such that all distances could be covered in ten minutes (Fig. 41) [42]. In practice, however, it seems that this goal could be achieved to a limit of 60 minutes which is a very natural one for the natural City of Anthropos (Man) [43].

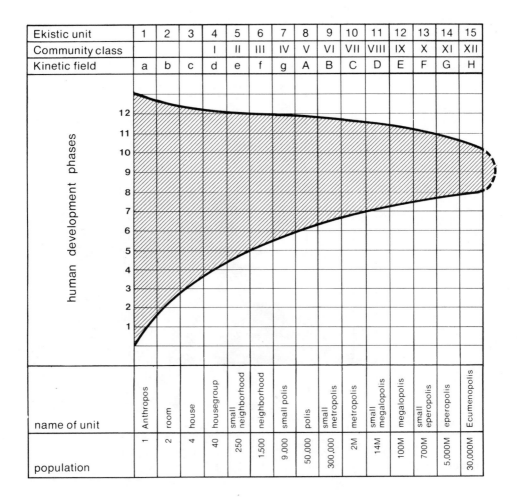

| Ekistic unit | 1 | 2 | 3 | 4 | 5 | 6 | 7 | 8 | 9 | 10 | 11 | 12 | 13 | 14 | 15 |
|---|---|---|---|---|---|---|---|---|---|---|---|---|---|---|---|
| Community class | | | | I | II | III | IV | V | VI | VII | VIII | IX | X | XI | XII |
| Kinetic field | a | b | c | d | e | f | g | A | B | C | D | E | F | G | H |
| name of unit | Anthropos | room | house | housegroup | small neighborhood | neighborhood | small polis | polis | small metropolis | metropolis | small megalopolis | megalopolis | small eperopolis | eperopolis | Ecumenopolis |
| population | 1 | 2 | 4 | 40 | 250 | 1,500 | 9,000 | 50,000 | 300,000 | 2M | 14M | 100M | 700M | 5,000M | 30,000M |

(y-axis: human development phases, 1–12)

## 40. mobility in space by development phases
conquering the world and then stepping back

Thus, when we plan correctly for mobility within the city we will help Anthropos (Man) to overcome the difficulty he has been facing. He is now forced to spend more time on the road than he did two centuries ago, even after a long effort of millions of years to reduce this time and energy spent on the road to an optimum percentage of his total time and energy (Figs. 42, 43, 44 and 45) [44]. We should not forget that Anthropos (Man) spends as much time moving today in the big city as he did in the Neolithic era, although later he managed to reduce this time greatly. From this we learn his desires.

| Ekistic unit | 1 | 2 | 3 | 4 | 5 | 6 | 7 | 8 | 9 | 10 | 11 | 12 | 13 | 14 | 15 |
|---|---|---|---|---|---|---|---|---|---|---|---|---|---|---|---|
| Community class | | | | I | II | III | IV | V | VI | VII | VIII | IX | X | XI | XII |
| Kinetic field | a | b | c | d | e | f | g | A | B | C | D | E | F | G | H |

| name of unit | Anthropos | room | house | housegroup | small neighborhood | neighborhood | small polis | polis | small metropolis | metropolis | small megalopolis | megalopolis | small eperopolis | eperopolis | Ecumenopolis |
|---|---|---|---|---|---|---|---|---|---|---|---|---|---|---|---|
| population | 1 | 2 | 4 | 40 | 250 | 1,500 | 9,000 | 50,000 | 300,000 | 2M | 14M | 100M | 700M | 5,000M | 30,000M |

minutes 10

0

■ walking     ≡ machine C

▨ machine A     ⦂ machine D

||||||| machine B

41.     the ultimate terrestrial city from the point of view of kinetic fields

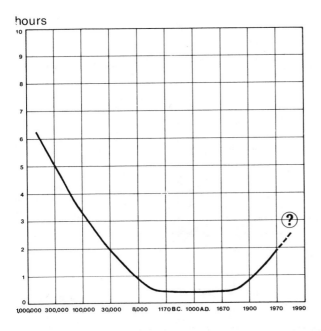

42.  time spent for Anthropos' daily movement

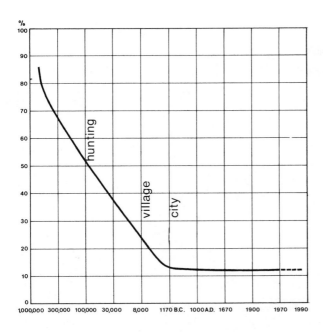

43.  human muscular energy
     spent tor Anthropos' daily movement

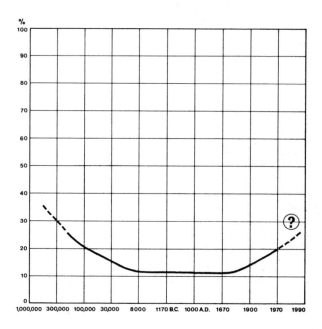

44.     energy spent for total movement and transportation
        as a percentage of total energy used by Anthropos

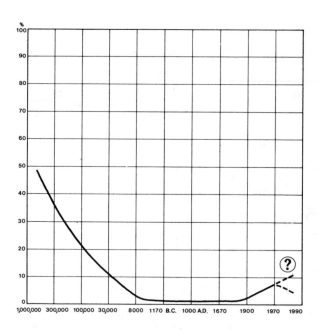

45.     energy spent for daily movement of Anthropos
        as a percentage of total energy used by Anthropos

## Ability to move

To be free to move is very important provided we can define how to move in order not to create chaos. If we all go out with our cars at the same moment and move in all directions without any controls and regulations, chaos would be the result. We do not need our city to be a prison nor do we need it to be chaotic.

*Hypothesis fourteen:* Anthropos (Man) should be given the opportunity to move by himself as far as he wishes without any assistance in every phase of his development and in the best possible way.

This looks like the previous hypothesis but it is not. One example is multi-story residential apartments. The young child has the opportunity to move to the garden by using the elevator, but then he depends on a machine. If his mother stays on the twentieth floor, she may not let the child go out and if she does, she may be nervous and the child unsafe and in danger. The strider has to see his neighborhood and to learn about Society, but he should not be let out of it alone with access to the highway and be killed or lost.

Anthropos (Man) needs to conquer the world, but this has to be done in an organized and safe way, serving his individual development, and thus we trace a second curve (Fig. 46) which shows how far out people can and should go without the use of machines, assistance or supervision. This is a goal which exists for Anthropos (Man) even without science and technology, it is the goal of natural mobility. Such a hypothesis increases our responsibility for shaping the small terrestrial units in a way helping everyone to achieve this. For the phase already mentioned this means that the toddler has the right to walk out to the garden without use of an elevator. Only thus is he a free member of the community.

This is the stage at which we must remember that Anthropos (Man) is able today to go far out, but at the same time he has lost the human scale close to him; this is what he has to re-establish. This is directly related to a contemporary American problem where parents produced "happiness is walking to your neighborhood school" signs [45].

Such thoughts make us look more seriously at one basic human right, the right to walk to many places without entering a machine (elevator, car, etc.).

## Safety

To move as far out as possible (hypothesis thirteen) without any assistance (hypothesis fourteen) is not enough. To be free to do so even in an organized way does not satisfy Anthropos (Man) unless he is safe. The maximum of choices without controlling the results they may have could lead him to disaster. If we leave young children the choice of jumping over a cliff, they may well do so.

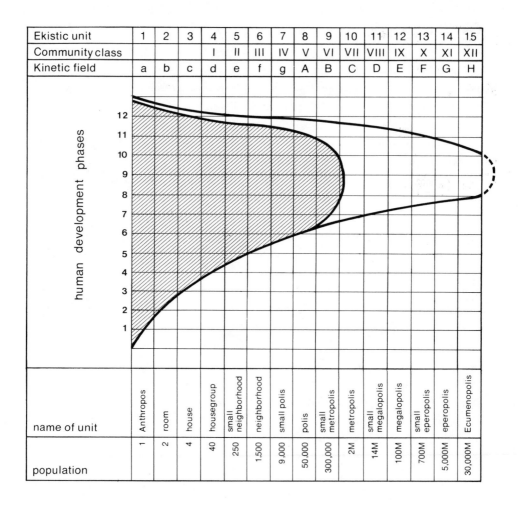

| Ekistic unit | 1 | 2 | 3 | 4 | 5 | 6 | 7 | 8 | 9 | 10 | 11 | 12 | 13 | 14 | 15 |
|---|---|---|---|---|---|---|---|---|---|---|---|---|---|---|---|
| Community class | | | | I | II | III | IV | V | VI | VII | VIII | IX | X | XI | XII |
| Kinetic field | a | b | c | d | e | f | g | A | B | C | D | E | F | G | H |
| name of unit | Anthropos | room | house | housegroup | small neighborhood | neighborhood | small polis | polis | small metropolis | metropolis | small megalopolis | megalopolis | small eperopolis | eperopolis | Ecumenopolis |
| population | 1 | 2 | 4 | 40 | 250 | 1.500 | 9.000 | 50,000 | 300,000 | 2M | 14M | 100M | 700M | 5,000M | 30,000M |

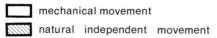 mechanical movement

natural independent movement

## 46.   mobility in space
conquering the world the natural way

People should have the maximum of choices within a well-structured city which can also protect them when they need protection.

*Hypothesis fifteen:* A city must guarantee everybody the best possible development under conditions of freedom and safety and thus it becomes a specific goal to fit the city to Anthropos (Man) in the same way that a tailor fits a suit to our body and not vice versa. We always have to think how the city can best be built to fit human needs. This means that the Anthropos-built (Man-built) environment (Shells and Networks) should protect Anthropos (Man) physically from adverse exposures to his physical environment: this also should apply to Nature, with its various aspects, all serving Anthropos (Man) as structures and as functions.

We are beginning to see that the city should provide opportunities for a gradual increase of freedom and challenge each person as it changes in size, structure and quality, so that these gradual changes will enable the population to gain the maximum benefit by their gradual exposure to more challenging environments, and the greater potential dangers that these environments present with greater freedom.

We should not forget that the manner in which people develop best is shown by Nature. In their first phase, all mammals are completely protected within the womb. After they are born, they not only need a closely protected environment but also seek the greatest possible protection of their mother's body, from which they separate only gradually. This can be seen not only in the marsupials (kangaroo, opposum, etc.) but also in our own children who feel happier when held at their mother's left side, because then they can feel the beating of her heart, thus connecting themselves with the protected environment from which they originally came.

The difficulty begins with the young child who has to learn about the reality of the world, as the poet Pablo Neruda tells us:

> "The child's foot is not yet aware it's a foot and wants to be a butterfly or an apple" [46].

We cannot leave the child to think it is a butterfly and get killed when he opens the door of his house and steps out. Although accidents on the street in many cities of the world are decreasing in relation to numbers of inhabitants, they are increasing in relation to children who are crossing streets or using bicycles and motor-bicycles.

Our big challenge is to build the city where the child will be both free and safe and this requires great wisdom to keep a child from doing certain things. "There is no game if there are no limits" Erikson said and, "The big question is where to set the limits and how" [47].

Today when we see children crossing the street by turning into a long serpent-line (Fig. 47) [48] we have to remember that the child should not only be safe in the city, but also feel safe, and this really means the freedom to move without being interrupted and endangered by any force. It is time that we realize what happened in the past and what is happening now in the street (Figs. 48 and 49) and try to overcome the problem of Anthropos (Man) squeezed between Shells and machine Networks. The very fact that we call the human part of the street "side-walk" is frightening. If Anthropos (Man) is on the side who is the master?

To achieve our goal of freedom to move in a safe way we must plan that the degree of exposure in every phase of Anthropos' (Man's) development comes in a gradual way. Since Anthropos (Man) is born completely safe in terms of spatial exposure and completely enclosed we cannot lead him from zero exposure to 100% exposure overnight. Nature shows the natural trend of exposure by allowing not only the body but also the senses and mind to grow. Nature does not lead Anthropos (Man) from 100% exposure to zero (death)

47.    the battle for survival

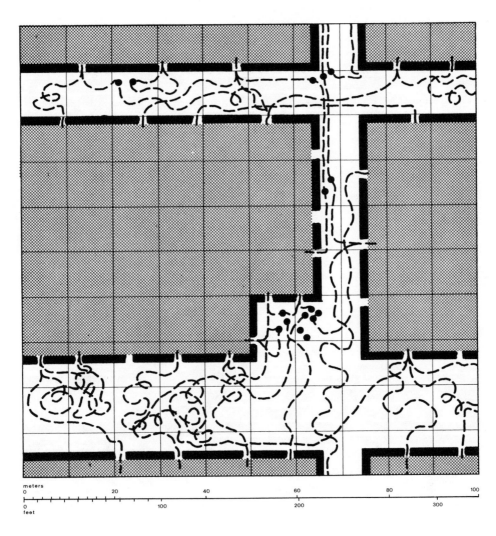

meters
0            20            40            60            80            100

0            100            200            300
feet

⌒⌒ human energy

▬▬▬ mechanical energy - automobiles

▨▨ built-up area

## 48.    Anthropos in the street of the past
he was free to move and to communicate

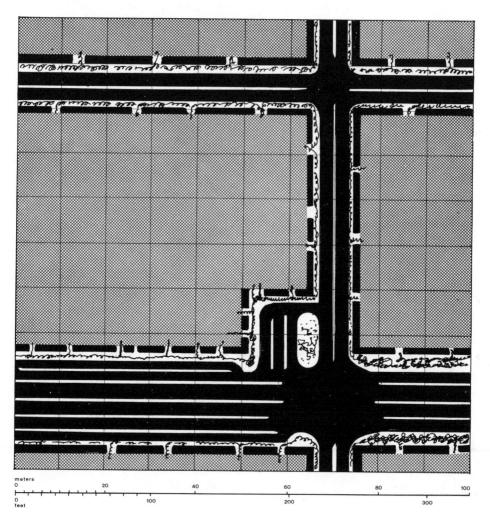

meters
0              20            40            60            80            100

0                         100                200                300
feet

human energy

mechanical energy - automobiles

built-up area

## 49.     Anthropos in the street of the present

he is not safe, he is not free to move
and to communicate; he is squeezed

overnight, but gradually reduces Anthropos' (Man's) ability to see, to hear, to walk and thus decreases his exposures and involvement.

This means that the earlier suggestions about mobility in space (Figs. 41 and 46) now need further elaboration (Fig. 50). We do have to move far out, in a natural way, but we must gradually be exposed to larger units and be prepared to enter them initially with protection and dependence and then by ourselves.

In the same way we can assume that, since the child is created and grows in a completely enclosed space, we must help him to move and understand spaces from the completely enclosed ones — a room closed on all six sides — then gradually to open ones. He can then be exposed to a courtyard open on one side, that is the upper one, and closed on five until one day he will feel himself to be secure in the desert — open on five sides (Fig. 51); and eventually he can become a parachutist or a swimmer — open on all sides.

The big question is, how can we help the child which has already spent nine months in the womb and several months in a small bed in a room enclosed on all sides, to enter the wider open space? A reasonable answer is to let the child first become accustomed to a very small, enclosed room (Fig. 51a), then the courtyard which is open at the top (Fig. 51b), then different types of courtyards and gardens (Figs. 51c, 51d). He could then be exposed to the road (Fig. 52a) which is enclosed only on two sides (like Fig. 51d) but has parallel walls, thus giving the child direction for his expansion and eliminating the dangers. In this gradual way the child can then move to a big square (Fig. 51e) or an open promenade by the sea (Fig. 52c) and finally to the open field (Fig. 51f) or the desert or wide open beach (Fig. 52d).

Such considerations help us to understand two things; the type of space we are in and the dimensions related to it. What we need is a gradual exposure to more meaningful space in terms of character and dimensions.

We can continue with similar approaches and think of gradual exposure to flora and fauna — from one flower in a pot and a house cat, to a courtyard and garden with trees and plants, birds and other small animals and finally to the wilderness or the jungle with its wildlife. How can we help the shy child to meet the world? How else can he develop close human relationships and feel secure in his environment?

We can be assisted greatly to achieve such goals if we manage to conceive human relations in space in a series of very detailed sketches such as those for Infant-Mother relationship done by R. Lourie (Fig. 53) [49] or the relation between men, women and children as suggested by the Family Planning Program (Fig. 54). Such approaches can help us to develop the desirable relationships in exact physical scales into a system.

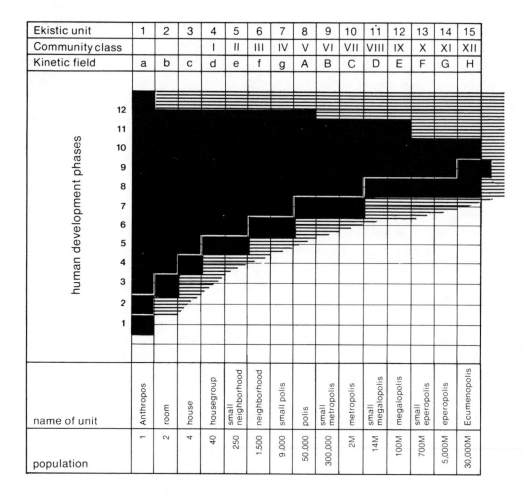

| Ekistic unit | 1 | 2 | 3 | 4 | 5 | 6 | 7 | 8 | 9 | 10 | 11 | 12 | 13 | 14 | 15 |
|---|---|---|---|---|---|---|---|---|---|---|---|---|---|---|---|
| Community class | | | | I | II | III | IV | V | VI | VII | VIII | IX | X | XI | XII |
| Kinetic field | a | b | c | d | e | f | g | A | B | C | D | E | F | G | H |

human development phases (12, 11, 10, 9, 8, 7, 6, 5, 4, 3, 2, 1)

| name of unit | Anthropos | room | house | housegroup | small neighborhood | neighborhood | small polis | polis | small metropolis | metropolis | small megalopolis | megalopolis | small eperopolis | eperopolis | Ecumenopolis |
|---|---|---|---|---|---|---|---|---|---|---|---|---|---|---|---|
| population | 1 | 2 | 4 | 40 | 250 | 1.500 | 9.000 | 50.000 | 300,000 | 2M | 14M | 100M | 700M | 5,000M | 30,000M |

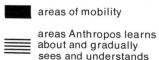 areas of mobility

≡ areas Anthropos learns about and gradually sees and understands

50.   gradual exposure to space so that Anthropos can be and feel safe

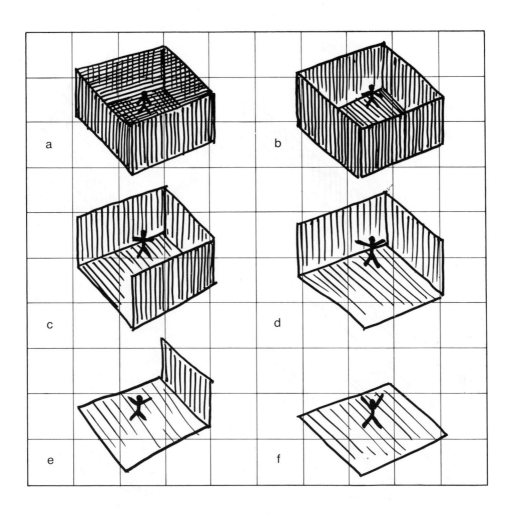

51. human space can be enclosed on all six sides or not enclosed at all

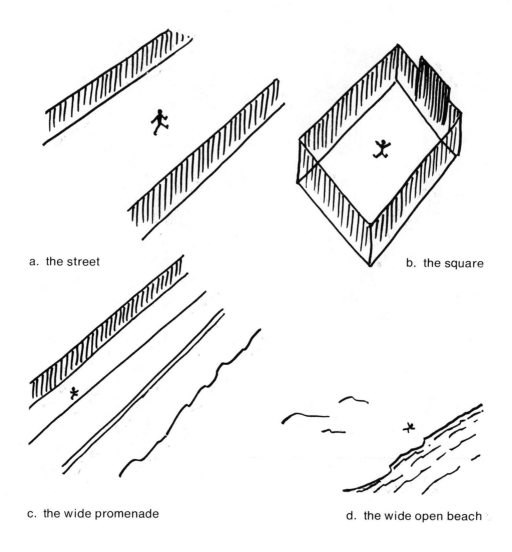

a. the street

b. the square

c. the wide promenade

d. the wide open beach

52.　human space can be enclosed or open in different
　　　ways or dimensions

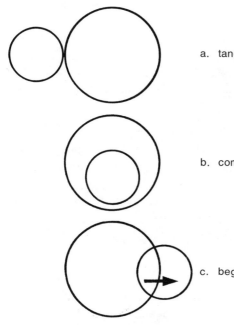

a. tangential relationship of newborn to mother

b. complete dependence of infant on mother

c. beginning of independence of infant from mother

53.　infant-mother relationship in the early months of life

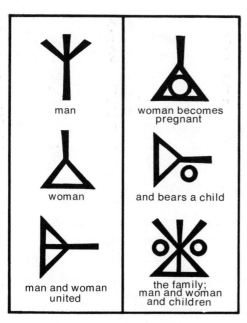

man

woman

man and woman
united

woman becomes
pregnant

and bears a child

the family;
man and woman
and children

design by Harold E. Sannason, for Family
Planning Program, Human Resources
Administration

54.　symbolic designs of people

## Quality of life

We do not need to state that our life is losing quality in terms of the physical environment of the city. It is enough to state that such problems of pressures (noise, density, etc.) which existed in the past in the central areas of small cities now cover much larger areas and are going to spread to even larger ones (Fig. 55). We only have to realize that we can now have a well controlled climate inside a house and a building while the contaminated air is thrown out into the streets; then we will understand that the smaller ekistic units of our environment have higher quality (not necessarily esthetic) than in the past while the larger ones are losing it. We also have to remember that many things happen around us today not for the sake of Anthropos (Man), but just in order to show off. A middle-aged man makes noise in an airplane by playing cards; a young one creates noise and danger with his motorcycle or car in the street; and the big corporation by building its very ostentatious towers where we do not need them. "A tower may represent male desire", Erik Erikson said [50].

*Hypothesis sixteen:* The Anthropopolis must create a system that can challenge every citizen to enjoy it and develop to his maximum and this can only be a system of quality that transmits the notion of order. This can be done if it has the proper quality at an optimum level, not too low and not too high and intense, with the larger part of the system representing order and parts of it disorder. We cannot expect civilization to be created within the jungle, although a garden in a city can be like a jungle within a broader and orderly urban system. This quality should be related to the natural, physical (created by Anthropos — Man) and social environment.

The big question is, what is quality and how do we measure it? We can state here that this is the most difficult question to answer. Anthropos (Man) receives messages from the space around him in many ways, from its dimensions and the freedom of movement that it allows him (body), to the feeling of safety (mind, soul), from the climate (body, senses), from the esthetic appearances both static and dynamic at all levels (eyes), the sounds and noise (ears), the smell (nose), the feeling from touching (skin), taste (tongue), etc.; and many of these messages which Anthropos (Man) is subject to are beginning to be measured in many ways through old and new sciences like "thermography" or "sentics" [51].

People are beginning to be aware of all these aspects as they affect them directly or indirectly when they want to enjoy themselves, or work, or sleep. They are also beginning to be aware that many tensions of body and senses are due to the impact of their environment. Anthropos (Man) is beginning to react and to classify the problems, as was done recently by an opinion poll of western

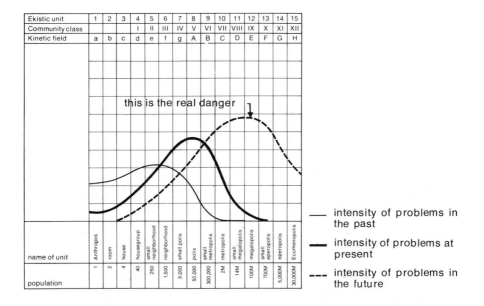

| Ekistic unit | 1 | 2 | 3 | 4 | 5 | 6 | 7 | 8 | 9 | 10 | 11 | 12 | 13 | 14 | 15 |
|---|---|---|---|---|---|---|---|---|---|---|---|---|---|---|---|
| Community class | | | | I | II | III | IV | V | VI | VII | VIII | IX | X | XI | XII |
| Kinetic field | a | b | c | d | e | f | g | A | B | C | D | E | F | G | H |

this is the real danger

name of unit: Anthropos / room / house / housegroup / small neighborhood / neighborhood / small polis / polis / small metropolis / metropolis / small megalopolis / megalopolis / small eperopolis / eperopolis / Ecumenopolis

population: 1 / 2 / 4 / 40 / 250 / 1,500 / 9,000 / 50,000 / 300,000 / 2M / 14M / 100M / 700M / 5,000M / 30,000M

—— intensity of problems in the past

—— intensity of problems at present

--- intensity of problems in the future

## 55.  problems of quality of physical environment by ekistic unit

European leaders, 68% of whom agreed that the problem of industrial effluents is considered to be the most serious environmental problem and then, that conservation of water resources was the second worst environmental problem, in the opinion of 64% of these leaders [52].

Although concern about problems of quality begins to be apparent, the major problems created by the city of the present are not yet understood.  I will concentrate on one of them in order to illustrate my point;  it is related not to what we breathe, but to the messages we receive from the city's structure.

When we look at the city from the lower floors, no matter whether we are in the street or in our apartment or office, we get one message:  There are no people in this city and machines are our only neighbors (Fig. 56).  Why should we allow parking to be seen from the street?

Second, when we look at the city from the top, from our apartment or office, we get a similar message:  Anthropos (Man) and house have disappeared and thus machines and isolated structures are in control of the situation (Fig. 57).  Why should we be so far out of the physiological, human scale?

Third, as a result of the previous phenomena and many others, the city transmits one message:  there is no order in our life system (Fig. 58).  This message is worse at night (Fig. 59) because one more element has been added to the dominance

there are no people to be seen and  machines are our only neighbors

56.     the city as we see it from lower floors

*Anthropos* and *Home* have disappeared; machines and isolated structures are in control.

57.     the city as we see it from upper floors

58.     the city transmits one message:
        there is no order in our life-system

*Anthropos* and *Home* have disappeared; machines and isolated structures are in control.

59.     the city at night as we see it from upper floors

of the heavy structures and machines which differentiates one part of the city from the other, this is lighting. Now, if I am rich, I can show off even more and eliminate many other natural and human, social and cultural values. We have left out only two more ingredients: to allow advertising to use sound and perfume in the streets in order to impose even more messages on us. It is interesting to note how children look at their city today (Fig. 60) [53]. Up come the blocks of flats, in front of us we have the machines and somewhere in between are the old symbols of Nature and Religion.

The time has come for a proper evaluation of the total relationship between Anthropos (Man) and his city. This does not simply mean what Anthropos (Man) receives from the system (as many people still think) but also what he does for it in his daily life. Only in this way can we have an evaluation of the total system of interaction. This is the most difficult job of all in the field of ekistics and it has taken me forty years to conceive and develop a model that is designed for a total evaluation, where we can insert the degree of satisfaction from every situation and action in a static or dynamic way.

The basic model contains even in a simplified way over one hundred million combinations and helps us to classify, measure and understand every case of satisfaction from Nature, Anthropos (Man), Society, Shells, Networks and their

60.     how children look at their city today

combinations. For example, we can see on this model (Fig. 61) what the impact of a new industrial plant may be, show where it is negative (pollution) and positive (employment, income, etc.) and finally indicate the degree of satisfaction in every ekistic unit in space. It is impossible to give details about the type of relationships that exist and their evaluation but I will mention one case which can give us an insight into what happens in a city in one respect and how we can face it. I cite one of the many cases I personally have studied which has led me to a better understanding of the very great complexity of our system of life.

This is the case of my one week's stay in an old house on the Greek island of Hydra, in order to understand how people feel when they live and work in it. I tried to work in its beautiful upper floor and studied all of my possible locations in it. What I learned is certainly personal following the Danish saying "the seen depends on the eyes that see" [54], but experience shows that such personal observations are slight variations from the average relationships which exist although there are certainly some few extreme ones, but I don't deal with them in any case.

My basic observation was that my work depended on the visual relationship between the city and myself. The view was excellent and constantly attracted me, I therefore did not want to close the doors and windows (Appendix 1). On the other hand, if I was exposed to the view I could not work productively. My conclusion was that I needed the visual contact, but that it had to be completely controlled. Although many people insist today on windows that cover a whole wall, for any balanced relationship in times of work we must have much smaller visual openings than we usually thought.

These conclusions were confirmed when I made similar experiments for my relationship with the auditory space around me. There I had a great shock because I was not prepared for the impact of the noises of such a beautiful town, which was really built like a theater and therefore even people who lived high up and away from the harbor could hear the opening of a bottle of wine at night in a boat! Visual beauty is not necessarily a pleasing auditory experience! Total evaluation is very difficult indeed.

Such observations confirmed my previous fears that over-exposure can have disastrous effects on Anthropos (Man), even if it is an over-exposure to beauty. How do we allow so many messages to be transmitted to us through signs? Aren't we destroying Anthropos (Man) in the Constitution Square of Athens, the Piccadilly Circus of London and the Broadway of New York? Is it coincidental that the primitive ape escaped from the jungle and evolved to Homo sapiens in a much simpler, natural system without so much information constantly being thrown at him as the jungle does in every respect?

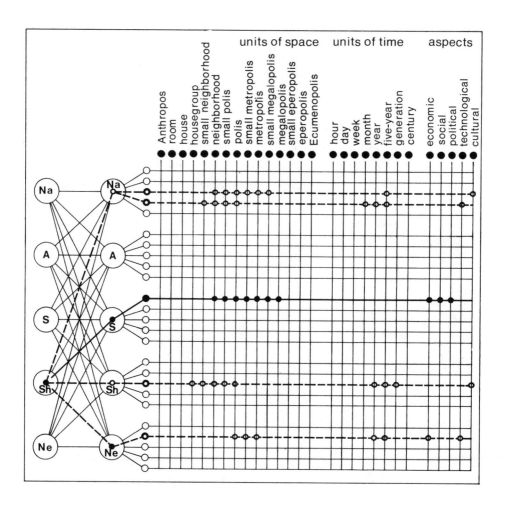

- - - negative effects
——— positive effects

The creation of a new plant in a city has positive effects for certain people because it brings jobs and therefore can be evaluated as an important contribution from the economic, social and political points of view. It also has negative effects for certain groups of people living nearby and for all people of the area because it creates problems like in water supply, sewage system, etc. Through such an evaluation we can locate the incentives leading to the decision to create the plant, but can act in order to reduce its negative effects.

61.    evaluation of the impact of a new plant in a city by the use of a complete model of the world of Anthropos

## Human contacts

The quality of the city is not only measured in terms of its physical environment but also in terms of its social interaction; that is the kind of contacts between people, depending upon numbers, intensity, quality and many other forces. There is no question that today Anthropos (Man) has the opportunity for many more contacts than at any time before, and therefore has many more choices; but there are also times when he is overexposed to contacts and tries to escape. This is a very important and complex problem as on one hand we want to maximize our potential contacts (first principle) and on the other we try to optimize our protective space (third principle). We begin to have cases where people suffer from too much stress from continuous contacts and, being poor, they cannot easily escape from the city walls. There are also cases where young children become frightened by the big city or the foreign city when they are abroad. We have statements that important painters like De Chirico may paint in a disconnected way because of his childhood memories and too much exposure to foreign environment[55]. Lately the idea has been more and more supported that the secret of an artist's creative work can be found in his childhood[56].

We are in the middle of a crisis, the causes of which cannot be avoided (first and second principle). The question is, what measures can we adopt to solve the problems in a creative but not utopian way — avoiding the big city — and how to control our exposure, especially that of the growing child, without reducing our choices. The only possible answer follows:

*Hypothesis seventeen:* Anthropos (Man) always needs to maximize his potential contacts with people and minimize the energy required, but this has to be accomplished without endangering the quality and optimum quantity of his contacts. This requires a gradual exposure to the city and its people, with an optimum situation for every development phase allowing for the possibility throughout Anthropos' (Man's) lifetime of exposure to any area with a different type and intensity of contacts.

To achieve this we must realize that people feel lonely if left alone in space and, therefore, they tend to come closer together to form communities and an organized society. But these efforts may result in squeezing them too close together so that they suffer. Thus the goal of the city is to bring people close enough together to benefit from their contacts, but at the same time to form a proper structure that can keep them sufficiently far apart, so that the exposure to and the danger from each other is minimized. Thus we can ask ourselves whether or not we have now reached a dangerous density on the whole earth (as some people pretend) and whether there is an optimum overall relationship of Anthropos (Man) with space.

The basic question which arises when we speak about Anthropos (Man) and space is: can a balance be created between them? Experts disagree on the desirable and optimum ratios and some refer to densities as the criteria of these balances. This problem is a very difficult and confusing one and can be viewed as a matter of dimensions of space and numbers of people in abstract terms, or as a problem of resources. These problems can be answered in different ways at each different scale of unit of space, because the meaning of density is different in a room, a city or a country.

I will deal here with the meaning of density in the units of countries and the whole globe where today the average person has about one hectare (10,000 sq. meters or 2.5 acres) of habitable space for himself. This ratio does not look at all dangerous if we remember examples in history where civilization, arts, and democracy have been developed in countries and areas with the same or much higher densities, where people occasionally lived of their own free will at much higher densities. An extreme example is the island of Delos forming a small state by itself where the density on the island itself was more than 87 persons per hectare (36 persons per acre) or Delos together with the nearby island of Rheneia where the average density was 17 persons per hectare (6.9 persons per acre) which is 17 times higher than the average density at present.

Today we have countries where people live at high densities as in Bangladesh with 4.9 persons per hectare (2.0 persons per acre), Java with 4.8 persons per hectare (1.9 persons per acre), the Netherlands with 3.6 persons per hectare (1.5 persons per acre) and Japan with 2.6 persons per hectare (1.05 persons per acre) or places where outsiders also go for vacations like Puerto Rico with 2.89 persons per hectare (1.17 persons per acre) and Lebanon with 2.11 persons per hectare (0.85 persons per acre). I do not speak of the single city-state of Hong Kong where we have the highest density of any separate state of the globe — 37 persons per hectare (15 persons per acre), because we do not know whether its inhabitants are forced to live in such high densities because they have no other choice.

The problem of the ratio of people to space on the whole globe at present, is not a problem of surfaces — seen as abstract dimensions — the earth could easily contain many times more people. It is a problem of resources, because all of the countries mentioned above import at least some resources from others and some, like the Netherlands, even use other countries' space-resources for their residents' vacations; they do, however, get a lot of visitors in exchange. We do not have any sign at present of an imbalance between people and space on a national scale, if we exclude the question of resources.

Although I will not deal here at any length with this problem of density, I do have the obligation to make one statement: This problem is not as simple as people believe. Density alone without the consideration of many other factors, from energy to the motivational ones, does not explain many situations by itself and can become a confusing oversimplification.

The question of the optimum relationship of Anthropos (Man) and space is an even more complex one when we realize that people sometimes like a very high density but only want it for a certain limited time with proper motivation and they occasionally prefer a very low density, again for a specific time and motivation. We can only deal here with typical situations which are apparent within the average developed settlements where people live at an average distance of 6 meters (20 ft.) from each other in houses, and 16 meters (53 ft.) apart in the total surface of the large cities; and this figure increases in the metropolis (Fig. 62) and even more upon the whole globe (Fig. 63).

Within this whole complex system of our globe we can now state that the number of contacts, which was at its highest at home and gradually decreased in the larger units (Fig. 64), is now dropping rapidly in Anthropos' (Man's) neigh-

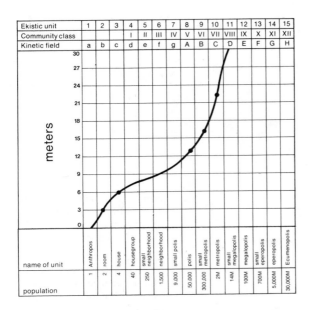

**62.    contacts between people**
theoretical distances between people within the built-up parts of human settlements

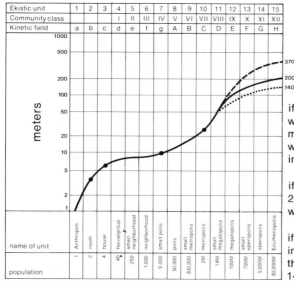

if the people presently on earth were to live at distances of 370 meters from each other, they would spread all over the earth, including the oceans

if they were to live at distances of 200 meters from each other, they would spread all over the land

if they were to spread all over the inhabited part of the land, then they would live at distances of 140 meters from each other

## 63.　contacts between people

theoretical distances between people in each ekistic unit from room to the whole globe based on average types of ekistic units

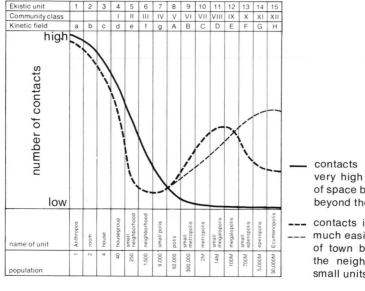

—— contacts in the past were very high in the small units of space but greatly reduced beyond the unit of town

- - - contacts in the present are much easier beyond the unit of town but very limited in the neighborhood and the small units

## 64.　contacts between people

average comparisons of person-to-person contacts in the past and present in every ekistic unit

| Ekistic unit | 1 | 2 | 3 | 4 | 5 | 6 | 7 | 8 | 9 | 10 | 11 | 12 | 13 | 14 | 15 |
|---|---|---|---|---|---|---|---|---|---|---|---|---|---|---|---|
| Community class | | | | I | II | III | IV | V | VI | VII | VIII | IX | X | XI | XII |
| Kinetic field | a | b | c | d | e | f | g | A | B | C | D | E | F | G | H |

exposure to:

unknown people

distant acquaintanceship

acquaintanceship

friends

family members

semi-isolation

complete isolation

| name of unit | Anthropos | room | house | housegroup | small neighborhood | neighborhood | small polis | polis | small metropolis | metropolis | small megalopolis | megalopolis | small eperopolis | eperopolis | Ecumenopolis |
|---|---|---|---|---|---|---|---|---|---|---|---|---|---|---|---|
| population | 1 | 2 | 4 | 40 | 250 | 1,500 | 9,000 | 50,000 | 300,000 | 2M | 14M | 100M | 700M | 5,000M | 30,000M |

numbers of contacts, intensity, quality, time, etc. presented by different degrees

## 65.   exposure of Anthropos to other people
(tentative presentation)

borhoods and almost as much in the large city. We do not learn what is happening nearby but we read and hear and see from radio and on television the disasters further away. This is not natural. The time has come for the correct measurement of Anthropos' (Man's) exposure to people, intensity, quality, time, etc. and this can be done if we use matrixes as in Fig. 65.

At this stage I have to make a proposal to determine the optimum number of contacts in every phase of life. In the U.S.A. I heard some experts advise that the number of children invited to a birthday party should be equal to the age of the child. If this idea is in the right spirit, could we not say that the optimum number of participants could be, let us say, 10 for a play group, 40 for a nursery, 150 for an elementary school, 500 for a high school, 2,000 for each college within a university of 10,000 etc.? Would this not be consistent with gradual exposure to greater numbers?

On this occasion we can recall the case of people being squeezed between machines and walls that has already been presented in a different way (Fig. 49). In terms of contacts we can now determine that although people were moving at lower densities in streets and squares they had more contacts in the same space than they have now. The reason is not density and distances but concern: People now are trying to survive in the street and to move out of the city quickly, this was not the case in the past. In a different way we can also now state that person to person contacts have been reduced or eased at home because of television. We can state this about Greece where television was only introduced recently and we learn that the tensions between older family members are now reduced. Here again is a new search for optimum conditions.

Such observations can be made easier in micro-scales where we can quickly see how multi-story buildings reduce mother-to-child contacts (Fig. 66) and the neighbor-to-neighbor ones (Figs. 67 and 68). But everybody needs these contacts. Isn't proof of this the success of the Sesame Street television program in the U.S.A.? The child needs to participate in this humane environment, the city has now taken it away and returns it as a spectacle. This program is a very good step in the right direction but the viewer does not participate as he could in a humane street! Isn't it dangerous for the child to become an observer of events and not to participate in them?

We have enough experience from those new towns where there is no chance for proper contacts; they are boring to children. An appropriate study was carried out recently in Germany where it was found by psychologists that "the children gauge their freedom not by the extent of open areas around them, but by the liberty they have to be among people and things that excite them and fire their imaginations. The children want to be where something is happening" [57]. And this also seems to be true in extreme cases like in Dublin, Ireland today, where in the Divis Flats district, which is in the areas of action, the children themselves at the age of 12 organize the resistance [58].

All these remarks should not lead to the wrong conclusion that the maximization of our potential contacts (first principle) is not natural and important. The

 anxiety

nervousness

a multi-story residential building creates problems for mother and child who cannot contact each other if the child is in the garden and the mother high up or if they are both enclosed

## 66. contacts between people
mother and child contacts in high and low residential buildings

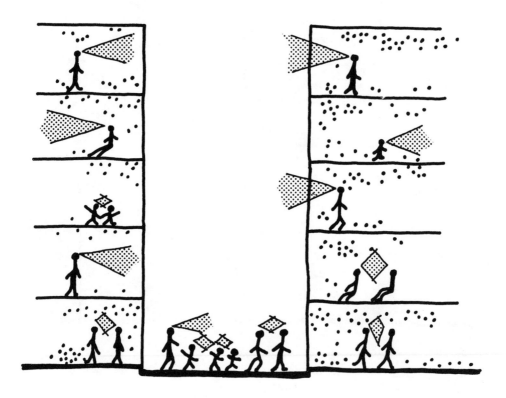

— contacts are easy at the same level where people communicate

— contacts are much more difficult and most often impossible at different levels

## 67.     contacts between people
neighbor-to-neighbor contacts

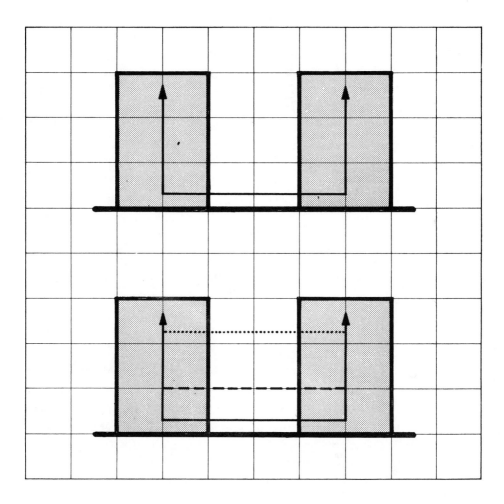

— high buildings create separate vertical circuits which do not allow normal contacts between people

— it is better to allow for circulation of Anthropos in as many directions as possible

## 68.    contacts between people
neighbor-to-neighbor contacts

best proof is that through increased mobility and contacts people are now becoming aware of age-old problems which were hidden in the past because of insurmountable distances. We have many examples of these and I mention one here about the experience of American youth: "The exposure of thousands of young, middle-class Americans to the conditions of poverty through their enlistment in the domestic volunteer program, VISTA, has sharply 'radicalized' about one third of them and moved most others toward a 'more left' social and political posture, according to a government study. The 170-page evaluation, 'VISTA and its Volunteers' completed last March under a contract with Volunteers in Service to America by Prof. David Gottlieb, a Pennsylvania State University sociologist, is based on lengthy questionnaires sent to about 22,000 persons — half of them former VISTA volunteers" [59].

In the big contemporary City of Anthropos (Man) we are able to open our eyes to the world and this is a very big advantage; the problem is, how are we going to open them again in our neighborhood?

## Creativity

If we manage to give Anthropos (Man) the proper physical system which will give him freedom to move in the way he wants and safely, within an area of good quality and with the proper human contacts; then we can hope that he will have the chance to develop properly and not have to limit his potential by exposing himself to a system that puts him in danger or squeezes him (Fig. 69).

To achieve this we must understand the need to assist every aspect of human development: not only the system of body — senses-mind-soul — but also its specific, dynamic directions like education, order and creativity. To present these dynamic aspects more clearly I will try to explain the case of creativity in an illustrative way that may make sense to those who understand spatial human relationships or also — symbolically — social ones.

Creativity can be seen as an explosion of a certain kind of energy which is biologically conditioned (Fig. 70a). This graphic presentation is a picture of creativity over a certain time period. One explosion may occur in one direction; later in another direction other explosions may be in different directions simultaneously. The sum total can be seen as an explosion of energy in the space (physical, sensory or intellectual) within which the individual lives.

If this space is empty (Fig. 70b,c,d), we can consider that the individual who has a creative explosion will begin to lose his energy and his interest for more explosions. If he is not challenged by anything, no matter how long we can keep him alive biologically, he will begin to lose his creative energy. This will

space has to help Anthropos to develop himself
in conditions of safety

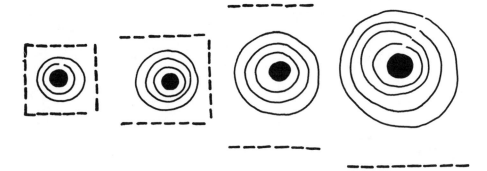

instead of limiting his potential by exposing him
to greater dangers in a very open space
or squeezing him between structures

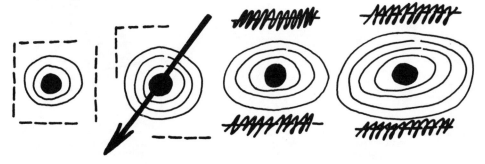

## 69.    human development and physical space

continue until he will lose any ability for further explosions of energy and at the
end there will be no energy at all left in the individual.   The individual will die,
not only as a creative person but in the end as a living organism.   If his explosions
meet with insurmountable boundaries — let us say the walls of a prison cell or
the heavy pressures brought about by a family unit, or by Society — then again
his creative explosions may begin to lose their intensity and the process will be
the same as before:   the individual may die without any creative energy left in
him.   On the other hand, the reflected energy from the boundaries may begin
to heat up the whole atmosphere and lead him to even greater explosions of

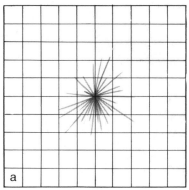

a

starts as an energy explosion

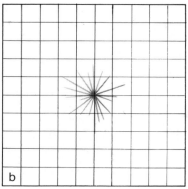

b

if the explosion takes place in a vacuum the source will begin to lose more and more energy

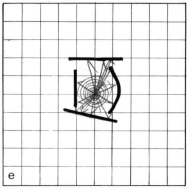

c

if the explosions remain in a vacuum, at the end there is no more energy

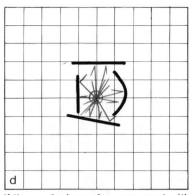

d

if the explosions of energy meet with insurmountable boundaries they begin to reduce their energy

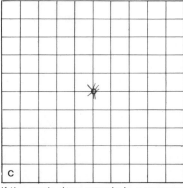

e

if the boundaries remain insurmountable the reflected energy may begin to overheat its source

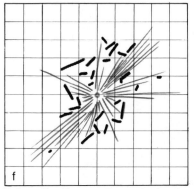

f

if the situation continues to be the same, the source is either burnt out or bursts

70.    creativity

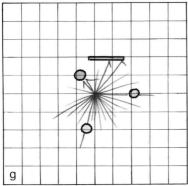

g

if the explosion of energy can over-come some hindrances and chal-lenges, the source is stimulated to further explosions

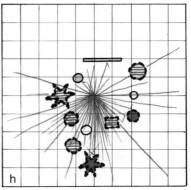

h

the next explosion produces more energy which can overcome greater difficulties and challenges

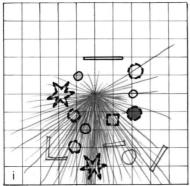

i

at the end the explosions produce much more energy in some direc-tions; the source becomes very strong

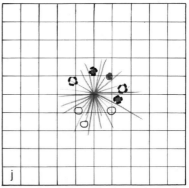

j

the task of the city is to help the source of energy respond to all chal-lenges

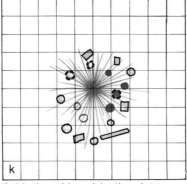

k

if this is achieved in the right way, then the source will be stimulated and develop new strength

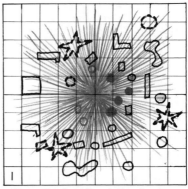

l

with continuing stimulation the source will be strengthened more and more and conquer wider spaces energy. If such a situation continues uninterrupted, the source may explode (Fig. 70e,f). It may break the walls, physical or social, which surround it and the result may be anything from complete success to utter disaster. In both cases Society loses a large percentage of creative individuals; many of those who lead to an explosion do so to the detriment of themselves and of the whole system.

However, if the explosion of energy is neither in an empty space nor within a space surrounded by insurmountable boundaries, but in a space with hindrances, boundaries and challenges, there is a great possibility that the source will be strengthened and made more able to proceed to its next explosion. As the explosions continue, the source finds itself able to produce more energy and to overcome greater difficulties and challenges. Such a process leads at the end to explosions which continuously produce more energy, but probably only in certain directions (Fig. 70g, h, i). If we now ask what the task of the city is in relation to the creativity of the individual (we can parallel creativity with initiative and other aspects of individual expression) the answer can be as follows.

*Hypothesis eighteen:* The task of the city is to help the source of energy — that is the individual — to respond to all challenges and to develop and meet as many new ones as possible. If this can be achieved from the individual's first relationship to his environment, then the source of his energy becomes stronger and can overcome even more hindrances. Such a well developed source of energy will finally be able to conquer the whole space, physical, sensory and intellectual which surrounds it, although this does not necessarily mean that it can conquer all obstacles or hindrances within this space (Fig. 70j, k, l).

If a city can achieve this goal, it will no longer be true that only the fittest can survive, there will be a development of all sources of creativity in all directions. This poses two questions. First, is it possible to develop every source of creativity, not only in some directions but in all directions, so that it can overcome all its challenges and develop up to the limits set by its biological genetic inheritance? Second, is it possible and useful for a city to achieve this for all its citizens and not only for the fittest?

I do not know the answer to these very difficult questions. I can only say that it must be an important task of the city to help every individual to develop his own creativity to the fullest, and that we must leave it to life itself to prove whether this can lead to the survival of all and not only of the fittest. Personally I believe that we cannot allow ourselves, for moral and other reasons, to help only the fittest, or to help individuals develop in one direction only. We have at least the moral obligation to work to provide the kind of city that can help everybody to develop in his own best possible way.

# 5. Specifications for the City of Anthropos (Man)

## The need to build better

We have made the hypothesis that Anthropos (Man) has to satisfy four of the human principles while building his city: maximization of potential contacts, minimization of effort, optimization of protective space, optimization in the relation of the city's five elements. The big question for a builder like myself is how Anthropos (Man) can satisfy his fifth and most important principle: a balance between the other four. What I have learned in practice is that it is relatively easy to satisfy the first four principles separately; a good analyst can satisfy the first and second separately, and with serious effort a good architect can satisfy the third and a very experienced one the fourth. What is very difficult is creating a balance between all four and this is where we produce very great mistakes from which we suffer most. To solve this problem is our great task if we seriously intend to build a better future.

We cannot achieve this until we write specifications for everything that we need. We certainly, as I already said, are not prepared for all of them right now but we do add every morning something new to our system based on the repetition of old concepts and the unsystematic insertion of new ones. The solution is not to escape by theorizing but to write the specifications and apply them, to learn from our mistakes and to constantly try to resolve them. By his actions, Anthropos (Man) has created a great laboratory of human settlements in which he is both the research director and the guinea pig. If we would only open our eyes, we can learn a lot by simply observing Anthropos' (Man's) action in this laboratory, and by studying his history there. At the beginning, Anthropos (Man) only moved over small areas of land and, through trial and error, acquired much knowledge of how to shape these small units — knowledge that we now need to regain. Later Anthropos (Man) created machines which helped him to conquer much larger areas of space as well as make greater and more intense use of this space. These achievements, coupled with Anthropos' (Man's) increasing ability to communicate over ever wider areas of space, have led to the erroneous conclusion that the globe is shrinking. It would be preferable to speak about an expanding Anthropos (Man) but even this would not be completely exact, as Anthropos (Man) bodily does not occupy more space; he still has much the same physical dimensions as primitive Anthropos (Man). It is his field of movement — his kinetic fields — and his sensory system which brings him much more information, that have expanded. We can speak of expanding Anthropos (Man) but be conscious of what this means, what we should avoid saying is the fashionable statement that the earth is shrinking, because it is wrong in every way.

This means that we should develop a system which helps not only Anthropos-the-giant, Anthropos (Man) who with his extended arms, body, sight and hearing covers the whole earth as some people think of him, but Anthropos-the-human, who is able to live in all scales in all units of space. The relationship of the unborn child to its mother remains exactly the same in space as in primitive times — in the womb. The relationship in space between the mother and the newborn child remains the same. So does the relationship between husband and wife, between close friends, and between all people who want to have personal, face-to-face contacts. These relationships in space do not change, though other relationships which depend wholly or in part on the use of machines change enormously. It is imperative that we develop a system which will help us to comprehend the relationship of people to space in all phases of their life or as Erikson says "from womb to tomb".

Such considerations lead to the question of the relationship of Anthropos (Man) to the total space within which he can move. While at any given moment his body and physiological system of senses only occupy a limited area, he does move around and benefits from a much larger space. In terms of human development, what are the dimensions of total space needed for Anthropos' (Man's) movements? Before he is born this space is confined to a specific part of his mother's body. After birth his space needs increase from his crib to the room, house, neighborhood and city. It is our task to write specifications on all scales and for all requirements.

To achieve this we have to organize our space as its dimensions have blown up and we still do not understand its units. Anthropos (Man) has been using terrestrial space for over two million years. He has lived in parts of it, formed or molded some of them and destroyed others mostly by exposing them to fire and recently new mechanical and chemical elements and has moved across certain areas of space. These actions have occupied different spatial units, from the cave (or room) to the whole globe. Such units can be classified in a system starting with Anthropos (Man) as the smallest unit of ekistic space (we should never forget that Anthropos (Man) is the measure), moving to a room (as the smallest physical space formed by Anthropos — Man) then to the house, neighborhood, small and large cities, metropolis and up to the whole globe which, in this classification corresponds to unit No. 15. We can add that Anthropos (Man), having moved beyond the earth, has now created another unit, No. 16, but as our study is concerned with terrestrial space we retain the 15 units. I have already used these fifteen units in previous diagrams; I only come back to them here in order to justify and explain them as they are the key factor for understanding Anthropos' (Man's) spatial relationships [60] and in order to present their meaning in terms of the physical dimensions corresponding to them and the scales in which we can study them (Fig. 71).

With the proper organized concept of space we now have to find out what this means for Anthropos (Man), because specifications can be written on this basis only. The first criterion for such an evaluation is the time that Anthropos (Man) spends in every unit of space; that is the time he is exposed to it. This must be done first for every phase of his life and then for every person and case. I only deal with the first here in the spirit of this whole study and suggest this same method for every single case. In this way we can measure how many hours any type of person spends in every unit of space, calculate the average for a family, etc. (Fig. 72), and then calculate how much time Anthropos (Man)

| ekistic units | 1 | 2 | 3 | 4 | 5 | 6 | 7 | 8 | 9 | 10 | 11 | 12 | 13 | 14 | 15 |
|---|---|---|---|---|---|---|---|---|---|---|---|---|---|---|---|
| scales in meters | Anthropos | room | house | housegroup | small neighborhood | neighborhood | small polis | polis | small metropolis | metropolis | small megalopolis | megalopolis | small eperopolis | eperopolis | Ecumenopolis |
| 100,000,000 | | | | | | | | | | | | | | | |
| 50,000,000 | | | | | | | | | | | | | | | |
| 20,000,000 | | | | | | | | | | | | | | | |
| 10,000,000 | | | | | | | | | | | | | | | |
| 5,000,000 | | | | | | | | | | | | | | | |
| 2,000,000 | | | | | | | | | | | | | | | |
| 1,000,000 | | | | | | | | | | | | | | | |
| 500,000 | | | | | | | | | | | | | | | |
| 200,000 | | | | | | | | | | | | | | | |
| 100,000 | | | | | | | | | | | | | | | |
| 50,000 | | | | | | | | | | | | | | | |
| 20,000 | | | | | | | | | | | | | | | |
| 10,000 | | | | | | | | | | | | | | | |
| 5,000 | | | | | | | | | | | | | | | |
| 2,000 | | | | | | | | | | | | | | | |
| 1,000 | | | | | | | | | | | | | | | |
| 500 | | | | | | | | | | | | | | | |
| 200 | | | | | | | | | | | | | | | |
| 100 | | | | | | | | | | | | | | | |
| 50 | | | | | | | | | | | | | | | |
| 20 | | | | | | | | | | | | | | | |
| 10 | | | | | | | | | | | | | | | |
| 5 | | | | | | | | | | | | | | | |
| 2 | | | | | | | | | | | | | | | |
| 1 | | | | | | | | | | | | | | | |

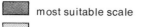

■ most suitable scale

▢ next to most suitable scale

## 71. physical scales

units of space and range of most suitable scales
for the study of relationships for each ekistic unit

104

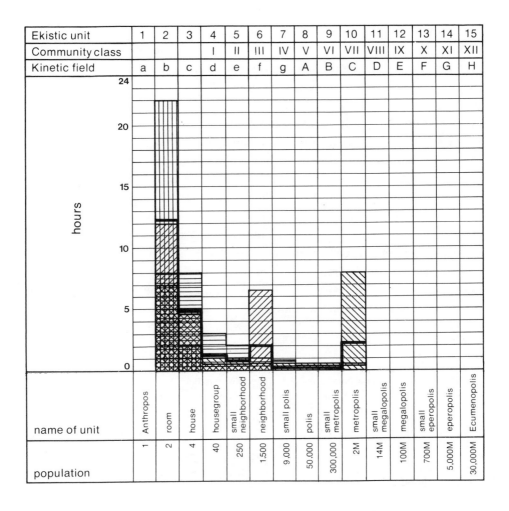

| Ekistic unit | 1 | 2 | 3 | 4 | 5 | 6 | 7 | 8 | 9 | 10 | 11 | 12 | 13 | 14 | 15 |
|---|---|---|---|---|---|---|---|---|---|---|---|---|---|---|---|
| Community class | | | | I | II | III | IV | V | VI | VII | VIII | IX | X | XI | XII |
| Kinetic field | a | b | c | d | e | f | g | A | B | C | D | E | F | G | H |
| name of unit | Anthropos | room | house | housegroup | small neighborhood | neighborhood | small polis | polis | small metropolis | metropolis | small megalopolis | megalopolis | small eperopolis | eperopolis | Ecumenopolis |
| population | 1 | 2 | 4 | 40 | 250 | 1,500 | 9,000 | 50,000 | 300,000 | 2M | 14M | 100M | 700M | 5,000M | 30,000M |

[[[[]]]] infant

≣ mother

▨ child

◪ father

━ family

72.    lifetime spent daily in different units of space

spends per unit of space in a city where the family carries on an average style of life in a community that has not lost its human characteristics (Fig. 73).

In this way we can now follow every person or the average person and, having calculated how much time he spends in every unit of space in every phase of his life, thus reach conclusions about the exposure to each unit of space (Fig. 74). There can be no question that what is important for Anthropos (Man) now in this way of examination, is not the monumental building of government in the metropolis but his room, home, etc. Needless to say, these needs differ from culture to culture, case to case, etc. but I doubt if there are cases where the image is very different from the general one given in this figure.

The second criterion is the importance of every unit of space for Anthropos' (Man's) life. He may spend an equal time in his W.C. (15 minutes a day or 1% of his lifetime) and his conference room (one hour a day for a fourth of his life, that is again 1% of his lifetime) and he has to decide which matters more. A third criterion is how many people spend time together in space. In this sense, a conference room has much greater value, if not for the individuals, then for the group.

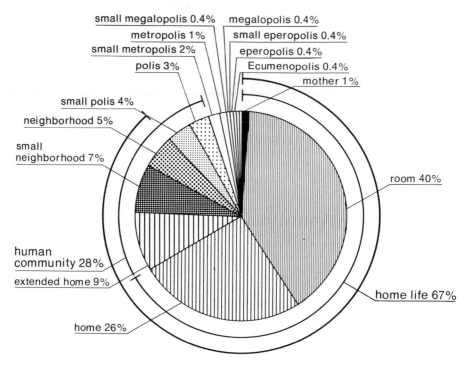

73.    lifetime spent in different units of space

| Ekistic unit | 1 | 2 | 3 | 4 | 5 | 6 | 7 | 8 | 9 | 10 | 11 | 12 | 13 | 14 | 15 |
|---|---|---|---|---|---|---|---|---|---|---|---|---|---|---|---|
| Community class | | | | I | II | III | IV | V | VI | VII | VIII | IX | X | XI | XII |
| Kinetic field | a | b | c | d | e | f | g | A | B | C | D | E | F | G | H |

human development phases — 12, 11, 10, 9, 8, 7, 6, 5, 4, 3, 2, 1 — total

| name of unit | Anthropos | room | house | housegroup | small neighborhood | neighborhood | small polis | polis | small metropolis | metropolis | small megalopolis | megalopolis | small eperopolis | eperopolis | Ecumenopolis |
|---|---|---|---|---|---|---|---|---|---|---|---|---|---|---|---|
| population | 1 | 2 | 4 | 40 | 250 | 1.500 | 9.000 | 50.000 | 300.000 | 2M | 14M | 100M | 700M | 5,000M | 30,000M |

■■■■IIIIII| | | the intensity shows the percentage of time
spent in every unit ot space

## 74.   time spent in different units of space
in every phase of life

For every such unit we can finally estimate for every single, average person
what it really means in each phase of his life (Fig. 75). With these estimates we
can conceive the model for calculating the total importance of every unit of
space for Anthropos (Man) (Fig. 76). This again differs from individual to
individual and culture to culture but this figure does make us recognize the very

| Ekistic unit | 1 | 2 | 3 | 4 | 5 | 6 | 7 | 8 | 9 | 10 | 11 | 12 | 13 | 14 | 15 |
|---|---|---|---|---|---|---|---|---|---|---|---|---|---|---|---|
| Community class | | | | I | II | III | IV | V | VI | VII | VIII | IX | X | XI | XII |
| Kinetic field | a | b | c | d | e | f | g | A | B | C | D | E | F | G | H |
| name of unit | Anthropos | room | house | housegroup | small neighborhood | neighborhood | small polis | polis | small metropolis | metropolis | small megalopolis | megalopolis | small eperopolis | eperopolis | Ecumenopolis |
| population | 1 | 2 | 4 | 40 | 250 | 1,500 | 9,000 | 50,000 | 300,000 | 2M | 14M | 100M | 700M | 5,000M | 30,000M |

*human development phases* (vertical axis, 1–12)

● ● degree of importance of every unit of space for the single individual

## 75.  the meaning of every unit of space in every phase of life
tentative suggestion for one individual

big importance of the smaller units which we have overlooked.  We no longer live in ancient Sparta where the great emphasis was participation in the state life for the achievement of the state's goals, a situation which did not recognize the goals of the individual.

By using the above models we can now calculate every aspect of life in every

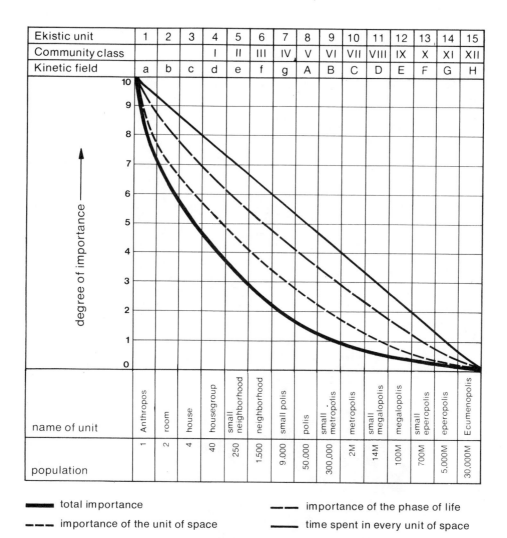

| Ekistic unit | 1 | 2 | 3 | 4 | 5 | 6 | 7 | 8 | 9 | 10 | 11 | 12 | 13 | 14 | 15 |
|---|---|---|---|---|---|---|---|---|---|---|---|---|---|---|---|
| Community class | | | | I | II | III | IV | V | VI | VII | VIII | IX | X | XI | XII |
| Kinetic field | a | b | c | d | e | f | g | A | B | C | D | E | F | G | H |
| name of unit | Anthropos | room | house | housegroup | small neighborhood | neighborhood | small polis | polis | small metropolis | metropolis | small megalopolis | megalopolis | small eperopolis | eperopolis | Ecumenopolis |
| population | 1 | 2 | 4 | 40 | 250 | 1.500 | 9.000 | 50.000 | 300.000 | 2M | 14M | 100M | 700M | 5.000M | 30.000M |

degree of importance →

▬▬▬ total importance    — — importance of the phase of life

– – – importance of the unit of space    ▬▬▬ time spent in every unit of space

## 76.    total importance of every unit of space
tentative suggestion for one individual

unit, for the individual, the family, the community, etc., assign values and find out what we must do for every single case. We can use our model first with the criterion of desirability and then feasibility (Fig. 77).

With such approaches we reach the point at which, having conceived human development and its balance in every phase of life (Fig. 33), we can now define

| | | feasible evolution in relation to present situation | | | | |
|---|---|---|---|---|---|---|
| | | -- | - | = | + | ++ |
| desirable evolution in relation to present situation | -- | -2 · -2 / -4 | -2 · -2 / -4 | -2 · -2 / -4 | +2 · -2 / 0 | +1 · -2 / -1 |
| | - | -2 · -2 / -4 | -2 · -2 / -4 | -2 · -2 / -4 | +2 · -2 / 0 | +1 · -2 / -1 |
| | = | -2 · -2 / -4 | -2 · -2 / -4 | -2 · -2 / -4 | +2 · -2 / 0 | +1 · -2 / -1 |
| | + | -2 · +1 / -1 | -2 · +1 / -1 | -2 · +1 / -1 | +2 · +1 / +3 | +1 · +1 / +2 |
| | ++ | -2 · +2 / 0 | -2 · +2 / 0 | -2 · +2 / 0 | +2 · +2 / +4 | +1 · +2 / +3 |

the figures in every small triangle correspond to the *degree of probability* of every feasible or desirable type of evolution and range from −2 (very improbable) to +2 (very probable)

the figures in every large triangle correspond to the *attention* that must be given to it and range from the highest degree of +4 to the lowest of −4

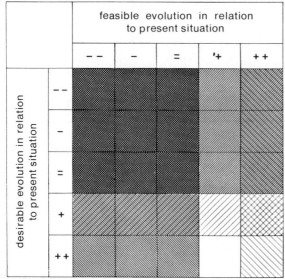

| | | feasible evolution in relation to present situation | | | | |
|---|---|---|---|---|---|---|
| | | -- | - | = | '+ | ++ |
| desirable evolution in relation to present situation | -- | | | | | |
| | - | | | | | |
| | = | | | | | |
| | + | | | | | |
| | ++ | | | | | |

the shades in every square correspond to the attention that must be given to it and range from the highest degree of +4 □ to the lowest of −4 ▓

## 77.  the desirability-feasibility evaluation model
an example of the method on energy

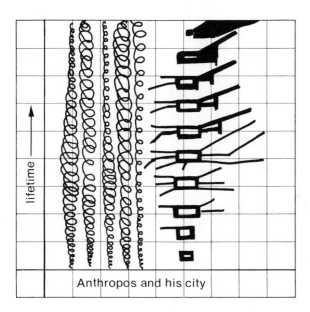

Anthropos and his city

78.    Anthropos has and needs a different balance
        in every phase of his life
        with his city or his system of life

and achieve the balance needed between Anthropos (Man) and his city by creating a system that can as a whole serve every citizen (since it cannot change for each one) and by its parts assist every group or individual in every phase of his life (Fig. 78) without simply helping some people or institutions to show off.

How can we achieve this? I can only answer as a bricklayer, and my answer leads to the proposals in the following sections for the city we need specifically, and can build for every phase of our life. This is the city we will build with bricks, exactly as Mallarmé meant to write poems. One day the painter Degas complained to his friend, the author, Mallarmé, of the difficulties of rhyming. "What a job", he said, "I've lost an entire day on one accursed sonnet without getting anywhere, and it's not that I am missing ideas. I have enough of them, more than enough". "You don't make sonnets with ideas, Degas, but with words", replied Mallarmé[61].

## Prenatal phase of life

We can now try and define the specifications of the total space used, or potentially used, by Anthropos (Man) in every phase of his life together with his period of exposure to this space in order to clearly define the units of space Anthropos (Man) needs at each period of his life. On the basis of such considerations, I propose a system of graphs corresponding to 12 phases and the many sub-phases in the life of a person up to 100 years.

In the first, prenatal phase, the spatial needs of Anthropos (Man) are very limited and his whole potential space is confined to ekistic unit No. 1 (Fig. 79) since Anthropos (Man) really lives only within the body of his mother.

There are many questions which arise during this phase and I do not know any answers. I therefore present them hoping to start a dialogue. We cannot deal with the needs of the unborn baby in the city but we can deal with the mother.

The first question concerns the unit of her room and its furnishings. We do not know well enough which type of furniture or which type of room is pre-ferable for her. There are certainly all sorts of cultural differences but the question is whether the body and senses during pregnancy must have any special kind of environment. I do not know.

How far away from home should a mother go? Very probably not as far as before pregnancy; the baby moves with her in a natural, dependent way.

How should she move? For example, when she walks is it better for her and the baby that she walk on a paved area only or also on a non-paved one (Fig. 80)? What type of movement is preferable for reasons of safety (paved areas), but also for transmitting to the baby a certain rhythm? If the mother walks only on paved streets, is the baby going to be a good walker or a good dancer?

When mother moves only by car from her kitchen door to her destination, is she helping the baby or depriving it of some abilities?

My proposal is, that because we may not yet know the answers, we must be conservative in changing the system too quickly. Therefore, we must give the mother not only the freedom but also the challenge to walk and not just drive (if she has a car, which most mothers do not). This will allow her to walk either on paved streets to reach where she must go (bus-station, job, corner shop, etc.) or on completely natural ground designed to be safe so that she goes because she feels like it. She must be challenged to go there, so there must be an alternate route for her; a road which provides places of pleasure like beautiful gardens with plants and birds or open-air exhibits or games. But this must also be possible in bad weather when a mother also needs to go out which means that a system of walking inside a covered natural landscape should be available. This has to be added for countries with long, heavy winters.

Safety demands much better material for sidewalks and garden paths.

How about her visual world? Is it better for her to be exposed to a variety of views or not? The assumption is that variety is best, but then the distant

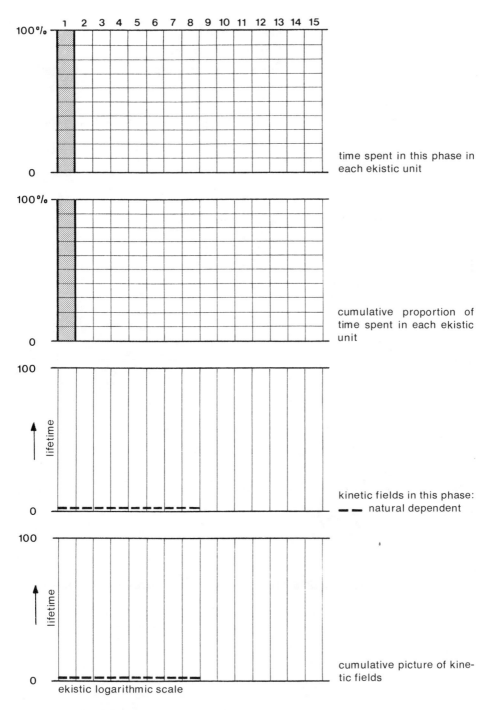

time spent in this phase in each ekistic unit

cumulative proportion of time spent in each ekistic unit

kinetic fields in this phase:
— — natural dependent

cumulative picture of kinetic fields

ekistic logarithmic scale

79.　time related to space
　　　first phase: prenatal or fetal (-9 months to 0)

park is not the answer as she cannot go there easily. Infiltration of the system by Nature is much better for her than the inaccessible park (Fig. 81).

How is she affected by the sounds around her and the noise? Is she not in a more vulnerable state when pregnant? Should she be exposed to all city noises or the smells and the walls she touches?

How can she maximize her potential contacts? Certainly not in the multi-

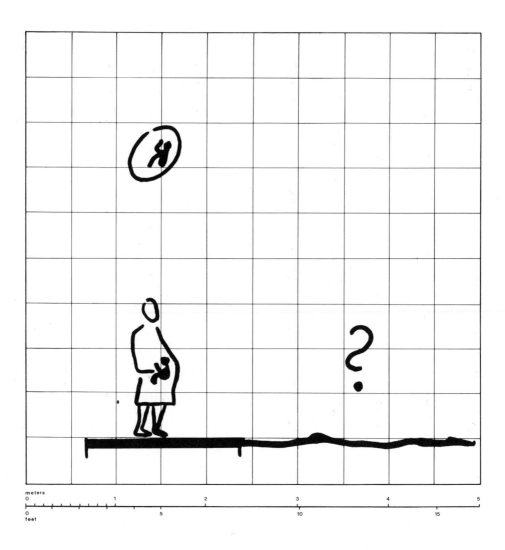

meters

0    1    2    3    4    5

0    feet    5    10    15

80.    spatial needs — first phase:
       prenatal or fetal (-9 months to 0)

story building. It has not worked so far[62]. All signs indicate that it is better for her to live in a one or two-story building but should she be isolated from others because of big distances between houses? Certainly not, because then she cannot speak easily to neighbors. She needs very close contacts. The best provision for these that I have seen are in the narrow streets of the small towns of some Aegean islands. The husband leaves very early and a few

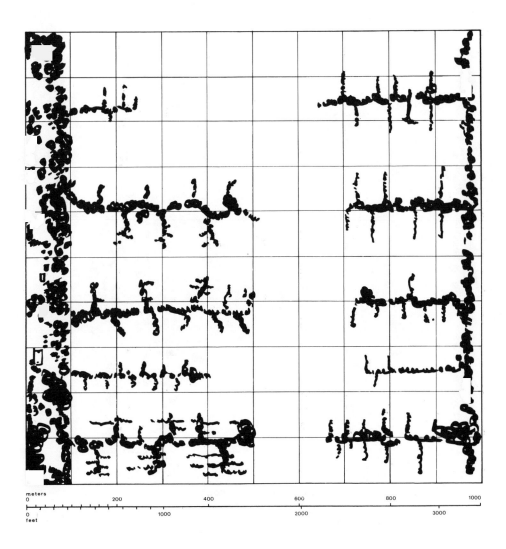

meters
0     200     400     600     800     1000

0     1000     2000     3000
feet

81.  infiltration of Nature into the human settlement is much better than a large park

minutes later the wives meet across their door or gateways which provide cover from sun or rain and they can gossip without being overheard (Fig. 82). In a few minutes some of their problems are over. This is the best type of application of principles one and two (for the easiest contact with open doors) and principle three for isolation (by closing the doors). Some people may say that such nearness creates problems but the answer is that "Even disagreeable treatment is better than total neglect and blandness in the environment"[63].

We need the narrow street for the proper contacts for mothers. It is here

82.     meeting across the doors

that principles one and two are satisfied in the best possible way. It seems that people come out to breathe fresh air and to see others and they also might happen to meet a neighbor and talk. This is the probable explanation for why this does not occur in the corridors of multi-story buildings. We seldom move outside our door just for one reason, just to gossip. But when we can also enjoy the beautiful street, the climate, the flowers and birds and learn from the passers-by then the value is different. When the discussion fails to satisfy us, we close the door and thus we follow the third principle.

This is the meaning of a balanced system.

## Breast dependence phase (0 to 6 months)

I hope that the experts will excuse me for using this phase as a separate one and not as a sub-phase. The reason is, when I look at Anthropos (Man) in space, I can clearly see this phase as distinct from the infant in the womb and the child on the floor. In the spirit of this study it made sense to me but I also saw it used as a separate phase in the last World Health Organization report on human development[64].

This is the phase that starts in the hospital and lasts for a few months when "Basic Trust versus Basic Mistrust"[65] (see page 314) develops; when the baby sees itself as part of the mother, and begins to feel a significant relationship to one maternal person by the time he is 3-5 months old[66]. Some cultures, like some Indian tribes in America train their infants to be suspicious, then when masochism begins to develop the mother does not understand how to re-spond[67]; separating a baby from his mother or her subsitute which the baby uses as mother may delay the process of connections between his own senses.

The infant is not yet free to move and depends on his mother who has to move him so as to initiate his sensory stimulation, but not too much and not without her. I was told by Spyros Doxiadis that one of the worst cases of retarded development that he has seen is a child of a very rich family who has grown up in a very luxurious room with a nurse and practically complete iso-lation from any other unit of space and without any other kind of exposure. Lately I read about the efforts of Jaroslav Koch[68] who studied many children in this and later phases and came to the conclusion that motor stimulation of infants has a profound influence on future development. In spite of this need, we can state that in many cases, the infant really spends this whole period in his room and at home (Fig. 83). In this way we have the first demand: since the infant needs exposure, the house should not be only another room or series of rooms, or a balcony on the tenth floor from which the child cannot

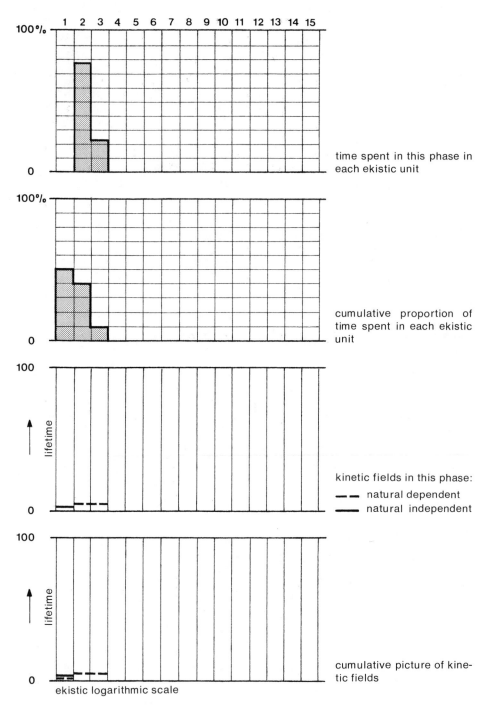

time spent in this phase in each ekistic unit

cumulative proportion of time spent in each ekistic unit

kinetic fields in this phase:
-- natural dependent
— natural independent

cumulative picture of kinetic fields

ekistic logarithmic scale

83.    time related to space
       second phase: breast dependence (0 to 6 months)

see or understand anything. The house must have the maximum possible types of exposure; this means at least some rooms (6 sides closed), a courtyard or atrium (5 sides closed) and a garden (2-4 sides closed or some semi-closed) as I have already explained (Fig. 51).

In this house the infant spends most of his time in his special crib and with his mother (Fig. 84). I do not intend here to restyle mother and I do not know whether it is preferable for the infant to see her in a white dress only or a black and white one (it would seem that initially he might understand or prefer exposure to black and white patterns rather than color or colored

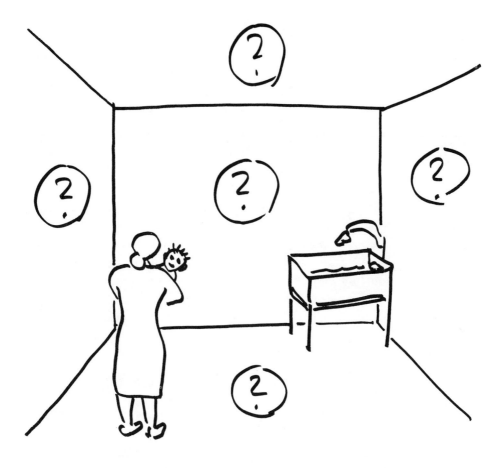

84.　　breast dependence phase — what kind of room?

dresses) [69]. There are groups which begin to speak of the importance of certain colors and state that they have, "a decisive influence on the child's mental performance", but we do not yet know enough on this subject [70].

Since the infant spends so much time in his crib, we must understand and specify the best kind of crib for him and, although there are many types in the market which are considered very good, I have questions to ask in order to be consistent with the earlier principles. As the infant is now making his first move from the womb to the open world, does it make sense to give him the feeling of more enclosed space? There are experts who begin to study such questions[71] but we do not yet know enough. We know that later he likes to go under tables or into cupboards, so at this stage he might like to feel as though he were inside a box without really being in one. Couldn't this mean covering the crib at a certain height to create a ceiling and should this ceiling be solid with the sides of the crib open, or the opposite, that is a grid as a ceiling and solid sides?

What colors are preferable, what materials (for touch or taste), what sounds?

Should we place a television set or a microphone next to him to observe him and to inform us in the other rooms of what is happening?

Should we control his climate in any way? The infant emerges from a standard, even climate where it has spent nine months and some day he is going to cross the Sahara and climb on Mount Everest. How about this phase? Does it make sense to consider it an intermediate one and try to develop the equipment that keeps him in a climate where temperatures do not differ by more than 5 °C (9 °F), if in the next phase or some of the next ones he will live in a climate with variables in temperature of up to 20 °C (36 °F) or more?

How do we stimulate the infant at this stage? We hear a lot about good and bad toys[72] but not enough about his whole system of life. These are questions we have to answer.

## Infant's phase (7 to 15 months)

The infant begins to want to separate from his mother[73] and to move by himself. It is the phase when the infant crawls in the room (ekistic unit 2 with normally two people) in a natural, semi-independent way, perhaps in the whole house (ekistic unit 3 with one family and three to seven people) in a natural, dependent way and looks out (Fig. 85), when he begins to "Perceive and Interact" (see also Fig. 53) and watch the interplay in the world around him. The infant certainly needs to feel that he is entitled to move like the others, but like whom, the older children or grown-ups? Equality is essential, yes, but how is it applied?

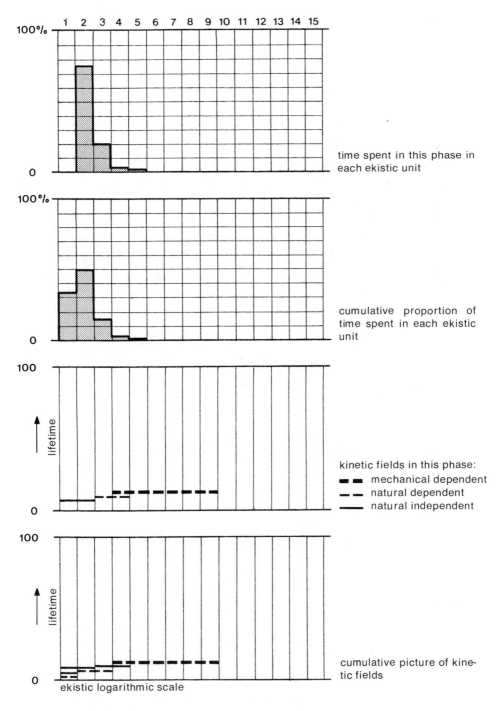

time spent in this phase in each ekistic unit

cumulative proportion of time spent in each ekistic unit

kinetic fields in this phase:
▪ ▪ mechanical dependent
– – natural dependent
— natural independent

cumulative picture of kinetic fields

ekistic logarithmic scale

85.   time related to space
      third phase: infant (7 to 15 months)

121

In order to apply this principle is it better to allow the infant to move only with others like himself? Where is the challenge for his development then?

Certainly, if there were any doubt about the need for courtyard and garden in the previous phase, there is no doubt now. The infant needs to start moving out of the house and seeing the world from the garden. This is his space. We must give its specifications by enumerating the smallest to the largest units, provided he moves by himself; because we do not need to design the highway for this infant — he will go there in a car with his parents, at least at present.

We started with the crib. Do we need anything more or less than in the second phase? If our assumption about an enclosed crib is right, should we now widen or open it at the top?

The infant now also needs his own space to move and we give him (higher income countries) the playpen (Fig. 86). Is this right, to give the infant the impression of such an enclosed space, or is it preferable to give him low, round or shaped tables to play at (Fig. 87) and close the door of his room? Or perhaps are both these solutions right, provided we use the playpen first, slowly reducing the length of exposure in it and increasing his exposure to the tables where he is not inside but outside? I think this assumption makes more sense in the spirit of gradual exposure to larger units. In such a case shouldn't we design round or oval playpens instead of square ones, since we know that human beings and animals do not start with rectilinear, geometric movement but rather with natural forms closer allied to round ones?

If we believe what Pope Paul VI said, "children play what the adults live"[74], and begin to study how children play in a systematic way, we must design the gradual transfer from womb to crib, to all sorts of playpens (small prisons) and tables (small assistants for walking). We must look at other pieces of furniture in the same way, and the challenges and problems they create. For instance, when we speak of cupboards, we must remember that the infant at this age catches hold of the key in the door in order to be able to stand up and then pulls it out and falls. Isn't it better to have handles at his height and the keys placed above one meter (39 inches) high?

The most important question is perhaps whether the infant needs a special very small room to live in or whether he should live in a common room alone or with his mother. We know that children go under tables, beds, stairs and unfortunately also into refrigerators and build what we call dolls' houses. Do they build them for their dolls or for themselves? Is the construction and the pleasure derived from inhabiting a miniature house not related to the children's need to occupy a space which corresponds more to their dimensions? In building the cities for adults who, however, represent only slightly more than

50% of the total population in high income countries, have we not completely overlooked the needs of children to develop in units of space corresponding to their dimensions and to their expectations?  Should we not treat space as we treat clothing, creating units corresponding to the needs of each individual?

There is no question that here we deal with a very basic instinct, the question

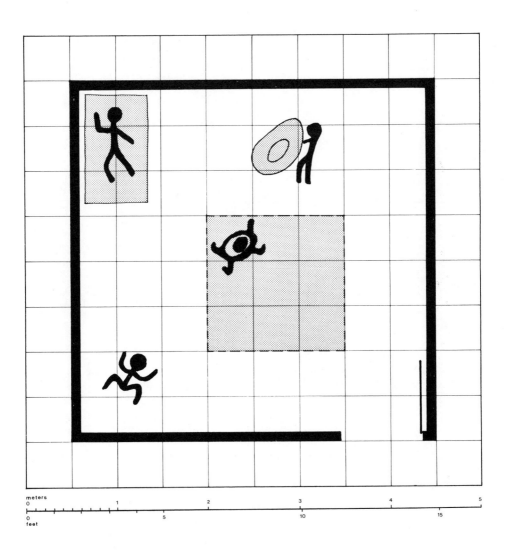

86.    spatial needs — third phase: infant (7 to 15 months)

is how to serve it. To start the dialogue I propose that we need a very small room 2.40 by 2.40 meters (8 by 8 feet) for the infant to live in, sometimes with his mother and sometimes alone. We must also build in some other place adjacent to this room, in the corridor or even in the kitchen or living-room, a much smaller room, not larger than 1.50 by 1.20 and 0.90 meters high (5 by 4 feet, 3 feet high) for normal play with doors that can apparently close but that will

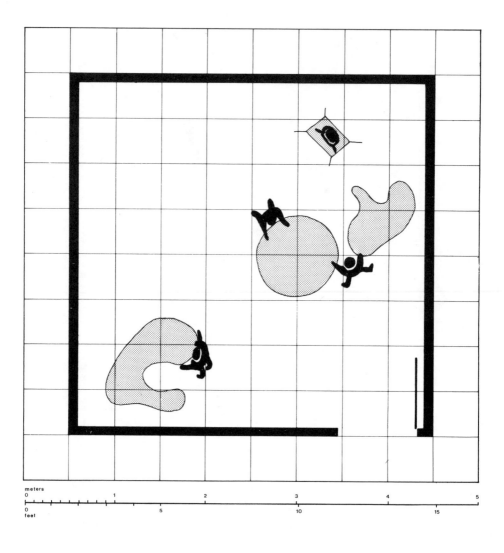

meters

| 0 | 1 | 2 | 3 | 4 | 5 |

0 feet | 5 | 10 | 15

87.     spatial needs — third phase: infant (7 to 15 months)

always open when pushed from inside. This must have holes allowing for continuous ventilation, for light to come in and allowing the infant to call out. When there are no longer children who need this space, it can be used in many ways, or its ceiling can be taken out and the whole space transformed in order to serve later phases and finally united to the room or corridor to which it is attached (Figs. 88 and 89).

88.    infant's play-room — first phase

Staircases should not be considered as open spaces accessible to all, but should always be designed to allow for the addition of a door when the child needs it badly at a young age for reasons of safety.

The notion that the infant should spend all his time in this phase within a room which is all enclosed (six-sided) is not correct as the infant would then feel he is a prisoner (Fig. 90). I have already explained in the previous phase that even the breast-dependent infant needs a courtyard (five sides) and a garden (3-4 sides). This need is now far greater and therefore I explain exactly what I mean by a courtyard or the ancient Greek aithrion (Roman atrium): I really mean a room without a roof. It is a room in dimensions and shape with one difference, it is exposed to the weather from the top, not to winds which never

89.    infant's play-room — second phase

90.    the room as the infant sees it

enter but to sun and rain (Fig. 91).  It is the first degree of exposure, not to foreigners, not to the road, perhaps not to plants and birds but certainly to open weather.  Safety in terms of mobility is absolute.

The garden, in the sense in which I am using the word, is different.  Instead of being inside or behind the house and having high walls, it should be in front and surrounded by a one meter high wall on all its sides that are not covered by the house itself (Fig. 92).  The infant (and the mother) can now see the world outside, that is, Nature, other houses, neighbors, etc.  Safety in terms of mobility is almost absolute if we have a correctly designed gate.

The courtyard opens the house to weather and the garden reveals the neighborhood.  We can expose the infant gradually in terms of time of exposure and freedom to be alone, first in the room, then the courtyard and finally the garden.

Are we still prepared to defend the multi-story blocks of apartments?

91.    the courtyard as the infant sees it

## Toddler's phase (16 to 30 months)

This is the phase when the toddler moves gradually out of his room, conquers his home and his garden and looks beyond them into the housegroup (ekistic unit 4 with around 40 people or about eight to ten families). In this phase he still spends the longest part of his life in his room, a large part in the house and only a very minor segment outside it where he is certainly dependent on assistance (Fig. 93). Thus his kinetic fields have now extended up to the boundaries of the house in a natural independent way, and beyond the boundaries of the house in a natural dependent way. Probably it is at this stage that the mechanical dependent movements begin, i.e. it is in the toddler's interest that he should

92.　　　the garden as the infant sees it

be taken by carriage or car beyond the family territory in order to get acquainted gradually with the neighbors and the neighborhood.

This is the phase as Erikson says of "Autonomy versus Shame, Doubt" as well as the phase of "parental persons". I assume that this means a safe base from which the toddler can begin to expand his environment.

This is a phase when the toddler gains in muscular coordination and begins important locomotive development. It is the phase when the mother has to say "NO" so often, as Erikson said [75], that the toddler's development goes wrong; all doors have knobs that only adults can open.

This is where the big question arises: what can we do for this toddler? Should

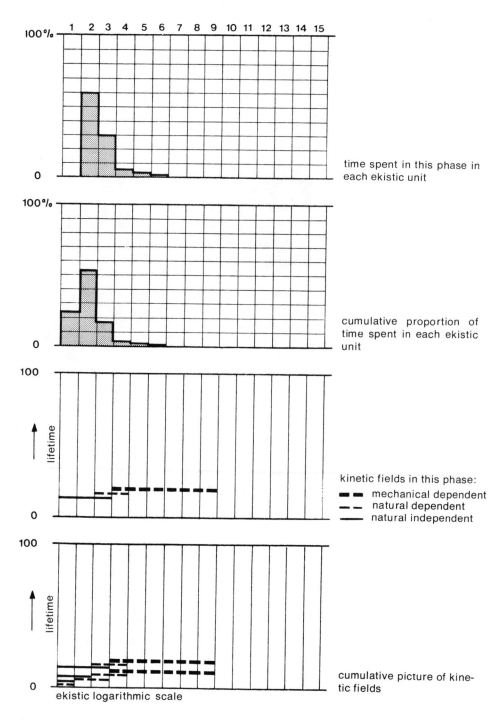

time spent in this phase in each ekistic unit

cumulative proportion of time spent in each ekistic unit

kinetic fields in this phase:
▬ ▬ mechanical dependent
– – natural dependent
―― natural independent

cumulative picture of kinetic fields

ekistic logarithmic scale

93.   time related to space
      fourth phase: toddler (16 to 30 months)

we place door knobs lower and let him be free? How far should a toddler be free to go by himself? I think that a good solution could be achieved in the following direction: let the toddler move freely in the house by placing a second lower knob, which will operate with the upper one, in all the doors that lead to places where the toddler can safely be by himself. This would require a new type of knob allowing mothers to decide when the toddler can operate them (green light), and when not (red light) depending on the ability of the toddler, the safety of the space they enter and the hour of the day. The limit for the most able toddler is the gate opening to the street, it cannot have a lower knob, this is the limit of his kinetic domain in this phase, but not of his visual and auditory range as the toddler can walk to the garden by himself (Fig. 94) and see people passing outside and talk to them without going out or letting them in (Fig. 92).

The house presents the same problems and possible solutions in this phase as do the room and the furniture, in the previous infant's phase. The difference is a slight one of dimensions and the first house equipment for a toddler has to be added as the toddler begins toilet-training. Should we have a special toilet for him, a special corner in the house toilet or bathroom or a movable one as we now provide? I do not know but we must find out. Whether or not we can afford to explore this question at this time I do not know, but we must remember that our purpose is to define what is desirable and only then find ways to make it feasible.

The big change in this phase is that the toddler enjoys very much going beyond the boundaries of home and meeting the world. This cannot happen if the world is controlled by cars and unsafe, but it can occur in a small, corridor-like pedestrian street, the home-street (Fig. 95) with a safe gate at the end. In this way the toddler moves out of the family, into the extended family, at first with his mother and father or brothers and sisters and then eventually by himself. It is here that we can hope that he reaches the optimal level of res-ponse and learning as Donald Hebb expressed his views on the need for a certain amount of excitement[76]. For this phase he has to conquer the world safely as no gate to any other house or from the home-street out will have low accessible knobs and must not be left open under any conditions. I suggest new specifications which are easy to realize mechanically and electronically. These results cannot be expected in the corridors of a block of apartments — the toddler will see only monochrome walls and doors. If he does go out of his home, it will be to enter a prison-like corridor. He is not challenged to go there, the quality of what he enters gets lower. This is not our goal.

It is in this home-street that we can challenge the toddler to face steps without any protection such as the staircase in a two-story house where a door

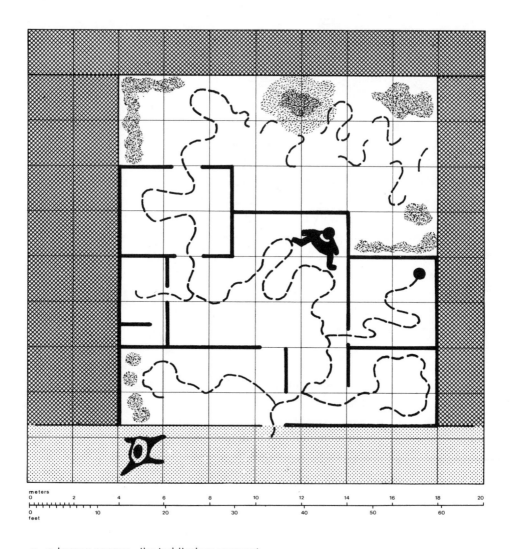

meters

0    2    4    6    8    10    12    14    16    18    20

0    10    20    30    40    50    60

feet

〰 human energy – the toddler's movement

94.    spatial needs — fourth phase:
toddler (16 to 30 months)

95.     the home-street

is necessary.  Conquering stairs must occur at some stage and if there is doubt about the toddler's ability during this phase it should be accomplished in the next.  Stairs in the street with wide steps are very important for training purposes and perhaps (although I cannot prove it) they help the toddler acquire a rhythmic movement as I have already mentioned on page      At the beginning (Fig. 96) he will climb when we hold him by the hands on both sides — he may be frightened as the stairs are new to him, but if we start helping him to jump over one step he will be interested to try the second, hope to achieve the third and be enthusiastic about the fourth.  Something new is frightening at the beginning, but if we know how to help him we may turn fear into conquest. The toddler will then learn to move by himself and the steps should be low and

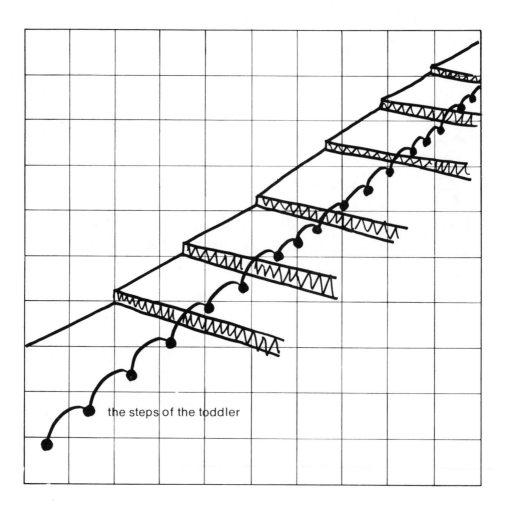

the steps of the toddler

## 96.      the stairs in the street can help a rhythmic movement

wide — so if he falls no great harm will come to him as he will only fall down
one step. To teach toddlers to climb and descend a full staircase we had better
start with such easy steps.

The home-street can end at a home-square, gossip-square, play-square
(Fig. 97) inside the extended family area which can have eight to ten families.
Such a square will be the symbol of the extended family and serve many purposes, with the supervision of one mother or grandmother at certain hours of
the day — it helps the toddler and the community formation. At this stage we

97.    the home-square is also a play-square or
       a gossip- square

have to understand how art can appeal to the toddler, as (Fig. 98) to this little
girl kissing a statue[77].

 We thus, can conceive and build the extended family or housegroup system
(Fig. 99) for pedestrians with a maximum length of 100 meters (330 feet) or a one
minute walk.  If there are any objections, let us remember how far we walk
in a multi-story building from the car to the entrance, elevator and corridor.
For any objection to this one level concept of housegroup we must emphasize
that high-rise dwellings do not offer any real advantages except to land owners,

98.     art and the child

but they create many disadvantages for Anthropos (Man), Society, Shells and Networks.  I illustrate two of these (Figs. 100 and 101) to show that buildings are not only pictures we see in magazines (such as street elevations) but elements of a system of life for people, and only if we see the people inside them — represented by their system of spheres (Figs. 28-30) — can we understand where these buildings do serve Anthropos' (Man's) needs and where they do not.  What contact can you possibly have with Nature, trees, etc. from the tenth floor which ostensibly gives you a view?  View of what?  Of towers or mountains!  Of the city or Nature but too far out — beyond the human scale — especially for the toddler.

We cannot have the Anthropopolis with high-rise blocks of apartments.  We

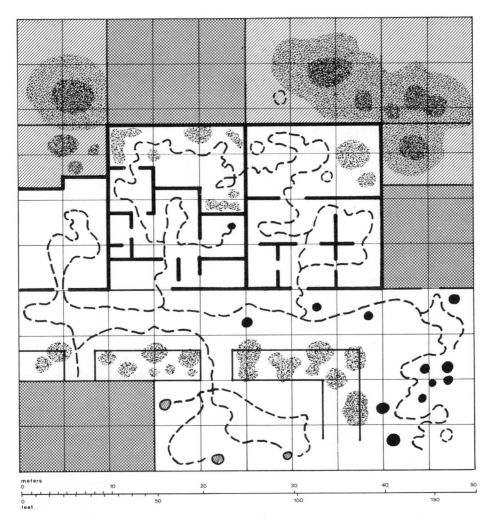

meters
0          10          20          30          40          50

0             50             100             150
feet

~~~ human energy – the toddler's movement

built-up area

green area

99.      spatial needs — fourth phase:
            toddler (16 to 30 months)

the contacts between children and between children and Nature which existed
in the past. . . . . . . . . .

. . . . are now lost

100.   the high-rise buildings work against Anthropos himself,
       especially against the child

the low density in the streets of the past

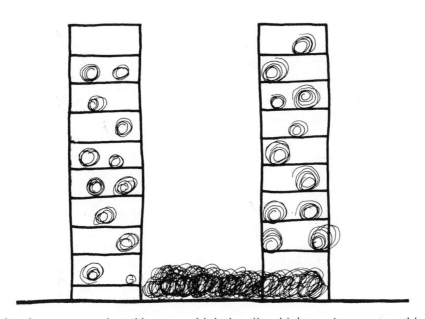

has been now replaced by a very high density which creates many problems

101.    the high-rise buildings work against the networks of
         human interest

had a special symposion on this during the 1971 Athens Ekistics Month [78] and a great movement has started since then presenting the many detrimental aspects of these buildings by many experts from all over the world [79]. The best response to this effort came from doctors and mothers and even from the door-men of these high-rise blocks of apartments; they are the witnesses of the daily tragedy. It is only with a one-level system (perhaps with one- and two-level one-family houses) that we can help the toddler move out, into the world in a secure way.

## Strider or play-age phase (2.5 to 5 years)

The strider grows and moves further out from the housegroup, from his contacts within the extended family, and his conquests of the small neighborhood (ekistic unit 5 with 250 people or 50-70 families). His contacts with people and the city increase. This is the phase Erikson says, of "Initiative versus Guilt"[80], the phase of basic family. I assume that with this foundation the strider begins to try and conquer the next unit: the large neighborhood. At the age of four, in the middle of this phase, the strider is ready for a kind of school, which may be only a play-group.

The total picture of the strider's kinetic field shows (Fig. 102) that since he has entered the play-age he begins to spend time with other children in the home-square or the play-group or nursery, situated in the middle of a small neighborhood which may be up to 200 meters (660 feet) long. It is in this phase that the strider needs both types of common spaces; first the one where he can safely be with only other striders and a temporary mother (play-group, nursery, etc.) and second the one where he can be in contact with all other age-groups (neighborhood square, etc.). The gradual conquest of these larger units of the city-space (Fig. 50) is the main subject for this phase of development.

At the beginning I thought that the strider might be able to leave the safe home-street I have already described, and walk not through but along the streets with cars (Fig. 103). Now I cannot see how this is possible. It is still too early for this. I do think that during this phase the strider ought to be allowed further out than before but we have already established that in order to have the proper contacts he has to move alone. Therefore his kinetic field should not contact any cars (Fig. 104). His movement should lead him in the opposite direction from the cars, towards HIS own center, that is the home-square with a small corner shop, the playground or nursery, etc. Cars should enter such areas, although they can first approach the houses from a different street which is inaccessible to children. This would be the street which serves

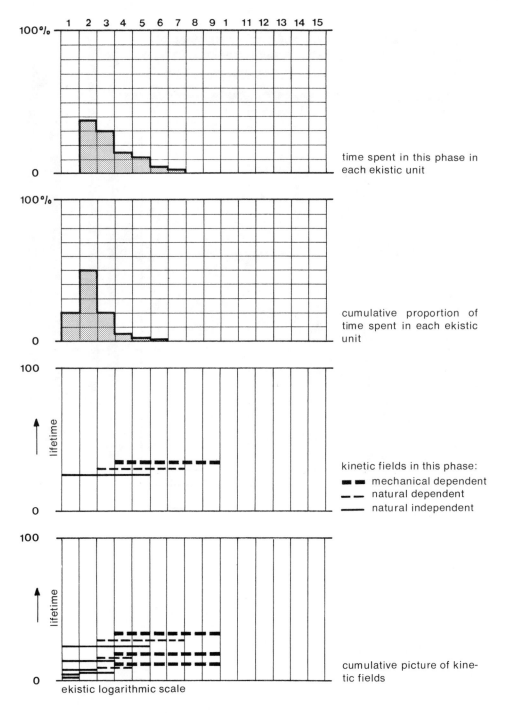

1 2 3 4 5 6 7 8 9 1 11 12 13 14 15

100% — 0

time spent in this phase in each ekistic unit

100% — 0

cumulative proportion of time spent in each ekistic unit

100

lifetime

0

kinetic fields in this phase:
- ▬ ▬ mechanical dependent
- ─ ─ natural dependent
- ─── natural independent

100

lifetime

0

ekistic logarithmic scale

cumulative picture of kinetic fields

102. time related to space
fifth phase: preschool age (2.5 to 5 years)

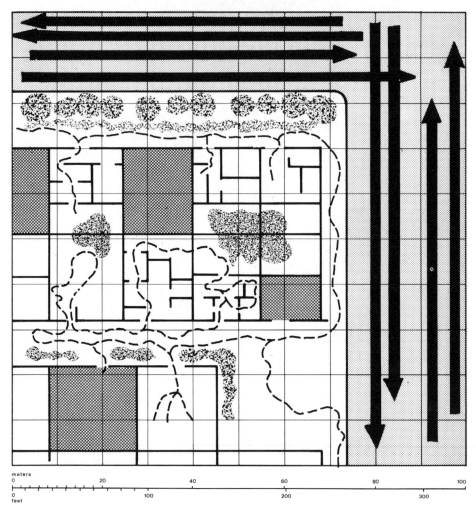

meters
0              20          40          60          80          100

0                 100             200             300
feet

∼∼∼ human energy

▬▬▬ mechanical energy — automobiles

▨▨▨ built-up area

▨▨▨ green area

separation of Anthropos from machine
creation of the home-street

103.     spatial needs — fifth phase:
          preschool age (2.5 to 5 years)

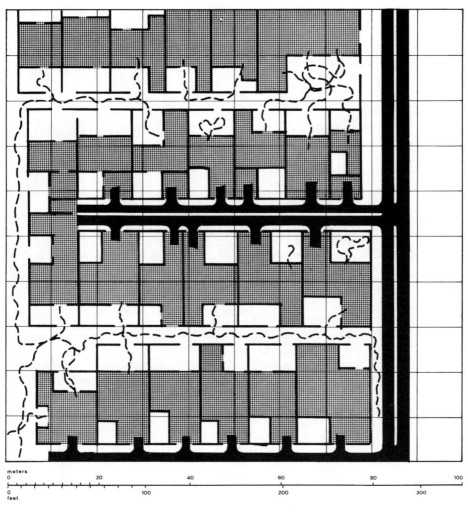

meters
0          20          40          60          80          100

0          100          200          300
feet

human energy — Anthropos as a free individual

mechanical energy — automobiles

built-up area

104.      separation of Anthropos from machine
creation of the home-street

143

105.    the exit from home-square to mechanical street

the home from the courtyard behind it (Fig. 91) to be called a "mechanical-street" (or mecstreet) versus the home-street in front.  At a later stage (one to two generations from now) cars will disappear from the surface of the city and go underground, then the human, home-streets, shopping-streets, etc. will remain at the surface of the earth with car or mecstreets underground.  Hasn't this happened already with water lines and sewers?

In the present phase the strider will know about cars and machines from earlier phases but should not contact them alone.  The first free contact will be a visual one as in the home-street where the home-gates do allow a visual contact with the world outside.  Now, when the strider moves to a neighborhood street to reach the playing-square or corner shop, he will see new gates, again safely enclosed but allowing him to see the cars outside serving the neighborhood (Fig. 105).

This is probably the phase during which the strider is really interested in moving freely within his neighborhood, in discovering it and in acquainting himself with it. The time has come to recognize that we cannot build standard houses which look similar to each other as we then transmit the message of confusion — the strider cannot develop the notion of a different identity for every house and family — he may perhaps receive the message that he was born in a society of bees. I heard that a five-year-old when asked how he draws, answered: "First I think and then I draw a line around my think"[81]. I was very impressed with this, because if this happens at this age, it is certainly time for us to realize how early the strider connects his thinking with specific forms. It is our obligation to transmit the message of a free world consisting of many different, individual elements tied together well into one unified system.

The concept of neighborhood, which is age-old for all cultures that I know of, is definitely a basic one from this phase on. This is a concept which has been lost in very high income countries and areas with many cars and is beginning to diminish in others. But we need it badly for all age groups and especially for the strider as this unit is his world. Why should we allow ourselves to eliminate the neighborhood and lose all its values that we need and that have been created in the past? There is no excuse for it. There are people who say that it is also the isolated village which has created good values (villages of artisans or dancers) but they forget that though this village is a unit in a human scale it very seldom gives its inhabitants all the choices they desire and very seldom leads them to a creative future. It is only the small unit within the city which can satisfy the demands for quality and safety (third, fourth and fifth principles) and the need for maximization of potential contacts with a minimum amount of energy (first and second principles).

It is the neighborhood in the human scale that must become a major goal for the City for Human Development (or Anthropopolis). When we say this we must remember again that the neighborhood does not consist of buildings only, it is really a system of life. When we state this, we will recognize that collecting 200 families in four multi-story buildings does not help people to interact. To understand the change we should not look at photographs of towers but at the system of human interaction as it was in the past and as it is now (Fig. 106). People now really meet in the street (but only for seconds), with many people and cars. It does not help either to keep people further apart by isolating the houses from each other as we do in suburbs. What results is that either people do not easily meet (Fig. 107) or that when they do meet they

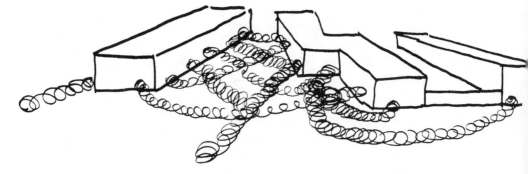

.... in the low buildings of the past

.... in the towers of the present

106.    the system of human interaction

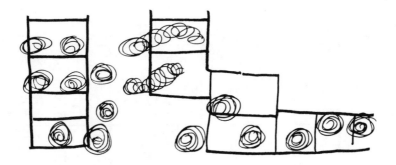

in the past the connections between people were easy

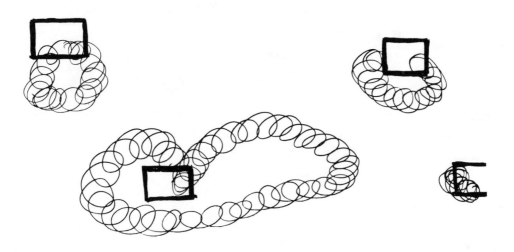

but not any more, if the density is very low because of the dispersed buildings

107.    the system of human interaction

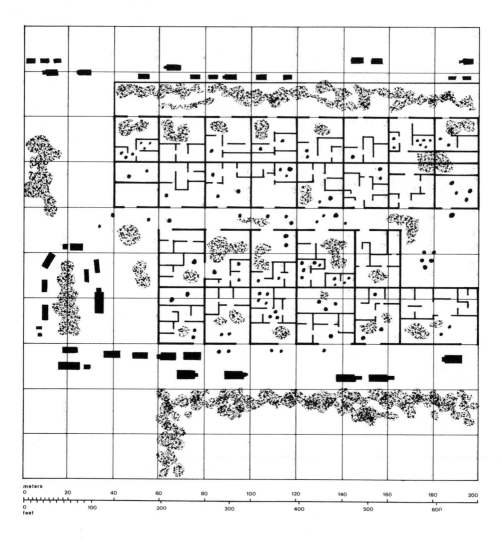

meters
0   20   40   60   80   100   120   140   160   180   200

0   100   200   300   400   500   600
feet

●   people
▬   cars
▓   green area

108.   spatial needs — fifth phase:
preschool age (2.5 to 5 years)

are isolated and squeezed between cars and fences; this is not a neighborhood, it is a building complex that does not care for people. The low densities of the suburbs are the same as in some farming villages, which did not have compact systems of life and were not known for their success!

It is time we understood that as there is an optimum distance between child and mother in every phase and an optimum one between mother and father for the child to be conceived and happily born and raised, there is an optimum density as well for the system of life of the neighborhood.

The task for the city corresponding to the needs of this phase is a double one: first to readjust the dimensions of furniture and room for the strider, and second to recreate his spatial unit — the human neighborhood in human scale with human safety (Fig. 108).

## School-age phase (6 to 12 years)

The child has to go to the elementary school without assistance. By now he must have become accustomed to meeting many people and machines as he moves within ekistic units 6 and 7 corresponding to a full neighborhood (1,500 people and more) and a small polis (9,000 people and more). He gradually spends more of his time in larger units as the slow increase of his kinetic fields shows (Fig. 109).

It is the age at which the child begins to be well acquainted with home, school and neighborhood stores and therefore all the lines connecting them — with a whole system. It is the age of "Industry versus Inferiority" as Erikson tells us and the age of the "Neighborhood School" [82].

In this phase the child cannot and should no longer move dependently only within spatially controlled areas with gates. It is time for him to be free to choose his own road. This brings him in contact with all sorts of units from the room, home, extended home, small neighborhood to the small polis. By now his needs have increased. His furniture and room have to be different in dimensions but not in purpose from those of the previous phases. The courtyard or garden has to accommodate not only play needs but also athletic training with the correct equipment. Most of this will be done in school and in his neighborhood courtyard-sportsground which must be open and supervised continuously. This is probably the time for him to participate in groups such as the boy-scouts; these groups could start taking over the responsibility for the operation of such play areas during certain hours.

As this is the time of free exposure to all sorts of buildings, this is the moment to insist that specifications for all buildings open to the public do not

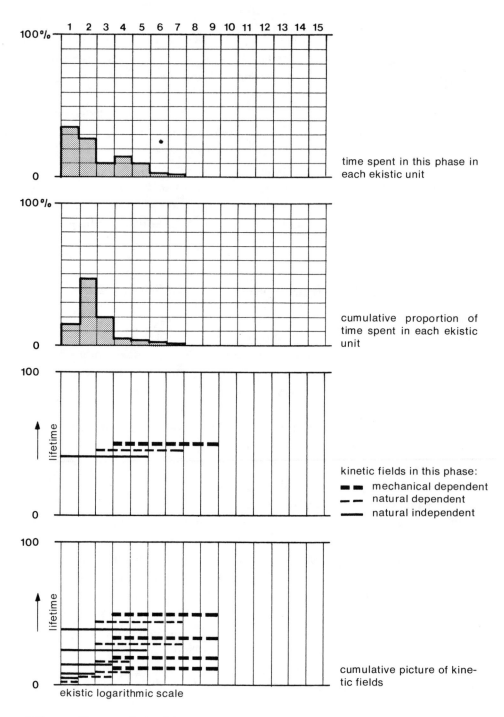

time spent in this phase in each ekistic unit

cumulative proportion of time spent in each ekistic unit

kinetic fields in this phase:
▬ ▬ mechanical dependent
▬ ▬ natural dependent
▬▬▬ natural independent

cumulative picture of kinetic fields

ekistic logarithmic scale

109.  time related to space
sixth phase: school age (6 to 12 years)

allow for any irrational and dangerous design. If an adult person without children wants to design a home or workshop that will not protect a child (low rails around balconies, etc.) he must be free to do so provided nobody can enter this home, it must have a locked gate. Any place, though, that can be visited by all people has to protect them in all phases of their lives.

The great change that occurs now is that the child will be exposed to machines and must still be kept safe. This requires specifications as the following:

*First*: There should not only be the narrow home-streets and neighborhood streets for pedestrians but also some central human streets (or hustreets) for walking and interaction and all vehicle traffic has to be banned from them. It is not the first time in history that these have been provided when men realized their great mistakes. Such traffic was not only banned from big cities like ancient Rome, with one million people, but also from small cities like Herculaneum near Pompeii where all vehicle traffic was probably banned from Decumanus Maximus, its main street [83].

*Second*: The sections of the streets controlled by vehicles should not be readily accessible. They should be enclosed by a low wall of one meter (3.3 feet) high so that people can see the bypassing cars and be seen by the motorists without having easy access to them (Fig. 110). There is no excuse for such a proximity of people to moving cars without protection from them. People should contact cars only in parking areas, first in front and later below the entrances of major buildings or groups of buildings.

*Third*: We must decide whether or not people should have to cross a street by the negative measure of the red light. When we advise that mother should not always say "NO", why do we allow the city to tell us "NO" in two-thirds of the cases when we reach intersections; red and orange lights take two-thirds of our adult walking time or one-fifth of our time, if as children we walk quickly or run. Are we sure that this is not one cause of the nervous strains that we create? Isn't it better to build passages above or under the streets with all kinds of small shops? We could economize in city-space without stopping children and people. This is meaningful from every point of view until the cars can be operated underground.

*Fourth*: If we must have cars on the streets and cross at the same level with them, we should no longer allow cars to move in both directions on any street of the world unless they are short, dead-end streets where low speed is imposed by itself. Up to now allowing two-way traffic has been disastrous, since most of the cases of pedestrians' accidents happen to people who get confused by two-way traffic. This would benefit car drivers also. Only when there is a very wide avenue with an island in the middle, wider than three meters (10 feet) should cars be allowed to move in two directions. Only then can the child get used to the changing direction from which the danger comes.

*Fifth*: The speed of cars should not be controlled simply by regulations and policemen. We do not protect our homes or banks with policemen at all times, but we have the right to stop any thief from entering them, and we can take his picture. The same should apply to offenders on the streets. We must have cameras which will automatically record everything at intersections and automatically take to court anyone disobeying the regulations. It would even be

110.     the mecstreet
         this is the first phase of the effort to turn it into a tunnel

the values and symbols of the past are lost because the machine scale controls the human one

## 111.    art in the city of today

better if we ruled that every car should have government equipment showing its speed, and then automatically reporting it to a speed-control center.

With such measures we can guarantee several goals, much greater, almost absolute, safety for the child and pedestrian, much better quality of urban space (much less noise, optical interference, etc.) and a revival of the concept of the neighborhood which we have lost because we have broken the human space by really raping it by machines.  We can no longer allow art and symbols to be ridiculed as happens with statues in the cities (Fig. 111) [84].  With these specifications we can build the correct units for the child (Fig. 112) and create a total, safe pedestrian system until machines go underground (Fig. 113).

In such a way we can now guarantee that the child will identify himself with his larger neighborhood and small town, whether surrounded by green

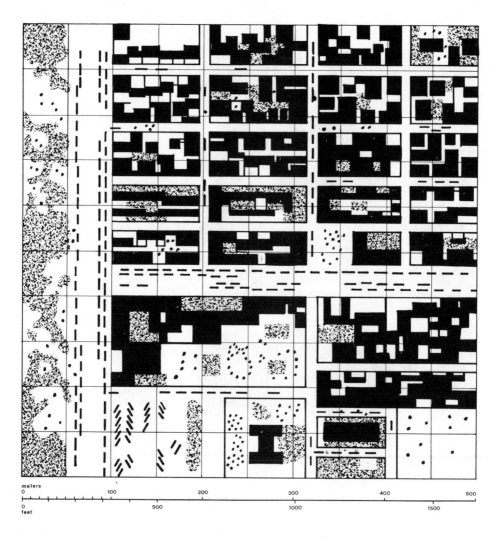

meters
0              100           200          300          400          500

0              500          1000          1500
feet

- •   people
- —   cars
- ▪   built-up area
- ▨   green area

112.     spatial needs — sixth phase:
           school age (6 to 12 years)

154

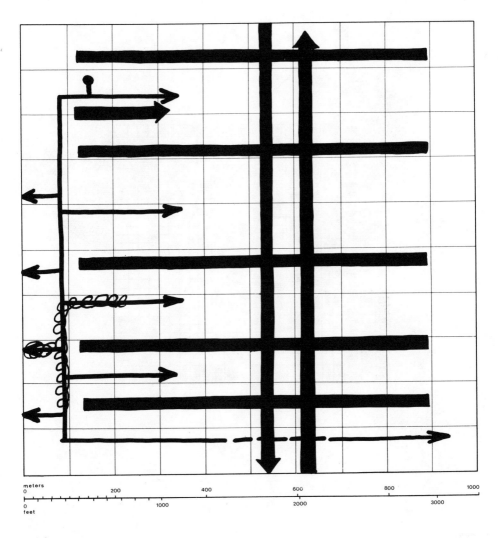

meters
0      200      400      600      800      1000

0      1000      2000      3000
feet

_ℓℓℓ_ human energy

▬▬▬ mechanical energy

113.     spatial needs — sixth phase:
            school age (6 to 12 years)

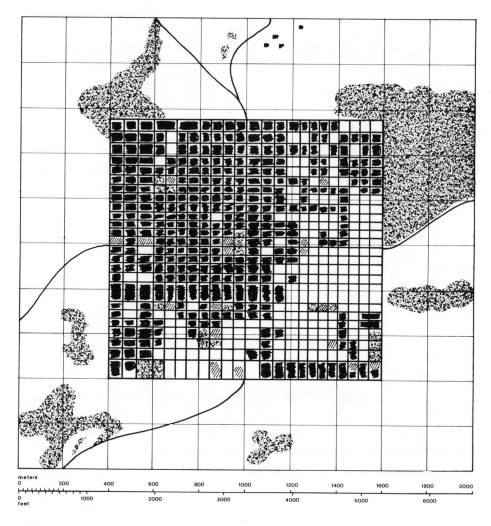

meters
0    200    400    600    800    1000    1200    1400    1600    1800    2000

0    1000    2000    3000    4000    5000    6000
feet

■■■ built-up area

▓▓▓ green area

this square corresponds to the traditional small town or organized community;
it is subdivided into traditional city blocks

the green areas come up to the edge of it

114.    spatial needs — sixth phase:
        school age (6 to 12 years)

areas — as existed in the old days (Fig. 114) and still does in certain areas — or surrounded by but properly separated from other small towns, all of them forming together the big city.  We cannot and should not isolate the different urban communities, but there is no reason whatsoever why we can't separate them with a green wall (Fig. 81).  Doesn't Anthropos (Man) separate himself by walls of rooms and houses?  Why not use walls for all sorts of communities?  Provided that Anthropos (Man) is free to enter or go out, is this not the correct solution?  Anthropos (Man) has always organized his city in order to be happy and safe.

## Adolescent phase  (13 to 18 years)

This is a very difficult phase as the adolescent has to conquer the polis (ekistic unit 8 with around 50,000 people and more), the small metropolis (ekistic unit 9 with around 300,000 people and more), and the metropolis (ekistic unit 10 with around two million people and more).  All of this has to be accomplished successfully in six years' time.  This means that the adolescent who enters this phase used to walking up to 1000 meters (3300 feet) in each direction, is now going to reach a radius of 50 km (30 miles) for his normal movement, first by using public transport and gradually moving to his own motor-bike or car.

In this phase, the adolescent spends a lot of time in larger units corresponding to the community unit which supports a high school and even, perhaps, a technical or junior college.  His kinetic fields have greatly expanded (Fig. 115).  By his natural independent movement he is likely to go well beyond the "small city" limits.  By his natural dependent movement with organized groups, under proper leadership, he can go on longer excursions.  Now mechanical, independent movement has also started to influence his life as he can at least use his bicycle over longer distances.  The mechanical, dependent movement can also take him still further out to begin discovering the wider world.

This is a phase of very great exposure to a wider world — from a community of about ten thousand people to perhaps five million, or 500 times larger.  In the previous, sixth phase the jump was to a population 30-50 times larger and in the fifth one the same.  It is today that the exposure is so great and I fully agree with Erikson who names this the phase of "Identity versus Confusion", because as I see it in terms of space the dimensions change enormously and the radius of significant relations is with peer groups and outgroups, the phase of models of leadership[85].

I think that such an exposure to huge numbers and areas really leads to this great confusion of which we have so many signs.  It is the age at which adoles-

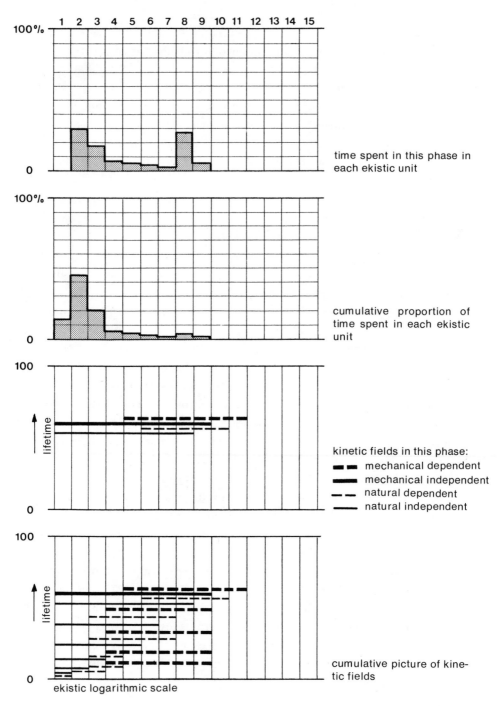

time spent in this phase in each ekistic unit

cumulative proportion of time spent in each ekistic unit

kinetic fields in this phase:
■■ mechanical dependent
▬ mechanical independent
– – natural dependent
— natural independent

cumulative picture of kinetic fields

ekistic logarithmic scale

115. time related to space
seventh phase: adolescence (13 to 18 years)

158

cents want a spatial change from the color of their room to the structure of their family, relations, etc. It is the phase in which they badly need their own, personal room and this must become a special goal for every family, even if the room is small. From experience in college dormitories we know that there is a much greater preference by students for even very small rooms, provided that they can be alone. Why not achieve this in the house? Correct design can allow for small rooms to be rejoined into a big one and then separated again; the home needs such a new type of modulus and structure.

Since the adolescent does not know exactly what is really preferable to him, he experiments in many ways. I have seen many suggestions, proposals, and designs for new types of rooms for this age-group which do not make any sense if we understand what a room really has to be[86]. As this is a phase of gradual adjustment to a much greater world, I think that we must learn from all past cases of adjustment to new worlds and build with this experience. Personally, I learned a lot from the gradual adjustment of the Bedouins with their nomadic desert life in tents, to the construction and life in a house by abandoning the tent and living in a house: it did not happen overnight. Life in the tent of nomads coming to the city was originally at a distance of hundreds of meters from the city, then these nomads moved, taking their tents closer to the city, and built one wall out from it for protection from the wind, then two walls, then four walls (with the tent on top) and finally the roof, and the courtyard, etc. This is an important lesson in gradual evolution and I think that we must apply what we learn from it to the process of the adjustment of the adolescent to the big city: we must make gradual changes in the larger ekistic units and their institutions which may be of revolutionary importance, but must happen in the right time-scale. We cannot move instantly from the small corner drug store, where people communicate, to the very large, impersonal one which is only approachable by car.

We need much better shopping streets which are only for pedestrians. From the past success of the single store concept, we should realize that we must go back to the solution of a scale from the small ones to the huge, impersonal ones. It has now finally been recognized what big mistakes have been made by private or public action for revolutionary changes in city centers[87]. It is time that we recognized the grave mistakes brought about by urban renewal in the U.S.A.[88]. It is much better to remember and design our new systems like the ancient Greek stoa where people could constantly interact. We do not know whether democracy could have been born without it. The change from feudal system to democracy did not happen inside or outise castles, but only in open areas which allowed the free interaction of Anthropos (Man) with his fellows.

Such remarks bring us back to the traffic system. Up to now we have been trying to protect the strider from approaching it and the child from being dangerously exposed to it as a pedestrian. We now have to protect the adolescent who rides his bicycle or motor cycle or drives a car. One solution is to separate the areas where they can drive from those of the community at large. I think that up to now this has not been attempted or even suggested, but if we believe in the principle of gradual exposure then we know that a person who is given a machine for the first time should not be allowed to travel immediately at the highest speeds.

To solve this problem there are two possibilities: first, allow the adolescents to maintain only certain speeds corresponding to their ages; 50 km (30 mph) at 16, 60 km (36 mph) at 17, 70 km (42 mph) at 19 and 100 km (60 mph) and beyond the age of 20. Such a solution requires the automatic control machine to have the identity card of the driver inserted — in any other way the car cannot start.

The second way we might solve this problem is to create separate streets for motor cycles and lower speed cars where young learning adolescents will be obliged to drive, where adults will also be allowed if they choose and where people during old age will again be obliged to return. This same measure can be applied for those whose eyes, ears, or bodies do not allow them the use of the maximum speeds allowed to others.

Related to these last remarks, is the need to control not only the speed of machines but also cut down noise, exhausts, etc., and all these can be achieved by automatic control equipment in every car. The need is imperative. Why allow people to conquer the world without controls? The Anthropopolis is not structured for Mongolian invasions but for conquest without harm to the conquerors or to all others.

Such considerations lead gradually to the following concepts.

*First*, the city must have a hierarchical transportation system with increasing speeds but the same degree of safety — a condition which we do not have now. The best safety from the transportation point of view we have managed to obtain so far is in the house and on the well-designed highway. We need the same safety in the units in between.

*Second*, the city must be organized into communities of a certain hierarchical system, the basic one of which is the traditional human community corresponding to the small polis. We have to respect this concept and organize every spatial unit, like a metropolis (Fig. 116) or a daily urban system (Fig. 117) or even Ecumenopolis on this basis. We should not forget that the smaller the territory the greater the identification of a person with it. Margaret Mead

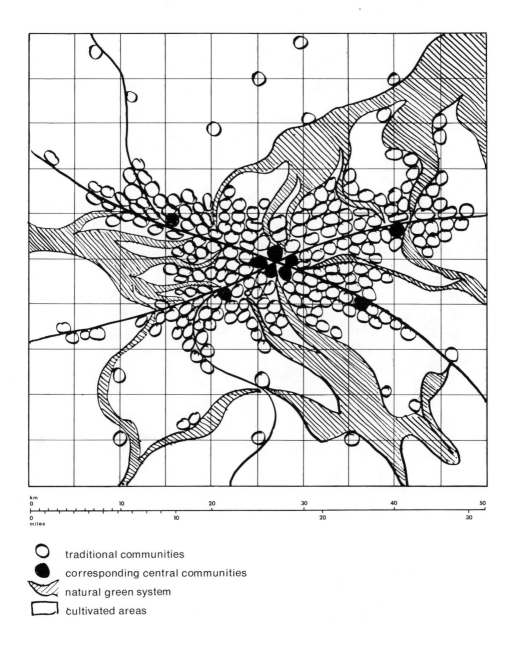

km
0          10          20          30          40          50

0                    10                    20                    30
miles

○  traditional communities
●  corresponding central communities
〰  natural green system
▭  cultivated areas

116.    traditional metropolis organized in communities,
        infiltrated by a natural green system

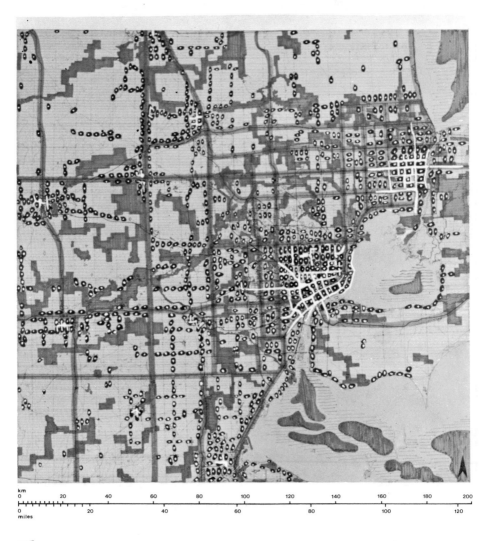

km
0        20        40        60        80        100        120        140        160        180        200

0        20        40        60        80        100        120
miles

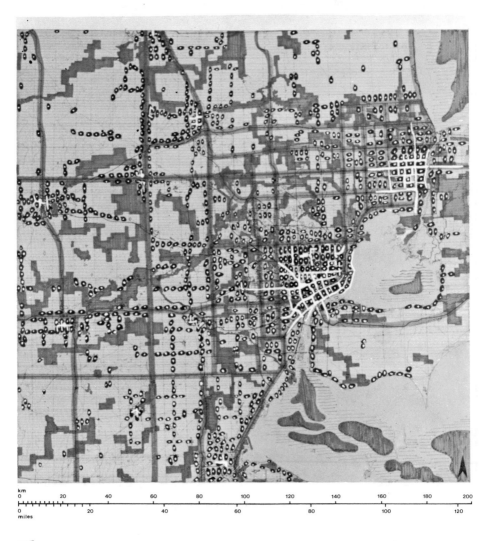 nature

human energy

commercial forms of energy and their impact on nature

117.   the future Urban Detroit Area with traditional
       and new communities in larger scale
       everything can be at the human scale

told us that the smaller the state in the U.S.A., the stronger the feelings are of the people for their locality and she cited the state of Rhode Island as the best example[89].

*Third*, the city must respect and keep the human scale which humanity had developed for long periods in many cultures and civilizations. When we see bridges full of shops over rivers like the Ponte Vecchio in Florence or like the architecturally very well built Banks of the Avon in Bath, England we must remember that Anthropos (Man) once had the courage to solve problems in a human way in eras of lower incomes and less technological development.

Why not now?

## Young adulthood phase (19 to 25 years)

This is the time when Anthropos (Man) may conquer the world. It is the age when many young people want to reach as far out as they can and may cover the whole globe from huge urban systems (ekistic unit 11 with several millions of people), megalopolises (ekistic unit 12 with tens of millions of people), small eperopolises (ekistic unit 13 with hundreds of millions of people), eperopolises (ekistic unit 14 with several billion people) and the whole earth (ekistic unit 15 with more than ten billion people) (Fig. 118) as they see it; the limit may be Nepal, the Himalayas or some islands of the Pacific — Alexander the Great was 22 years old when he started his campaign to conquer his world. This is the age when many other people started their own campaigns and battles.

At this stage a young person spends much more time in the larger ekistic units (9, 10, 11): the small metropolis, metropolis and small megalopolis or daily urban system — where his college or university or factory is located. His kinetic fields have become extended more by his natural, independent movement than his natural, dependent one. His mechanical, independent movements extend beyond the metropolis as our young adult now drives a car which he owns, in the high income countries, or borrows or steals in many cases. The use of the airplane in mechanical, dependent movement enables him to reach the limits of all the terrestrial space up to unit 15 (Fig. 25). He can now contact 3.5 billion people or several hundreds of times more than in the previous phase of a few millions. The jump is equally big with that phase.

This is the phase of young adulthood where the psychosocial crisis is "Intimacy versus Isolation"[90]. It is in this phase that big questions arise and many young people try to give their own answers. I was interested to see in·the QUICKSILVER TIMES (June 9-19, 1970), a magazine by young people which I was buying at a corner of Wisconsin Avenue in Georgetown, Washington D.C.,

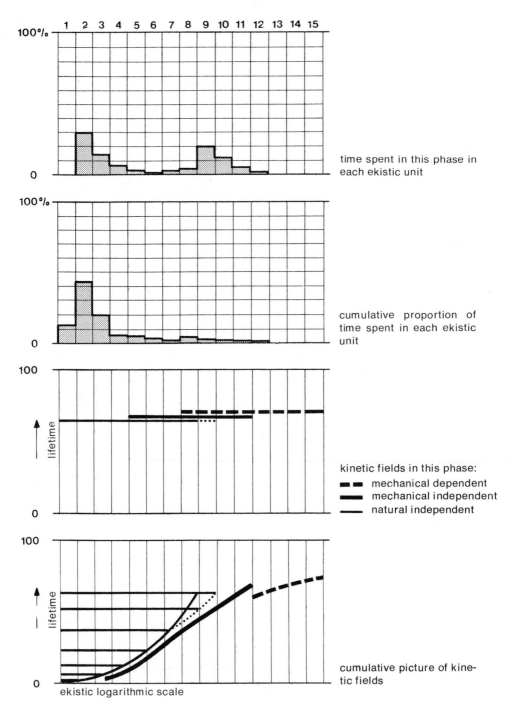

time spent in this phase in each ekistic unit

cumulative proportion of time spent in each ekistic unit

kinetic fields in this phase:
 mechanical dependent
 mechanical independent
 natural independent

cumulative picture of kinetic fields

ekistic logarithmic scale

118.  time related to space
      eighth phase: young adulthood (19 to 25 years)

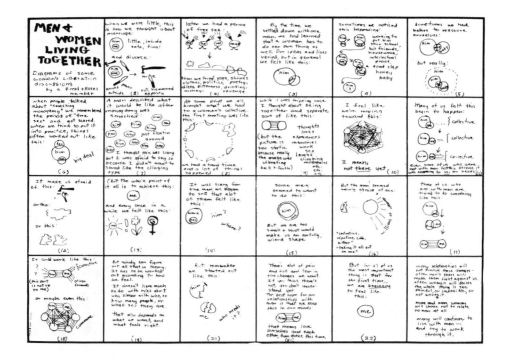

## 119.   men and women living together

an article trying to explain how men and women are living together (Fig. 119).

In this phase the young adult begins to have a very different relationship with space, not only from increasing his kinetic fields but also by conceiving and living or trying to live within different systems.   One of them is the neighborhood, and we should not forget the Rive Gauche in Paris, or Greenwich Village in New York which are or have been in certain phases mostly inhabited by young adults.   It is true that they are trying at this stage to go out farther but it seems that instead of this and not because of it — they really need to be closer, to be able to connect better with each other and so they revive the concept of neighborhood especially in areas where it has been lost.

It is for this reason that we must pay much greater attention to the university campus as a physical system of life and reverse three basic errors which have become very common all over the world.

*First:* The campus should not be a fortress turning its back to the city, thus creating a negative relationship [91].   The campus should infiltrate the city and be infiltrated by it (Fig. 120).

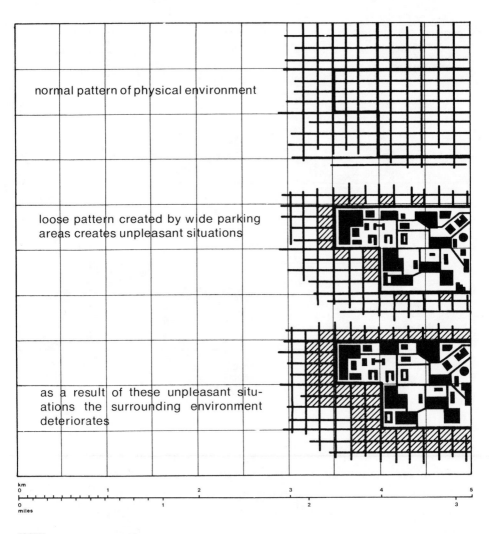

normal pattern of physical environment

loose pattern created by wide parking areas creates unpleasant situations

as a result of these unpleasant situations the surrounding environment deteriorates

km
0          1          2          3          4          5

0                    1                    2                    3
miles

////// areas controlled by cars

**120.    detrimental effects of a university campus on its neighborhood**

loose pattern controlled by cars

*Second:* The campus should not consist of isolated, monumental buildings serving as graves to some people who have departed. They should be interconnected into a tight physical system of buildings and courtyards where everything will be alive. The room is for isolation, but the building is not. Correct analysis will show how close students' rooms and university facilities should be[92].

*Third:* Towers cannot serve a university campus and its students. They do not allow the interconnections that are badly needed by young adults who require both isolation (room or work shop or library) and all possible contacts.

The next problem which requires our attention is opening the big city to this group of people. It is not a question of freedom to move that should worry us — they have it anyway — it is a question of having the ability to move, especially for those in the lowest income groups. It is here that enlarged public transportation systems with lower fares are imperative. It is the age when the young adult wants to try to move more but has the least amount of income with which to do so.

The units to be covered at this time are very large — from the big natural valleys which were the frames of the first city-states or the natural primitive societies like the Balinese one where everything they do daily is in relation to a mountain which provides their complete orientation and security[93], to the modern daily urban systems[94] and even beyond them, up to the whole earth.

We can understand this aspect of daily urban systems if we know how far modern Anthropos (Man) moves in his space every day. Such an image is transmitted by the kinetic fields of eleven U.S. cities which were selected as samples (Fig. 17) which shows that the radius of the average city was 92 kilometers (51 miles) in 1960 increasing at 2%-3% a year [95].

If we understand these present systems, we see that we must plan their future in a systematic way and so we are led to the alternatives selected by urban systems like the Urban Detroit Area (Fig. 121)[96], where a new type of balance is being created between Anthropos (Man) who has to reach out along high-speed corridors, and Nature which has to be saved. No longer should we have the wrong concept of a green belt — we do not need belts — what we do need is the correct infiltration of the city with Nature[97].

In this way we begin to realise that in order to help the young adult conquer the world we need three things:

*First*: An organized type of neighborhood which allows young adults both to go far out and to stay united when they need it.

*Second*: A network of "hospitality and travel", as Margaret Mead sugested[98].

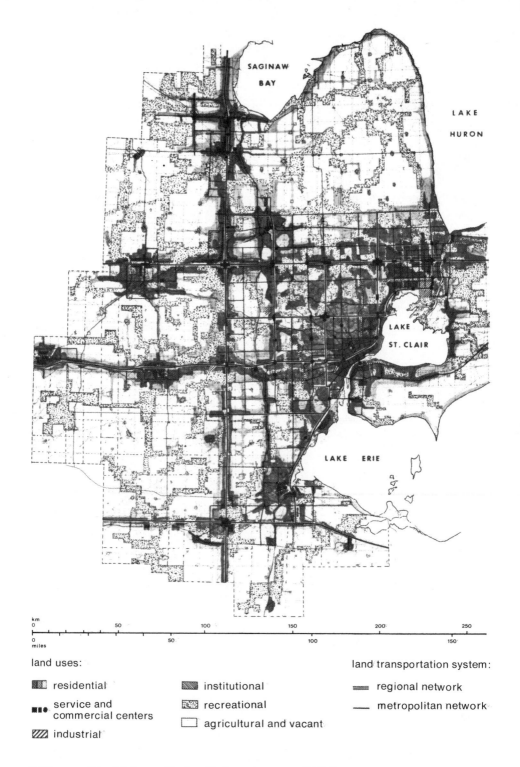

land uses:

- ▨ residential
- ∎∎● service and commercial centers
- ▨ industrial
- ▨ institutional
- ▨ recreational
- ☐ agricultural and vacant

land transportation system:

- ≋ regional network
- — metropolitan network

SAGINAW BAY

LAKE HURON

LAKE ST. CLAIR

LAKE ERIE

km
0       50      100     150     200     250
0       50              100             150
miles

## 121.    the Urban Detroit Area, year 2100

*Third:* A high-speed system available to those who need it most.

In some way this can be a repetition of what the great Moghuls did in India some centuries ago — they built a system of caravanserais every 18-20 kilometers (11-12 miles) or one day's journey. It is time to understand that the private hotel or motel is not the only necessity — they are in many ways coincidental and serve certain groups only — it is the private expression for the individual that we need. Parallel to that, though, we also badly need a whole organized system and this has to be done by inter-governmental agreements so that every 200 kilometers (120 miles) as we see distance today if we use private cars, we will have stations — also perhaps, learning centers that can help Anthropos (Man) move to conquer new areas and learn.

Only with such systems can we cover the needs of an expanding human race. The big question still remains, how can we challenge Anthropos (Man) in this phase of life to try and conquer something very difficult, be it Nature (mountain, desert, jungle, ocean) or city or science? We are still not prepared to define this goal correctly, but if we can manage to help the young adult conquer terrestrial space with a network of youth stations; then we may give this young adult the organized spatial exposure to the different aspects of the contemporary world where he may find the challenges he needs. Aren't students blocked today in a downtown campus, and isn't it natural to revolt from time to time? Would it be the same if every student could be exposed to the poverty of Calcutta and the difficulties of the desert before ending his studies? Would he not then be challenged to conquer the areas of poverty and fight them by hard work or invention? One thing I do know, young architects are still asked in many universities to design utopian, personal monuments, they have not yet learned to build the houses that humanity really needs.

## Middle adulthood phase (26 to 40 years)

This is the phase when Anthropos (Man) has conquered the earth in terms of kinetic fields — he has gone, if desirable and feasible, up to its limit — but he has not managed to control it (Fig. 122). It is the phase which requires hard work by him to control any area which he thinks is part of his own domain whether territorial or intellectual. It is the phase of "Generativity versus Stagnation" or self-absorption [99], the phase when some basic decisions are made. This is the time when Anthropos (Man) can go beyond earth to the moon, but this happens very seldom, therefore, the greatest amount of his energy is spent for the consolidation of his conquests.

It is in this phase that more of Anthropos' (Man's) time is spent in the larger

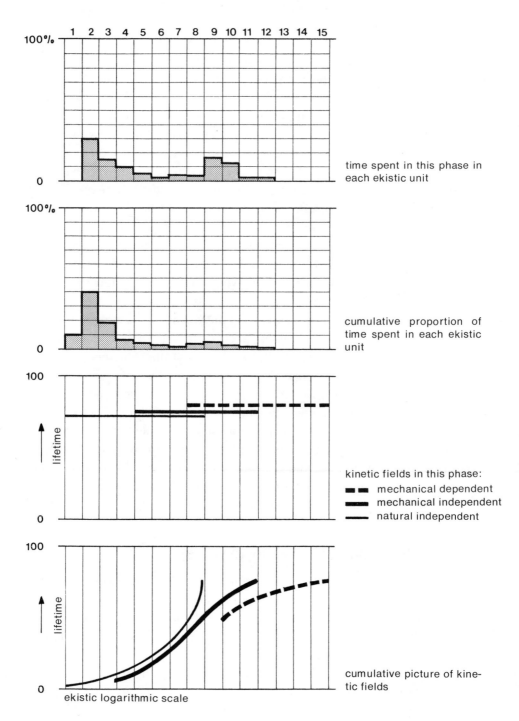

time spent in this phase in each ekistic unit

cumulative proportion of time spent in each ekistic unit

kinetic fields in this phase:
▬ ▬ mechanical dependent
▬▬ mechanical independent
—— natural independent

cumulative picture of kinetic fields

ekistic logarithmic scale

122. time related to space
ninth phase: middle adulthood (26 to 40 years)

ekistic units and his kinetic fields extend far out by mechanical dependent and independent movement. On the other hand, his natural movement does not extend beyond ekistic unit 8, that is the town or its equivalent, such as the area of Champs Elysées in Paris, the City of London or an area covering from ten to fifteen streets of Manhattan or ekistic unit 8 or up to the small metropolis (ekistic unit 9) at a maximum for some few people because Anthropos (Man) seldom walks beyond the limits of a small city, or 20 minutes walking time. It is the area where some people may run a few miles for reasons of health and training.

The very small community only is no longer satisfactory except for a few people. Even the women who used to be content to talk to each other from their doorways are now moving further out, at least to the market-place, either to the natural Greek agora, in a street or a square, or to the very organized shopping center or New York's 5th Avenue. This is the area where we have made the biggest mistakes as this has always been the place for the greatest interaction (in terms of numbers of people multiplied by the time of exposure to each other) between adults. It has now become an area of greatly shortened visits where contacts are no longer easy and natural.

A sweeping reform is now badly needed because this area must be returned to its old function of free interaction for all. This requires us to remember that the market-place should not be a system of buildings isolated from the city as most of the modern shopping centers are (Fig. 123), nor the area where we now bring people to be squeezed between buildings and machines, as the great shopping avenues do (Fig. 124), but it should be a place of interaction of people in a balanced network between buildings and Nature. It is human energy that must be in control. To achieve this we have to recognize the three great mistakes of our time and reverse the present situation.

The first great error that we commit is that we have allowed machines to isolate people from their city (Fig. 123) or from each other (Fig. 124) and this has to stop. Machines should stay out of the picture and this can be done in two steps; first by covering all parking lots and turning the desert (Fig. 123) into an oasis which will be one level higher and then in new developments by taking the machines underground (Fig. 125).

To solve this problem only is not enough as we have committed two additional mistakes, we build tall, multi-storied monuments and we forget that Anthropos (Man) can only interact successfully on the ground floors of the city.

It is a crime to build monumental buildings in areas of human interaction [100]. We don't need palaces and fortresses [101] but buildings of interaction where people can enter and exit freely. Even old churches and cathedrals allowed

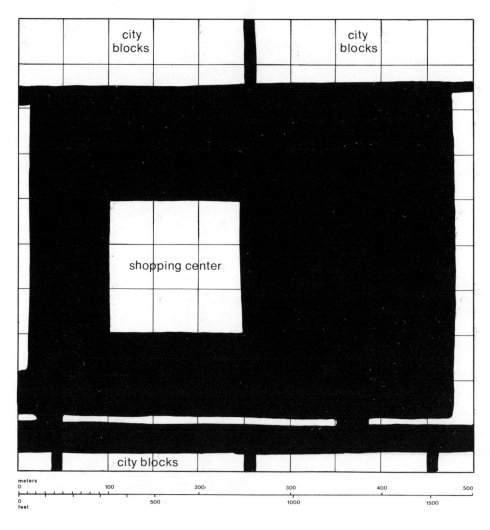

area covered by machines

123.    the modern shopping center isolates people from
        each other and the shopping function from the city as
        a system of life

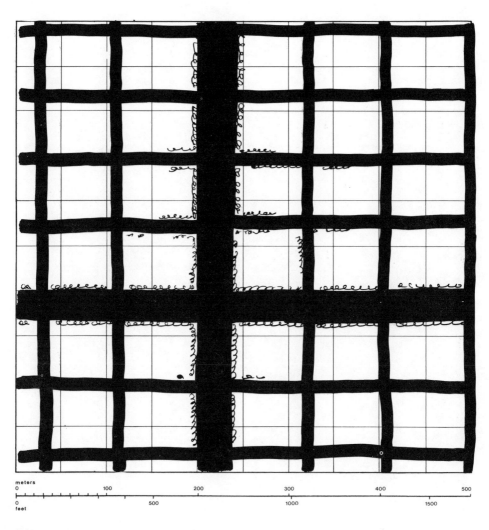

meters
0               100            200           300           400           500

0                       500               1000              1500
feet

■ area covered by machines

people moving around

124.     the shopping areas are controlled by machines and
people are squeezed between them and walls

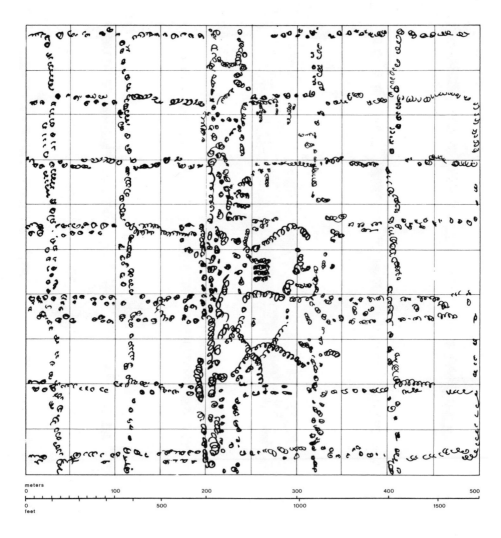

meters
0 · · · · 100 · · · · 200 · · · · 300 · · · · 400 · · · · 500

0 feet · · · · 500 · · · · 1000 · · · · 1500

CQ̸℧ people and human energy

## 125.     the humane shopping center

people are in control
human energy defines the system
machines are below the level of Anthropos

174

this but now the big banks and corporations open one door at certain hours of the day and then the fort is closed. Hitler did not manage to build his triumphal arch which, for the first time in history, would have been enclosed, but many others have since built them under different guises. Even human avenues like the Champs Elysées are beginning to lose their cafés and restaurants. Many ground floors are taken over by big companies like airway and automobile showrooms which exhibit and sell — this is a show-off which is sometimes attractive but only briefly. Very few people enter; the majority remain outside!

To solve the problem of the human "market" is not enough as Anthropos (Man) goes way beyond it but this is a key area in the life of the adult. It is here that he has to interact even if he is not a merchant, official or administrator — Anthropos (Man) is always the consumer of goods and ideas and the ideas he needs are not only those from the institute and university campus — in a free and developing Society these ideas are often found in the street and the market.

The case of the "market" is the largest unit where human interaction is possible. People do not interact when the physical dimensions are beyond what they can naturally and physiologically see and hear — then interaction is controlled by telecommunications networks. It is, therefore, very important to save the "market", our largest unit of free, uncontrollable human contacts.

Beyond these, we have to create very high-speed systems connecting all units of physiological human scale — from home and neighborhood to the large markets in the best possible way. This can only happen if we take all transportation underground and this is feasible first for the large branches of our transportation systems [102] and eventually for every home. This should become our ultimate goal and then the city will become natural and physiological again — the surface will be Nature with free Anthropos (Man).

Thus we now must ask, what will happen to Nature? This can only be answered in one way. Our task is to save Nature. When Anthropos (Man) has tried in the past he has succeeded. He must start by eliminating pollution. This is not a new trend. More than a century ago Europe started the movement against surface sewers and succeeded in placing them underground. Anthropos (Man) will soon be successful and eliminate air, water and land pollution.

The second task is more difficult: to achieve a balance between city and Nature, but Anthropos (Man) has done it in villages, city-states[103] and monasteries [104]. If we again gain control of the situation, we can build the same balances as in the past with one exception: the scale will be different and the relationships will no longer be single-level but multi-level ones. In simple terms this means a multi-level network through which Anthropos (Man) will enter areas of Nature, whether walking or moving by underground systems, and will have different types of relationships with it. In the neighborhood garden he can use Nature to satisfy his esthetic desires, while in the big, natural areas he will not be allowed to enter even by bicycle or to cut any grass or disturb Nature in any way. In between he will have the whole range of the areas of Nature from fabricated imitations to natural virgin expanses.

## Real adulthood phase (41 to 60 years)

This is the phase during which Anthropos (Man) as an individual has already managed to conquer the world, or part of it, and very probably will no longer try to conquer anything beyond his area — although he may in fact be doing this through the organizations that he manages or creates. The fact that some single individuals, usually among leading intellectuals, continue to expand does not mean that the average individual of whom we are speaking wishes to do so.

This is the age during which the adult stabilizes what he has already conquered and may begin to pull back from attempting any larger efforts. To achieve this he probably spends approximately the same time as before (perhaps more for some people or less for others) in the larger units of space. Therefore, his kinetic fields probably remain the same with a tendency (I assume) to be reduced because of age, weakness, illness and other diminishing forces (Fig. 126).

This is the age at which the adult begins to feel many small problems of health and tries to overcome them by starting — if he has not already done so — to exercise, but he can only do this over the weekend which may not lead to the results that he desires. What is needed is the opportunity for continuous daily exercise at no cost in terms of time and money because excesses in both these factors can eliminate its realization. To drive a car to the golf club or to the sea to swim is reasonable only for those who have the time, the money and a car.

What is imperative is that he should have the occasion inside the small units of space to exercise and this can be at least partially achieved by providing some stairs in public roads and squares. There is no question that if you have to climb steps frequently the lower part of your belly will benefit, it will have stronger muscles and less fat. I proved this myself by experimenting on the island of Hydra, and it is probable that people living in such areas suffer less from heart diseases. I don't have scientific data to reinforce this idea, but this is what local doctors tell me.

Here it is also recognized that a completely horizontal city deprives us of one important dimension, one which existed in Nature from which we came; and one that we have gradually eliminated. It is time to understand that what we defined before for the small units. the human scale, also requires a third dimension.

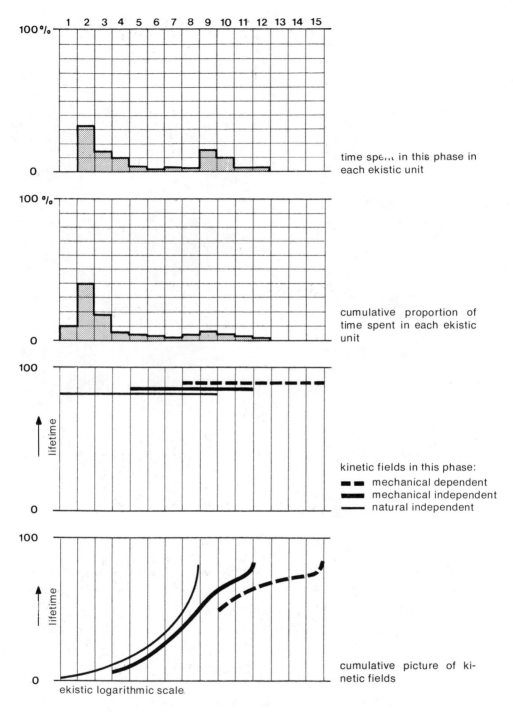

time spent in this phase in each ekistic unit

cumulative proportion of time spent in each ekistic unit

kinetic fields in this phase:
- ▬ ▬ mechanical dependent
- ▬▬ mechanical independent
- ── natural independent

cumulative picture of kinetic fields

ekistic logarithmic scale

126.  time related to space
      tenth phase: real adulthood (41 to 60 years)

177

127.   the home-street as a three-dimensional structure

Either by accident, design or necessity people need to be given the opportunity to make a minimum effort.  By only using cars, on the mecstreet or later in the underground tunnel, and never walking, they will have great problems.  The front-street has to be kept human, and by human we now see that this means three-dimensional (Fig. 127).  I could not find any animal that has developed a kinetic field which is only two-dimensional.  Why should we turn Anthropos (Man) into less than any other animal?

In this phase Anthropos (Man) needs to interact not only in the very small units like the extended family and neighborhood (he may spend the minimum percentage of his time in them in relation to other phases), but also in the city center.  During this phase Anthropos (Man) has to be given the incentive, not always to abandon the city center by five p.m., but to stay there and bring his companion as well, or find one.  This requires the imperative need to eliminate the fortress-like and monumental qualities of the central city, or restrict them to a few buildings only.  Otherwise the city center loses its human character.

We have to go back to the ancient agora in the broadest sense of the word and recognize the need for a complete remodelling;  to serve a mixture of functions for which no segregation can be allowed.  This means that all such regulations, which define a street only for shops, have to be eliminated.  People very often need their homes above these shops to facilitate their full participation in the life of the central city.

## Early old age phase (61 to 75 years)

This phase I have called "early old age" in order to comply with the traditional definition of old age, but also because I have to respect the new fact that there are now people in their 60's and 70's who look young.  There is no question that Anthropos (Man) is beginning at this age to retreat in terms of his movement. It is true that some people will continue to move out, perhaps for a round-the-world trip when they get their pensions or those special trips for American widows who survive their husbands by five to six years;  but these are not the kind of people who try to conquer the world — they will probably only visit it once.  Therefore we can still conclude that the average Anthropos (Man) of this phase is really beginning to step back.

We can recognize that at this stage Anthropos (Man) moves in an independent way with his car within the large urban system (ekistic unit 11), walks within the city (ekistic unit 8) and begins again to spend more than a third of his time within his room (Fig. 128).

The room requires much greater attention now than before, especially if it is the one planned for retirement.  It has to be larger, especially for those who do not have any special study or workshop, and it has to give the maximum of advantages in terms of esthetic choices, from collections of photographs, souvenirs and books to the proper view outside of the garden or city.  I question whether or not it is proper to look at the city from the top as in so many old-peoples' or senior citizens' homes.  With such a perspective we lose the real view of the world and look at it as birds do — static birds — not ones that are flying and see energy and life.  The city is dead from the top vantage point and only pollution is apparent, this dismal picture therefore leads to pessimism (Figs. 57, 58 and 59).

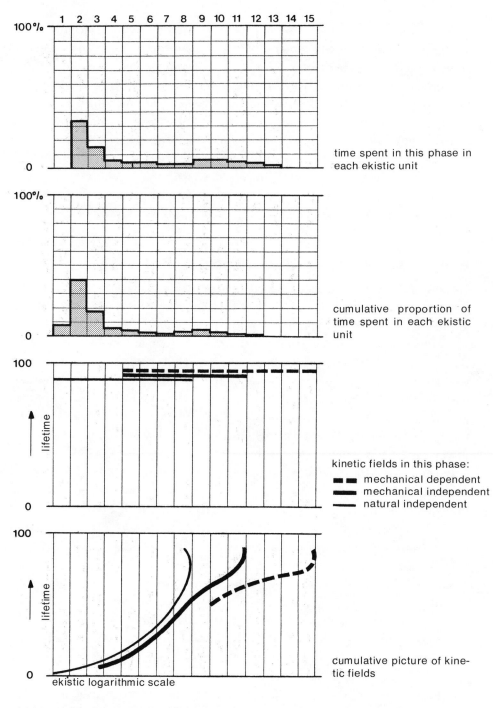

time spent in this phase in each ekistic unit

cumulative proportion of time spent in each ekistic unit

kinetic fields in this phase:
- - - mechanical dependent
━━━ mechanical independent
─── natural independent

cumulative picture of kinetic fields

ekistic logarithmic scale

128. time related to space
eleventh phase: early old age (61 to 75 years)

The house now requires greater attention, the courtyard becomes much more important and requires a repetition of the whole nature of our earth within it. This cannot possibly be planned within the house as Nature is missing from it in most respects, but the courtyard can have the whole earth included in it; land, water (even a pond without water reminds one of it) and air, plants and animals of all sorts. In the courtyard of our office in Athens we tried this in a 18 × 10.5 meter area (60 × 35 ft) and it is successful; there are three kinds of trees, ten kinds of bushes, cats, a pond with fish and even birds (Fig. 129).

129.    the Doxiadis Associates courtyard in
        Athens, Greece (1973)

130.    the courtyard as the old man or woman needs it

The same can be achieved in much smaller dimensions (Fig. 130) let us say a
square of 6 × 6 meters (20 × 20 ft) as in the ancient days, or even narrower plots
as in medieval and later days.    There are even courtyards 4.50 meters (15 ft or
5 yards) wide in the planned community of Georgetown, Washington D.C. where
parties are given.    To complete this small facsimile world we need symbols not
only of Nature but also of Anthropos (Man) and his culture; this means reviving
sculpture, mosaics and other expressions of art whose value has been demonstrated by old cultures, especially those of the Middle East.

In the same spirit we must now look at public squares and parks.    We have
recognized the need for special areas for children, where they can play without
mixing with adults.    Old people are also entitled to the same privileges.    We

must provide quiet, protected areas for the elderly and private places where they can retire for some period of time daily. Everybody needs a place for contacts, but they also need occasional isolation, individually or as a group.

The road out of the house gains even greater importance with one difference; in earlier phases we needed steps to train the child (Fig. 96) or help the adult keep fit (Fig. 127), now the home-street must also be accessible to those who cannot climb steps. The solution for the future is the mechanical tunnel, but for the present it can either be the mechanical motor car behind the house or — more important — the home-street itself, which can be designed with stairs to challenge and train, and without to help the sick and the aged (Fig. 131).

131.  the home-street as a three-dimensional system
training and helping people to move

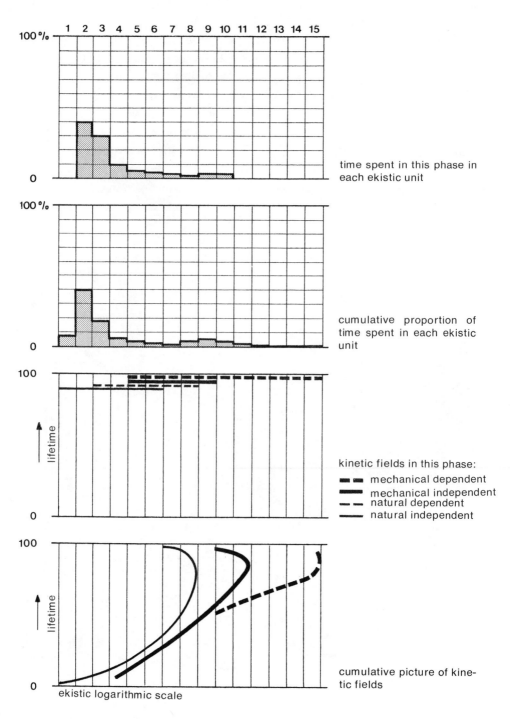

time spent in this phase in each ekistic unit

cumulative proportion of time spent in each ekistic unit

kinetic fields in this phase:
▬ ▬ mechanical dependent
▬▬ mechanical independent
– – natural dependent
—— natural independent

cumulative picture of kinetic fields

ekistic logarithmic scale

132.   time related to space
       twelfth phase: old age (76 to 100 years)

# Real old age phase (76 to 100 years)

By now Anthropos (Man) has definitely retreated back to the smaller unit. With very rare exceptions, he does not walk far and he is no longer professionally involved in wider spaces (Fig. 132). Anthropos' (Man's) kinetic fields have shrunk and folded back.

By the 100th year of his life, Anthropos (Man) has normally retreated to the smallest unit, which by then is often, at least in lower income countries, covered with flowers. After starting out from the very small unit and conquering the world space in different ways, he reaches the maximum possible to his own natural and mechanical kinetic fields and then folds back to the smallest unit of size (Fig. 133).

What has been required before for the room, house, courtyard, garden, home-street and home-square is even more important now. It is in this space unit that Anthropos (Man) eventually dies, so here he needs every aspect of his life to be taken care of. First in his surviving years we must provide health services close by in organized buildings and communities, then make his surviving years happy not only with a big room, but also with the rich courtyard even though it may be small. God in several forms may need to enter it by now.

The home-street and home-square are still imperative to create the opportunities for contacts between the young and the old. It seems that in terms of man-hours spent per person in the same spatial unit, the best contacts are between those who have the longest exposure to each other. A city cannot support any imposed segregation whether it be racial, religious or age discrimination, although certain specialized functions require it by nature such as the school or the office or the laboratory where segregation by age is imposed. But the home-street and home-square are not specialized, they are the first basic unit of the city structure.

A last question arises in respect to the grave and where it should be located. Children living in villages are much more realistic about death as they have seen it from an early age in every burial procession. Very often they follow their mothers and grandmothers to lay flowers on graves. This reality becomes much more obscure when the cemetery is very far from home which necessarily enables children to visit it very rarely. Thus, when later they have to view a grave for the first time it is a much greater shock than it had to be. Death is death, but our exposure to it may train those surviving to visualize it better. If these thoughts are correct, should we not now revive the small community cemetery where the dead are close to the living and consequently benefit everybody alive?

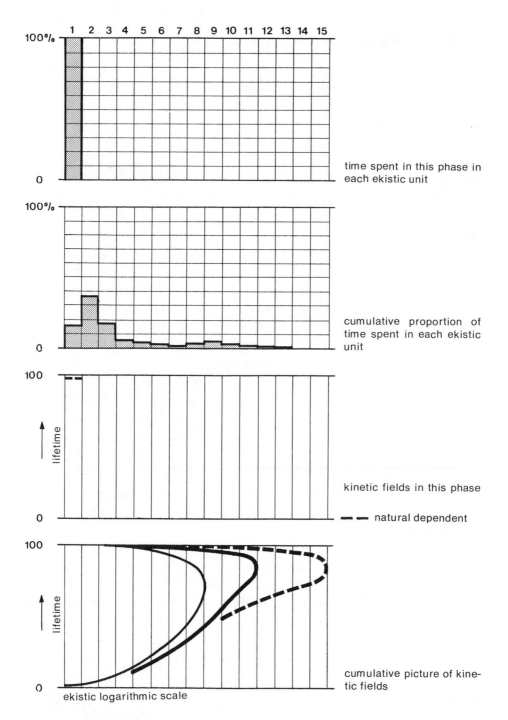

100%

1 2 3 4 5 6 7 8 9 10 11 12 13 14 15

0

time spent in this phase in each ekistic unit

100%

0

cumulative proportion of time spent in each ekistic unit

100

lifetime

0

kinetic fields in this phase

— — natural dependent

100

lifetime

0

ekistic logarithmic scale

cumulative picture of kinetic fields

133. time related to space
twelfth phase: old age (76 to 100 years)

There is no question that in old age at least Anthropos (Man) thinks of retirement and death. If he thinks of the cycle he has completed in his lifetime with wisdom, which has certainly increased over the years, he certainly thinks of its end. There are people who try to build their own graves in advance — there are actually "do-it-yourself" tombstone kits and many other attempts to overcome the difficulties after death for those surviving, such as the attempts in northern Italy to build multi-story cemeteries. But is this human? Has Anthropos (Man) not tried to keep his dead very close by? He probably did at the beginning when he kept them inside his cave or his home, it was not until quite recently in relation to his two million years history that Anthropos (Man) buried his dead in cemeteries.

We do still have some cases where a family wants the dead person near by; during the last war when regulations were not enforced in all instances we had families who buried their dead in their gardens. What does this mean? Is it reasonable to separate the dead from those who are living? I have not found an answer to this question and I am simply posing it in the hope that we can examine it — whether or not separating the dead from the living is any more unreasonable than separating the very old in towers, away from everyone else. The explanation for what we do is a direct result of the explosion which takes us apart; but this does not mean that we cannot face it. We can come close to each other again in one respect by decreasing the distance from the dead to within a natural, physiological human scale.

If we create community cemeteries in ekistic unit 7 or 8, that is for a few thousands to some tens of thousands of people, they will be small; they will not only create a better balance between individuals but also between Anthropos (Man) and Nature — some of the best natural preserves are cemeteries with all sorts of plants and birds. We need them close to us for biological and cultural reasons. National parks are very useful, but they are too far away from us to clean the air that we breathe daily. We need them closer to us also, and thus small cemeteries will lead to better balances.

This is the end; the cemetery provides the return of Anthropos (Man) to Nature and a certain means for re-establishment of Nature and survival of Anthropos' (Man's) culture.

## Creation of a total system of life

We have followed Anthropos (Man) in his life and movement in space from the very small units to the whole earth. The relationship of Anthropos (Man) and space, or, now that we know that Ecumenopolis covers the whole earth, the relation of Anthropos (Man) and his city depends first on the dimensions and quality of every unit of space and second on the relationships between the different units of space. The reasons for this second statement are two:

*First*: Anthropos' (Man's) happiness depends on his mobility, otherwise he is a prisoner in a room or a national state if he is not allowed to move around of his own free will.

*Second*: One principle is true from times past, for the small, and recently for the larger units of space, their own quality depends greatly on their relationships to each other. This is true not only for the room, that has to fit in the house, but also for the global oceans which can be polluted from the actions in some of its corners.

If we want to face any problem related to Anthropos (Man) and his space, we must create *the total system of life* that we need. This system must make sense from the smallest to the largest units of space. This is the great task ahead for the realization of our Anthropopolis, and it is a very difficult one.

Three examples can illustrate why it is important, how it will be difficult to achieve and the spirit in which this great human system can be created.

The first is the room itself, this basic unit of space, in which we spend from one third to one half of our life, is so often overlooked. We have already specified that the room has to be small for the child and large for the aged. So, for whom shall we build the room? Our tendency is to create a standardized room, somewhere half-way between both necessities, this, in a statistical way, makes a lot of sense but it does not help human development in the best possible way. It is a compromise.

In the high income countries — I refuse to call them developed — people up to 20 years of age represent slightly more than 40% of the total population; in lower income countries they reflect almost 50% of the total population. If we add other people who cannot easily use the larger spaces created by Anthropos (Man) because of old age or illness, we come to the conclusion that about 50% of the population of the earth does not have physical dimensions which correspond to the size of the big units we are building. One half of the lifetime of humanity is spent in a room. Is it therefore reasonable to create the room and so many other units of space on the basis of the dimensions of the average Anthropos (Man), that is of a normal, healthy adult? I do not believe so.

The argument against this theory is that the greatest part of humanity cannot yet afford different types of rooms, some of which will remain empty when there is no child or old person. Despite this, the answer can be a new house type with the modulus of a very small room, let us say of a width of 2.40 meters (8 feet) so that four young children may have four rooms and when two depart to study or marry the others remaining will have a room with a width of 4.80 meters (16 feet). When, some day, no child remains at home the aging parents' bedroom may grow from 3.60 meters (12 feet) to 6.00 meters (20 feet) and the other units may be turned into guest rooms or transformed into a new, separate home unit which yields income and can later be reconnected with the previous one, forming once again a single home, with changing sizes of rooms. We need the changing, modular home as well as convertible furniture (Figs. 88 and 89).

The second example is the road. There are difficulties but also possibilities of creating a solution for every other unit of space. The road, as we have seen, needs different types of forms and uses, from the narrow home-street to the avenue, the highway and tunnel. But even the home-street, which is of the greatest importance for the developing child and can be very pleasant for many adults — especially women and old people — may be unpleasant for others who, returning from jobs or belonging to a minority, like a homosexual, may not want to see people or be seen in every phase or movement of their life. Sections of the home-street also have to be different as already stated, part with many steps and part with none. The solution is the duo-approach system, the home-street for walking and contacts and the mechanical street or mecstreet (and later the tunnel) for no contacts at all, either with Nature or people. A variant possibility is the creation, at the periphery of every small neighborhood, of special streets for cars and pedestrians separately where movement and contacts are so many that they become impersonal, as Fig. 110 illustrates. Then nobody cares or really follows up. This may be the first step until we reach the tunnel phase and it may be necessary until then to have impersonal streets where the pedestrian remains separated from the machine.

The third example refers to the system as a whole and I focus now on the question of security with a very specific suggestion for a key. It is time that we conceive a very specialized key that can open only one room, my room, but also one home, my home and one home-street, my home-street and one neighborhood. In this way we can create a safety system with one key per person. We can even increase its efficiency. Anyone who does not insert his key and his specially made identity card at the extended home or neighborhood gate cannot enter — if anyone tries to, the guard or the resident in charge or the police will be automatically warned by signals on a plan or map and a photograph can be taken automatically of the intruder. This idea is given only as an example of how we could create a new meaningful, hierarchical electronic nervous system for our system.

In similar ways we can now create a synthesis of Anthropos (Man) with his total environment and, after studying who needs what and where in his cities, try to create every unit for all those who use it, the room for its one or two masters, the home-street for its one hundred masters and the total City of Anthropos (Man) for its billions. If we do it in a hierarchical systematic way, we can respect both the individual and Society as a whole by ranging from completely individual solutions to universal ones; serving every culture and the whole earth where Nature creates the laws.

# 6. Time for action

## In the middle of an explosion

There is no question that we have entered into a phase during which we are suffering from the mistakes we have made in the treatment of our environment. I would even go so far as to say that it is a pity that this fact has been repeated over and over again to such an extent that it is now becoming commonplace. From the one extreme at which we stood in the early sixties, when we said nothing about the problems for which we were responsible, we are now switching to the other extreme, and we constantly lament over the state of affairs that is emerging. Lamentations, however, are only justified when they lead to a better path of action.

There also is no question that we are in the middle of an explosion [105] of many forces from great numbers of people, economy, energy and the knowledge that we use. As with any other explosion, the present one not only takes us far out but also destroys many existing structures; those of the cities and many natural.

landscapes as well as many existing values and cultures [106]. From history we learn that big action and often many big changes appeared after the complete destruction of some cities; people had to start from scratch and rebuild with the same processes or attempt new solutions. But what are we doing now? Our cities are not destroyed but we do not act properly to save them.

It is quite clear that we have been frightened by the explosion and we are trying to escape, first by attempting to stop the growth of cities, then the growth of population, and the economy and the energy. In doing this we forget that it is not feasible to accomplish such action by force nor will anything be achieved overnight, because population growth follows biological rules and city growth has never been stopped by force even by autocratic regimes. What are you going to do with the first child born beyond the stipulated number allowed in the city as defined by intellectual or political autocrats? We also forget that such action is most often undesirable as with the forces of energy and economy. What other hope do we have for countries with primitive economies and underprivileged minorities?

What else can we expect from people in the middle of an explosion? We are genuinely frightened and confused and we do not know where to go or what to do. Several serious efforts are beginning for the clarification of this situation but it is still very difficult to comprehend the entire dimensions of the whole problem and cover its different aspects even in a simplified way. When, some years back, a serious effort was undertaken by a medical school to discuss the subject of "A City for Human Development" in a two-day meeting [107] I tried at the end to summarize the sectors and dialogue we had covered during our presentations as we do during the Athens Ekistics Month [108]. Some aspects of the whole system, such as Nature, were not covered at all (Fig. 134). This was nobody's mistake, it only illustrates how difficult it is to cover all of this complex and confusing subject.

How can we move now and select the correct path; we, the frightened and confused people? This is the great question. There is only one path to take and help ourselves and this has to be with the proper understanding of our present situation and the correct action to overcome our problems. In physics or biology we can experiment in seconds with gravity or in minutes and hours with polypods, but this is not possible in Anthropos' (Man's) situation, the only hope is to turn back and learn from human history. This is really what has guided the present study; a combined attempt to learn from Anthropos' (Man's) long history and from my personal experience and finally from my forty years of professional life in the big laboratory of the world in which we live and work.

We have started the process of understanding our situation and thus we have

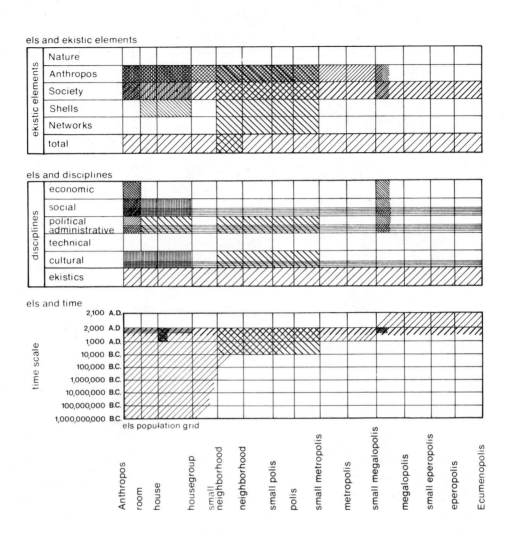

els and ekistic elements

els and disciplines

els and time

els population grid

(every type of hatchmark represents the area
covered by one speaker)

134.　　sectors covered during a symposion on the City
　　　　for Human Development by different speakers

to ask ourselves, what should we do next in order to start the action we need in order to implement what we described? I can only answer from this personal experience which has led me to see the necessity for utilizing the following points:

— We need courage.
— We need order.
— We must define who should act.
— We must define what action should be taken.

## The need for courage

Since we have already admitted that we are frightened, we must now develop intellectual and moral courage. The reason is clear; we are not at the end of the explosion but in the middle of it and a difficult future lies ahead. We can certainly face it scientifically [109] but this is a difficult task. Physics was developed first and biology came much later because it deals with phenomena of much higher complexity; we can understand that the scientific approach to the most complex system of all — human settlements — will take a longer time. To avoid a disaster in the meantime we need courage, this is our great challenge.

There is no reason to be pessimistic about it. Anthropos (Man) once managed to have courage when he undertook to organize relations between his village and the surrounding fields. He saw to it that the village did not grow to such an extent that the fields available could not support all of the village dwellers, and that the water supply was equitably shared between all the peasants to meet the needs of all their farms, thereby establishing an equilibrium in the unit "village". He exhibited similar courage when building up his city-states where he likewise established an equilibrium or by bringing about balance in the Middle Ages between the monastery and its farmlands. Similar courage was shown by certain states which sought to organize relations within the nation-state. Today our courage has to be expressed in several ways as can be illustrated by three examples.

*First*: We must recognize the true dimensions of the contemporary city, which was born in 1825 in England, when the first railway added a new mobility to the people. Today we live in a city which is many tens and hundreds of times larger than the traditional city of the pedestrian but we still accept the old one as the only unit of our organization and this is completely wrong. We escape by waiting for metropolitan government to be created and to act, but we forget that Anthropos (Man) first created new settlements and then recognized them as facts. It is time to remember that the Athenians had the courage to create the new city of Piraeus and connect it by long walls with their city into one physical system in the 5th century B.C., that Anthropos (Man) had the courage to create a huge axis out of the small city of Teotihuacan at the beginning of the 2nd century A.D. and thus established a very big city completed in 600 A.D.; that Peking was a planned city of one million people in the 15th century. We also forget that Washington D.C. (Fig. 135) was conceived in 1791 in a big plan,

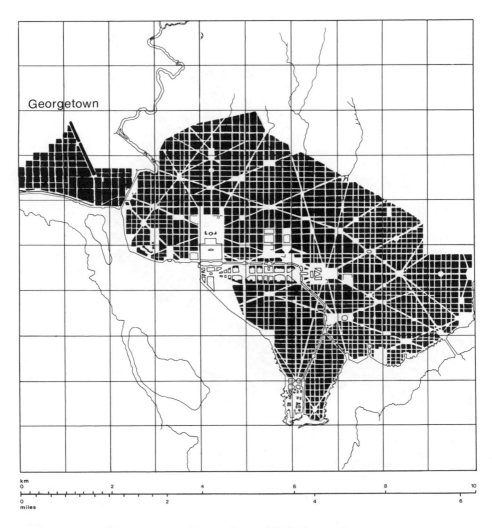

Georgetown

km
0       2       4       6       8       10

0              2              4              6
miles

## 135.    Washington D.C., U.S.A. (1791)

L'Enfant's plan covers an area ten times
larger than Georgetown to the west

although the inhabited area was only small Georgetown. Paris was remodelled in a rational way between 1853 and 1860 and Barcelona conceived in 1859 (Fig. 136) as a large city (compare it with Washington D.C.) although there was only a small walled city in the south and few villages to the west, north and northeast. Thus these cities were planned for a size ten times larger than the areas inhabited at the time. It is time to recognize that we must adjust our thinking

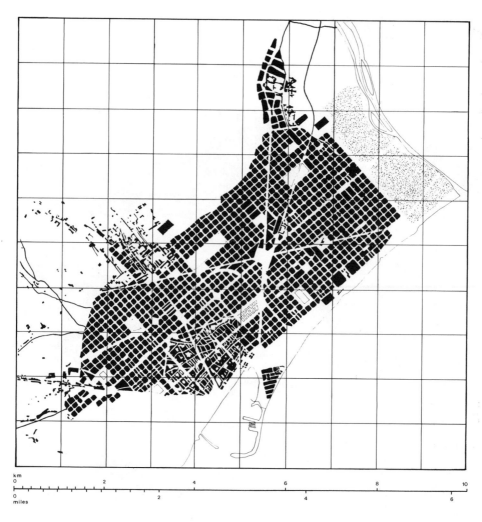

km
0            2           4           6           8          10

0                    2                         4                         6
miles

## 136.   Barcelona, Spain (1859)
the new plan was ten times larger
than the contemporary built-up area

to the real City of Anthropos (Man) which will lead to daily urban systems with a radius of over 100 km. This requires just the same courage as that which led to the creation of the city-states of Greece more than 26 centuries ago.

*Second*: We must remember that a problem like pollution is not only a contemporary problem and Anthropos (Man) has learned how to deal with it in the past. It started with pollution from food and dead bodies but people discovered how to burn or bury the remains. Anthropos (Man) has also learned how to start exposing himself to the energy which he needed and then learned to control it. The great source of energy, fire, polluted the air for hundreds and thousands of years until Anthropos (Man) placed it in fire-places with chimneys. Electric wires were first fastened on the surface of walls and now they are inside. It is time to remember that we will use more and more energy necessitating greater control, and we eventually will have to make use of underground networks for all our transportation and utilities.

*Third*: We must not be afraid of feasibility studies which show that our solutions cannot be implemented. A common feasibility study today is usually based on a small number of years, but the cathedrals of mankind were not built overnight. Such a project as ours for the proper City for Human Development cannot be implemented within an annual budget or a five-year plan. Some of it will eventually be accomplished within one generation's time and the remainder in a few generations. As we pay for insurance to protect our children, so we must also be prepared to pay for insurance for the future of human settlements. This future can be ideal after a few generations when we will again be in balance with Nature and culture. We must fight the defenders of only temporary solutions, because mankind can do better than this if we are not afraid to make decisions. We need only courage.

At times, though, we often lose the opportunity for action because we fail to reach an unanimous agreement on many critical issues. Because we do not have an accepted science of human settlements and because there is no objective system for evaluating the situation, we cannot convince any large group of society of some truths and, lacking the courage, we settle for compromises. But cities cannot be saved through compromises, although they may have been good enough solutions for a village that grew in a natural way — this is not enough for the future City of Anthropos (Man).

## The need for order

Since we know that we are not only frightened but also confused, we not only need courage, we also need order. This is very important because without

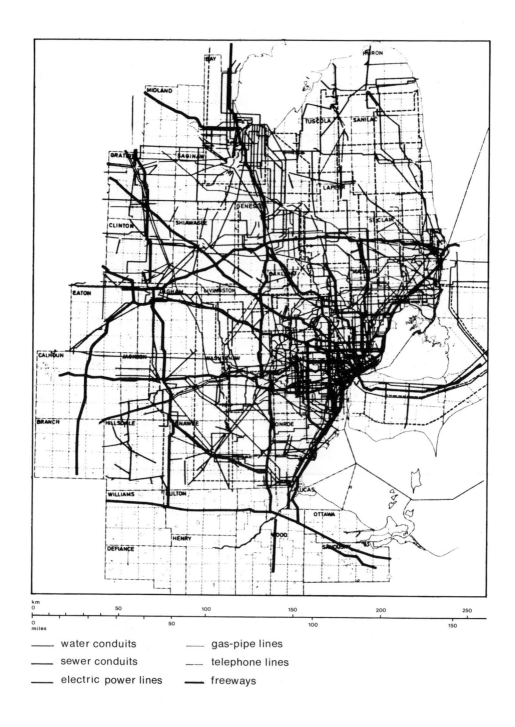



_____ water conduits  _____ gas-pipe lines

_____ sewer conduits  _ _ _ telephone lines

_____ electric power lines  ▬▬ freeways

137.    Networks of the Urban Detroit Area, U.S.A. (1970)

order even our courage will be lost through continuous conflicts and compromises, if, in ancient times Anthropos (Man) had sufficient courage to impose a plan like the Hippodamian one on a city with a radius of one kilometer (0.6 miles), because it was conditioned by the pedestrian who wanted to walk only for ten minutes, then we should have the courage today to impose a plan on a system with a radius of 50 to 100 km, since there are inhabitants who travel over such distances.  But this means order within a larger unit.  We have not yet realized the need for this order, and it is imperative now to decide how to achieve it.

This question of order is a very difficult one and we so often have missed it completely, since our tendency is only to think of Anthropos (Man) the builder instead of Anthropos (Man) the organizer who really precedes him.  Anthropos (Man) first decides to cultivate certain lands and settle on a certain part of them in order to use their resources to his best advantage and only then does he build his village.  Anthropos (Man) has always tried several solutions before creating a city.  During the Chalcolithic period in the Jordan valley (around 3300 B.C.) people tried to live closer together but at the same time maintained distinct hamlets on their own mounds[110] and the Acropolis of Mycenae was surrounded by small but separated neighborhoods where Anthropos (Man) had not yet formed a compact city[111], which was probably invented much later.  These are two examples of Anthropos' (Man's) attempts to come together towards centralized settlements without realizing their real needs for a compact structure.

In this way we can see that today Anthropos (Man) still does not understand the order which is mandatory for the formation of a complex but continuous urban system.  Today he is experimenting, trying to understand the new dimensions, the higher and lower densities and the new organization that is required.  The time has come to remember that basic order is secured with proper coordination of all Anthropos' (Man's) networks into a pattern that can save the natural resources and create corridors of high energy functions, saving the natural and cultural heritage among them.  There are examples of urban systems which had the courage to analyze their situation, like the Urban Detroit Area, which contained as everywhere else many unco-ordinated networks (Fig. 137) and led them to proposals for better developments which demonstrate the order we need in a large scale [112].

We can look for order in this same way on every scale from the large regional and urban systems down to the small units where we can see the order of the small city surrounded by Nature as was the case of ancient Athens (Fig. 138).  This can be repeated in today's modern city where the balance of Nature and Anthropos (Man) now has to be achieved by the penetration of the one into the

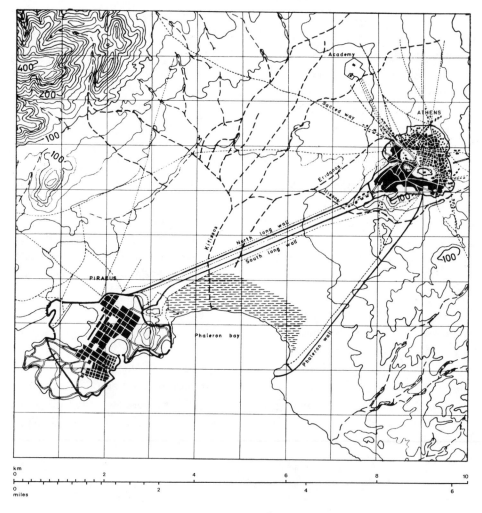

138.    ancient Athens and Piraeus in the 5th century B.C.

other at many different scales, like the example given in Fig. 81 for 1 km (910 yards).

Moving down the scale of dimensions, we reach the point where we find the order between Anthropos (Man) as an individual and his environment, an order which requires both the conservation of the physiological human scale in all the old parts of the cities and the re-establishment of it in all the new parts, our buildings, our streets and squares. This is the only way in which we can hope to create a new balance between Anthropos (Man) and Nature that will help him to survive in the huge urban systems. We had in the past unhealthy cities of high densities like the fortified ones but then most of the people lived in the countryside. But now the opposite is true and we need even more a balance in our big cities and a harmony which is not apparent at present. Otherwise mankind will suffer enormously as the population tends to become global and has to survive.

To reach such systems of order, and harmony we have to work hard and, since we are still confused, we need to develop all possible alternatives to find the proper road for each problem. Then we can select the best one, this is the correct method. It is the proper method not only for science where Anthropos (Man) first began to use it, but also for art as we learn from Stravinsky, "To proceed by elimination, to know how to discard as the gambler says, that is the great technique of selection. And here again we find the search for the One out of the Many" [113].

## Who should act

Who has the responsibility to act with courage and order? This is where we all try to escape: Private citizens accuse their governments, city governments accuse state governments, each profession accuses another (such as architects accusing civil engineers), liberals accuse plutocrats and vice versa. Each group blames the other and there is no end. This has to be stopped as we are all responsible and the only way out is for everyone to act at least in his own sector.

If we leave it at this point we will have failed again; since we are all responsible let us not hesitate to act — we have to mobilize over 3.5 billion people. We had better start acting immediately by ourselves or in groups. Our responsibility is very great.

Can we make decisions on everything? Certainly not, but we can make recommendations on everything we know about and then ask questions of experts on subjects we do not know. We should not forget that the most important part of creativity is to ask the right question. If we do so, others, who know some subjects better will answer.

But there is something even more important than the total answer: The city is not a one-scale system: if we pose the right questions and challenge Anthropos (Man), many decisions can be made and acted on tomorrow morning because many citizens will make their own individual efforts such as:
— Mother can decide which furniture to buy and how the cupboard should be designed.
— Wife and husband will choose which house to buy or build.

— Groups of neighbors can close their streets to cars or remodel them into dead-end streets, thus converting them into safe home-streets.

— Citizens' groups can work to improve their community, city, region, state or nation.

— Citizens can crusade and work for solutions for broader parts of the world.

Let us each act and many will profit. They will take over and ask their own questions and work to satisfy their own needs.


## What should be done

*First:* We have to learn more about every single aspect of the whole system of human settlements. There are millions of questions to be asked and several can be answered by one discipline like ecology; which, for example, can tell us the effect on the birds living in a valley if we eliminate the forest there to build a factory. Each science has to cover the components related to its field.

*Second*: We have to learn how to connect sciences, build bridges and cover the great gaps between their tunnels of knowledge. We have, for example, to connect physiology as concerns optics with architecture and building. We still do not understand why the eye tries to avoid some curved surfaces although we suspect we know. We have to create connections between genetic and environmental (natural and social) aspects. How else are we going to understand cultural needs?

*Third*: We have to learn how to connect all previous knowledge into a system, the science of ekistics, that can lead to the city we need. It is not an easy task but people did face it in the past and succeeded although in smaller scales.

*Fourth*: We have to estimate what is really needed; how much air, how clean, how much oxygen, etc. per person, type of person, phase of life, etc., and proceed to all necessary calculation for the system we need. This can be done if we start designing for every builder's action from room to Ecumenopolis by starting with human activity expressed as a system of energy and only then placing structures and walls instead of learning to do the opposite as we still do today (Fig. 139).

*Fifth*: We have to clarify in our minds what we need and how. For example, we need to walk and this certainly has to be done on the surface of the earth and not below. We also need to move by machines and this can certainly be done in tunnels for high speed driving — speeds could then be increased much more and make people safer than on the surface or in airplanes. Today Anthropos (Man) needs different things for himself, the question is what these are and how to get them. His supplies can all be moved in an orga-

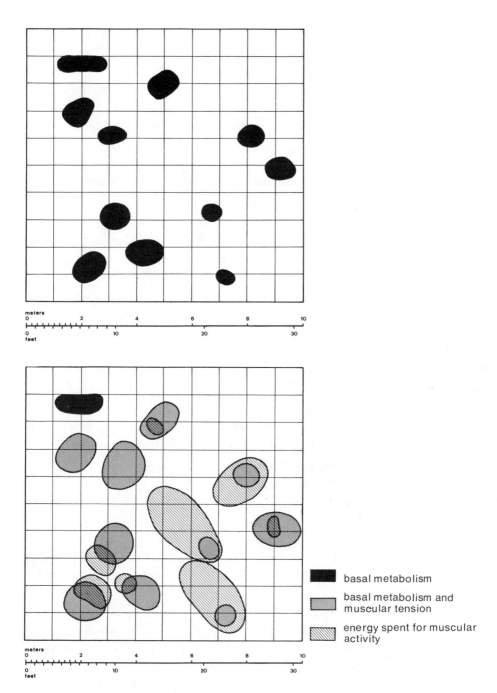

139.    a static picture of a group of people as given in plans,
        whereas the real picture of the same group is given by
        energy measurements

nized way underground. The big trucks will be seen in a few generations as the dinosaurs of the past — total movement of goods and utilities will be through tunnels and pipes.

*Sixth*: We should learn how to experiment and this has to follow the examples of medical practice. We cannot experiment with unsafe medicines or unsafe balconies and roads. We have to prove that they make sense and do not create any additional danger — that, on the contrary, they lead to improvements; then try them on those who want to take the chance. We cannot always invent new processes; we have to understand the natural ones and express them better — as soon as we can.

*Seventh*: We have to develop regulations, not only specifying what is not permitted as we do today the world over, but also what is ideal or preferable, then what is acceptable and finally what should not be permitted at all. We cannot hope to lead to a better world with red lights only.

*Eighth*: We have to clarify that all regulations will serve the poor nations, the farmers, the weak and the developing persons and not only the rich nations and their luxuriously equipped citizens.

Today the world is still using regulations corresponding to the rich and strong. When I had the occasion to serve the Iraqui people of the slums with new schemes providing water supply and sewage systems I found that the rich, industrialized countries had influenced the government to use only steel pipes for sewers. "Why not your own clay pipes?" I asked. "Because," foreign experts replied, "they do not last long." These foreign experts probably had not visited any museums with excellent pipes thousands of years old.

## One example of action

There are several ways we can create much better situations if we first conceive our goals and then try to realize them. This will not be difficult at all, provided we have the moral and intellectual courage to proceed and to create a City for Human Development.

We first have to understand the necessity for proper planning for a very clear division of landownership and delegation of the responsibility for action.

We should define land and properties ownership and clarify the notion of horizontal or space ownership [114]. Why should we stick to the old notion that if we buy land we also buy the air? We should build common utility corridors — not every authority and company choosing its own! The economy and order is much better. We should create the mecstreet-corridor (where we hide the machines forever) and the garages. The community should build concrete dividing walls for each lot, and thus we guarantee forever safety from fire, and much better isolation from noise and privacy. Every family should build its own house. We can have freedom for the creation of really individual solutions and for their continuing change. Anthropos (Man) will then be free to create and live but his community will also be human, safe and respected.

Then the big question arises: how about the houses and streets we already have? Are we going to forget them? Not at all! We can gradually change most of the existing situations into much better ones.

## How we can start the process

We need a revolution to achieve our goals but we cannot succeed overnight. We deal with a biological process and we have to guide it in order to speed up the change.

To achieve this we should not forget that the only criterion for change is human interest and benefit. Many urban renewal projects are initiated forgetting that they first have to rehouse the slumdwellers and then eliminate the slums. This process is reminiscent of Nero's program for action[115]. Many cities tend to eliminate slums. They destroy and eliminate buildings in order to build better ones. In the process they push the weakest minorities out, reduce their housing supply and their access to the central city. They create new monumental fortresses, with no one left at night to protect them. What they forget is that the goal is not to *eliminate* anything but to *serve* Anthropos (Man) better. You do not eliminate the heart of a patient, you try to make it work better.

The whole process of action needs revolution but this has to be carried by evolution towards a better system. We need revolution in our thinking for better evolution of the system of life, with the criterion of continuous amelioration of the system of life.

# 7. Epilogue

The time for action has come, not only for those who are guided by profit-making principles and build monuments and towers but also for those who feel a responsibility to Anthropos (Man).   We must act.

For this we must recover our courage and then we will find the order we need.   Apollo will be with us again restoring the harmony that we need.   He will not come from the North, as in the old days in ancient Greece, but from the mountains and isolated islands — from those who have not been frightened and still know the true value of the human scale.   The Oracle of Delphi will function again, not to make forecasts for the future but "to give guidance to the human spirit when in doubt"[116].   Then Anthropos (Man) will not elect his leaders only for their political talent or administrative ability as he now does, but will select those leaders dedicated to new creative action for the benefit of Anthropos (Man), that is his demiurge (δημιουργὸς) — an autonomous creative force or decisive power, or a Platonic subordinate deity who fashions the sensible world in the light of eternal ideas[117].

# Part two

# Symposion on the
# City for Human Development

# 8. Introduction

The symposion on the City for Human Development took place on July 6-8, 1972 in Athens, at the Athens Center of Ekistics. It was organized under the auspices of the 1972 Athens Ekistics Month, in memory of Apostolos and Evanthia Doxiadis.

The participants were:

*René Dubos*, biologist, Emeritus Professor, The Rockefeller University.

*Erik H. Erikson*, psychoanalyst, educator and artist, Emeritus Professor (Human Development and Psychiatry), Harvard University.

*Dennis Gabor*, physicist, Emeritus Professor, University of London.

*Reginald S. Lourie*, child psychiatrist, Professor of Psychiatry and Child Health and Development, George Washington University.

*Margaret Mead*, anthropologist, Curator Emeritus of Ethnology, American Museum of Natural History.

*Conrad H. Waddington*, biologist, Professor of Genetics, University of Edinburgh.

*Thomas A. Doxiadis*, physician, Director Medical Department, Evangelismos Hospital 1951-1972.

*Spyros A. Doxiadis*, pediatrician, President, Institute of Child Health, Athens.

*C.A. Doxiadis*, architect and ekistician, President, Doxiadis Associates, Int. Co. Ltd.

The symposion was organized by the Athens Center of Ekistics and Kyrkos A. Doxiadis with Margaret Mead acting as chairman.

In this part we present the addresses given by the participants, the discussion among them and the questions asked or answered by a few people from the audience. The letters and the comments we received are too many and cannot be published. They remain in the archives of the Athens Center of Ekistics. One letter by Dr. Gordon Tripp referred to a special aspect of the whole subject and it is presented in Appendix 2.

Margaret Mead described the symposion in her opening statement in these terms.

This part of the whole ekistics presentation was designed as a discussion among a particular small group of people. The important thing about it is the interaction among them. It is not designed as a panel presentation to an audience, in which the audience is then expected to make highly amplified responses, nor is it designed as a group of people. It is the original panel idea that each person on the panel represents a segment of the audience. When panels were first invented, each person represented a discipline — so that an architect would speak for all the architects, and a biologist for all the biologists: so that you would have youth, women and agriculture on the panel.

Now [this panel] wasn't designed that way. It was a group of people who had been working together . . . on the same problems, who had grown interrelated to each other.

Therefore we cannot have much time for questions from the audience. I am going to ask the panelists also not to be primarily influenced by the audience, but to be primarily influenced by what they, as individuals, want to say to each other, and [the audience has] the privilege of listening in. However, we don't want to waste the audience, as we've got them here. Therefore, I have arranged that if anyone wants to put a written question in, they can turn it in [by the recess]. These will be reproduced and given to all of us so we will have some chance to respond to all the members of the audience.

# 9. "A City for Human Development: eighteen hypotheses"

## C.A. Doxiadis

Although one of the members of our group opposes the definition that I am using of the goal of the city, I have been impressed from my youth by the definition given by Aristotle, who said that the goal of the city is to make Man (Anthropos), the citizen, happy and safe. I have read a lot in forty years of professional life and found many other definitions. But I have concluded that this is the only one that I can hold to, with one major difference; the population of the ancient Greek world at the time of Aristotle had reached a levelling-off point, and probably Aristotle was not at all concerned about zero growth of population and energy, because they had already reached their maximum. This means that today Aristotle's goals are not sufficient by themselves, because of the colossal explosion of forces in the fields of science, technology, energy, population, etc. It has therefore become imperative that Man (Anthropos) should develop, so that he can manage to remain in balance and therefore feel safe and happy in the new world around him. Just as Man (Anthropos) was obliged to adapt himself to new conditions when he created the first cities, he must adapt himself now that he is building dynapolis, which is turning the metropolis into megalopolis and laying the foundation for Ecumenopolis. Aristotle was also probably not concerned about the notion of: Where we go from here? But today, we are in an earlier development phase in our civilization and therefore I think we have to add that the goal of the city is to make Man (Anthropos) happy and safe and also to help his human development.

All right but how far forward do we look? Can we consider Man (Anthropos) a thousand years from now? This seems absurd and probably the most we can seriously consider is the next three to five generations. These are the reasons why a decision was made to hold a gathering of a few scientists who are interested in the fate of Man (Anthropos) in order to discuss whether it is within our ability to create a city which will make Man (Anthropos) both happy and secure, as undoubtedly all would want, and which would also help him to develop in a more satisfactory manner, as is being envisaged, or at least anticipated throughout the world.

In order to facilitate the discussion I have drawn up a proposal which faces this problem from the point of view of a craftsman who builds houses and cities, and who feels the need to develop them in a responsible manner.

The report is based on the following hypotheses:

*Hypothesis one:* We are dealing with a very complex, dynamic system of life on the surface of the earth, where every part has an influence on the others. These influences follow certain principles and laws, some of which we know and some we do not, because of their complexity. But the whole is a dynamically changing system (it was not in the time of Aristotle), that has positive or negative effects on its parts depending on the criteria we use. I want to insist on this. We have to talk about the most complex system created on this earth.

*Hypothesis two:* Throughout human history, Man (Anthropos) has been guided by the same five principles in every attempt he makes to live normally and survive by creating a settlement which is the physical expression of his system of life.

The first principle is maximization of Man's (Anthropos') potential contacts. If the black dots (see Fig. 5) represent clusters of people and somebody wants either to create their capital city, or to supply all of them with goods, or to deliver any services, he will certainly select the location shown. This is true from ancient days to the present; Man (Anthropos) seeks a maximization of potential contacts.

The second principle is the minimization of energy (Fig. 6). Biologists and zoologists may be able to show that not only Man (Anthropos), but also animals observe this principle. Actually, a donkey going uphill, tries to discover the best possible path for minimization of energy.

The third principle, which is also probably common to other animals is that we create around us an optimum protective space (Fig. 7). When we talk together, when we sleep in bed with the other sex, when we move away from something that annoys us; each time we seek an optimum dimension. This is just as true of city building which always has optimum distances: not maximum or minimum distances but optimum ones.

The fourth principle is that we seek a balance between the five elements that form the human settlements: Nature, Man (Anthropos), Society, Shells, Networks (Fig. 8).

The fifth principle is an optimum synthesis of the previous four principles, based on time and space, on actual conditions and on Man's (Anthropos') ability to create his own synthesis. Fig. 9 shows a simple expression: a room. We think it is so simple to create a room but it took Man (Anthropos) tens of thousands of years to achieve it, and it was a great invention. A room is a place in which Man (Anthropos) can maximize his contacts with family and friends with minimum effort (opening a door); he can optimize his protective space (by closing the door); he can optimize his contacts with Nature, Society, Shells and Networks (by adjusting doors and windows to control view, temperature, etc.).

*Hypothesis three:* Man's (Anthropos') attention to his whole system of life is indirect. His main direct interest is his own safety, happiness, and, at times, his development. Balance, on the basis of human satisfaction, is Man's (Anthropos') ultimate goal when dealing with his system of life. Our goal should be to reach a new balance between Man (Anthropos) and Nature corresponding to the many changes which have occurred as a result of Man's (Anthropos') new needs and development. This balance cannot now be expressed only at the village scale (as was the goal ten thousand years ago) or only at the city scale (an additional goal over the last five thousand years), but at all scales from Man (Anthropos) himself to the whole earth. This means that the system of Man (Anthropos), Nature and other elements must all change as they move towards the same goal.

*Hypothesis four:* The settlements created by Man (Anthropos), guided by the first four principles, have been more successful, and have made their inhabitants happier and able to live longer whenever the fifth principle of a balance between the other four has been well applied. I have chosen a simple example from primitive man (Fig. 12) showing how he gradually moved from the notion of isolated huts to a sequence of straight walls separating adjacent rooms. This is the sort of way that Man (Anthropos) has resolved many of his problems.

*Hypothesis five:* Human settlements will be created in the future by Man (Anthropos) guided by his own five principles which should not and cannot be changed by anyone.

*Hypothesis six:* The big city is inevitable; it is already growing and it is going to grow even more since it has now become a multi-speed city. Our task is to discover and understand why the city is changing at present and where this continuous change will lead. In the past we had isolated cities or villages (Fig. 13) dependent on human energy. But then came the different systems of mechanized energy — the railway and the automobile — and mankind moved to another type of city: People can now move at higher speeds and in this way their commuting fields, which are parts of their fields of movement (kinetic fields), grow to form systems of cities which give birth to new ones where these kinetic fields overlap. The old, static city is turning first into a dynamic one, the polis into dynapolis, and finally into an urban system.

*Hypothesis seven:* The future city is going to be much more complex in every respect for very many reasons — from new technology and new dimensions to the three forces which condition its shape. These three forces, which increase the complexity beyond those created by the multi-speed systems, are the attraction of existing urban systems, the existing and new lines of transportation and esthetics.

*Hypothesis eight:* The future city is going to grow much more than the city of the present because of the growth of (a) population, which will take time to slow down, (b) income and energy and (c) Man's (Anthropos') mobility.

*Hypothesis nine:* The main crisis of the city is due to a lack of balance between the five elements (Fig. 1). There are certainly many reasons for this but the basic ones are the increase in its dimensions (people, area, energy, economy) and the changes in its physical structure.

*Hypothesis ten:* The inevitable evolution in the structure and the dimensions of today's cities are leading to a universal city, Ecumenopolis. This evolution is going to occur by stages in the next few generations. The spread of present-day urban systems is inevitable. Their foundation stone was laid in 1825 when the first railway ran with passengers in northern England. Urban systems are already 147 years old and they are going to become much larger. The trouble is that we do not understand these facts. We close our eyes in fear and let our urban systems remain without proper structure, leading more and more towards bad conditions and a poor quality of life.

We can easily foresee, that if we avoid any major catastrophe, that we will have to deal with a universal city whose population will tend to be stable in numbers but increasingly more developed intellectually and socially, which will dispose of much greater quantities of energy and achieve greater social interaction.

What is going to happen to Man (Anthropos) within this complex system? We have to consider "Man (Anthropos) within his City", and my next hypothesis states:

*Hypothesis eleven:* The first goal of human development must be to help the average person develop to the maximum of his potential (as we do now for longevity), and the second must be gradually to increase the level of this potential to its maximum in order to help humanity develop to its utmost.

214

*Hypothesis twelve:* The greatest difference which exists in the relationship of Man (Anthropos) and his settlements is the difference between people in varying phases of their life. Any grown-up can walk in the street with cars; even if he has not seen one before he can adjust to them. But a two-year-old cannot. I have been hearing all my life about racial segregation, religious segregation, etc., but the largest difference I have found in the relation of people to the city is by age-groups because a black, a white or a red man can cross the street but their small children cannot. From this, I tried to find how people are divided by age-groups, and here I can cite the divisions in Sanskrit philosophy and those made by Shakespeare and several experts, including Dr. Erikson who is with us. I then took the initiative, not as an expert on Man (Anthropos) but as a builder of cities, to see which phases of our life are related to the city in different ways (Fig. 34). We start with the prenatal or fetal phase; then the breast dependent infant; then the toddler, preschool childhood, school age etc., until we reach old age. Having clients of all these ages, I could see different needs for each different group.

*Hypothesis thirteen:* Man (Anthropos) should be given the opportunity to move out as far and to as many places as he needs in every phase of his development. This, for the average person, means to start from the minimum distance — the body of his mother — and to expand to the whole earth or even go beyond it and then, gradually, reduce to the smaller areas corresponding to actual needs and interests. This is an ultimate goal facilitated by modern science and technology (Fig. 46).

*Hypothesis fourteen:* Man (Anthropos) should be given the opportunity to move by himself without any assistance as far out as he wishes and in the best possible way for him and in every phase of his development. I asked myself whether one could speak a bit more clearly about this, and Fig. 46 shows two curves, one delineating the areas within which we can move by walking, having an independent natural movement, the other the areas for which we have to use machines. Figs. 90, 92 and 95 show the gradual exposure of the child to his environment. First, only the room as seen from his small bed, then the house and garden, gradually the small street and wider areas.

*Hypothesis fifteen:* A city must guarantee everybody the best possible development under conditions of freedom and safety and thus it becomes a specific goal to fit the city to Man (Anthropos) in the same way that a tailor fits a suit to our body and not vice versa. We always have to think how the city can best be built to fit human needs. This means that the man-built environment (Shells and Networks) should protect Man (Anthropos) physically from adverse exposures to his physical environment: this also should apply to Nature, with its various aspects all serving Man (Anthropos) as structures and as functions.

*Hypothesis sixteen:* A City for Human Development must create a system that can challenge every citizen to enjoy it and develop himself to his maximum, and this can only be achieved by a system of quality that transmits the notion of order. This can be done if the system has the proper quality at an optimum level (not too low and not too high and intense) with the larger part of the system representing an order and the smaller parts a disorder. We cannot expect civilization to be created within the jungle although a garden can be like a jungle within an orderly system.

The relation of Man (Anthropos) to space is not so simple. For example we can enclose the child in a room but open it at the top (the atrium); open it also to the garden; open it more and more so that we can see the complexity of the system related to the energy explosion of the small child (Fig. 51).

*Hypothesis seventeen:* Man (Anthropos) always needs to maximize his potential contacts with people and minimize the energy required, but this has to be accomplished without endangering the quality and quantity of his contacts. This requires a gradual exposure to the city and its people, with an optimum situation for every developmental phase, allowing for the possibility throughout Man's (Anthropos') lifetime of exposure to areas with different types and intensities of contacts. If we have insurmountable boundaries, as in a prison, the energy has no outlet and it may blow up (Fig. 70).

*Hypothesis eighteen:* The task of the city is to help the source of energy — that is the individual — to respond to all challenges and to develop and meet as many new ones as possible. If this can be achieved from the individual's first relationship to his environment, then the source of his energy becomes stronger and can overcome even more hindrances. Such a well developed source of energy will finally be able to conquer the whole space — physical, sensory, intellectual — which surrounds it, although this does not necessarily mean that it can conquer all obstacles within this space. Fig. 74 shows that in stage one all the time is spent inside the mother; then most of the time is in the room, then in the home, then school and high school, then downtown business or factory, at some distance away; but the system as a whole emphasizes that we spend nearly 80% of our time inside our home and in the small area around it.

We can proceed and speak about the meaning of each unit of space for every phase of our life. It is clear that the room and the house and the immediate environment are of the greatest importance. If we have noise there, we suffer. If we have noise on the highway which we cross to go to work we care much less.

The importance of space in each different phase of life related to its total importance shows that what really matters are the smaller units. And I began to ask myself, as a builder of houses, whether we are sure what it is we want the small child to see in its early phase. On Fig. 84 I put question marks on the walls (the colors, the light). And then let us try to look at the courtyard, as the child sees it. Here the child is safe but it begins to see the sky instead of ceiling; it begins to learn to contact strangers without danger to itself (Fig. 91). We can then think of the further units of human scale within which the child can move by itself (Fig. 97) and the broader units and the broader system of balances (Fig. 104) up to the whole system corresponding to the world of the young adults who can drive all over it (Fig. 117).

In the past we had centers of power and centers of religion but we dream of a future where hospitable centers for learning and human development in the broadest sense *(paideia)* are going to be at least of equal importance with the centers of power. We cannot turn the philosophers into kings but we must always attempt to give them enough power to influence Man (Anthropos).

# 10. "Great city versus small city"

# Dennis Gabor

## Uniformity versus diversity

I must reproach Doxiadis for having a somewhat *too* logical mind. He starts from not less than 18 "hypotheses", which are all of the nature: optimize desirables, minimize undesirables. I have no quarrel with any one of his hypotheses; fortunately they are too vague for leading unescapably to an optimum solution. I say fortunately, because if they were definite enough, they would lead to one city, and this would be a distressingly uniform world!

We have already too many "optimum" solutions, admittedly with the low purpose of reconciling acceptability with maximum profits. The chain stores, the gas stations, the supermarkets, the Hilton hotels and of course the high-rise slab, these are all such regrettable optimum solutions. We do not want more of them, we do not want the optimum city either. What we want, among many other things, is more diversity. This is a principle, which, I believe, ought to override not only profitability but also the quest for optima.

Now Doxiadis has presented us with essentially one solution. It is in many respects an attractive one. I like particularly the idea of the "home-street" and the "home-square". His solution is also an ideal one from the point of view of the safety of little children, and a reasonable adaptation to the "seven ages of Man". Of course, what is ideal for the infant is not necessarily ideal for the parents. It is, essentially, a suburb, and brings with it, unavoidably, all the sufferings of the lonely suburban wife. May I add to Doxiadis' 18 hypotheses my own, which is that modern men and women have become very intolerant of boredom. They have in their home the telephone, the radio and the television set, all things their ancestors had to do without, but these have only raised their expectations of the excitements which life has to offer. And the suburb offers very little.

There is a hidden hypothesis among the explicit ones of Doxiadis, and this is that women like chatting with their neighbors. This was undoubtedly true in villages, it may still be true in working-class quarters, but in English middle-class suburbs people often carefully avoid making friends with their neighbors — because they cannot get away from them. Experienced pursers on pleasure cruises know this very well, and try never to give one table to people who come from the same district. The suburban woman prefers to choose her friends from all over the town, and chat with them through the telephone. I have a little invention for alleviating the misery of the lonely suburban house-wife, who cannot do her housework while having the receiver pressed to her ear: an improved loud speaker telephone, which allows her to walk about and attend to her household duties with both hands while conversing with one friend, perhaps even with several of them. This is the sort of thing which Alvin Weinberg calls the "technological fix" of social troubles, though I do not of course suffer from the illusion that technology can fix everything.

## City or suburb?

Human habitations do not make a city. I am sure that Doxiadis knows this as much as anybody, if not better, but my impression is that his city is top-heavy with human habitations. Perhaps he has gone a little too far in condemning the architectural crimes of the past?

I am entirely on his side by condemning the construction of high-rise buildings from an esthetic and human angle, but I am afraid, I have to play the *advocatus diaboli* in bringing in a strong argument for the persistence of the "gigantic inanity" as Lewis Mumford has called it. Oil will be running out in about a couple of hundred years. This may appear a long time, but a steep rise in the price of oil can be expected before the end of this century. Even before this, the fact that two-thirds of the world's oil reserves are in Arab countries will produce painful political tensions. But heating small houses with oil is so comfortable that people will stick to it even if the oil price will double or treble, thus producing grave financial trouble for countries like the U.S. I foresee there-fore, that the governments of such countries will favor, by taxation or even stronger means, the building of compact towns, with high-rise buildings, be-cause these can be much more easily heated with the reject heat of atomic power plants, or with heat pumps. I am truly sorry to have to play the *ad-vocatus diaboli!*

I must disagree with his condemnation of dispersed buildings, and unconnect-ed buildings. I am fully aware of the beauty which the beautiful old towns of the past have gained by their connectedness. But if (for the reason mentioned before), we are *forced* to build high-rise slabs, these are by far more agreeable if they are separated by green strips than if they are built side-by-side.

I agree with much of his condemnation of monumental building. I agree that corporation headquarters need not be monumental. I even contend that the gigantic corporation headquarter is a silly technological anachronism in the epoch of the telephone, not to mention the picturephone and the computer console. Only a small fraction of the people in these gigantic buildings ever talks to a live customer otherwise than through the telephone. They could be just as well dispersed in small towns, in a radius of hundreds of miles. But it is the monumental building (not necessarily a giant building), which makes a city something which expresses civic pride. Can we do without a substitute for cathedrals?

I forcibly agree with his condemnation of the anti-human city because I am on the side of Man. But has not Doxiadis sinned against this by displaying, in my eyes, an unwarranted defeatism in the matter of the great city versus the small one?

## Great city versus small city

Here are a few quotations from Doxiadis' original report:

"Because of science and technology the city is changing in a very natural way, but we are still confused and talk about improbable things such as the desirability of the small city, although we know that mankind will always abandon it, and run to the big city."

Will mankind always run to the big city, and is this forced on us by science and technology? I refuse to believe this. Why do people run to the big city? Doxiadis gives an interesting argument; a minority of "blue people" can find their like in a big city. I admit this only in the case of very undesirable "blue people", such as homosexuals, criminals, drug addicts and drug pushers. They need the big city to hide in! It is true that more desirable "blue people", such as scientists, philosophers, painters also find their like in a big city, but would they not find them easier in smaller places, such as university towns or painters' colonies?

The normal citizen, I believe, runs to the big city mainly because he wants job security. It is easier to find a job, or change it, in a big city, though when the job changes, this leads to the phenomenon of thousands of commuters crossing through the town center every day, from one end of London or New York to the other. A smaller number, especially young ones, drift to the city in search of excitement, but there is hope that this slightly pathological symptom will not always be with us. Many young Swedes already are starting to prefer small towns, or even rural districts, to Stockholm.

I query even more the statement that the drift to the big city is a consequence of science and technology. Certainly, science and technology have enabled crowded multi-million populations to be provided with transport, power, water and food, but how unsatisfactory is the solution of transport! In cities like New York the commuting time is almost independent of the distance. Consequently, it is not the city proper that is growing, but the suburbs. The populations of the inner cities are already decreasing in the U.S. with well known disastrous con-sequences for the town finances.

Doxiadis is, of course, right in recognizing the trend towards giant conurba-tions. But let me ask him (with Lewis Mumford), why he takes a trend for a com-mand? Why does he abandon so lightly the small city, into which his plans would fit so much better? Modern technology can replace commuting by communi-cations, and by the placement of key industries one could make small cities as job-secure as great ones.

There is another argument, which makes me believe that Doxiadis is too rash when saying that "Even if we assume that we could do the impossible and effect an immediate levelling-off of the Earth's population, the urban population would still increase to three times the present size." And "... we should not, and in any case cannot, control the influx of rural people to the urban system." The argument is that crime and drugs are increasing so rapidly, especially in the big cities of the U.S. that responsible parents ought to accept even a small reduction in living standards (which is not at all necessary) to keep their children out of crime and clear of drugs. Small towns (especially newly built ones which have no slums) can be so much more easily policed than big ones.

This question of the unavoidability of the growth of big cities is evidently of the greater importance, and we must thrash it out in the discussion.

## Age grouping

There is another of Doxiadis' tacit hypotheses with which I cannot quite agree, that people should associate with others of the same age. Of course, little children ought to play together, but for the somewhat older ones we are already doing enough by putting them into the same school. The principle becomes downright dangerous when applied to university students. At this age they ought not only to stride out through the world, as Doxiadis rightly emphasizes, but they ought to get used to the idea that they are not a compact class opposed to all the rest.  Are we not widening the "generation gap" by forming communities of 20,000 or more people of 18-23 in giant universities?

I do not much like the idea of old people's communities either.  There are now "senior citizens' villages" in the States, but for me this is a dismal idea.  In my book, *Inventing the Future*, I have advocated exactly the opposite idea, and it does not discourage me that it was received, at best, with an indulgent smile.  This was the revival of the multi-generation house, which was once the privilege of the aristocracy and of a few successful people.  A large manor, with ample grounds, where three or four generations of a family live under one roof, and where the older people enjoy a sort of immortality by having young ones of their own blood under their eyes.  A house from which the young men go out in the world, for years of work and travel, but in the end proudly bring back their young brides, because there is no better place in the world.  Of course, I must admit, that our civilization has become intolerant not only to boredom, but also to older people and that a change of this attitude is still nowhere in view.

## Economics and ecology of the city

I am surprised that Doxiadis nowhere seems to mention that the city is for work, not only for habitation.  I cannot believe that he thinks only of dormitory towns. I gladly admit that his city is much superior to the usual American "housing development", but this would be measuring from a very low level.  John Aldridge, in his book *In the Country of the Young*, speaking of the confusion and aimlessness of American youth writes: "What better can you expect from people who have grown up in housing developments?"  Indeed, what other window have these poor people on life and civilization than the school and television?

The dormitory town is largely an unwelcome creation of the motor car, combined with the economic insecurity which drives people into proximity of big cities.  My ideal is a town in which the working place is within walking or at most cycling distance.  It is true that modern Man does not like to walk, but perhaps he can learn again.  It will do him a lot of good.  There is much talk nowadays about people not going to work at all, but doing it at home, at a computer console.  This, as well as the other great "future shock" invention, that the housewife should do her shopping at a television screen, and order the goods by pushing some buttons, I consider as unmitigated psychological nonsense.  Most people, except perhaps craftsmen and some creative artists, need to get out of the home to do their work, and the housewife needs the walk to the shops and the gossip with others in the shops and markets, or else she will get the typical suburban claustrophobia. But neither is it necessary to travel 10, 20, 30 or more miles to one's working place. The modern light-industry factory need not be ugly; in fact in many small American towns these are the only buildings with some pretension to beauty. They are light, white, pleasant structures, surrounded by well-kept parks.

As regards shops, Doxiadis claims boldly that, "Man can only interact successfully on the ground floors of the city". I hope this does not mean that he approves of the horrible one-floor shopping centers which are now sprouting up in or around the main roads of small American towns? To me they are an architectural eyesore, much worse than the "Emporia" in the English suburbs. Perhaps he has the old-fashioned market place in mind, at the centers of some beautiful German towns? I do hope he will be able to give us a vision of something equally attractive.

The small city must be economically sound; it must not live by exporting labor. In order to assure job-security it must have mainly basic industries which are not too subject to fashions and fluctuations, such as food processing, textiles, clothing, furniture, artistic crafts. Most "modern" industries, such as electronics or aircraft, have too sharp ups and downs.

Ecological soundness can mean very different things. The minimum requirement is of course that the city must not pollute air or water. The problem of pollution has created quite unnecessary heat, because on the whole, in the industrialized countries, it takes only one and one half to two per cent of the GNP to keep air and water clean. If for some industries, such as the paper industry it means an extra cost of 15-20%, let them add it to the cost of the product! Most of us would be quite happy with that much less paper polluting our writing desks.

But ecological soundness can mean much more than absence of pollution. In a country like Denmark, where agricultural land is already scarce, it may mean strong pressure towards high density town population. Most countries, especially the United States, are still far from this stage, but as I mentioned before, there may be some pressures toward higher density by the wastefulness of oil heating of single, small houses as compared with the ease with which densely populated centers can be provided with central heat. We know how violently the developing countries are reacting to the ecological principles which are now propagandized by the industrialized countries. As they are mostly in hot zones, they can congratulate themselves that at least they will be free from the headache of house heating.

Ecological constraints are, unavoidably, restrictions in the efficiency of production, and they cannot fail to be painful. Unless we are very wise, the greed which is now ruling the industrialized countries will lead to an ecological catastrophe, or, conversely, it may require so much *dirigisme* that we shall have to give up democracy in the Western sense. In a very thoughtful article, Arnold Toynbee wrote: "... we cannot be sure that even in Britain parliamentary government is going to survive the fearful ordeal of having to revert, on the material plane, to the stable way of life" (THE OBSERVER, June 4, 1972). This is a fearful problem, too enormous to discuss in our small symposium, but we must keep it in the back of our minds.

## The challenge of the city

Giving the word again to Arnold Toynbee, without an adequate challenge no civilization can survive. Doxiadis has summed this up very well in his *hypothesis sixteen:* "A City for Human Development must create a system that can challenge every citizen to enjoy it and develop to his maximum. This can be done if it has the proper quality at an optimum level, not too low and not too high and intense."

Is it not too much to expect from the city architect? Can buildings (Shells and Networks) "create" a challenge? I am inclined to doubt it, especially if one accepts Doxiadis' condemnation of the monumental building. Is Paris not an exciting and challenging town because of its monumentality? One can certainly enjoy a garden city, but will it challenge the young people to develop to their maximum? If they want to develop, they will escape from its uniformity as fast as they can.

I may be lacking in imagination, but the only adequate challenge of which I can conceive is competitive pride. Let small cities compete in their diversity, let them try to be different from others and pride themselves on their individuality. Let them take a pride not only in their local football team, but also in their local stadium. Let them put up schools competing in beauty and luxury. Let them cultivate their own architects, with distinctive styles. Perhaps in time they will also develop distinctive apparel?

I am glad that I can end on a note of agreement with Doxiadis. He deplores, rightly, the shortness of the contacts people make in the modern "market place". Our ancestors knew very well how to make long contacts in the café! Make ample plazas for pedestrians, and even if the shops cannot be on one floor, the cafés and open-air restaurants can spread out. And let each small town have its pleasure gardens, its Tivoli or Vauxhall or Ranelagh Park. (It was not the English climate which killed these, but English puritanism). Modern technology can help by giving them the right sort of climate in every sort of weather.

We have indeed committed many crimes. Have we built in the last hundred years a single city in the industrialized countries of which our descendants could be proud? There are of course excuses: industrialism, population increase, the spreading of egalitarianism, that is to say the desire to give decent shelter quickly to the teaming new millions and perhaps worse than all, the motor car. I am afraid these pressures are not likely to relax of their own accord. They can be countered only by farsighted architects and by a gradual education of the patrons. Perhaps they can be educated at least to be determined to build nothing for which our descendants will curse us!

# 11. "Comments on the City for Human Development"

## C.H. Waddington

I want to start by saying that I think there are some other biological needs of Man which ought to be taken into account in designing a City for Human Development. I am not going to pretend that they are firmly established, because one of the extraordinary things about biology is how little we know about Man, how little we really know what his basic requirements are. But there are a few that I think should be considered, and the first is Man's need for muscular movement. I think that Doxiadis does not put enough emphasis on this. Although he provides steps on the streets for people to walk up, I think we would not get nearly enough opportunity or challenge to indulge in muscular movement. This is one of the major reasons why we find today so many degenerative diseases of middle age.

Let me bring into discussion the possibility of much greater development of the bicycle. The bicycle is a wonderful machine for getting about, over distances of three to four miles. In its present type, there is no protection against the weather and it is certainly uncomfortable in rain or wind, but there is no obvious reason why it should not be enclosed in a plastic bubble. There is no reason, even, why it should not be reasonably airconditioned, if you want this. There is no reason why you should not have a little supplementary engine if you have to go uphill or against a high wind. All these improvements can be made if we have adequately designed urban transport routes for it. If it is prevented from getting mixed up with 124 horse-power motor cars, there is no reason why the bicycle should not be a pretty safe way for people to transport themselves. It could in fact be protected with a plastic cover, with about the consistency of cartilage: something that would be slightly bouncy and resilient, so that if the bicycles did run into one another the people would not really be hurt very much.

I think that there is a lot to be said for having three types of human transport: the pedestrian, the bicycle and then highly mechanized, fast, long distance automobile transport. In any case I think we ought to design for men and women to have much more opportunity for taking muscular exercise in the normal course of their life.

There is another thing which I would like to emphasize in the bringing up of the infant. Doxiadis has talked about its space requirements. Another thing it has to do is to learn to perceive. There is a considerable evidence among animals, such as cats, that they have to learn to perceive certain definite types of shape at quite a young stage. For instance, they have to see edges from different angles, not just from one. One can probably safely say that people have to learn while still quite young, to perceive a sufficient variety of different things, and things that are fairly definite. This seems to me to mean that they need an environment which is both visually rich, but rich in things with definite shapes. I believe that early experience, what is available to the perception of the young child, probably has a considerable influence on its later visual capacities.

The third factor I think we want to take into account is something which Doxiadis has obviously considered but which he does not explicitly state. This is the sense of "time". Modern urban people, on the whole, don't naturally think in terms of processes going on through time. A child in a natural environment is always surrounded by things that are growing: plants that are growing, animals that are growing. He is surrounded by things that vary over short or longer periods, or with the changing of the seasons. His attention is directed to a whole series of things extended in time. It is very important that this sense of processes going on through time should be reinforced and developed. We are becoming more and more convinced that biology is dependent to an extraordinary extent on rhythmic processes. We are all conscious of highly intimate biological rhythms of digestion, excretions, monthly rhythms and so on. I think the maturing human mind needs to come across many experiences of rhythmic processes and their extension into continuous developmental processes in time. I believe something of this kind could be incorporated into the way cities are organized.

To turn to quite another point, there is the question of why people move into cities. I want to link this with certain other stages in the life cycle that Doxiadis sketched, certain stages which I think he rather under-emphasized. In connection with city development, he didn't lay very much stress on the two periods which he calls adolescence and the young adult. But I think the people who go in the cities are very largely from this age-group. I believe that the immigration into the Greater London area is predominantly from this age-group, and these young people go into cities by choice, largely, I think, to find excitement. Discussions of cities tend to be based on thinking of people as being all the time very sensible, good, worthy citizens. But most people go through periods of being rather irresponsible, and periods of not putting their civic duties on the top of their list of priorities. A great many people go to cities just because cities are exciting. They are exciting because one can meet a lot of people, because one can change jobs, because one can meet very different sorts of people without one's parents being aware, without one's neighbors being aware; away from the intensive social system of the small place. Young people like to go somewhere big, where they can get mixed up with all sorts of things; and of course this young age-group has quite a lot of spending money. It doesn't control great fortunes that can build enormous slabs of apartment blocks, but it has the money to rent apartments in these apartment blocks. In fact the young have probably more uncommitted spending money than they will have a few years later, when they start having their own families and settling down. I think, therefore, that their demands have a very considerable influence in shaping the city.

I move to another point. Someone raised the question of whether specialized areas should focus on particular age-groups. I quite agree with Dr. Gabor that there is something to be said for having areas where there are a lot of families with young children. But there's certainly nothing to be said for segregating the older people. There may be something to be said for areas focussed on the young adults; partly because they like to get together, and partly because they tend to be a nuisance to everybody else as they like to make a lot of noise. So, on the whole, there is quite a lot to be said for having Chelsea, and the Left Bank in Paris, and other such places where young people can get together and amuse themselves in ways that are not always so amusing for older or younger people.

Doxiadis talks about the location of working places but not much about their character. His discussion is mainly devoted to the nature of the dwelling house and the home street and the small dwelling region. But I think we have to give serious consideration to the character of the work place, because this is almost certainly going to change. The assembly line is almost certainly going to disappear, partly because people in reasonably well-off countries will no longer be willing to work at it. In Britain, West Germany and France, almost the entire labor force in mass production car assembly lines are recent immigrants, largely from countries that are less well-off. The actual Frenchman, and certainly the actual Swiss, won't any longer undergo this sort of mass production work. That is one reason. Another reason, of course, is that with the rise of automation and with better communications systems there is no particular reason why anyone in the world should undergo this form of labor. Particularly as we move towards a more stable society, we are going to want things which are made to last much longer. It may be that you are going to pride yourself not on having next year's model automobile, but on having an automobile that was built so well 15 years ago, that it is still running just as well as it did to start with. It is the sort of pride some people take in Rolls Royces; and if you run a Rolls Royce that was built in 1935 everybody knows you have got a superlatively good car. We may have to go through the world with much more of these sort of values. So I think the character of the work place needs a lot more discussion.

Finally, I was glad that Gabor raised the question of what he called monumental buildings (though I should prefer to call them focal buildings or focal areas) as substitutes for the cathedral. At the moment the substitutes for the cathedral in most large American cities are banks, and there is one bank that builds the biggest, tallest building in every city along the West Coast. But surely banks are not wholly representative of our civilization, and I agree with him that cities do need some other visible focal center. We need a worthy focal center which people will take pride in, and we haven't at the moment really got anything to put in this place.

# 12.  Discussions

The participants decided to concentrate their discussion on the following points:
1. increasing the *density*
2. monumental buildings
3. segregated communities (by age groups)
4. shopping, ground floor interaction
5. diversity — small city competition
6. muscular development
7. character of work-places
8. crime and the city

**C.A. Doxiadis:** During the intermission, our panel decided to concentrate the dialogue on the above eight points.  Several more of importance were brought up this morning, but as some of our members are going to speak more about them tomorrow, they will be brought up tomorrow or the day after.  So the Chairman has asked me to write this down:  these points have been selected by us to speak on this morning, and she told me that we should answer in a short way the first one and then we will have the discussion.  Am I right, Mme Chairman?  I follow orders.

Now on the first point:  Dr. Gabor told us that for a specific reason we should build compact cities and increase their density.  I agree with him one hundred per cent for two reasons:  First, because humanity has tended historically that, although they all started in some very compact settlements, where there was not even space for streets (like in Asia Minor 4,000 B.C., people had to enter all houses from the roof), or by bearing low density, like some Neolithic villages in North-Western Greece, they have always tended as far as we are able to find, to compact settlements of an average of 200 persons per hectare, eight persons per acre.  Now, we are spreading again, and when we were talking about financial aspects yesterday, I came in with a strong proposal to make our cities more compact, because I believe that historically Man has proved he has an optimum and today we have lost it.

**Mead:** Now, who would like to respond to that? Dr. Gabor?

**Gabor:** Yes, one hundred per cent in agreement. There's not much point in responding.

**Waddington:** Could I make a remark to this? I can entirely agree with the desirability of compact cities, but I don't think that you can discuss them without also discussing the size of area of the compact part of the settlement. I mean, a compact settlement is fine (I think I would agree with Dinos) (C.A. Doxiadis) up to an area you can walk across in ten minutes to a quarter of an hour. But if you have a compact settlement and the compactness goes on for mile after mile, then you are in, I think, an appalling situation. I think the point about compactness is that it also has got to be combined with loosening, loosening between the compactness, loosening the network structure.

**S.A. Doxiadis:** I would like to ask people who might know, we have come to realize during the last two years the relationship between animal behavior and the density of the group in a certain confined space. Does anybody of the panel know if similar observations exist on human beings, in prisons, institutions, camps?

**Mead:** One of the most astonishing things that we have found is the amount of compactness that human beings can stand, if it is culturally regular or associated with hope. And this seems to be far more important than any kind of measurement that you can put in. You can put 15 student volunteers in a five-passenger motor car and they will come out unimpaired.

**S.A. Doxiadis:** Are you sure?

**Mead:** Well, but you couldn't put Europeans in for a short period of time without their being impaired. Only, on ships that went to Israel from concentration areas from various parts of the world, the density was utterly unacceptable by anything we know medically and nobody got sick because they were moving from something worse to something better. This seems to be so much more important than the kind of studies they make on rats, where they can make qualitative predictions.

**Lourie:** I think that's an important point, but it is very dangerous to extrapolate from the studies on rats and so on to Man. I suppose that the greatest density of Man per acre at the present time, I think, is in Hong Kong and similarly there are two densities to consider. There is the density per acre of land area, there is also the density per room. And this need not be the same thing. But in both cases, in Hong Kong at least, they are far greater than anything we would consider normal, and the average density in Hong Kong is by ten times the maximum allowed by British laws. But the Hong Kong people put up with it. Now, Margaret made the point, Man can put up with a lot of things; if he has found it worthwhile for some other reason this doesn't necessarily mean that it'd be the optimum for him. The Hongkongians or whatever they call themselves, the Hongkongees would probably like more space, but they put up with it under the circumstances. Man in contrast to the animal is much more adaptable. And I don't know whether we can talk about an interpreting Man, but in the earliest years, as I'm sure C.A. Doxiadis will be telling us, there is patterning set up and expectations. And if we bring up a youngster in crowded conditions, this is what they have been able to incorporate in their picture of what is natural and what is desirable. As a matter of fact, in some of our inter-city populations, where we've moved families out into new houses, after they've been living in very crowded conditions, giving them a room for each child, we find that in some of those families the children refuse to sleep alone in their own rooms. Even if some of the adults would have been brought up in very close living conditions they abandon their rooms and insist on sleeping with others. So it depends on what we want to bring up Man to adjust to. And it is the change later on in life. If you put a man in prison, who has been used to living in a defined space, you'll find that he finds it very difficult to adjust to the very crowded conditions. And that gets into this whole question of additional expectations, because if in the crowded conditions he is exposed to crime, exposed to violence, his expectations are that there will be crime and violence. If in the clumped group of families there was crime — I'm not sure just how close living existed with Adam and Eve, but there were some expectations that Abel and Cain evolved in their relationships and I'm sure their interest in violence didn't arise purely from themselves. There must have been some learning that went on there.

**Gabor:** Crowding can have two completely opposite effects. In England and in Holland for instance, colossal density has brought a lot and a missing amount of self-restraint, and a very good city spirit. We know, gentlemen, that it can have just the opposite effect. I want to mention an interesting example. During the war, the East and West Ends crowded together, as they were particularly exposed to German bombs. They crowded together in underground stations where they slept under unbelievable conditions together. But after the war, they left with great regret, because a community spirit developed in the shelters, people talked to one another, which suburbans don't usually do, and they were perfectly happy.

**Mead:** But this does bring us back, of course, after we have said all this, to the question: what is optimal and what are the possible ranges? And to Dr. Gabor's statement: that he wants diversity. Now this carried to a proper extent would mean that we'd take some parts of the world and permit them to be spread out and have all the virtues of spread-outness — you know, communing with nature, preferring a large amount of space and quiet, and not getting to know very many people ever, and then we have other parts of the earth, like modern Holland or modern Britain, where we develop some of the other virtues. We might find that there are some virtues in the suburbs, which I doubt, but it is possible.

**C.A. Doxiadis:** If we make a scale of space, from room to the very big city, to the megalopolis, and consider density, we find that the optimum is constantly decreasing. In a single building we can have many people, but as we add streets, squares, factories, etc., the overall density drops. The same applies if we substitute time for space. We can be squeezed very tightly for a short time to buy tickets for the theater, but the longer we stay, the more we must have lower densities. The interesting thing is that we may also want minimal densities for short periods: to spend a weekend alone on a mountain.

**Waddington:** Could I take up a point about diversity in density? Supposing we do have cities of considerably different density: some very, very highly built up, some much more dispersed, different like Manhattan and Los Angeles, or something of this kind. Now, when one talks of diversity of cities, at least the image in my mind is of cities in which people spent their whole lives. There are either Florences, or Sienas or Venices, or cities of this kind, but is it possible that in a sort of more flexible world with many more opportunities and different sorts of jobs, that people will tend to move from one type of city to another during their lifetime? The diversity wants to be thought of not only as diversity of life styles, that you can adopt for your whole life as has happened in the past, but as a diversity of life styles (as reflected in densities) which you can move between during your lifetime, when you are having your children, when you're settled, when you're old, when you're adolescent, and so on.

**Dubos:** If you do not mind, I would like to return to your allusion to experiments on crowding in animals. Now one of you was referring to John Calhoun's studies: I am not sure whether they are the most famous, but they are the most talked about, in which he showed that following after certain levels of population density, not only in rodents, but also in other animal species, there are all sorts of abnormal facts of behavior change in biological character, sex failure to reproduce and that kind of thing. No one will have any difficulty in repeating these experiments: many of us have. But there is one aspect of Calhoun's experiments which, I believe, limits the relevance of Man to the human condition and which one can even find, using the same animal species and almost the same experimental conditions.

And let me just, in two words, state that a change of experimental conditions will bring about results profoundly different from those of Calhoun. Those of you who are familiar with John Calhoun's studies will recall that he has a big room in which he lets animals multiply freely and they soon reach a population density in which all sorts of abnormal biological manifestations become obvious. But if you take exactly the same room and provide the animals with exactly the same kind of satisfactory nutritional and sanitary conditions, and just introduce sub-sections, you can achieve a population ten times (not 10%, but ten times) higher without any of the biological disturbances which Calhoun so beautifully describes. So I think that by design of the human environment, one can really change the effects of crowding (if you use human density as a definition of crowding). I add this because I think crowding involves very much more than population density.

Dr. Lourie talked about what we are trained to expect through early conditioning. If you buy animals of the same species (of the same genetic constitution) from different breeders and put them in one cage, even at a very low population density, you get all sorts of conflicts, all sorts of biological destruction. But if you let the animals multiply together, they achieve some quality of togetherness, through conditioning in early life, which makes it possible for them to reach a very high population density. And then, of course, as soon as we move to Man, and I suspect it applies to animals, living under crowded conditions one learns to develop all sorts of protective mechanisms as we all know (all of us who live in undercrowded conditions) like the kind of space bubble, which Ed Hall talks about. And that can go very very far. I believe that whenever one speaks about crowding and the effects on Man, one should at least quote that extraordinary letter of Descartes, in which he states this so explicitly. He was asked: Why did you go to settle in Amsterdam (or Rotterdam, I can't remember which one of the two cities)? It was at the time the most densely populated city in the world. And he says very explicitly: "In Amsterdam (or in Rotterdam whatever it is), there are so many people around and they are so busy with their own affairs, that I can move about unrecognized and undisturbed whereas in Paris I can't." This sort of problem of crowding is a very ill-defined phenomenon, and if I had time (if I wanted to take the time, and perhaps I shall on some other occasion), I would express my conviction that when we talk about crowding, we are never or hardly ever referring to density of human beings, to the density of motor cars, of radios, of televisions, and all the noises that come from technology and that accompany human life.

**Erikson:** I think we are now talking about subjects, and this one is density. I would like to anticipate with something that will have to come up later, when we discuss development. After all whatever Doxiadis showed this morning had to do with specific spatial requirements, at each stage of life, and I would like to say this morning, the discussion mostly referred to seven ages, but that is Shakespeare. And if you look at Shakespeare's Seven Ages, you would not come out with any city plan, I think. Well, Doxiadis really speaks of 12 stages, and it may be good to return to them in discussion now and again. What was said right now seems to be very important for children and one should be able to discuss, when we get to it, for various childhood stages.

You see, let me interrupt and say, when you look at architectural drawings, you usually find only one person in them, and that usually is to show the scale in which the whole thing is built. Even your sketch of speech dealt with houses full of people; it showed anyway the desirable degree of density that children really absolutely need for development. What we should discuss eventually is development, which always means that one just has been in a stage, just is in one, and just is about to go into another one. One needs to be surrounded by people, who have been, who are in the one in which one has been, who are in the one in which one is, and are in the one in which one is going to be — to bring in actually evidence of some of the time perspectives which Mr. Waddington has talked about. Because this is the way a child very early gets an idea of what the potentialities of development are. It is obvious that in the stage where a baby only needs a mother primarily, he doesn't care how many people are in the room, and yet, maybe very soon, he needs beyond the mother, who is within his limited perception capacities, needs to know the others, and also perceive distant people as well as close people, and so on: so we may want to come back to that.

**S.A. Doxiadis:** Well I'm pleased with these points of view because they come back to my question and the implications of my question: That we cannot possibly have a very arithmetical, numerical definition of density. There are so many variables that, unless one defines very clearly what one means, any type of ratio is of no importance at all. Talking about babies for example, we know that you can have equal deprivation in a room with three babies and in a room with one baby, depending on the amount of time spent and the quality of care taken. So here we have an entirely different ratio of persons to space, and these babies could equally be deprived. So it is a multiplicative factor which determines the good or ill effect of crowding.

**Lourie:** Talking from the point of view of the behavioral sciences — I don't know whether you would call that an unnatural science in contrast to the natural ones — we try to match up the information from the biological sciences with the behavioral sciences, we see that there is a tendency to clumping, even when you are dealing with the smallest of the natural units. Cells tend to clump and people tend to clump. And there are points at which this clumping takes place.

We look at the human developmental process: The first phase within the family doesn't require the child to clump, to group, but in the next phase the child will look for other children and will form groups, if you make these other children available to him. The boys will group with the boys and the girls with the girls, between the ages of five and ten to twelve. With adolescence there is the same kind of grouping, only it begins to break down the sexual division which had evolved before then. But we need to have provision for the school-age child to form his groups. And that's one component that goes across some of these lines from density to segregation in age-groups. We need to have provision for the child to learn how to function outside of his own family, the extended family. He needs to check up with age groups, learn how the rules which he learned within the family fit outside, in the neighborhood, in the school, in his immediate community, and I don't think that we need to have separate places for the adolescent. If we do, I think they will tend to disregard them, they will find their own places, because as a group they're testing the value systems that have been the traditional ones we've brought them up in. I said that we should make place for them, I meant the opportunity to have a place, because they'll find their own place to carry out these experiments with variations on our traditional value systems. And from that point of view I'm very much in agreement with this need even if we give the adolescents a latitude to select it themselves. But we must give them the privilege of the place to experiment, if they spare us from the noise, as Margaret pointed out.

So that you can't think in categorical terms of specific ideal densities, we need to have a range of opportunities for a range of densities at different age levels.

**Mead:** I think, you know, we're up against a very difficult problem here, and Dr. Dubos pointed out that when we move from the rat to Man, there are all sorts of complications; and Dr. Spyros A. Doxiadis points out that you can't talk of densities, you can't even talk of ratios, because of the great variety.

And then we keep coming back to little statements like school: I mean, who said that human beings have to go to school or are going to go on going to school? Or we come back to the particularities of England or the United States or Greece.

As I understand the presentation that C.A. Doxiadis made here, he means it to be for the human race. As we are building now, any building we do anywhere in the world affects building in the rest of the world. It's only because you do it, if nothing else. Therefore, we've got to think in some kind of generalized terms even though we give them extraordinary limits. Even though we may say that a man needs the space an Eskimo needs, or only the space that a Dutchman needs and you can live in each, then we have to go on and say if you're raised like an Eskimo, what are you going to do if you're stuck in with the Dutchmen. Or if you're raised as Eskimos and have a Dutch architecture, what's going to happen to you?

Most of the things that we've been saying here have been points about a culture of particularities and what can be told about it under certain conditions. For instance, C.A. Doxiadis starts with that baby in the room. And how about the people where the mother bears her baby on her back? And the baby goes everywhere, in which case the baby doesn't need a room. How about putting the baby on a cradle board, so it saves enough room so you can dump it down in the middle of a very large group? Or hang it on the wall, so it can see everything? The modern mother now puts that baby on her back and tries to climb into a car; she bumps the baby's head, because she wasn't brought up that way and she doesn't know anything about her back anyhow, and she can't allow for the baby on her back. Somehow, we are going to have to bring these things together.

Now, I think of some point Dr. Dubos made when he qualified the Calhoun studies. It's a sort of a meeting point. Because you were talking about something that can be generalized for the whole world, whether you use a large space or whether you subdivide it. And that can be thought about in terms of the mud hut with its many little cells in Iran, or can be talked about in Hong Kong, for what you give a Chinese family in Hong Kong is place where they can make their compartments. If you give people space that's already compartmentalized, they can't do things with it. Somehow we ought to hope to come out of this with a biological guidance that we call human, that ought to be taken into account, as well as prescriptions for diversity. How we're going to keep these in mind all the time on a two-dimension diagram is really one of the big problems.

**Gabor:** The point several people have made here, and especially Dr. Dubos, seems to suggest that it's not so much density which is critical, but it's the size. Of course to a natural scientist the idea comes very naturally, that there is a critical size for towns as there is one for uranium. Many become explosive. And this is something we ought to come back to. We should not talk only about density, but of the size of the towns to give density.

**Erikson:** Margaret, could I quickly tell one little story which most of you probably know? Of the Jewish man who was wrecked on an island and was finally found, and he lived in a very nice little house that he built for himself. Then a few feet away there was another shell and they asked him, "What's that?" He said, "That's a synagogue where I pray." And over the hill there was another shell, and they said, "What did you build that for?" He said, "That's the other synagogue in which I wouldn't be caught dead." I simply mention this, that he had all the space, there was no density there, and yet he had to build himself. . . you see what I mean, that what you call human is simply a little more complex.

**C.A. Doxiadis:** I only want to say that if we take into consideration all statements made in the last 25 minutes, we have an excellent image of what density means for Man. Because all these aspects have to be taken into consideration. We now have the time to formulate it exactly in one page, but I think we have covered the subject and we have opened our eyes so as not to over-simplify such complex problems.

**Mead:** You want to go on to the next point now.

**C.A. Doxiadis:** Monumental buildings. This was brought up by our two speakers, with a big question: Where is the monument that we lost? I was planning to bring up an answer to this question from a one-day two-man symposion that we had four years ago with Dr. Harvey Cox, the Harvard theologian in Washington D.C. on this issue. He was insisting that we need a monument, and I was only answering that at present the monument we need is the City of Man whom we are not serving, and that the monument of the new culture will come later replacing the first monument, the feudal tower, and the second monument, the cathedral. But I have a strong suspicion that the secret services are involved here, because when I went up to my office, I found a letter from Dr. Harvey Cox which just came, I will read it to you:

"Dear Dinos,

Last year at Delos Nine you strongly recommended that we stop constructing human shells of more than ten stories high. I think this week I would urge that they never be more than one. In trying to paint my summer home here before flying to Athens for Delos Ten, I placed the ladder insecurely and the whole thing — ladder, paint and myself — tumbled down."

So he cannot join us. He's heard about our subject though, since the secret services passed the information:

"I am especially sorry this time since your thoughtful invitation for me to comment on the future of religion while we are at Patmos was a fascinating one. Notice that in the text of the Revelation of St. John there is no 'temple' (i.e. no monumental structures) and that the kings and the ordinary people seem to mix quite freely in the streets (*Apocalypse 21*). Notice also that according to verse 17, the whole city is built 'according to the measure of man'! Whatever its details, I am still glad the Bible ends with the vision of a city — not a sea or a cinder or a topless tower or even a wilderness."

So we have here the statement of the theologian who doesn't insist on a cathedral, and allow me to say that I stopped being a consultant of a city where they wanted us to design the city hall at a cost which could give houses in simple forms as rooms to 2,000 families out of the 5,000 homeless people. I believe we are at the beginning of a new culture, we have to serve Man first, and then he, one, two or three generations later, will find his symbols.

**Waddington:** For the sake of the discussion, let me put in two points in connection with this: two experiences of mine. Shortly after World War II, I found myself visiting Warsaw, which was practically a heap of ruins. What did the Poles do first? They totally rebuilt the old central city, stone by stone, according to the drawings they still had in their possession, long before they built any houses. The other thing they did was to turn all the cellars into night clubs, so that they could enjoy themselves. This was a very typical Polish response, but it was not the response of first building housing.

One has to think whether it is the people's desire first of all to build housing accommodation of an ordinary kind. One comes across a lot of tendencies in the human species to create some sort of a symbolic focus of settlements. In the past, this focus has nearly always symbolized power. Big cathedrals were built when the church was powerful. Present-day banks represent financial power. We are now moving into a world which is not so power-centered. And

I think the symbols that the people are going to like in the near future are not going to be symbols of power. This is what makes the idea of monumental structure very paradoxical at the present time. Communication centers could be symbols. Cathedrals were not only great structures which you could see from all over the city, they were also places where you went to mass and after mass you sat around and talked a great deal. They were human interchange places and this is an important function of a symbolic center. I don't think we've at all solved what forms monumental structures could take in the cities of the future, but I do think they should be considered as an important part of it.

**Mead:** I saw an instance lately in Australia that sums up some of these problems very nicely. There was a small new town and its center was to be a golf course. The golf course was going to provide open space, air, all those requirements and, coming from America, I said that I thought this was a most unsuitable symbol, because it's something for a mature man, and on the whole a mature middle-class man, who sits too much. They said, oh! no, here the children start playing golf at four or five and the women play as well as the men. Now, in a sense this sums up the changing aspects of a symbol or a monument — if you move it from one country to another it wouldn't be understood.

And also I'd like to go back to this point you made several times about children's experience. I don't think you'll ever get a group of people to build a magnificent anything that sums up what they once were, if they have never seen anything magnificent that sums up something else. Now we have an example of a little island in the Pacific, where all the aristocrats were killed or drowned on the way there and nobody arrived except commoners, low-class people. It took them three generations to re-invent a king, but they had a language and every single point said good, better, best, good, better, best, what's the top, what's the top, what's the top . . . and that's all they needed to work on. But in most of New Guinea no people anywhere have ever been able to invent a high, so called, point because they have no historical background for it, they haven't got it in the language, it isn't anywhere.

**C.A. Doxiadis:** I agree, Margaret. But I want to make the point of the difference between symbol and monument. I am for symbolism in everything, also in the small scale, also at home. We need a symbol of what we believe in, a picture or whatever, but not at this stage, we do not need to invest huge resources just to let big operations show off in the central city or waste the city money for a big city hall if the people do not have water in their homes.

**Mead:** Does anyone want to add more on this monument point? Otherwise I'll ask Doxiadis to go on with the third point.

**C.A. Doxiadis:** Now both our speakers again brought up in different ways the question of segregation by groups. They both insisted that we should not allow it. I thought they would agree with a variation of this expression: that the city should bring all age-groups together, by giving the chance to everyone to isolate himself for certain periods like in the nursery schools, the sports ground, or the youth club. If we speak of every society, we have understood the variation that we need. In the street and the square, we should all be together, and in isolated units we should give the chance for special groups. I will mention two cases: between the two world wars, the French built houses for the old and then learned their mistake, and then this mistake was repeated in the U.S.A.; houses with segregation for old people. It is a big mistake. That's one case. The other is the campus. I think it is a very big crime, Dr. Gabor, to build symbolical walls around the campus. I have always defended this idea and I want to show you why I think the campus leads to problems, because by building walls around not only have they isolated the young people inside, but they made all these areas lose value. They lose value in land first, then in quality, and then we have the problem of Columbia University because of its growth. Therefore, as we build campuses now this way, the solution we think is this: The center of the campus should be dedicated only to its activities, but the campus should have branches spreading into the city, so that when the student or the faculty member goes for lunch he can see other people around. The citizens will interact with them constantly, they build houses where they rent rooms to the students next to their families, and therefore, instead of having a tower with walls around, we have a system within a system.

**Gabor:** This reminds me of the situation which existed in England in the 18th century. The English were very suspicious of the foreign (kings), the Hannoverians, and did not allow the soldiers to live in barracks. And nowadays we feel the students may become similarly dangerous, if they are to be allowed to live in the campus.

**Mead:** Dr. Lourie raised the point that children and youngsters tend to segregate by age. We know this can be made pathological, but I suggest that people do aggregate by age, whether or not this is socially encouraged. We know it can be dangerous but I want to know whether there's a real biological base for it.

**Gabor:** No, that can be very dangerous. . . . . . . . . . . . . . . . . . . . . . . . . . . . . . . . . . . .

**Mead:** We know it can be dangerous. I want to know whether there's a real biological base for it. Did you say there was one?

**Lourie:** I don't know any biological base for it. And I think Man is such a peculiar species, that even if I did know one, I wouldn't have taken it very seriously.

**Dubos:** Margaret, I'm sure you're asking me a question because you know the answer. And the answer of course, as you know far better than anyone of us, is that the segregation by age has a very peculiar rhythm of development in European history. You know there are. What's the name of that book, Philip Arius, which shows that so very clearly.

**Mead:** I don't know anything of the sort. We found that very very primitive societies are segregated by age.

**Dubos:** That there are many societies that do, I don't question it. We do, we are a society. But that it is inherited in the biological nature of Man? I don't see any evidence for that because there are many societies that do not, and European societies did not until very recently. Now I would like just to ask a question about the campus. I'm very surprised that you should so emphasize the danger of segregating the students. There is some danger of that. What I find far worse is the fact they've been segregated in losing all awareness of what the real world is about. I think the campus has destroyed the social awareness of the faculty even more.

**C.A. Doxiadis:** I'm not a professor anyway, so I don't have to answer this, but we do have professors.

**Lourie:** Well, there's no question that the influence of the grouping, the segregation by grouping, doesn't stay within a group, because we can see the pressure from the student group on the faculty. In recent history in Europe and, I think it started in Europe, in France, in Germany, and in South America, the influence of the students on the thinking of the faculties is considerable. But it's only fairly recently that the faculty has begun to take notice of this and the thinking has influenced first the younger people in the faculty, and it reaches a point where, we talk about noise, the noise cannot be disregarded and at that point, I think all the faculty members begin to pay attention. But there is a need for segregation by age-groups that has developmental importance. Erik was alluding to it when he said that there needs to be the opportunity for the younger to watch the next older and the next older to watch the still next older and pattern themselves from that point of view.

But as a group, to get back to the question that Spyros asked earlier, even in prison there is this kind of normal segregation that takes place by age-groups, in the prison yards, as the groups form, you'll see that it's very often by age-groups. But also this question of grouping as a natural phenomenon is very clearly demonstrated in the way prisons function, or people function in prisons.

But one further point which I think maybe ties our discussions together. Why are these universities so big? Is there a need for bigness as part of a value system, and is this part of a need maybe to change value systems in terms of how the world wants bigness whether it's in the form of monumental buildings, big universities or whatever. In other words, we are in process of (the fact that it has come up here is evidence) a change in our values and very much of it is being forced on us, as the more senior citizens, by our youngsters.

**S.A. Doxiadis:** I would like to bring up a point raised by Dinos and this is that segregation by age-group should combine times when they can be segregated and times when segregation is not necessary, as a matter of fact is not desirable. You remember the story of *Lord of the Flies*. Some of these eight to twelve-year-old boys went to the extreme of criminal activity, because they were together all the time. They wouldn't have done it if they were together for five or six or seven hours a day and then in the evening went back to their families.

So it is desirable, if possible, to have some activities together and some activities apart. This is, I think, very important. The importance of not segregating all the time small age-groups within childhood became very evident to pediatricians under two contexts which could be studied, more or less experimentally. In hospital wards we used to place sub-groups together, babies together, toddlers together, young children together, all the children together. Now (if we exclude the two extremes: adolescents and new borns) we found by clinical experience that this is not a good thing. That in the ward of six beds it's far better to mix younger and older children. It is better for the younger ones, who are looked after by the older ones when the parents are not there: better for the older ones because they develop more responsible behavior, than they would have all alone. The other thing, which again critical experience has taught, is in children deprived of normal families. Experience has taught that the best way for these children to be brought up is not to be segregated by age-groups in institutions, but to create an artificial family of a couple, with six to eight children, but of different ages.

**Waddington:** When I went on talking this morning, I was talking about segregation. I suggested that the adolescent young adult age-group was the one for which I saw some point in having segregation. I wasn't thinking of the universities in particular (and I think this business of the divorce of the university staff from real life has nothing to do with spatial segregation, it has something to do with concentration on the specialities). Segregation of the young adult group — not just for a few hours a day but possibly for weeks on end — is because they are exploring the world to make something new of it. This is difficult if they have to come home every night and be submitted to the criticisms of their middle-aged parents. I was thinking of the characteristic youth culture of Kings' Road, Chelsea, where they have developed their own clothing style, their own discotheques, their own restaurants, and where you practically never see anyone over the age of 25. When they are making the new world of the next generation I think that they don't need to have this diluted every evening by mixing with the old ones. And I think they are the one age-group for which provision of a certain quarter to themselves part of the time (not that they'd never meet anyone else) has something to be said for it.

**Mead:** Now look Wad, you said something terribly dangerous at the beginning of that statement. You said that the segregation of the faculty from real life has nothing to do with space. Now that challenges this whole discussion. If it has nothing to do with space, if where they live and where they walk and whom they see and whether they need other people and whether they ever talk to their brother who's a baker, if all this has nothing to do with space, what are we here for?

**Waddington:** Well, because in Britain at any rate, I don't know about America, the faculty practically never lives on campus. The faculty lives in houses all around the town. They are not specially isolated from the rest of the real world. If they become isolated from the real world, I don't think you can attribute it to space.

**Mead:** But wasn't the style set by the faculty behavior in the U.K.? Wasn't it set by Oxford and Cambridge where they were heavily isolated, where the town gown position was historically clashing?

**Waddington:** That was 50 to 70 years ago.

**Mead:** Right. Where did you grow up?

**Waddington:** I grew up in Cambridge and I was surrounded by the whole town. It wasn't a total campus at the University. I was for some years living in a student dormitory with about 200 or 300 students and about 20 staff. But this was surrounded by the town. It wasn't like living in the middle of a university campus or anything of that sort.

**Mead:** Now, you know, I think this is much more serious than that answer gives us. I mean because . . .

**Waddington:** Margaret, I think the isolation of the university staff from real life is due to the competitive concentration on narrower and narrower specialties in order to do better than the next man in some refined aspect of some intellectual subject. Now I think it has been the push towards specialization within the intellectual world that has meant that you had to drop everything else. And I don't think this is closely connected with living in groups where you never meet anyone but other specialists.

**Mead:** Yes, but the point that Dinos is raising (and I'm going to spend a little time on this for a minute) is whether the way you arrange your space and the degree of interpenetration of different kinds of living and whether there are walls or not that segregate one group from surrounding groups, such as we find in American cities around almost every institution (hospitals just as much as universities) whether this sets a style. And I think we've got to accept or reject this proposition. We are talking about what a builder does, as he affects things. Now we can't, as Dinos, stop specialization or low concentration by revising the curriculum. But we can ask him to tell us how he thinks a city could be devised, so there would be less of it.

**Waddington:** But the walls around the campus are primarily walls around the students, not primarily walls around the faculty. In most universities the faculty lives all around the town in suburbs. The students may in some universities live in large student residences because, on the whole, the university expansion has gone so rapidly that there are no longer lodgings for them to go into in the town as there were in the old days.

**Mead:** Now what I meant was that we were being too specific about one culture and one period and one illustration. Spatial arrangements of this sort is what I understand Dinos has been saying and I think we've got to stick to it. You weren't really just talking about universities or universities in one period, but you were talking about where you put walls or where you don't put walls and where people live. What we have to do is to try to relate this in a more generalized style. You see, just the same as you were saying, Regie (R. Lourie), prisoners in American prisons segregate by ages. So what? They segregate by ages outside, and it doesn't tell us anything much about human nature that they do the same thing in prison that they do outside. Unless we can look at prisons all over the world as a form of constricted space, and then see how it relates to people of different cultures and different periods. Or am I overdefending you, Dinos?

**C.A. Doxiadis:** No, I think I will speak afterwards.

**Erikson:** Well it's getting pretty complex here, because we are using words like segregation obviously in many different ways, which illustrates how many meanings words can have. Are you segregated because somebody builds walls around you? Are you segregating yourself and building walls to protect yourself? Do you want to break down other peoples' walls? And for what purposes? All of this has a lot to do with what goes on in youth. And it goes all the way from, let's say, a kind of a snobbish criminality on the one hand and a criminal snobbishness on the other. That means whether you feel you belong to a class of youth that (now let me say one thing about youth which already implies what a big term this is) wants to be noisy and congregate in illegal or at any rate disturbing forms, or a snobbish youth that wants to congregate and keep all other people out? But if we turn to the developmental stage, what seems to be involved there in all of this is really that youth has to experiment as you pointed out with these values to see what values they can as a group agree on and to develop an *ethos* which is not just based on the moral prerequisites of what they brought along from childhood, but on what they can try out, experiment with, agree on and most of all provide leadership to each other.

This is why I like also that remark of children which should be down on the record as important for future discussion. At what point do children take responsibility for other children? Because, as I would like to come to later on, because I really believe, nothing of what we are discussing here can be materialized without some change in the whole moral climate as to who is responsible for whom, and on what basis of common discussion, common experience and so on, can one affirm certain values? Not because one has been told not

246

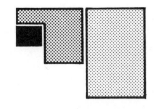

a. land use planning
   brought in segregation

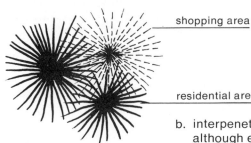

shopping area

residential area

b. interpenetration of functions
   although each has a center

140.    segregation and interpenetration of functions

to do certain things, but because one has learned to affirm certain things.   In that sense it should be said about (I don't know how much of the audience has seen your (Doxiadis') book) these things on which apparently Margaret and you agree:  namely these hospitable centers all over the world where young people disperse and learn about other countries and so on would be terribly important here as a mode of self-education, not just academic learning.

**C.A. Doxiadis:**  I don't see any problem, Margaret.  I think I can understand that in some universities especially of some countries the faculty is dispersed within the community which therefore leads to the following:  With your permission, I'll make a sketch showing in a simplified way what 40 years experience has led me to.  When cities started growing too much, we find a pattern of land use zoning with separated areas for houses, factories, shops, schools, etc.  You can still see city maps showing such a complete segregation of functions which leads to disasters (Fig. 140a).  The solution that I have begun to understand is to have some areas which are only residential which are allowed to spread out into other areas.  Similarly shopping centers have to infiltrate other areas as some small shops are needed near homes (Fig. 140b). Although the city is a system of centers, we cannot have the different functions (education, etc.) divided off by walls: No confusion, no segregation, but interwoven functions.

**Mead:** But we still have the question: How much can you influence by the arrangement of space? What are the limits of spatial imposition of opportunity? Which is one of the things that has been suggested here. You see, that was the point that I was trying to raise, that Professor Waddington was talking about something that grew up of itself and could not be influenced profoundly by the arrangements of space. But this conference is dealing with what we can do with space, how space spoils things, or how space can permit things that we regard as human and important.

**Waddington:** Margaret, I think, if I may go on to the next topic, I think this question of influence of space becomes very intuitive. This was written down as shopping and ground floor interaction. I would like to bring in the size of special units. A large factory or a large general store is already as big as you want to walk across. This question that Dinos had just brought up of the interlacing of things is quite easy to do if the shops are about the size of a house. But it seems to me that technology is tending to produce single elements which are already too large to be intermingled in the same sort of way. I think this is a very general problem of the influence of space on limitations set by scale. If you have a really big steel plant or chemical works or automobile works or something, it imposes a great deal of constraint on how it can be incorporated.

**Mead:** Anybody else who wants to do anything with the shopping centers? Or horizontal interaction?

**C.A. Doxiadis:** As point four is related very much to points six and seven, and we don't have the time to discuss all of them, and together they are important, I suggest if you approve, we take up point five brought in by Dr. Gabor about the small cities. We should be given the occasion to compete with each other in order to help us to avoid uniformity and standardization. Do you approve?

Dr. Gabor, I'm grateful to you for bringing it up. If you ask me today what worries me most is this continuing trend towards uniformity. We have been trying to understand how it was in ancient Greece that they managed to keep their character and to give occasions for every location to develop something of its own. We try to find the basic town in ancient Greece, that is what Aristotle called the natural town. And to our amazement, we find the following: Greece had about 750 basic towns developing their own local culture. Politically some of them were unified, such as the city-state of Athens. But even if we think politically, there were at least 550 city-states. Now in a small country like Greece, one of the smallest of the present-day world, we had more than 500 political units, and more than 700 natural cultural units. Let me insist on one point. We are finally convinced that the Greek culture is due, among other things, to the possibility of ancient Greeks to challenge and fight each other on many issues — but still to come together (in Delphi, in Olympia and other places) with an agreement not to fight during certain weeks of the year. This double possibility of being separated and together was something very important.

How can this now be translated in our modern city which, with the development of transportation technology is becoming more and more unified; and we cannot stop this technology with all its advantages. I think this is the most difficult problem of all for humanity, much more difficult than pollution. I can see only one way to begin doing it: to strengthen very much every local culture which exists and put all our available resources to help every small island and every small city-state, to express itself. At present everything we do around the world is to repeat the existing systems. When we build schools in our village, they are repetitions of the city schools. I saw in Aspen, Colorado something awful (and it is a center of many intellectuals): a school without windows! I said, why? They said: Children should no longer see any urban landscape around them. Therefore, there was no more urban landscape! We need a movement for cultural isolation within the cities that can tend to unify us all.

**Mead:** I think there is still a question between what Professor Gabor said and what you would say. Professor Gabor was advocating little cities one hundred miles apart that developed while Doxiadis was thinking of the Greek urban system with centers of diversity within it.

**Gabor:** The second is a natural thing for Greece and the first for America.

**Mead:** You mean one hundred miles apart?

**Gabor:** In America you could have cities one hundred miles apart, and the country wouldn't be full with 500 million people. In Greece, of course, it is very different. Technology is not the enemy. Modern technology has made it perfectly possible to have the small towns. The enemy is the economy, because there is no doubt that it is cheaper to repeat exactly the same chain store in one hundred towns than to appoint a good architect, a good town-planner to produce something different.

**C.A. Doxiadis:** Yes, what I want to say is that we cannot stop science, technology, economy, which needs always a new hierarchical system. What I want to emphasize is that if we leave all the new forces of a high level, we would be lost, culturally, maybe we will be living in 1984 forever. And that is a very big obligation. In the same way in which we begin to fight for Man in all the stages, we have to fight for the human scale which existed in the cultures we had created in the past in city-states of Greece, in city-states of Renaissance Italy, in isolated islands of the Pacific, etc. In the same way in which women started the Women's Lib movement to save values which are forgotten, we must start the movement to save the lower levels of the hierarchical pyramid created by the brain we are now developing.

**T.A. Doxiadis:** Between these two sorts of small cities (the American ones and the Greek ones) there is a difference and a similarity. The difference is that in Greece we had city-states, but in America there are many small cities belonging to the same state. The similarity is the common language. That is a tool which is very important for the development of many factors of happiness for the people.

**Dubos:** The only thing I want to do is not to mention faith, which would take too much time to document. I know that everybody goes about the world seeing that things are becoming the same. I have made it a profession for myself to go about the world and see how places differ. Whereas everybody emphasizes the forces that make for uniformity and homogenization, I see strong forces creating centers of differentiation which are the result in part first of natural climatic factors, which affect not only what can be done in a place, but the way people do it; which affect the way you walk in the street. I know that when I walk in France, I walk very differently from when I walk in London or in the United States, and when I walk in California, if I ever walk in California, it's very different from the way I do in New York. I think the extraordinary kind of physical expression of the New York environment in the way people move is really very powerful. For many years we had an apartment across from the Rockefeller Center in Manhattan and my wife, when she didn't have anything else to do, would watch people walking into the Center. She found she could almost always identify where the people came from. Regionalism is something which I think is far from disappearing; it is beginning to re-emerge in the world, affirming itself as an essential force of mankind. Since I cannot develop that theme here (though I have published a book on the subject), I'll just mention a single example. Many of us who travel all the time by airplane from one continent to the other, travel on the same jet planes with crews operating according to the same international rules and then, despite all the uniformity, when you land at Kennedy Airport, you know that you are not in France; when you land at Orly, you know that you are not in England; when you land at Leonardo da Vinci, you know that you are not in Germany; when you land (I can't remember the name of the airport) in Sydney, Australia, you know that you are not in Europe; despite all those forces of homogenization that come from the technological equipment. I repeat that I believe that there is a very powerful movement to reaffirm the identity of each place, the genius of a place.

**C.A. Doxiadis:** I'm very encouraged by what René told us, but still seeing what happens in several parts of the world, I think we must create some positive policies to help these forces because if we had not stepped in on the island of Mykonos or other islands, like Hydra, it would be changed completely; because I remind you of the big force of the landowners versus the culture of the people. So I'm all for what you said as I simply want us to take the necessary measures in the first phase of technological infiltration, because a generation later the people will revolt against this invasion, so our task is to help them now.

**Waddington:** I have for the last 20 years lived in a country in which this question is very much in many people's interest. I am English by birth, but I live in Scotland. The Scottish nationalist movement is a very important constituant of Scottish intellectual life. It starts, of course, from the basis that the homogenization of the British Isles has gone a very long way.

When I was a child, I was brought up in a rural district and the way I spoke English would be totally incomprehensible to any of you. And also in fact quite incomprehensible to somebody living even in Yorkshire. The local dialects were very strongly developed and if you were clever enough at listening to speech sounds you could tell within four or five miles precisely where a man came from. This has changed. It is as a reaction to this general homogenization that the movement for separating Scotland much more from England and making it rely on its own traditions has a very strong force. But of course it is always conflicting with the other thing that is going on, that must go on, namely the creation of world Man. We have not only got a loyalty to mankind as a whole. I think everyone probably agrees there is great value in both of these, but it is very difficult to find just the right way to balance these two opposing tendencies. But this is, I'm sure, one of the major things going on in social development at the present time, that people want both to have individuality for their society and universality. And I think there should be both in theory, both are synthesizable, but actually synthesizing is quite a job.

**Mead:** And I think there's only a touch in this volume, but C.A. Doxiadis' whole emphasis on networks of power distribution for instance would make it possible to have diversity. If you're going to have your argument between Scotland and England or between New South Wales and Victoria in Australia conducted as to whether you can have different gauge railroads and all the passengers have to go out and have to get into another car: we're going to have different single gauge railroads and everything else. But if we can see that the single gauge railroad makes it possible for you to have some diversity in the two places — now we only have in this volume just one map of Detroit, with the suggestion that even Detroit could have some diversity, if the power and the highways and all those things were rationalized. That is, I think, one of the things we'll be discussing, although it's very slightly touched on in this volume. And if you get Scotland there to a position where they can't use the electric light bulbs made in England or somewhere else, then we're back in trouble again, aren't we?

So this is the end of the first day's session and we will reconvene tomorrow morning.

# 13. "The biological basis
# of urban design"

## René Dubos

Close to one hundred billion human beings have lived on earth since the late Paleolithic period. The immense majority of them have spent their entire life as members of very small groups. For example, the breeding communities of the Paleolithic hunter-gatherers, the villages of the Neolithic farmers, the nomadic bands of pastoralists, rarely consisted of more than a few hundred persons. A similar demographic structure persisted in most communities of Europe and America until the Industrial Revolution. And it still persists now in most of the world. India today consists of 565,000 villages and less than 2,000 small and medium-sized towns. The genetic determinants of behavior, and especially of social relationships, have thus evolved in small groups during several thousand generations. They cannot possibly be altered in the foreseeable future, even if the world were to be completely urbanized and industrialized.

Doxiadis' original report, *A City for Human Development*, deals with some of the problems of urban planning which must be solved in order that the human environment be adapted to the fundamental characteristics that modern Man has inherited from the biological and social past of the human race. My own views of the ideal urban settlement are very similar to those of Doxiadis; I shall therefore discuss only the few aspects of his report which appear to me somewhat controversial.

Doxiadis states that "the goal of the city is to make citizens happy and safe". As I shall mention later, happiness and safety have rarely if ever played a significant role in city design. At this point, however, I shall limit my remarks to the question of safety. Concern for security and safety is rarely a compelling determinant of human behavior. All over the world, people return to areas which have been devastated by floods or volcanic eruptions even though they are still threatened by such natural disasters. Similarly, the residents of Los Angeles joke about their smog, as do the residents of other cities about their own forms of environmental pollution.

Extensive publicity concerning the damage done to Man and to his environment by the automobile has not decreased automobile traffic anywhere. Some 150,000 persons are killed annually in automobile accidents and close to 2,000,000 are seriously wounded. In Great Britain, the automobile kills four times as many people a year as the Luftwaffe did throughout World War II. Yet we continue to build cities as places for motor cars to pass through rather than as places for people to live in. Almost any form of positive value such as climate, scenery, financial gains, or fashion is far more influential than awareness of environmental hazards in the selection of ways of life and of urban environment.

Children, in particular, seem to be endowed with a higher degree of behavioral adaptability to external dangers than could be surmised from Doxiadis' report. On the Navajo reservation, preschool children tend sheep and goats almost in solitude; in New York City they play games in crowded streets, unconcerned with automobile traffic. Most of the children who grew up among the countless hazards of the small family farm, or of the Lower East Side in New York, developed into well-adjusted adults and many have become highly successful in various walks of life.

I doubt, furthermore, whether as Doxiadis implies, we are now exposed to more contacts and more stimuli than in the past. Life in wilderness, in the family, or in the 19th century tenements meant an immense range of stimuli which are rarely experienced in the modern world. The stimuli to which we are exposed are different in kind from those of the past, but they are not more numerous or more intense. The problem of crowding illustrates how environment stimuli change in kind rather than intensity. Population density was extremely high in the Neolithic settlements, the medieval towns, the tenements of the Industrial Revolution — higher in fact than in modern European or American cities. The stimuli derived from the human encounter are now less intense than they used to be; but on the other hand the stimuli derived from encounters with machines are obviously different, and are probably far more traumatic than those of the past.

In another place Doxiadis states that the goal of human development is:
1. "to develop the maximum of the person's potential (as we do now for longevity)" and
2. "to increase the level of this potential."

Contrary to general belief, longevity has not increased for many decades. The expectancy of life is greater at birth, but not past the age of 45, and longevity is actually decreasing in some of the most prosperous countries: whether adults and older people are now healthier than was the case in the past is still a moot question.

It is also questionable whether it is possible, or desirable, to arrange for a maximum expression of a person's potential. Each one of us is born with the potentialities to become a thousand different persons; but he can usually give expression to only a very few of his potentialities. We kill one of our potential selves every time we make a choice which causes our life to evolve into a certain direction instead of another. Differentiation and organization usually interfere with subsequent reorganization. In practice social mores and aspirations impose constraints on the development of most of their members. Urban settlements can be so designed as to increase the range of options in the development of human potentialities but they can hardly raise the level of these potentialities. From earliest times, urban planning has been based on institutional considerations rather than on efforts to "make citizens happy and safe".

The medieval settlements were planned to serve as fortresses against invasions and also as sites for religious ceremonies. The 19th century settlements reflect the necessity to provide adequate amounts of labor and management for the Industrial Revolution. The 20th century settlements are increasingly designed as centers of transportation, mass media, and other means of communication. Traditionally, planners and architects have thus been primarily concerned with designing settlements for political Man, social Man, economic Man, industrial Man. But they have rarely paid much attention to the fundamental needs of biological Man or psychological Man. The satisfaction of biological needs and the development of human potentials are concerns which have come to the minds of planners only during very recent decades. In fact, much of planning reflects a rather static view of Man. Despite overwhelming evidence that social demands are constantly changing, modern settlements are built as if our societies were committed to the present forms of behavior based on the present forms of technology enduring forever.

Surprising as it may seem, one of the reasons for the failure to provide adequate environments for biological Man or psychological Man is that his needs have never been clearly defined, let alone his potentialities. In theory, the environmental requirements for physical and mental health are well understood; moreover, they are essentially the same for all members of the human species; but in practice, the patterns of disease differ from one civilization to another and the conditions for optimum development are culturally determined. Much is known also of the social structures, systems of belief, and behavioral patterns characteristic of the various human groups which have been studied by social anthropologists; but this knowledge applies to specialized situations and not necessarily to mankind as a whole.

In contrast, I shall attempt here to define some of the fundamental needs which are shared by all human beings, irrespective of time or place. The immense variety of cultures are but as many different ways to satisfy these needs — within the constraints imposed by local conditions and traditions.

Some understanding of Man's fundamental needs can be derived from the fact that his genetic constitution has not changed significantly for some 50,000 years. His physiological requirements, anatomical structures, and psychological drives are still governed by the genetic equipment he acquired during the Stone Age, and this equipment will remain essentially the same for many generations. Tastes change rapidly, but not fundamental attributes or needs. The ways of life and the design of human settlements must therefore be compatible with the attributes and needs which have characterized our species since Cro-Magnon times.

I shall focus my remarks on a few aspects of urban life as they relate to perception of physical space, human relationships, and self-creation of personality.

Man began to develop his humanness when he emerged from his shelter in the forest into the luminous and open horizons of the African savannah. Ever since, he has retained a biological and psychological need both for protective enclosures and also fairly large, open vistas. The various forms of architecture and planning constitute as many forms of creative adaptations to the environment by which Man has attempted to satisfy the complementary needs of relation to space — enclosed and open — which he has inherited from his Stone Age ancestors.

Even when living in uncluttered environments, with unobstructed views of the sky, Man has tended to place and orient his constructions as if he wanted to maintain emotionally some visual contact not only with natural surroundings but also with cosmos as a whole. One of the supreme achievements of archaic civilizations was the skill with which they placed their monuments in the landscape. The megalithic structures of Stonehenge and Karnak were oriented to enhance the perception of the sun and the moon at critical times of the year and probably also to serve as dramatic points of departure or arrival for processions into the surrounding country. The trials of Egyptian pyramids at Giza, the placement of the Parthenon and other temples on the Acropolis, the Tibetan monasteries overlooking valleys or deserts, the Christian churches on the summit of hills from which they dominate human settlements, are but a few among the buildings which owe a large part of their majesty to their natural settings and their profile against the sky. All over the world, the great buildings of ancient and classical cultures thus commonly express a preoccupation with the yonder world of the sun, the sky, the clouds, the mountains, the sea, the horizon — world to be experienced emotionally and visually, even if it cannot be reached bodily.

Where natural topography did not provide large open vistas, the landscape architects created an impression of infinity by manipulating the environment. This art developed on a large scale in late 17th century France. The view from the Château de Versailles beyond the Grand Canal fades into a seemingly endless countryside. In Versailles and other creations of the same period, landscape architecture thus manages to produce from a rather undistinguished nature the magical impression of a boundless scenery — *la magie des perspectives infinies*. The English landscape-architects aimed at a similar, but more intimate impression of open space by letting the view sweep on large bodies of water and down vast slopes of meadows. The longing for large open vistas has continued to be a powerful emotional factor in human life. In Europe this longing was richly expressed by literature, music and other forms of art celebrating vast landscapes, preferably in distant places such as the American Far West or the steppes of Central Asia. The prospects of space travel have now given even larger scope to imagination.

Early Man took advantage everywhere of natural shelters such as caves, and he organized his life around them. The lasting associations of groups of people probably constituting extended families, with particular locations may have begun the attachment to place which we now express with the word *home*. Throughout the Stone Age, different caves in close proximity to each other were occupied for prolonged periods of time by human groups, each with a characteristic style of tools, pottery and other artifacts. As Stone Age people were never quite sedentary, it would appear that the sense of property was respected, at least as far as habitation sites were concerned, even in the absence of the owner. The sense of home, symbolized by the hearth, seems to be deeply rooted in religiomagical reasons.

At a very early period, Man also developed different skills for the creation of artificial shelters. Inner courts existed in some of the private houses built in Sumer, Ur as far back as 4,000 years ago. The igloo with its highly effective design against the arctic winter can be regarded as an architectural creation of genius especially in view of the fact that snow was the only insulating material available to the Eskimos. In contrast, in the tropical forests, various groups of pre-industrial people developed open types of dwellings, so oriented as to receive maximum ventilation from the winds and a minimum of insolation. In the American Southwest, the Pueblo Indians resorted to thick adobe walls, a type of construction which insulates dwellings against both the blazing sun during the day and the cold at night.

Almost everywhere in the world until our times, men have thus empirically created shelters adapted to local resources. As one travels from North to South in the United States and especially in Europe, it is easy to recognize that the shapes and sizes of roofs, verandas, and patios, the orientation and width of the streets, the design of public grounds and buildings, the location of civilian monuments and places of worship are influenced by local factors such as insolation, temperature, rain, snow, topography, the distance of the horizon, and last but not least, the collective beliefs and aspirations of the community.

I believe that these two complementary aspects of space are both essential aspects of human settlements. I believe I could also demonstrate historically that each age, each civilization, has attempted to satisfy both of them, often fairly satisfactorily. But, since I cannot do this, I shall symbolize in terms of two persons of our time (although both of them are dead) how this has been a kind of preoccupation which has always been present in the mind of planners. The two whom I have selected are Frank Lloyd Wright and Le Corbusier, not because they are great architects (I wouldn't be able to judge that) but because they have been so explicit in their statement of these two fundamental needs. Frank Lloyd Wright, time and time again, has said: "The house is primarily a shelter where Man is protected from the wind, from the cold, indeed protected from light." These are his words — "protected from light" — and anyone of you who knows Frank Lloyd Wright's buildings will understand how he applied them in his designs. Then Le Corbusier states over and over again, how influenced he had been in his early life by walking across the Jura mountains between Switzerland and France and being exposed to all the forces of nature — to light, to the breezes, and, as he says, to the horizon. He concludes that the architect, the designer, must help Man to recapture the horizon.

In our times, the widespread desire for social separation from other human beings has led psychologists to formulate the theory that each individual moves around in a psychological "bubble of space", which marks the distance that he needs between himself and anyone else to feel comfortable. The optimum size of this psychological bubble of space is characteristic for each culture — large for North American, English and Scandinavian people, and generally smaller for Mediterranean people.

During the Old Stone Age, the hunter-gatherer way of life probably depended on a social organization built around bands of some 50 persons. Such population units were highly integrated and small enough that their members could closely interrelate and thus function as a true communal unity. It is probable that, in most cases, the hunting band was part of a larger breeding unit consisting of several hundred persons living within an area which permitted easy contact among them. The social organization based on the hunter-gatherer way of life lasted so long — several hundred thousand years — that it has certainly left an indelible stamp on human behavior.

Many more people, however, have lived since the end of the Old Stone Age than during the hundreds of millennia before. The earth population probably never exceeded ten million until the beginning of agriculture 10,000 years ago. Then it increased rapidly as the supplies of food became more abundant and more reliable following the domestication of animals and plants. Of the 80 billion human beings who have lived on earth, 70 billion have lived since the era of the cultivator and pastoralist. The biology and psychology of modern Man has certainly been influenced by the fact that, during the past 10,000 years, most people have lived in villages of some 500 inhabitants.

Increasingly, large settlements began to develop a few millennia after the agricultural revolution, and there have always been cities since the Bronze Age. But until our times, the largest numbers of people have lived in small communities close to the land. All cities, furthermore, have been largely populated by immigrants from the farming areas and they continue to depend for their survival and for their growth on this kind of biological transfusion. Despite appearances, the attributes which make for success in urban life are largely derived from the traditional virtues of peasant life.

The agricultural ways of life thus may have made as strong and lasting an impact on Man's genetic constitution as the hunting experience of the Old Stone Age. Man the hunter does indeed come through now and then in modern behavior, but Man the farmer is far more constantly influential in our existence. The biological memory of the hunter's exciting life unquestionably survives in our collective dreams; it urges us now and then to pack up, move beyond the hills, accept discomfort and even live dangerously. But the peasant's orderliness and austerity is also an important part of our biological and psychological heritage. The discipline of the peasant has generated the organized and predictable atmosphere from which modern civilization eventually emerged.

Irrespective of sophisticated communication techniques and changing tastes in social relationships as in other aspects of life, behavioral patterns established thousands of years ago still influence the size and structure of social groups. Modern Man is still psychologically conditioned by the range of human contacts that were possible during his evolutionary past. He spends much of his leisure time traveling in search of the village atmosphere and he endlessly illustrates it in novels and paintings. He even tries to recreate some aspects of it within the urban agglomerations — witness the appeal of block parties and the demand for neighborhood self-management. Much of the human charm of London and Paris comes from the fact that these huge cities still operate as if they were made up of a multiplicity of villages. Within their grotesque and obese structures American cities would benefit from the creation of neighborhoods small enough to be capable of achieving identity and local pride.

Modern Man still has a biological need to be part of a group and probably to be identified with a place. He tends to suffer from loneliness not only when he does not belong but also when the society or the place in which he functions is too large for his comprehension. Industrial societies will therefore have to find some way to reverse the trend toward larger and larger agglomerations and to recreate units small enough so that they can develop a social identity and a spirit of place. By cultivating regionalism, the United States could derive from its rich geographical diversity cultural values, and incidentally also forms of economic wealth, far more valuable because more humanly meaningful than those measured by the artificial criteria of a money economy.

Although Man has evolved in small social groups, life in the past was not always as relaxed and uncrowded as commonly believed. Most human beings during prehistory as well as history seem to have preferred human companionship to physical comfort. The largest and most traumatic cities of our times are also the ones that are the most glamorous and that grow the fastest, a fact which certainly has roots deep in the past.

The Neolithic settlements, Rome during the imperial period, pre-Spanish Mexico City (Teotihuacan), the pueblo villages of the Rio Grande, the medieval fortified towns, and the mushrooming cities of the Industrial Revolution, all had very high population densities. If present trends continue, human beings may become even better adapted to crowding as a result of being exposed to city life from the time of childhood. This adaptation will probably be facilitated by the fact that crowding is an ancient experience of the human race.

The deleterious effects of crowding do not seem to be caused by high density of population per se. More important are the biological and social disturbances associated with a *sudden* increase in density. During the first Industrial Revolution and again in our times, immense numbers of people from farming areas suddenly migrated into urban centers where they had to make painful physiological and mental adjustments to new ways of life. Increasingly, furthermore, crowding implies traumatic contact with mechanical gadgets and exposure to unnatural stimuli. Motor cars, telephones, radios, neon lights, are what the man in a modern crowd experiences, rather than the human encounter. Banning automobiles from an avenue or a park is sufficient, even in New York City, to create a relaxed environment in which human beings once more smile at each other.

The effects of crowding thus cannot be estimated from population density. They depend on social organization and on the nature of interrelationships between individual persons. Hong Kong and Holland are the most crowded areas of the world, yet their populations enjoy good physical and mental health because during centuries of experience with crowding, they have slowly developed patterns of behavior that minimize social conflicts and allow persons to retain a large measure of individual freedom. This does not mean that the density of populations can be indefinitely increased but only that the safe limits have not been determined.

In any case, retiring into "a room of one's own" is not the only way to escape from the world. René Descartes found crowded Amsterdam a congenial environment in which to cultivate his own thoughts, because he could move unrecognized and undisturbed among the busy townsmen of this mercantile city: "I walk every day among the confusion of a great people, with as much freedom and repose as you would have in your back streets, and I do not consider the men that I see there any differently than I would the trees that are found in your forests, or the animals that graze there." Even today, isolation can be achieved on the bench of a park among lovers, children, and nurse-maids — or even in the anonymous atmosphere of an air terminal.

But there is more to crowds than passive participation in them. As mentioned earlier, the great megalithic monuments such as Stonehenge or Karnak were probably the meeting places for large numbers of people who gathered to share a common experience. And so it has remained for all kinds of communal events all over the world, irrespective of the type of civilization. In our times immense crowds *had* to gather to mark the end of the World Wars, or to welcome Lindberg, or to grieve the death of President Kennedy, or to celebrate Apollo 11. Hundreds of thousands of people who could have watched the moon landing on their own television sets in the comfort of their homes, *had* to gather uncomfortably before a giant screen in Central Park not so much to see the spectacle as to participate in the collective emotion.

It is probable, in fact, that no society could survive without the opportunity — and the appointed place — for the sharing of communal experiences. The malls and piazzas of Europe like the dancing grounds of Indian villages, are the spatial frameworks of the tribal spirits.

Even while functioning as part of the social group, most human beings crave the opportunity to express themselves in a unique manner. All of us have much in common and human nature is very stable, but no two persons are identical genetically and furthermore each person's genetic heritage can express itself in many different forms, depending upon the environment. Social institutions and attitudes can thus change drastically within a few years, despite the constancy of Man's nature. Every human group and indeed every particular person harbors at the same time the Paleolithic hunter, the Neolithic farmer, and the Bronze Age city dweller. Don Quixote and Sancho Panza, Dr. Jekyll and Mr. Hyde are all simultaneously present in human societies. There is in each one of us Tartarin de Tarascon who dreams of hunting lions in Africa and the Tartarin who longs for his cup of chocolate in the comfort of his home.

The paradox is that Homo sapiens remains always and everywhere fundamentally the same, whereas his existential expressions and social aspirations constantly fluctuate. The existance in normal persons of such conflicting and apparently incompatible needs and demands naturally makes it difficult and perhaps impossible to create human settlements which are fully satisfying. The planner has the peculiar task of having to design environments which will permit the unpredictable expressions of individuality by anonymous Man. Since persons differ in their endowments and aspirations, each needs a particular set of opportunities and surroundings to act out his life, environmental diversity is more important than efficiency in the long run because it greatly helps the development of personalities and civilizations. Without diversity, furthermore, freedom is but an empty word since men can really be free only when they have options from which to choose.

Ideally each person and especially each child should find in his physical and social environments, settings on which to act out his life in his own way. A meadow, an ocean shore, the banks of a river, a peaceful village green, a secluded room, the crowded square of a city, or busy street displaying the multifarious activities of daily life, constitute as many different settings in which different kinds of human performance can be acted. Thinking of my own early life, I realize how much I have benefited from having had the opportunity to select among a hundred different persons I could have become — in particular by using as the stage for my life one or the other of the hundred different atmospheres in streets, parks and public squares of Paris and Rome. The famous cities of the world are uncomfortable and even traumatic, but they continue nevertheless to breed a wide range of talents because they offer a great diversity of stages on which very different kinds of people can act out lives of their own choice.

# Envoi

Stately parks and manicured gardens which once saw the pageantry of court life now serve as playgrounds for the general public. Palaces and mansions built centuries ago for frivolous or pompous activities have become government or business offices. Monastic buildings in which monks and nuns sought shelter from sensual temptations and social trivialities have been converted into distilleries for the production of liqueurs or into museums for the display of mundane art. Even the religious buildings which are still dedicated to divine worship have witnessed a change in public use. Gothic cathedrals are commonly settings for concerts but no longer for the miracle plays which brought the earthiness of the streets into their sanctuaries during the Middle Ages.

All over the world, ancient buildings and landscapes thus continue to be used, but commonly for purposes different from those for which they were built, centuries ago. They remain serviceable in modern life because they were designed not only to serve certain functions but also to meet fundamental, unchangeable traits of human nature.

In contrast, the present tendency is to emphasize the suitability of buildings and landscapes for the economic and political aspects of life rather than fundamental human needs. This may provide for transient efficiency according to modern criteria, but rarely for lasting usefulness. As in the case of living organisms, the creations of Man which are highly specialized cannot readily be adapted to changing conditions and therefore have a limited chance to survive. Yet, it may be possible for us, as it was for the planners of the past, to create designs which transcend ephemeral demands and fit the unchangeable needs of Man's nature.

All successful human settlements have included:

— Shelters against the forces of the external world (a room of one's own);

— A community organization through which the members of a neighborhood know what to expect of each other;

— Malls, piazzas or other public grounds where the human encounter can be enriched by contacts with crowds of strangers;

— Ready access to gardens, parks, and natural environments in which to experience animals, plants, and the pageantry of life;

— A variety of settings to provide stages on which different kinds of people can act out their own styles of life;

— And last but not least the opportunity to experience as often as possible the magic of infinite perspectives.

# 14. "The kind of city we want"

## Margaret Mead

I want to address myself particularly to points not of my disagreement with the design that Doxiadis has presented, but to supplement a few things, many of which I think have been taken for granted. For instance, Doxiadis has shown us a picture of every family living in a courtyard, each protected from noise and danger, but every family cut off from every other family. This is exceedingly frightening to an American, because our typical American design is to have an enormous lawn with no fence and then a big veranda, to let people in by degrees. We don't put up walls, as walls are frightening to us, although walls are considered protective in Greece and all through the Middle East.

The assumption of the courtyard diagram, basically, is that the people already know each other. This is not the way you build a city of strangers. This is the way of life in a delightful Greek village, where generations have lived there for centuries, and then the walls don't matter. You already know everything about the person next door, and their grandparents and their great-grandparents. You know just how they are going to behave and also that probably one of their children will have a harelip or something. These are the non-delights of living with the same people for a thousand years.

We have heard some discussion about the joys of living in multi-family households, but one of the reasons that people go to the city is because they are tired of all these people they have always known. They want to get away. They want to start a new life. We see this when we study the reasons people move to the cities in different parts of the world: one of the reasons is always to get away from the neighbors. Now, neighbors and relatives are taken for granted in Doxiadis' design. There is no discussion of where they come from or how you get them. You know that God gave them to you, and there they are.

To take another example of much the same thing, all the modern planning that is being done virtually all over the world is assuming the existence of the individual family as a unit, with no relation to anything else at all; and everyone had better be married, because there isn't any place for anyone else. We have had a discussion about what we do with adolescents. Do we send them all to Woodstock, or some related spot? (Certainly, I mean send them. They wouldn't go of their own accord if the society wasn't alienating them.) And what do we do with widows, what do we do with single people and divorced people, and childless people? There is no place for them in the kind of planning where every single house is supposed to be a family of perennially young children. I notice they never grow up. Every little family has lovely little children in a nice, close little spot; and then the baby moves out from there, slowly, until he finds another little family with some other little children; and then we don't know what happens to the family until they get aged. When they get old they use the nice courtyard again. But there's about 40 years in between that's left out; and in most projects there is no planning for the variety of people who make up what I would call a real community.

Real community is based on memory. It is based on people who have known each other over time. In a small community you get too much memory, and you want to run away from it, but nevertheless I am now talking about the ways in which societies are organized. What happens when young men bring their wives into their own small group, or what happens when the young men have to go into their wives' groups and make new friends. The community is based on shared experience over time, that is continually revivified by comment, by reference, by telling the story over again. People in small communities are not bored; the thing that is infinitely and absolutely boring is living among strangers shut in with a television set. In this condition you need something new every minute. Because life has no meaning, no past and no future, and there is no interest in repetition. The reason that nomadic people find it so hard to settle down into a nice well-organized proper settlement, is because it is so boring. In nomadic life there is continual interest in looking at every blade of grass and finding that every blade of grass is different. When I take my granddaughter for a walk she is searching for variety on every sidewalk. But then she finds a piece of paper that has been around some chewing gum, and you have to say: "Don't pick it up; it's dirty;" in effect, "stop looking."

I have been to two conferences in the last month dealing with the question of integration in the modern city, for it is of course one of our prevailing desires today to try to build a city in which the poor and people of different racial groups are not discriminated against; are not boxed up in the ghettos and denied access to all that the city offers, but have good housing and freedom to move around. But the discussion centers all the time on individual families, and we hear the parallel demand for the right of people to live near other people who are like themselves.

In many parts of the world we are so preoccupied with the horror of the ghetto conditions under which people have been forced to live (simply because they were black or red or brown or low caste or poor) that we have lost the other part of the picture; that they need to live with people something like themselves, and people with a past that they share, and that in the center of every community there need to be groupings of people who have come to know each other and have selected each other.

The two bases of close association, that we find everywhere in the world, are kinship and friendship. In very small communities, it is very hard to invent a friend that is not a relative. But it can be done, and people do it. A man or a woman can pick out one of their numerous relatives and say he or she is my friend. They may even swear blood brotherhood for somebody who is also a third cousin. But they have picked them out and made them different.

There was a motto that used to hang on the wall when I was a child, that said: "It is God who makes brothers and Man who makes friends". The right to select usually begins in adolescence (sometimes in play groups): the right to select people that you care about and wish to spend time with, and the acceptance of the relatives that the good Lord gave you — which is a way you learn to tolerate human life. And people who don't have to learn to accept those relatives that they wish they didn't have, lose one of the great capacities of humanity which is to learn to accept human beings (male and female in all ages) just because they are there.

What I would like to include in designs for the cities of the future is a way to make it possible for people to come together and form the nucleus of new communities, as well as to move around in the cities. This is taken for granted in Greece, in Italy, even in Calcutta. People move from one village to one spot in the city, where they find their relatives and friends; or where they hide from them, whichever they prefer. But if you are hiding from your relatives, you know they are still there, and you have not lost them; you are just staying on the other side of town. We have no allowance for this at present, for it means a good many other things. It means that people would not live in houses designed for nuclear families. But there would be "conjeries" of different kinds of houses. Some would be houses for a small nuclear family; some would be the right size for a couple who have no children, or for a couple whose children have left, or for a single woman or a single man; or for a bunch of kids who would like to put their sleeping bags down and do not want any more space at that moment. A group of older people might stay there more permanently.

We need to know at what age you need familiar surroundings. This is certainly true of small children, and it is also true of much older people, and these can provide continuity for the young people going out and coming back and going out again.

I think one of the reasons that 10,000 communes in the United States have failed in the last ten years (the figure varies depending on what you call a commune) is because they were all young people on the edge of exploration and change and seeking life styles of different sorts. There were no older people to give continuity, and you need older people both to provide continuity and to give the little children a sense of community. I will give a short story which I think illustrates this point rather acutely. I was walking along a street with my two-year-old granddaughter and we stopped in front of a flower shop, and she looked in the window and said: "Never be a cat." Now the usual approach of a visiting grandmother might be: "Yes, deary, and see the pretty doggie." Because she would not have a clue what the child meant. But I knew what she was referring to, because she had been sung the same song I sang her mother. This was a little children's song that has been sung in America for four or five generations: "Always be a pussy, never be a cat. They call me pussy willow, and what do you think of that." And there were pussy willows in the window (they are plants that have flower buds that look exactly like little grey kittens). Now, that is what a child needs. I mean, when she said: "Never be a cat" she expected me to know what she was talking about. And we are exposing children today all the time, everywhere, to adults who don't know what they are talking about, because they don't know what was said or sung yesterday; they don't know what happened yesterday.

The need to be bound to the past is, I think, a basic human need. To remember, and have somebody remember, that you had red shoes when you were two and you walked out in the snow with them. And this time when you are four and you have red shoes, you had better be bright enough not to walk out in the snow. This is what has made people human: this is what has made it possible for them to build rituals, because rituals are relationships to repetitive experience in your own life and in other people's lives.

When I went back to New Guinea after 25 years, to a village where I had lived for seven months, 25 years before, my various friends asked two questions: "Did you remember anybody?" and "Did anybody remember you?" Now, those are the most idiotic questions that you can imagine, in talking about people who, for the seven months I was there, knew what I ate for breakfast every day:

people to whom I could say 25 years later, when I heard the name of a place: "I don't think I ever went there." "No, you didn't." Or people would say to me: "But you remember him! Why, he was in the second row behind us at that wedding we went to in Patusi" (25 years ago in another village). And I do remember, because I learned those people, and all about them and how to live with them, with a terrific intensity, because they were the material that I was working with, and was going to work with for years. So our memories interact when I go back. Someone will mention a name and I say "I don't remember that name." "No, you called him so and so." (This is when somebody had nine names, and I used to memorize the nine, but usually only used one.) Or I come ashore and an old woman appears with a duck. This was in 1967, and I had been there in 1938, and the duck was in return for a pearl shell that my husband had given her dead husband in 1938. That debt had stayed in her mind all those years: one pearl shell deserves a return of one duck when they come back again. This is community. This is what the human race have lived with always. This is what people lose as small children if we take it away from them in the way that we compose towns.

Now, I don't think this means you have to live in the same place all your life, any more than I believe you have to own your house and stay there. But it does mean that you have to grow up as a child in a community that has some center and focus and set of relationships, and that has to be held together by the members of the third and fourth generations: not necessarily your own grandparents but somebody's grandfather. I don't believe that we are ever going to go back to the extended biological family, but we need three generations to give a sense of the past so that we can have a sense of the future. The unit of memory is about five generations: from my grandparents to my grandchild. Because I saw my grandparents, I can tell my grandchild about them. This is the human link in society, and if we rob people of this link, we rob them of a part of their humanity. I want to emphasize again that this means you have got to let people have their own kind of choice of where they will live. We have to have an openness which makes it possible for three young men who went to medical school together to say: "We'd like to live in the same town," or for people to live near their godparents, or their cousins, or whoever it is they care about and want to live near. This makes the difference between what Harlem was 40 years ago in New York, when it was still a neighborhood, and today. Then it was uncomfortable and miserable and there was bad housing, but people were human beings, and it was a gay place. Today nobody knows anyone else, and they're afraid of each other and they're pushed around from one spot to another, and community is lost; and we find this happens everywhere.

What do we have to do now, to try to prepare children to be able to build the kind of cities that we want in the future? Because the kind of cities we are dreaming of will not get built in most places tomorrow. How are we going to bring children up with some sense of the cities we want? And here I want to emphasize very strongly that, although babies may live in one room, everything around them comes into it. If there is somebody coming from the sea they smell the brine on their shoes when they come in, and if they are not taken up to the roof to see the stars, they see people who have been up to the roof. From the moment it is born, and probably before, the child receives an imprint of the total society that it lives in. This imprint may come in very specialized ways. But it is all there from the start. So that if you live in a town where there is no center, that child will grow up with a feeling that there are no centers anywhere: just as in the United States people who have grown up in the city find it very difficult to live in a small university town where there is not any "downtown". They are lonely. If you have lived near a river or lake you are imprinted to want water somewhere, and to feel the water when it is there.

The man-made city and the natural landscape become part of the child's world very early. We can demonstrate this by giving the child materials to build a world and see what it makes. So what are we going to do with children who grow up now in our anonymous and terrible cities? In the Natural History Museum of New York there is a flight of stairs that goes down to the big room where we have a great model whale and children just hurl themselves down those steps towards the whale. You see, they respond to this new kind of situation.

Fifteen years ago I thought that one of the most important things to do with children was to give them aquariums in the school or in the home, because there they could see a bounded life and they could learn about the boundaries of natural systems. Now I think the thing to do is to build some kind of biosphere filled with living things, where they can see the effect of their own breath when they enter the place, and see what happens with the change in temperature, and begin to realize that they live in a fragile world that is totally interdependent. We have to think very carefully about preparing the kind of children that we want to have live in the future.

One of the other points that I would like to introduce is the fact that Man, who has always been earthbound and will always be earthbound (due to the fact that he has got to lie down or stand or sit on a solid piece of space), now shares an atmosphere, which cannot be bounded, which cannot be staked out, which cannot be defended in war and which is completely shared around the earth; and that what we want to do is to build cities and towns in which that shared sky (the important thing is not the sky that you see through your window, but somehow we have got to get the notion of shared sky) must be protected for everyone or it cannot be protected for anyone. In the past, men have had to fight each other for space (I say have had to fight because, in one shape or another, that is what it has been, even though they managed to be peaceful for long periods), because if that is your town it cannot be my town and if this is my field of potatoes it cannot be your field of potatoes. So we have had a conflict between local loyalty and love of country; and love of kin and world citizenship and world loyalties. This is disappearing as we realize that we share the atmosphere and the oceans, and that these cannot be defended in the same way. We need to build cities, with the kind of open space and the kind of shared space that will give the future citizens of this planet a sense of this shared atmosphere, which cannot be divided by boundaries.

# 15. "Which way progress?"

# Thomas A. Doxiadis

I have read my brother's (C.A. Doxiadis') original report on *A City for Human Development* very carefully. What drew my attention from the start was Aristotle's definition of the city: "The goal of the city is to make the citizens happy and safe"; especially those last two words: "happy and safe". Reading on I saw that a very serious effort is being made (a radical one I should say) which, as the author puts it, is the outcome of 40 years of work to secure, from the standpoint of town-planning, the greatest possible measure of happiness and safety for city dwellers. However, besides town-planning, there are various other factors that may not have played any role in the past but which, today, under the influence of the fourth dimension, time, have gained importance with regard to the first concept: happiness.

To make myself clear I shall mention something that happened to me a few weeks ago. I was strolling with my wife and daughter through Central Park in New York. A couple of Coca Cola vendors passed us by and stopped at the sound of our voices, for we were talking in Greek. They approached us and for a few minutes we stood there in friendly conversation. It turned out that one of the men was from Patras and the other from Kokkinia in Athens. They had come to the States fairly recently; one had been there for six months and the other for twelve. Both felt miserable as they could not speak English and they intended to go to Greece. They offered each of us a Coke and refused payment.

Those two men had attempted to make a fresh start in life, but they were terribly disappointed when they found out that they lacked the most important tool for success: the ability to communicate.

There is no way in which members of multimillion nations can understand the difficulties and sometimes even the tragedy of those whose language is spoken by — relatively speaking — a mere handful of people. They wonder at our ability to use two or even three languages besides our own, but no one cares about the tremendous effort that has gone into learning them. Heaven knows how much "midnight oil" I have burnt to be able to talk to you in English today!

In earlier times people seldom moved far from their cities; they usually lived and died where they had been born. Since they all spoke the same tongue there was no problem. The problem appeared when cities started growing and travel became easier. I am certainly not going to forget that, especially during the last century, the great American republic was invaded by millions of immigrants from Europe, Asia and Africa. Most of them were illiterate people; often mere children. But they were hardy souls determined to fight and succeed. While the weak among them were lost in the bitter struggle for survival, the others eventually managed to learn the local language, though preserving their own at their national gatherings. As the Bible says:

> "And the LORD came down to see the city and the tower, which the children of men builded.
>
> And the LORD said, Behold, the people is one, and they have all one language; and this they begin to do: and now nothing will be restrained from them, which they have imagined to do.
>
> Go to, let us go down, and there confound their language, that they may not understand one another's speech."

*(Genesis* 11, Chapters 5, 6 and 7)

In the States the multitude of languages also gave their place to one, and this gave them power. The same thing occurred in Russia, where the various dialects spoken by its teeming millions have now been replaced by Russian. In India, on the other hand, a foreign language, English, has been kept as a universal medium of communication among its different peoples.

The language barrier was a terrible problem at the turn of the century. When I was a medical student in Berlin, no German spoke a word of French and no Frenchman knew a word of German. The iron curtain is nothing compared with the Rhine in those days. Each nation believed that its enemies on the other side were at least cannibals.

A Polish doctor, L.L.Zamenhof, tried to solve the problem 85 years ago by creating Esperanto, but it never managed to spread far enough. Now we have Leslie Jones and his Eurolengo, which he calls a language for Europe and describes it as a "manual for business and tourism". The first book in Eurolengo has already been published. At first sight it seems very easy. "Eurolengo is to tres fasil.  Le lengo habo un diskionarie de venti mil paroles.  It isto kompletik fonetik and le defisile sonds in le lengos de West Europe isto eliminado." Although it seems a very easy language I have great misgivings regarding its future success, for no artificial language has been able to prevail so far.  We have an apt example right here in Greece.  When we finally rid ourselves of Turkish rule 150 years ago, a number of pedantic scholars tried to revive an artificial language, made up of a mixture of ancient Greek, Greek as written in the Gospels and the idiom current at the time.  The experiment failed after it cost much time and effort.

I believe that the solution to our basic problem is coming of its own accord. Today, the English language is spoken in several areas outside the United Kingdom:  in the U.S.A., in Canada, Australia, New Zealand, South Africa, India (by the educated), in Africa and in Europe (again among the educated).  Gradually, it is turning into a universal language and it has the enormous advantage of being easier than others, and one can express oneself in it with clarity.  So, for those of us who speak one of the numerically minor languages, it would not be necessary to learn two or three foreign tongues in addition to our own;  English would be enough to solve the problem of communication with other peoples. Even though the language barrier would not be eliminated, it would become less bothersome.

Now let us turn to the second of those two words in Aristotle's definition: "safe".

With regard to this word I shall refer to my brother's hypothesis sixteen:  "A City for Human Development has to have the proper quality related to the natural, physical (created by Man) and social environment."  Being a doctor, I shall concern myself with the man-made physical environment.  Automatically, our thoughts turn to the word "pollution", by which we all mean car exhausts and industrial waste.  I am not going to discuss these two factors.  They are well known;  they are in the papers every day;  because they are sensational news items everyone is under the impression that as soon as we solve these problems, everything will be all right.

In my opinion the whole issue is much deeper and broader in its implications. In fact, it is related to the whole of the environment created by the revolutionary progress of life in the twentieth century.  Up to the end of the nineteenth century, life advanced at a snail's pace, if at all.  Both in Europe and in America the countryside unfolded itself like a huge colorful carpet whose continuity was broken at large intervals by small townships.  The sky was clear and the human eye could reach as far as the horizon.  Here and there small puffs of smoke came out of the stacks of a few toy-like trains.  Each town had its own large and beautiful cemeteries, where babies' and youngsters' graves abounded, for about 40% of the children passed away within their first year of life and many others never reached their twentieth birthday.

Disease, especially in its acute infectious forms, was a terror to parents. People suffered from bronchitis in the winter and enteritis in the summer, and doctors kept coming and going. Everyone dreaded a cold and took to wearing thick woolen underwear while avoiding draughts, the sun and water. For medicines they had quinine, iron, iodine, opiates, extracts from herbs and leaves, etc., while aspirin was just starting its triumphal march. People ate natural food: fresh meat or fish, herbs and vegetables from their gardens, a bit of milk, cheese and eggs from their livestock and poultry, along with bread, potatoes and pastry. Their clothing was of cotton or wool dyed with natural pigments, and they lived in their lime-washed cottages with their few wood-burning stoves. In war-time the officers rode their fine horses and brandished their swords while the poor privates followed them on foot, just as in the times of Alexander the Great. The only difference was that arrows and lances had been replaced by rifles, and they wore more impressive and colorful uniforms.

People traveled in horse-drawn carriages or aboard sailing ships; they traveled at leisure, admired nature, and avoided foreign countries as much as they could. When they went on a pilgrimage to the Holy Land it was such a feat to get back that they were entitled to call themselves "hadjis". The woods were full of game as well as robbers, and the Rhine had so many salmon that the police ordered landlords not to give their servants salmon more than twice a week. All Vienna danced to Strauss' waltzes and in Montmartre there was the Moulin Rouge and the cancan.

Suddenly, as though a good or evil witch had waved her wand, everything changed. Scientific research, whose foundations had been laid over the last two centuries, started yielding practical fruits. Progress was slow at the beginning but gradually gained momentum and is now proceeding at a fantastic pace.

Since I am a doctor, I shall start with the progress made in my own discipline. First of all I should say that, after we had acquired sufficient knowledge about contagious diseases; after we discovered microbes and put an end to theories about miasmas; we were then able to eliminate the great scourges that frequently invaded Europe and withdrew only after killing a large proportion of its population. Cholera, the plague, etc., were finally vanquished. Then new diagnostic methods made their appearance, which greatly facilitated and consolidated our task. We had X-rays, biochemical and microbiological laboratories. Then came the various vaccines, with which we were able to overcome diphtheria and rabies. Existing new knowledge and dramatic cures came in quick succession. We learned about the existence of vitamins and how to make them. We learned how to cure pernicious anaemia by administering liver extract. We discovered insulin with which to treat diabetes. We studied hormones and their curative properties. We discovered sulpha drugs, antibiotics, cortisone, cytostatics and tranquilizers, not to mention the possibility of dissolving gallstones and the whole series of vaccines that have changed human life completely.

All those things that used to terrify us are gone forever. Meningitis, scarlet fever, puerperal fever, pneumonia, peritonitis, typhus and typhoids, malaria, and especially tuberculosis, are no longer a constant menace. With improved asepsis anaesthesia, and the help of antibiotics, surgery has been able to improve its statistics, and it has even dared to expand into fields which, only a few years ago, were considered inaccessible.

Thanks to all this, there has been a tremendous drop in the infant mortality rate, which was 40% for the first 12 months of age. The same happened·with the rates for other age-groups and this is how we came to the "population explosion". This is how the inhabitants of the earth increased from 1,600 million at the turn of the century to over 3,500 million today and are expected to reach 7,000 million by the end of the century, if the present rate of growth is kept up. I said "if" because there are several biological factors that are still unknown and whose effects cannot be estimated in advance. We have seen and will still see changes in the growth rates of the various peoples on our planet. We shall see — and the "pill" will play its small role in this — the peoples who created this progress, the peoples who took 2,000 years of intellectual brainwork to achieve it, diminishing and suffocating under the tremendously increasing growth rates of other peoples. Isn't this biological suicide?

Nevertheless, since I am an inveterate optimist, let us forget about future dangers and turn to a survey of how mankind has developed over the past two-thirds of the twentieth century. First of all, thanks to the tremendous, even though artificial, increase in food-stuffs, very many people have been able to improve their nourishment. Regrettably, this is not the case everywhere but let us hope it will soon be. However, to revert to the main point: a large number of people have been able not only to eat more but to do so more systematically. The first effect of this has been a change in Man's appearance. Food which is richer in proteins and vitamin-saturated has supplied us with more energy; it has forced us to move about more; it has done away with excess fat and stretched our bones, especially by eliminating latent rickets. It has made men and women taller and more beautiful and, by prolonging their menstrual period, has allowed women to stay young much longer. What a great joy it is to admire the strong and beautiful young bodies of boys and girls and to think that they have reached perfection, only to be pleasantly surprised when one sees even greater beauty in the next generation!

Think of those famous beauties of earlier generations: Empress Eugenia or the lovely creatures who adorned the royal court in the days of Ludwig of Bavaria and whose portraits still hang on the walls of the palace in Munich; or even the beautiful ladies of old Athens, whose fame still lingers with us. Such exceptional beauty is not going to be seen among the younger generations for the very simple reason that all the young ladies of today are like fresh roses and equally beautiful.

To see the difference you only have to look at ladies' fashions over the past 40 centuries. Over a time-span of 4,000 years women have been willing to show a larger or smaller part of their décolleté — ranging from the bared breasts of Minoan times to today's more modest necklines — but they had never shown their legs. They were too clever not to know that their legs were ugly, and it was only after the second world war that their legs got better, because food improved and because women started taking jobs outside the home and had to go out into the sunlight and make greater use of water. It was only then that they decided to show their legs.

Based on that reasoning, I had predicted some years ago the advent of the mini skirt and hot pants, and here they are! Gone are the "Dames aux Camelias". No longer do we have those ethereal creatures of the past. The world is now full of Dianas rather than Venuses. Once we accept the fact that better nutrition has improved our appearance, what could stop the improvement from spreading to other tissues of the human body? Fat has dissolved; the muscles and skin are better; our glands are functioning more properly. But has there perhaps been any change in our brain? Do children mature earlier and learn more easily? Are people more intelligent? There is a whole series of such questions for which there is no ready answer.

Moving now from the question of probable greater or smaller intelligence, or maturity; is sufficient use being made of those beautiful legs of present men? Are they beginning to forget that they ought to walk in present-day cities; even more, to climb hills and mountains? It is true that many people engage in athletics but what about those who do not exercise? Don't they run the danger of gradually weakening the muscles of their legs? And those who are exercising; do they exercise their bodies with the natural exercise that is offered by walking, climbing, swimming or skiing? And finally, will physically and psychologically thin people, prove stronger than stocky ones, as Eugene Kretschner claims? How will the city help us in this particular problem?

We live in great cities together with thousands or millions of other people; cities which are full of exhaust gases from all sorts of engines. We live in large blocks of flats together with many others. The walls of our homes hide miles and miles of electric cables that set up a magnetic field around us and we are filled with electricity and sparks. Alongside the cables there are pipes that supply us with the water we need. The walls of the houses are painted with chemical substances and every so often they have to be repainted because the colors have faded. This means that minute particles of paint break away from their base and bombard their surroundings, that is our bodies. To an even greater degree, perhaps, this happens with our clothes. The clothes we wear consist of man-made fibres colored with artificial dyes. These, of course, fade and have some effect on our bodies. And then there is another bombardment. Our bodies are bombarded, for the first time in the history of humanity, with the different waves of radio or television. Has that been without any biological importance? It took years of research and observation to find out that the coloring substances they used to put in candy could be carcinogenic. Today, we consume a lot of canned foods, fruit and sweets which are very nice but contain infinitesimal amounts of chemical preservatives. Certainly, their use is allowed because they have been found to be harmless. But has anyone investigated what can happen to even a few people when the intake of these chemicals goes on, not for a week or a month, but for ten or twenty or forty years? These are all questions awaiting their answer. Let us not forget our sad experience with thalidomide or the prohibition of cyclamates. For quite obvious things, like the relationship between cigarette smoking and lung cancer, a whole century had to go by before anyone would even think of investigating the matter, and then so much effort and research were needed because this knowledge clashed with organized interests. In the same way, it took three quarters of a century of aspirin-taking before anyone related it to stomach bleeding. A lot of work combined with imagination and drudgery — real detective work — has been and will still be needed to investigate all the angles of recent progress so that humanity, after waging a victorious war on contagious diseases, will not succumb to man-made disease. Mankind must certainly not end up like the Sorcerer's Apprentice!

I should now like to conclude this talk with a few words about two things: tranquilizers and DDT. There can be no doubt that the discovery of tranquilizers was an advance in the field of medicine, and it helped a lot of neurotics for whom life was difficult. I am afraid though, that the tranquilizers have back fired on us. For I feel that some doctors, when faced with difficulties in diagnosis or therapy, tend — in good faith, no doubt — to diagnose the symptoms as due to a neurosis and are quite pleased when they can drown the symptoms in a deep "Sea of Tranquility". This entails several risks, however. First, there can be no proper diagnosis; the real cause is not traced and the disease is left to take its course until perhaps irreversible harm comes of it. Second, the doctor suggests to the patient the aetiology of the disease and so the patient tends to overlook his complaint, telling himself that "It's just a neurosis, that's all". Third, the use of tranquilizers over any prolonged period might eventually prove harmful to the patient. Every time I see someone take out a little box and carefully select one of the multi-colored pills in it, I am certain he is a "pill-addict" and I feel sorry for him.

Now about DDT. Some days ago I read in the papers that the United States is imposing an almost total ban on DDT. Now, I do not know the actual reasons that forced the Environmental Administrator to order this complete ban, but I am sure that they must be serious ones indeed. But please let me tell you a short story, the story of malaria in Greece. Before the last war Greece had a total of seven million inhabitants. Health conditions were deplorable. Typhoid fever, gastro-enteritis and malaria were rampant all over the country. We had a million cases of malaria every year, and the people's resistance to infection was lowered. In various regions, like Thessaly for instance, the people were thin and terribly pale while the children roamed around pot-bellied and ema-ciated. Tuberculosis was raging. I recall that, in 1925 or thereabouts, the recruits in the Corfu regiment were found to have the highest percentage of grey TB in Europe! Then the war broke out and those weak men were the first to put up a victorious fight against fascism. In the end, however, our country was conquered and one of the first things that the occupation forces did was to confiscate the Greek government's supply of quinine.

In 1942 we had over two million cases of malaria. So, when Greece was liberated, it was decided that we should serve as the first guinea-pigs in testing the effects of DDT. It was first used in 1945-46 at a village called Souli near Marathon, where the population had 100% malaria. The experiment was a success and the next year they sprinkled DDT all over Greece like salt and pepper. There was not a house, room or yard left without DDT, and the miracle happened. Greece and her population have changed. Our country is no longer infested by insects, vermin, flies and mosquitoes, and we have not seen Rachel Carson's *Silent Spring*. On the contrary, malaria is gone and the emaciated children have given way to the wonderfully healthy youngsters we see around us today. We lack malaria cases even for demonstration purposes in our medical schools. TB has also disappeared and — something that health experts say is unrelated — we no longer have typhoid fever. Today, Greece has one of the lowest morbidity rates for tuberculosis, etc. Speaking as a clinician, I have seen nothing over the past twenty-five years that could be ascribed to the ill effects of DDT. I have no doubt that there must be valid reasons for banning it, but I cannot help smiling when I read "letters to the editor" expressing the writers' concern for the fate of insect life as a result of that evil thing: DDT! Today, I feel this is the right spot and the proper moment for a respectful requiem to the greatest beneficient factor that has ever come to Greece.

# 16.  Discussions

The participants decided to concentrate their discussion on the following points:
1.  human contacts, social separation, bubbles
2.  community characteristics, organization
3.  work places, shopping areas
4.  easy access to Nature
5.  unifying Networks, communications, language
6.  definition of what Man needs from the city biologically, psychologically.

**Mead:** We have done the same thing that we did yesterday: that is looked up the course of the discussion during the first two hours and picked up points that need to be further discussed and amplified. We also have the questions that were turned in from members of the audience to include in these discussions at whatever point any participant feels that they can be comfortably included. Our first point of discussion is human contacts, social separation and bubbles.

**C.A. Doxiadis:** On this point we had several references, the clearest one and most challenging one came from René Dubos who said we probably still have the same number of contacts that we had in the past. I think it is a very good statement and useful for me, let me try to challenge it a bit, in order to clarify it. We have the same ability for daily or annual contacts, but in the past our selection, let us say, of ten close friends, 20 friends of second importance, 50 of third was made from a total of 500 people. We now see one million in Manhattan. Although in the past we could easily select without so many choices, today we have many more choices but a bigger danger from the huge numbers we contact daily. Walking along the Champs Elysées, one day I tentatively measured 20,000 people including 5,000 beautiful girls.

**Waddington:** Could I make a remark on this? Margaret Mead raised a very interesting point contrasting the layout of the typical New England town with the courtyard layout that Doxiadis has described in this book. We all know that people need both contact (community, continuity) and also separateness (individuality). And in a way you are getting to use two things by two different means. It is a question whether one is any better than the other or whether you can have sometimes one and sometimes the other. If you build courtyards, even a series of courtyards like the individual house courtyard or the closed home-street, bubbles of different sizes that Dinos' plan provides then you are incorporating the separateness in bricks and mortar: the walls around the courtyards. If you want to make contact, community and continuity you do this through psychological methods — the opposite way that Margaret Mead is referring to. You provide the continuity by total openness, with no walls separating the gardens or the houses, and if you want to have any individuality and privacy you have to do that by psychological means. So for the two things of separateness and community in the first case you are doing the separateness in the bricks and mortar on the community psychologically, and in the second case you are hurrying to make the separateness by psychological means, not by bricks and mortar. I would not know whether there is any particular preference for one solution or the other, but I think in both cases you are aiming at the same problem by totally different means.

**C.A. Doxiadis:** Not being a psychiatrist (in our home this is covered by my wife), I can answer only on the physical side as a bricklayer. Now what is our experience? Let us be clear on this. Humanity from ancient days never knew what it wanted, it was always experimenting and always selecting the best. The best proof of this and by now we can prove it mathematically, is the room. With every excavation in Paleolithic and Neolithic settlements we find new types of rooms. In Yugoslavia we have a unique room, entire settlements built with this type of room, never before seen, never after. So I would say that humanity tries several things and some of them develop early in time and others disappear as soon as Man learns about a better way. In this way we cannot say (now I am not speaking of rooms but of settlements) that we all know exactly what to do. I deeply believe that the Anglo-Saxons are wrong in opening their courtyards to everybody, because they do not help Man to have a gradual transfer

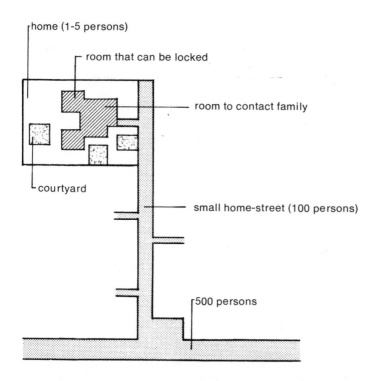

home (1-5 persons)

room that can be locked

room to contact family

courtyard

small home-street (100 persons)

500 persons

## 141. human contacts and social separation

from his room to the world as a whole. With the help of Dr. Erikson I made this sketch (Fig. 141).

We all need a room that can be locked; human evolution shows that we all need a living room to contact other members of the family. The older civilizations have learned that you don't need only a room to lock which has a roof, you also need a courtyard because you can be naked and have sunshine and enjoy nature without being seen. Also the child can have a gradual exposure to nature. As soon as you want contact with others, you can come out and then from the contact with yourself only you can go to say five other people, the members of your family. If you want more you can sit in front of your house and you will have 20. When you walk along your small home-street you will have one hundred, and so on. It is a biological system of gradual exposure.

In the same way we need the contact with greenness. One of the wise things of the Middle East is that in the very ancient days we had a very small pool in the courtyard with fish always, so the child learns from very early: water, plants, fish, cat, gradual exposure from the very small pool to the big ocean. Both human experience and practicality lead to the system.

**Mead:** Yes, but if you are going to talk about ancient cultures, let's have China for a change. They did not build low-walled units, they built units around great big courtyards — different sizes for different members of the family; three generations living together, this was the ideal, around a great open courtyard, all related to each other. All I am objecting to is your uniform little boxes that assume that every family will be the same size (which is just diagrammatic) and makes no provision for different kinds of people living together that are not families. The future is not going to be made up of nuclear families any more. That's really what I am talking about. Whether we like our psychological barrier between people or prefer a stone barrier which Wad brought up, this is again a matter of culture. You can have all three in Samoa, where the houses are all open around the outside, but the guest has a very nice curtain to protect him inside the family, while he sleeps in full view of the entire village and you can't take a step without conversation. The length of the village you have to say you're going bathing, yes, saving your presence. I am going bathing, and bathe, yes, I will go and bathe, bathe then! You say that to every person, that you should go and take a bath, up and down the village.

Whereas, you are going to have the kind of situation where you don't speak to anybody on the street. Now I don't believe that you can make one plan like that, it is not natural, and you're just about doing it, Dinos!

**C.A. Doxiadis:** I am trying only to transmit this message of the need for systems of gradual exposure. Because, as you have seen, most of the material is related to the first phases of life and not to the very old who may need multi-story complexes with medical services and other facilities.

**Mead:** But this is a place where you are imposing a design which is extraordinarily peculiar to your part of the world and undoubtedly the way they should live, they may have tested out everything so it's exactly right. It is suited to a world with a special kind of climate and special kinds of building materials available and it presumes a future of everybody living in families. Now, I mean where are you going to put your unmarried people? Where are you going to put your young people? There is nothing in that design for them.

**C.A. Doxiadis:** Then I need twenty volumes like this to answer this question.

**Mead:** I agree with you that you didn't get it all in one volume, and what I am trying to do is to discuss the other nineteen . . .

**Waddington:** The important thing he did get into this book is the people's needs for contact with other people and with Nature and so on, and changes during their stages of life. Now this solution Doxiadis has given is a typical Mediterranean solution, but the point is that it is related to a life history and this I think is an important contribution which we have not had before.

**Dubos:** It is most unusual for me to quote numbers. I am not at ease with numbers. But very recently I began reading into this design of houses and whether or not they should be isolated by some kind of structure of which you speak. I started from the assumption, which is very natural for a French person settling in the United States, that the landscape all over the United States is very open. There are no walls, you can look into everybody's backyard, you are looking at everybody's picture window. If you come from France it is obvious and an impression with which I have lived all these 50 years. Until I began noticing, during the past four or five years, that the structure of the American landscape is beginning to change.

I was not quite aware at first what was happening but then very soon it became obvious. Many people who could afford it were building a wall or building a hedge or any other such thing. I did look into it a bit by enquiring about the sale of any kind of material that goes to build partitions between houses. Do you realize that the sale of fencing is the fastest growing trade in the United States? It is growing at a rate of over 20% a year. It is incredible, the rate at which it is growing. In fact it was in Houston that I became aware of this. In Houston, everywhere used to look open to me. Now one begins to see hedges or fences. Admittedly everybody says this is caused by the fear of violence, but I do not think it is that only.

**Mead:** We've just had a survey made in Texas of people who are moving to new towns. They've put safety as their major reason for moving and I would say that this is a very important point. The rich have always had walls around them in America. They were one group that was afraid of thieves breaking in. Now everybody is afraid of thieves so they are all putting up walls.

**Erikson:** It would be interesting sometimes to draw a number of bubbles for one person. One would of course be the bubble of what is physically available, or what is built. The other one obviously would then be the bubble of what is traditionally permissible. Such as, let us say, in New England where there are no fences, the fact that there are very rigid rules as to where you should go. In other words (for houses, mansions, applying to rich people too) you would not cross the open space, you would go around to the front door. A child would learn very early that this is the way to get to the next house. So the question what walls will have to be built and what walls could be designed by tradition and by custom is very important. Then there is another bubble which we'll talk about tomorrow when we speak of development — what is cognitively available to the child — the room as a bubble or the available people? Cognitive means his intelligence, emotional contacts, it is a bubble which he needs and wants to go by. But then the whole concept of a bubble has something which always inspires me because it has no inner structure, it has no center. A bubble defines the emotion and cognitive from that point of view, the important thing is what you can indicate and what you can feel active in. A bubble is a wide area that you can vaguely perceive but you cannot actively fill. There is a German word — I am not sure of the exact translation — which is "spielraum" meaning play space, the space you can fill by activity because this is the only place in which we really feel safe and happy. So the question is what can one indicate in such a way that Man actively fills the bubble? It is very essential that we discuss it.

**Lourie:** Obviously the baby starts out needing to be part of somebody, in fact needing to learn as a first step what it is like to be close, what it is like to be part of somebody. Then comes the separateness which in the human takes place when he begins to reach outside of home and at that point you begin to see at ages six, seven, eight a need for privacy. Particularly in those settings where there is a great deal of crowding and families have to live very close together. Even in dressing at seven, eight or nine you can see this change taking place where the youngsters insist on being private, sometimes in very paradoxical ways, because if they have been brought up as boys and girls bathing together, you'll see them insisting on the others turning around while they undress and then they'll get in the bath together, boys and girls.

The next separateness that takes place developmentally is wanting one's own room and that begins as an early teenager. In fact teenagers want locks in their rooms to make sure that their precious possessions are not invaded. They start writing diaries and the diaries have to be locked, only they leave the keys around somewhere so that other people can see them...

But when there is too much crowding we see the same phenomenon that René Dubos described in terms of noise. You begin to lose what one appreciates in touching, in closeness. Where you see that most obviously is in the subway (in New York) where there has to be a kind of a personal element in touching. I suppose the answer to that is that a new kind of bubble has taken its place:

the car and when the car becomes the bubble, touching each other gets very expensive and we have to avoid this touching process. But I think maybe I could say a final word about how adaptable Man is. In terms of this kind of bubble, when one invites the opposite sex to share that bubble as a place for love-making, this changes the whole pattern, which in a sense shows the adaptability of Man.

**S.A. Doxiadis:** There has been some very important work on the effect on the young mother, not on the baby (whenever we talk about development we think about the effect on the baby), in the first day of her baby's life. Now there have been two groups studied, one with the traditional contact between mother and newborn every three-to-four hours when the mother feeds the baby which takes about 15-20 minutes, then three hours later the same thing; and the other was the experimental group. The mothers of the experimental groups were given their babies in addition to the feeding time for a total of 16 hours within the first three days. That's the first three hours after birth for one hour, the following three days for five additional hours. One year later there were measurable differences in the behavior of the mothers. We did not know what was the difference in the behavior of the babies, that was not our work, unfortunately, I wish it were, but the effect on the babies is not known as yet. The effect on the mothers shows that there are measurable differences in the behavior of the mothers between the control group and the experimental group. The only difference in treatment was the amount of contact between mother and naked baby during the first three days of life. Now Dr. Mead may know a lot more about it from her studies on primitive societies. This was done not in a primitive society but under an experimental setting. I mention this because these are the origins of social contact and it shows how early important attitudes toward contact from beings may be established.

**Mead:** I think there is one point that ought to be added here. Of course in primitive societies a baby is given to the mother at once. You don't measure it out in hours and in some instances she is entirely responsible for doing everything herself, cutting the cord, and everything that is done, but in any event she is given the baby and no one takes it away from her. Of course the baby is breast-fed and we can say this is the primary and proper way to do things until we realize that 50 to 60% of those babies die within the first two years. Many of them die during the first three days to six months. In other words, with that sort of system which made the baby absolutely dependent on the mother and the mother dependent on that baby, to be able to feed it (you had many other reasons for the death rate of course), but still in cases of the baby who did not fit the mother and the mother who did not fit the baby: the baby did not survive. It was a perfect system for testing out whether the mother and the baby fitted or not, and if the baby lost weight the mother lost her milk, the baby lost more weight and the baby died. And another baby could be born that perhaps did fit the mother. When we start saving all the babies or almost all babies (my aim is to save every baby) we are going to save an enormous number of bad fits. The question is whether we have to have more modulated differently managed relationships. I think this can be used as a prototype all the way through that we are saving individuals who would have died under these conditions — not of course the conditions Dr. T.A. Doxiadis talked about this morning as recent European, but under primitive conditions. We have never seen a blind child live in any primitive society, they would not put forth the effort to save him. When we include blind people in our system of society we have done something quite different and we make new inventions and everything changes. As Dr. Dubos says we have not changed our potentialities, but we have changed in our capacity to keep all of those potentialities alive.

I think if babies are going to be born in hospitals we have to look over again how are we going to handle them. How much will we give the baby to the mother? How much will we have breast-feeding, even though it is not adequate nutritionally, and all of these things have to be re-examined in the light of the knowledge of who's here now, who would have otherwise died, and of course there is the mother who could not breast-feed her child. The bad breast-feeding baby did not survive and the bad breast-feeding mother did not survive and the mother who was not good at having babies did not survive and you had a very different sort of selection from what we are having now.

**C.A. Doxiadis:** I am sorry to come back to the initial question of boundaries, because we may have to jump to the next question. We had the occasion to make one big experiment in the U.S.A. In 1962, when we won a competition for the Eastwick project outside of Philadelphia, the city council insisted that we change one thing. We must eliminate the fences and the compound walls. We had a dispute for eight months and the final solution was not to build them ourselves but to change the city regulations to allow the people to do so. In four years everybody had done so.

**Mead:** You laid the groundwork for them?

**C.A. Doxiadis:** We only made it possible for them to do it. We never saw anyone, simply it was a neighborhood of Philadelphia where the regulations allowed the people to build them.

**Mead:** Didn't you tell them that they could build fences? How did they know they could build fences?

**C.A. Doxiadis:** They knew the regulations. Man is learning, I am not educating him.

**(Woman's voice):** Just on the question of the form of space and privacy. I think an interesting thing is happening with the young people of the United States who have been brought up in homes where they usually had their own bedrooms and privacy. Now they seem to want to live communally and live together and are no longer interested in privacy, around the age of 20.

**Dubos:** There is a simple, quantitative answer to that. I do not know the exact number of American communes but it is well known that it is in the few thousands. However, the average commune has less than 30 people and the average life of a commune is less than one year. A recent study of those communes which have survived for more than one year has been made by a doctor at a Brooklyn hospital. He made a list of the characteristics of each commune (what rules have to be lived up to in that commune) and how long the commune has survived. The conclusion he arrived at is that those communes which survive (and there are not many as I just said) have the most bourgeois criteria of communal behavior that you could possibly imagine. In other words, communes survive to the extent that they are very "square", to use an American word.

**Mead:** We do not have time for any more questions, but if there is someone who would like to ask something on point one, please go ahead.

**Waddington:** Could I ask you a question, Margaret, which we could make a bridge to number two: community characteristics and so on?

In very many parts of the world, people live in community houses of some kind. My impression is that this usually concerns an earlier age-group than the people who are setting up communes in America. It is, I think, essentially a teenage phenomenon.

In Britain many go in for communal living in boarding schools in their teens — I was brought up in one myself. I think in New Guinea and other places, there are many communal systems of the boys and girls going away from their families

288

and living in communal houses. But I believe it is before the age of marriage.

**Mead:** Bachelor houses are for before marriage. However, there are also many villages that think that individual houses are just bedrooms. Therefore the house shrinks to a place for the wife and small children, where the husband visits them sometimes but he does not even stay for breakfast. These men will still spend a good proportion of their time in a man's house. Also in some Mediterranean towns men spend almost all of their time out of the house and only return at night. But I do not think you can make an age range. In some Islamic communities little boys go back and forth between the men's quarters and the women's quarters, and learn all about the women's quarters before they start going around with the men. In other places they segregate the boys for a long period. There are so many variations that you cannot insist on any one point as being necessary.

**C.A. Doxiadis:** Let's move to the next question.

**Mead:** We were moving to the next point. Wad just said this was a bridge; now we've got there.

**C.A. Doxiadis:** I'm late in following you, but I have a question which may be answered in several ways. If you ask me as a builder what aspect is the most difficult one when a new community or town is built I will answer that it is how to bring people together on the basis of what patterns, and not how to separate them by income, etc. I think this has been successfully answered by the patterns that you know, the interwoven patterns. But the big question is when people come to a new town or a new community, should we try to mix them by force or should we try to let them come in by groups and mix gradually by themselves? I have only one answer, based on our research of the past. I have not found any case where in the past they were mixing people by force, and nonetheless we know that finally all communities became integrated. Now they may have done this by force, but I could not find any case.

**Dubos:** I am not going to answer this question except that it gives me an occasion to return to a criticism of your report which I believe both Dr. Gabor and Margaret made, namely that you did not emphasize sufficiently that the city is not only a dormitory, but is also an economic institution; that it has its own ways of sources of income. So what I would like to suggest as a possible beginning to answer your question is that all cities in the past had begun as centers of occupation whatever the occupation might have been: a harbor, or an economic enterprise of some sort and this necessarily brought all sorts of different kinds of people, different economic levels. I would like to make a suggestion (although it is not mine, I'm just repeating because it has already been made by others) but if one wants to design new cities as is being talked about all over the world today, it might not be bad to think about starting the city with a variety of sources of economic activities and income and then different kinds of people will move into it.

**C.A. Doxiadis:** I'm all for it, René, there is no question that unless we understand the city as a system consisting of all these functions we will fail. We must always start a city this way and never, never as a dormitory. Let me only explain since Dr. Gabor brought up the point yesterday, that by necessity I covered only a few points and I tried to cover those points which we very seldom speak about: So I gave emphasis to this type of community. Otherwise you are completely right.

**Waddington:** Could I make a point in relation to when we talk of the city founded around its economic activities. Dr. Dubos brought this up in connection with community and organization, implying, I think, that the function or the economic function or the community is an important socializing, communalizing force. The question I want to raise now is the change in the character of work in the future. We have already seen that we no longer build the city around steel works or a coal mine. We are shifting away from this type of occupation to service occupations, to merchandizing. In some ways service occupations would seem to be an even stronger force for bringing about interpersonal communications and socialization than the standard production line. Working on an automobile assembly line is probably not a very good socializing force, but I feel that the more service type of occupation we move into may be even better in bringing people together in societies.

**Dubos:** I always try to avoid talking about France and never succeed. It happened that during the past three weeks my wife and I had looked at some new cities in Sweden and France where we spent only two weeks. For an outsider, the most successful new city is one in France which was built because there was a steel plant. Namely, it is the city of Ourville which is beyond Caen, between Caen and the sea. There is a very large steel plant which served as a nucleus for the growth of the city and now there have been added all sorts of activities. For example, the medical school serving the west part of France is being built there, precisely because the city has been successful. It is not a very small city, I think at the present it has 45,000 inhabitants and they told us it was to go to about 80,000 or 100,000 inhabitants. This is one single example, but it did interest me in contrast with the Swedish cities which, from many points of view, were much better designed, but which essentially had been developed as dormitories for Stockholm. I have discussed this matter with Serge Antoine, who is the person who runs the office for the Department of Environment. Mr. Serge Antoine pointed out to me the new city of Vaudreuil which is being built now. Before the city was developed they made sure that there would be five or six industrial-commercial activities that would be established there. The city of Vaudreuil is now jointly being planned by an American group which has a permanent representative in the Department of the Environment in Paris and in Vaudreuil and in New York. There was a very long article, published in the magazine SCIENCE last year or during the last few months (see the Bibliography). The deliberate effort is, I know, that several of the industries are being established and some of them are the most unlikely industries — for example the Pasteur Institute — have accepted to move all their production activities there (which are very large). The Pasteur Institute is the largest, single producer of drugs and vaccines in France. Now all is to be located in Vaudreuil and the city will grow after that, so this example may indicate to me that new cities will develop around activities. This is what I wanted to say.

**Mead:** I think it is also useful if you have several of the same things in the town and one of the reasons for Topeka, Kansas being the psychiatric center in the United States was that there was more than one psychiatric institution in that town. There was a big, private Menninger Foundation, there was a State Hospital, there was the Veterans Hospital, there was the State Home for Boys and the State Home for Girls and then there was another Neurological Institute put in, and then there was an air base psychiatric set-up. Everybody moved jobs if they wanted to without leaving town and that has a very soothing effect on the Institutions you are working for. So that gave the same kind of mobility that I have been asking for members of families and friends — that you could move around within an area of knowledge and friendship and habituation without having to leave. Whereas, if you have one steel works, when you have a fight with the manager, you have to leave town. If you had two steel works or three or four works where they could use the same kind of accountancy or management you would get a community that has much more possibility of openness.

**Lourie:** I think this question of community might be looked at to begin with from the developmental point of view because children begin to form a community in a sense as they reach school age. All it takes to begin a community is two children who get together and form a set of rules about how they will function. The first rule is usually how to keep a third youngster out of the little community that they are developing. This is a process that develops a structure with the core purpose of establishing a community.

In terms of the larger community we are interested in, there need to be some unifying forces to hold it together. Some of these can be economic, some of them can be shared interests. In some of our cities the soccer team or the basketball team becomes a rallying point around which everybody can be mobilized to fight the next town and their teams.

We also see the community organizing around the more basic needs of individuals; around safety, around services, around education, when there is a need for people to function together. I think how it is structured is probably best expressed by Arnold Toynbee in his *Study of History*. He has pointed out that helpless people who are kept in a dependent position function best with an autocratic kind of structure and government, and it is only when you have people who can think and function independently (in other words a viable middle-class) that you can have a truly democratic type of society.

The interesting phenomenon that we now see in some of our American cities is an attempt to reverse this process: to help the helpless (the poor, the dependent and the depressed) to arise from apathy and get into action, and become not only part of a community but determinants of what will happen in that community. All of this has many values; however, when one begins to open the doors to those who have been suffering pain, one finds that this is a Pandora's box and that the pains that people have long endured suddenly become unendurable if you give them a chance to have them relieved.

**C.A. Doxiadis:** Again, I have to be more specific because tomorrow morning we take decisions on three cities in Nigeria and so I lead to a proposal and welcome your comments. I propose the concept of a multi-level hierarchical system. Man needs organization at many levels.

**Dubos:** An experience I had in Canberra, Australia, illustrates what peculiar kinds of social forces and social accidents one can use to create a higher level of community organization. As you know, Canberra is an entirely new city, a few decades old. It is a multiple city of sub-centers, each one of which is separated by greens and all sorts of administrative units. From what we were told, it turned out that most of these individual social units really did not work very well. But they noticed that two sub-units were functioning much better than others as a community. In both of these, the integration of the community had come about because each had been faced with clear, well-defined difficulties (in the school system or some other kind of public service). Once these difficulties were recognized, a social apparatus began to take form to deal with the difficulty, and some kind of integration within the community then occurred. When we were shown that at the Office of Planning in Canberra, they told us what they were planning in the future. They were considering the possibility of introducing unresolved problems, if not built-in difficulties, so as to create challenges to the community, which would then organize itself around this problem. They hoped they could create problems common to each one of the sub-units so as to create a unified Canberra through the necessity of solving common problems.

**Mead:** How much in the cities that you are building are the people going to be able to participate in solving problems as they go along?

**C.A. Doxiadis:** I think that I have not seen any community where people have not been able to do it if given the opportunity. I have seen a very big success in Tema, Ghana, a completely new city. There by the way, one dialogue covers what you said about the French cities. An American sociologist was asking in the market place "Why has your city reached in ten years 130,000 people, while ours has not?" He was answered "I do not know, but we all come here because we want jobs and because we come, jobs come to us," which is how the city is formed. So Margaret, in Tema they invited the people to take over the small community hall. I have never seen any better social function in terms of life and activity. They had their committee and the community hall was functioning from early morning for mothers who went there to see a pediatrician to late at night when the young people were dancing in the same space. Give a chance to the people and where it is difficult to solve the problems of their nation or their metropolitan areas, they will solve them at the community level.

**Waddington:** May I ask what happens about the Networks services that spread right out of the local neighborhood? I can see it is fairly easy to arrange democracy at the level of the city: built-up community center and so on. But what about the sewers, the water, the pipes, the public transport services and so on? Isn't this one of the unresolved problems, as far as I know?

**C.A. Doxiadis:** Yes, and therefore I proposed the concept of a multi-level hierarchical system, because we cannot solve problems of the metropolis at the neighborhood level. This is no reason for not telling the people that the neighborhood belongs to them and the functions of social organization (community hall, etc.) have to be solved by them. The best way to help them to identify themselves with the community is to give them their own shops, because there they meet every morning and evening, and the interaction begins.

**Mead:** But I think that one of the questions that was asked by someone from the audience was "How do you involve people in building a new community?" How do you involve them soon enough? When you say that they are building the social organization this could be day-care centers, dances for young people, pageants, religious festivals, all sorts of things. But how do you involve them in any alteration in the space arrangement? Or do you have to make the space arrangement so rigid that there is nothing they can do about it? I think this is one of the things that people are very much interested in.

**C.A. Doxiadis:** We have two lessons from history on this. Ninety-nine per cent of the human settlements grow by themselves, a merchant builds a shop at a crossroad; somebody follows and the settlement grows. So, I would call it the naturally grown settlement and then we have the other kind where somebody — a government, a colonizing force — takes the initiative and creates a nucleus of houses and then the people gradually change things.

My answer is not to try to solve all problems from the beginning but to try to start a process by giving the people land and water and then letting it grow.

**Mead:** Now does that lead us naturally to work places and shopping areas? We have been working to some extent with work areas also. Is there anything more that you want to say?

**C.A. Doxiadis:** I want to insist again against segregation of functions. Some of the best commercial streets are the ones where the merchant lives above his shop and we have human interaction throughout the day; and in the backyards we find the small workshops, the handicrafts. These have a continuing function I think. One of the very big mistakes is the complete separation of commerce from residence, and if we want to revive the CBDs of American cities, if we want to make all parts of our cities habitable, we should bring work places and offices inside every neighborhood, unless the factory is too noisy or dangerous for health.

**Waddington:** I think one of the audience raised the question about the economies of scale. Of course what Doxiadis is saying is definitely rejecting the economies of scale. If you are going to have shops in the sense of enormous market places with computerized inventories and all the rest of it, they cannot fit in the ground floor of a private residence. I think there is a lot to be said for the point of view that we are paying in human values for these economies of scale, although we may be saving in pounds or dollars. But I think it must be recognized that to go back to the residential shop will cost a lot of money. Maybe it should?

**Mead:** I don't think we have begun to plumb the possibilities.

You can have standardized products. Every little village in New Guinea has the same things in it (packages of cigarettes, some kinds of soap, a few kinds of tinned food). These are imported on a very large scale and then distributed to smaller and smaller salesmen. I think it is an old idea that the small shop was uneconomical because it had so much individuality. What we want in the small shop is that people should meet each other there, that they should not have to walk so far and that they can take their babies with them comfortably (not having to push the baby all around a huge supermarket). I think that just as Bucky Fuller has made the point that modern technology makes forms of dispersal possible, that it is not necessary to say that. I do not believe that there is an economy of scale when you have a Children's Emporium such as we have outside Boston where you have to drive 25 miles and then find on a totally empty space, related to nothing, about 20 acres of everything that anybody could ever have for a child. I am not at all sure that if you consider the driving there and back, and the delivery of all those things we may not have as much economy as we thought.

**C.A. Doxiadis:** The first rank in the army was "captain", but captain corresponds to the small town. The U.S.A. gave five stars to a general to guide an army of millions, but they did not eliminate their captains. Humanity was increasing the levels of its organization; now a new force has entered and we have a new level which Wad is referring.to with its products. But we have no sign that we should eliminate the other units. We need a multi-level system in everything. My answer is that we need centers which will serve huge numbers of people; but this does not mean we don't need the small corner shops for many reasons, from human to economic.

**Waddington:** My point was that we may need them; and personally, I have lived in a town where I could walk up the street and buy some bread if I ran out or something. . . But the economic forces of the present-day seem to be eliminating them. Now Margaret may be quite right that we rarely record all the internal costs, and if we did then maybe the economies would not be what we think they are. Certainly it will be possible to decentralize controls a great deal more, with computers and communication and so on. But the point I was making is what is actually going on at the present time, has been going on for the last ten years or so, is that the corner shop is being driven out of business by the supermarket. I regret it, but one has got to face it and if we are going to reverse this trend we have got to take definite steps.

**Erikson:** Perhaps this would be the time to say something about men and women, and particularly women, because the question would be what is implicit in your town planning about the future of women. In your explicit text so far you have a number of references to gossiping women in the market place. I think one can assume that gossiping is probably one of the most important tradition-guarding activities. But the implication that it is mostly women who gossip is probably not quite justified and I think that men gossip on their way to work, and men at work have their own phones. I am sure this is a whole network and of course it affects the community. One tries not to become the person gossiped about. I am now asking about the implications for the future. Already very many women work, and if one looks at this town what provisions are there for the children? Or the women who work? Or perhaps the men will stay home when the work week shortens; and the men may stay home with the children, when men and women work on different days, and so on, assuming that this is only implicit in what you found out.

**Gabor:** I would like to say something about keeping an eye on the electronic experiment computer experts, because if they look at the organization of the retail shops they find it is the most uneconomic thing in the world, half of the business is done in one hour of the day usually in the small shops and all that. And we have of course wonderful technological solutions, the trouble is that they don't fit men. The solution is obviously to choose the television sale: you push a few buttons and your request is delivered by emissions and then the goods are sent with noiseless electric carriages during the small hours in order not to disturb the traffic. Well it is all very beautiful.

**T.A. Doxiadis:** How will the population of the small community be served in health problems? Will they have small out-patient departments from a central hospital, and what sort of a hospital will this be? Will it be one of those clinics (which are now flourishing in the United States) where minor operations are practically done on out-patients, and these people then go home? Should we have a small hospital for every community or a large hospital for many communities? In many large cities today, all the major hospitals tend to be in the same region of the city (like in Athens) because that suits the doctors very well. I think all these questions have to be answered in some way.

**Lourie:** I think these are very important questions, Thomas, but I would like to extend them a step further because I think we are learning that you cannot separate health from mental health and you cannot separate either of these from education or from the social and cultural forces that involve people and families and communities. We may have to think of putting our service systems into the same kind of pattern as do our shopping systems where we can combine our patterns of communication and service to enhance what the family has available to it. But at the same time (and this is a point I was going to make tomorrow but it comes more appropriately today) we must not forget Waddington's corner store. It may be only a kiosk, but it will be some place where the child, when he begins to be able to leave his home, can be in touch with commerce and can learn by himself about how one interacts with other people in terms of supplies and services. I would hope that we could maintain the personal, human touch at the same time as we think of how we can better organize service systems, because shopping really is just another one of our service areas.

**Erikson:** We have not discussed schooling at all, or pre-schooling. I think we could take some time to think beyond the traditional corner shop to possible shops where children can go in and learn and watch the people do what they are doing, and learn to do it, so that the corner shop in the future could take over a part of the schooling which schools cannot fulfil.

**Mead:** But there is one problem that is going to grow terribly in new towns in developed countries though I do not think it will be as bad in developing countries. The problem is that you build the town all at once, and of course it tends to break down all at once. When apartments were built when the United Nations was first set up, they were built so fast, and with such standardized equipment that all the door knobs came off the doors on the same day in one whole apartment house; every toilet broke down on the same day. Now, this situation was probably slightly exaggerated; but nevertheless things will be built with standardized parts, especially as regards hardware. But after five years, you will not be able to buy that hardware anywhere, the way life is going at present. This is true in New York City now; even in the best built apartments that you would really like to live in your hazard is that if a knob comes off a faucet, you never can find one again because they no longer make them. What I have been wondering is (picking up what Erik said) that if in the new town one could not build in a mechanics shop with all the tools and the skills necessary to replace those parts that are going to be breaking down over time and which, with our present system, are going to disappear. It seems to me very unlikely that in the present distribution system of the world you are going to be able to get anything old ten years from now. I do not know if this is possible — it would mean training for the children, i.e. training for a certain number of apprentices in all sorts of skills. It looks, in a sense, like turning backward to advocate an all-purpose shop like this, but it is one way of meeting this utter nonsense of everything going out of supply.

**C.A. Doxiadis:** I think that we have only one example from history where somebody tried to impose a system on the whole world and succeeded and that was the Roman Empire, which also imposed its styles. But for how long? A very short time. They sent their people, imposed their technology, their planning, their architectural styles, but look at the cities created by the Romans! Finally the expression is local. This is something that encourages me very much to believe that although the imposition is not through a social political system but through a technological one, we may have hope if we fight to revive all local forces, from cultural expressions to technical supplies. There is no reason why we should let the invaders' new technology take over everything, instead of accepting the best from the invader and creating a balance with all local needs, human community, etc.

**Waddington:** I want to emphasize again one more point which is implied in what I said before.

All advanced technology is now aimed at saving labor; and it is not aimed at creating alternative jobs for the people whose labor is saved. Automation has not yet actually broken over our heads, but it is almost certainly going to do so in five or ten years. When this does happen we are going to have to look very hard to find ways of employing people. I think we shall find ourselves going back to a lot of extremely labor intensive procedures, which are the sort of procedures that give human scale and human contact, although at the moment this may appear backward looking, or utopian. But I think the technology will force us to refuse to use advanced technology, because it is so one-sided in saving labor and not creating occupations.

**Gabor:** Yes, this is one of my old ideas. We shall emphasize how unpopular they are. But we must not go back to the manufacturing of the 17th century where people sat around a long bench and handled everything from the simplest tools with their own hands, and made things such as bracelets, hand-cut glass or individual bookbinding. We have to give satisfactory work to everybody; and indeed, if you let industry run on the principle of efficiency, we will have a terrific unemployment problem on our hands in not so many years. Just think of the American economy with two and a half million unemployed people under arms, and what will happen for instance if the two and a half million people are released from the army? But of course economy is against us.

**Mead:** Some of those unemployed people in the United States are people that had two jobs or women who are working. We build an economy that makes people work all the time to buy the things it made. I think we forget that if we had an economy where people did not have to buy so many things they would not have to be employed so many hours. The number of services we are not fulfilling in any society today could use all the unemployed people. It is really a question of the distribution and reorganization of labor. Basically, it is not an economic question but a social political question that we are faced with.

**Waddington:** It depends on what you call economics, Margaret. It is clear that you have cities that badly need re-building, full of unemployed people who would be perfectly competent builders. You cannot bring them together, because I think there is no way of paying them a wage to build the houses that they need.

**Mead:** Because of the unions and that is something that can be reorganized.

**Waddington:** It is only a bit because of the unions. It is much more I think because of the financial system. It is because we are dominated by a Phoenician invention of money, which is a very nice thing for trading when you go to market with a pig and want to buy a bag of flour or a couple of heads of garlic or something, but it is not really designed for long-term investments in things like cities. You cannot really invest in anything if you cannot get your money back in 15 years.

So you have this situation of people unemployed and obvious things people need, because money is really an inadequate invention for what we want to do.

**Mead:** I think this is a very modern definition of money. One of the things that also is not in the book that we are discussing is the extent to which it's been possible to get Detroit Edison and Toledo Gas & Power (who do think and are able to think more than 15 years in spite of money, because they have to deal with power plants and an environment), to realize they do have an investment and ought to plan for an investment way ahead. I agree that the financial system of the western world imposes certain difficulties, and the financial system of eastern Europe imposes another set. I do not doubt we would find that China has thought up a third financial system if we knew enough about it; but I do not believe you can blame it on money, because it is perfectly possible to express hundred year issues in money and that's been worked out over and over again. We are not dealing with pieces of gold and silver any more, we are dealing with a system of long-term commitment of communities. This is absolutely essential if we are going to build the sort of networks that will protect our small communities that Doxiadis has been talking about. We have to have a capacity to make long-term commitments.

**Waddington:** I agree with this. But it seems to me so far as I can make out, it is only very very big outfits that can do this — I think the great multi-national companies, great oil companies, some of the greatest banks, IBM and companies like that. They can seriously consider "shall we still be in business 40 years from now" and they want to try to arrange a world in which there will still be a place for them, 40 years ahead. But the ordinary sort of investor in housing and so on does not seem able to do it. Nations can do it, but this is where the political will has failed. I agree an enormous amount of this is a question of political will. One of the things political will has to do is to find some new way of handling its long-term financial arrangements. It is a matter of whether you call it economics or whether you call it politics; but it is something in that sort of general area that is breaking down — in the sense that we have obvious things we want to do, we have lots of resources for doing them and we cannot at present bring them together.

**Mead:** That I do not object to, just so you don't redefine money into the system because every time we have done that we have got into trouble. It does not provide a solution, what we need is an economic-political system. Now we have skipped Nature, we went into Networks in a sense with no Nature in between. Would you like us to try to deal with access to Nature?

**Dubos:** At least I want to make one statement which refers to one of the questions from the floor earlier this morning. I think that Man in the western world and in most of the world has not lived in Nature for 10,000 years. Wherever Man lives, he has completely transformed Nature. If you want you can limit yourself to Europe, but this applies just as well to America and probably to many other parts of the world. The earth was, until Neolithic times, covered with forests and with marshes. Wherever Man settled, he cut down the forest, he drained the marshes. There is one very interesting fact of natural history which was first recognized by an American geographer: namely, that all the plants we grow are sun loving plants, none of them are plants that grow in the forest. Man began, as he became Man and created even the simplest settlements, to clear the forest. And if you take the flight over the Amazon valley, the most densely forested area in the world, wherever there is Man, there is a clearing, so, Man does not live in Nature unless you add an adjective, he lives in humanized Nature. Now that does not mean that one should be ignorant of the ecological laws, if you wish to call it, but Margaret mentioned this morning, because humanized Nature is stable, is healthy, it can survive, it can serve Man, it can serve the natural world only if it has been humanized according to certain kinds of laws which in the past were satisfied through the kind of empirical wisdom that has made the most of western Europe, laws which now are being ignored because we intervene so fast into Nature. Therefore we will have to achieve this wisdom through scientific knowledge. But let us be clear that when we speak about Nature, we really are speaking about an environment that has been profoundly changed by Man. And as I recall the question raised by that lady from Wisconsin — I happen to know Wisconsin fairly well and you have to go a long way in Wisconsin before you discover undisturbed Nature. Wisconsin, like the rest of the American continent, has been completely transformed by Man. So, I speak about Nature but it becomes a very tricky word to use because it is Nature as modified by Man for his purpose, which implies a certain way of life, certain ideals, if you will, certain preferences so that you can have Nature emerging from the same kind of God-made land and looking very different. Anyone knows this who crosses the Channel from Great Britain to the northern part of France, where there is the same geological formation, the same kind of climate and yet where the landscape is so different because of historical and social influences which have expressed themselves in the creation of a new artificial ecology which we happen to call Nature at a given time and which is no longer Nature or was not that before.

**Erikson:** I take it when Nature, as you put it, infiltrates into your towns, it is still

Nature in the sense that you can only do a limited number of things with it. It exerts its own nature and insists on being treated in a certain way to produce food or even flowers. It seems to me in your book when you speak of the infiltration of Nature you left something out, undoubtedly thinking it is part of it: namely there should be places for children to go there, which would be an aspect of what we were talking about the shops and about the schooling which could be provided outside organized schools.

**Waddington:** I want to make one point about the access to Nature. We have in the past tended to think it was good enough for the urban dwelling child if they could keep a cat, or a pet mouse or something like this. I think one should realize that it is becoming more important that they should try to keep a bit of a natural system (this is the point Margaret was making about her aquarium). In the present situation of mankind, it is very important to realize that Nature is not just a single animal or a single plant growing in a window pot. It is a system and this is something very important to try to make available to children.

**S.A. Doxiadis:** I think we take this for granted, and I do. But why is it that easy access to Nature and knowledge of Nature is a desirable thing? Why is it? For esthetic reasons? For economic reasons? For biological reasons?

**Mead:** I think they are different in different periods. At the present moment I would say that the most important reason probably is that we do want children to understand the whole natural world as a system of which we are part. Now in another period in history, e.g. for the Japanese, it was certainly an esthetic consideration almost overwhelmingly. They had a tiny island, they wanted to see little delightful bits of Nature and they dwarfed everything so that they could accommodate Nature in small space and still enjoy it esthetically. But today it is the desire to have human beings (and especially human beings who grow up in western Europe and America) realize they're part of the living world and not something that dominates it and disposes of it without any reference to its laws. This is probably at present an overwhelming desire. Now there are also people who feel that our humanity depends on knowing this. I remember asking Konrad Lorenz once: "If we build a colony in space in which there is no kind of living creature, other than human, would the people living there be human?" He said that the first generation from Earth would be human, but the second generation would not be. I think this is a possible definition — pretty alien to people who have the idea that God gave Man dominion over Nature and the right to fix every tree.

**Dubos:** What do you think about the wonderful young lady who served as a guide to us yesterday when we visited the monastery and who was pointing out to us with such pride the wonderful trees that grew all around the monastery saying how wonderful natural vegetation was and I did not have the courage to point out to her that those were eucalyptus trees that have been imported and not so long ago. . .

**Lourie:** I thought that we should not leave without answering Spyros, and there is a child development story that I think would be appropriate. It is about a mother mouse walking with her brood of baby mice when suddenly they were confronted by a mean old cat. The mother mouse got up on her hind legs, stared the cat in the eyes and said: "Bow-Wow-Wow" whereupon the cat with this turn of events was scared, turned around and ran and the mother mouse turned to her brood and said: "Now do you see what I meant by the advantage of having a second language?"

## Questions on the session of Thursday, July 6, 1972 submitted by the audience

**1. M.S. Adams:** Language, semantic categories, meaning, etc. recur frequently enough in these discussions. I wonder to what extent each panel member would care to comment on the usefulness of *semiotics* as a research tool in exploring the City of Man.

**2. T. Durrani:** My comment relates to Professor Waddington's suggestion regarding the use of bicycles and the need for incorporating bicycle paths into the transportation system of cities. I think that in the non-mechanized countries there is also a great need for incorporating two other types of slow moving traffic used primarily for bulk transportation: the non-mechanized vehicles and/or individual beasts of burden, and the human laborer using the top of his head or his own back. In the latter case, even if he uses a hand trolley, etc., he does not have a separate or designated path to use.

**3. Fran. P. Hosken:** How — Where — At What Level should citizen and citizen group participation be built into a community?

As a spokesman for minorities (I am on the Board of the Housing Committee of the National Urban League and Chairman of the Subcommittee for New Towns)

I *know* that unless citizen participation is built into a community from the start as an *INTEGRAL part* of the community life, minority concerns are always left out (especially in the U.S.). By minorities I also mean the *young*, the *old* and the *non-conformists*, etc. besides *Blacks* and *Racial* minorities. Specific provisions for participation can be planned for and built also into the physical design. I should be grateful for a response of all panelists especially C.A. Doxiadis and Margaret Mead.

**4. J. Lawson:** Taking advantage of your invitation to submit relevant questions I would like to submit two on C.A. Doxiadis' proposals in regard to the limit (free) of two floors above ground and two below. Would it not be reasonable to extend this to four above ground to achieve 50% more capacity at little detriment to the environment? And as regards the tax on all floors above the limit does Mr. Doxiadis propose this on existing buildings? If not I would certainly favor this as it would provide a source of funds for environmental improvement not covered by present Municipal taxation. Now a comment. My impression is that the sessions I have attended yesterday and today have been concerned almost exclusively with the wealthy communities, including their poor population to the exclusion of the under-developed countries which contain the vast majority of the world's population. To cite two examples:

1.  When discussing basic housing Miss Tyrwhitt suggested the mobile home and that this could be *bought* and placed on a plot to be *bought*, a proposal quite out of reach of the majority of countries in the world.
2.  Mention was made that in Sweden paper plants could be rendered free of pollution for a cost of $1^1/_2\%$ of the GNP, compared with the 0.12 average of GNP spent on assistance to the underdeveloped countries. Again an emphasis on developing countries developing still farther while the under-developed are in relative decline.

Finally, C.A. Doxiadis suggested that I present the following facts in connection with his reference to average metropolitan growth rates of 3% and his land gift proposal. The growth rate for Lima is nearer 10% or currently 300,000 per annum, posing numerous problems in housing and jobs as the unemployment is 28.5%. To meet some of the housing needs the Government has allowed the occupation by 800,000 Provincial immigrants of some 1850 hectares of State land on the outskirts of the city on plots of between 105 m² and 120 m². On these the immigrants are building their own houses but with at present little prospect of receiving the basic services.

**5. E.F. Murphy:** One problem in this discussion has been that there have been few mentions of the concept of the economy of scale. Do the discussants reject its existence? Its value? Its likely continued functioning? If economy of scale exists and has value, this may explain why urban-industrial society has the super-market, the discount chain, the huge bureaucratic structures of corporations and government — and the multiversities — and, if this is so, then what has happened will tend to continue and to intensify uniformity.

**6.   R. Quinn:** Since the panel has clearly indicated that different satisfactory densities can be achieved, could they now, for the specific benefit and guidance of the physical designers, attempt to define the criteria which should be used in designing for an optimum density of 200 persons per hectare (80 persons per acre).

## Questions on the session of Friday, July 7, 1972 submitted by the audience

**1.   Robert Aldrich:** Question for Margaret Mead: The City for Human Develop-ment should be considered also from the standpoint of Man's spiritual develop-ment — or orientation toward some "god" or deity — Isn't this one of the governing principles that should be added?

**2.   R.A. Aldrich, Jr.:** I think everybody should *grow up* with opportunities to art, music, sculpture, etc. They must *see it done*, as children, *not* on T.V. In reference to Dr. Dubos' statement about people's need to express — discover themselves in *stages*, which I agree with emphatically, how, what, forms. In community? Home? City scale? Children must see it close and experience it.

**3.   Jose Jimenez:** Can you give us a scientific definition of a *city* and a scienti-fic definition of development?
    Unless we have these operationally defined, we cannot hope to get at a scien-tific approach to the question of building the City for Human Development.

**4.   Erik ter Meulen:** Three series of data exist which I cannot fit into the vertical hierarchy as proposed by C.A. Doxiadis.
1.   *Man's personal environment — bubble* (Fig. 142).
2.   *Man's different milieus* for his living, service, working, etc. How do these fit together? Is there any hierarchical relation?

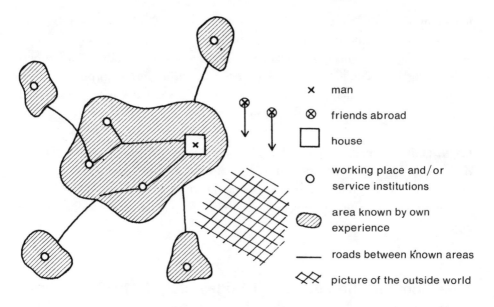

| × | man |
| ⊗ | friends abroad |
| ☐ | house |
| ○ | working place and/or service institutions |
| ⬭ | area known by own experience |
| —— | roads between known areas |
| ⬨⬨ | picture of the outside world |

142.    man's personal environment

3. *Conditions of accessibility:*

vehicle, time, money, absence of socio-psychological constraints.

All these conditions have to be met simultaneously. Otherwise the chosen commodity is inaccessible.

If these series are correct, then I can't see that Man lives his life in hierarchical series, but from the one specific milieu to the other.

In my opinion we should look therefore more to establish series of diverse milieus than to establish specific hierarchies.

**Third day: Saturday, July 8, 1972**

# 17. "Consideration for the young in a City for Human Development"

## Reginald S. Lourie

Man began as a creature of Nature. In terms of the life of the earth, it is estimated that Man is only the equivalent of six years of age. As six-year-olds we still have a tremendous amount to learn about the forces and still hidden secrets of Nature. We are trying to make Nature the agent of Man but we are far from controlling Nature. In fact, as we try to mature, the creature Man, like a six-year-old, is in the process of perverting Nature.

We began, like the other creatures of the earth, with two major interests and functions: survival and preservation of the species. As living became easier and easier, there was more and more opportunity for a range of other satisfactions. Preservation of the species, while still as important as before, has had to compete with more and more priorities and preoccupations of modern Man. Although the city is increasingly the place in which we rear our young, we have forgotten to build them with preservation of the species in mind. We must change the priorities in planning and return to the value system that puts human development in the forefront where it belongs. Keep in mind, in this connection, that 47% of the world population is made up of children and youth, and that by 1975 it is estimated to be more than 50%.

My personal emphasis is to have our new priorities begin at the beginning of human development. It is in the first years of life that the foundations of human development are laid. Poor foundations are a fundamental hazard to human development, as René Dubos points out in his concept of "Biological Freudianism". The child's first living environment is the womb, and here too Man has perverted Nature. As Doxiadis states in his original report: "The environment of the womb cannot be guaranteed to be perfect or without possible harmful, induced impairments to the possible future child. . . even if natural fertilization and the uterine environment have been selected over long evolutionary ages, still there are 'mistakes' in Nature and the uterine environment turns out to be harsh to many. The incidence of these 'natural' damages is not negligible. . ." Genetic mutations are constantly taking place, producing (by chance) changes in individual babies as Monod dramatically points out even though Einstein refused to believe that "God plays dice".

We are only beginning to be aware of the magnitude of disease produced by genetic or congenital abnormalities. Approximately $5/_{1000}$ newborns in the U.S. have major chromosomal abnormalities and $10/_{1000}$ have inherited metabolic disease. Thus, in the U.S. alone, 20,000 children per year are born with chromosomal or metabolic disorders. These are responsible for 25% of all hospital bed occupancy in the U.S. Science has made it possible for these children to live when in the past they died. Tagani Al Mahi, the distinguished psychiatrist in the Sudan, points out that the deaf cannot survive in the African bush, and that there are no stutterers there.

All this tells us how Man has perverted Nature in the earliest development of our young. The process of natural selection has been partially reversed. We can now keep more than 60-70% of our handicapped children alive and functioning, who earlier would have died or been born dead. There are experiments which demonstrate the possibility of taking a gene for a specific metabolic function from the bacterium and placing it effectively in the cell of an organism with a missing gene for that function. Therefore, if we are to be true to our too often violated ethics and value systems as they relate to the sacredness of human life, we have a dual responsibility as we plan the City for Human Development. On the one hand we have the mission to enhance the potentials of the normal "average" child as the founder of humanistic psychology. On the other hand, the humanistic city must take into account those who start life with defects in their basic equipment.

Nature, in the process of natural selection, has wisely produced the human who, in contrast to the other mammals, has a brain which is only partially formed at birth. It is not the blank "tabula rasa" postulated by John Locke, nor are all its abilities innate, as Gobineau contended. The infant has an unfinished brain.

It takes $1^1/_2$ to 2 years after birth to reach the level of maturity that is typical of the time of birth in other mammals. Beginning as a newborn with its genetic inheritance, the infant has an opportunity to add to the ability of its brain to understand and cope with the environment in which it is expected to function. To accomplish this, the brain is growing faster than it ever will again in these first two years; reaching more than two-thirds of its adult size. Appropriate environmental experience is necessary for the stimulation of the embryonic genetic mechanisms to complete their unfolding tasks. This stimulation must be available at appropriate times in development, the so-called critical periods or optimal periods for development of specific functions in the ever widening world of childhood.

Even though we are far from knowing all the answers about what goes into this developmental process, we know enough to begin to use our information in planning the City for Human Development. We know that there are three basic processes going on in the developing structure of the brain which, in addition to the genetic potential, determine the level of ability of the brain to function.

The first is that the number of connections that grow between brain cells is determined by the amount and type of stimulation available in the first years of life. The obvious implication is that the more of these connections (arborization of dendrites) which exist, the more possibilities there are for flexibility, integration of functions and information, creativity, and the possibilities for choice in the individual. This is particularly important in an increasingly complex, technologically advanced world with new levels of communication, energy, human interactions and planetary organization. And keep in mind that the time in which these connections are made is limited in terms of months.

The second is that the amount of blood flow to the different centers of function in the brain is likewise developed in (a still unknown) ratio to the amount of appropriate stimulation of each function. The amount of blood flow (vascularization) is far from complete at birth. In turn we know from a variety of studies that, for example in snakes, the more acute sense of hearing is probably reflected in the much increased blood supply to the cochlear nucleus in contrast to other reptiles. Many experiments of blindfolding or removing of both eyes of newborn kittens have demonstrated that there is later marked reduction of the blood in one or both sides of the brain. In the human infant there is already evidence that the density of blood carrying networks is much less at birth than later. In the human we know more about the results of deficient blood supply chiefly from its effect on the functioning of the heart.

The third process is that nerve networks and connections develop without an outer coating which must be formed before the nerve can be activated for use by the individual. This process, known as myelenization, is also considerably influenced by environmental stimulation, with significant effects on ultimate structure and function. The influence of deprivation on activity of specific functions can result in developmental delays and less than optimal functioning because of improper or deficient myelenization.

The slogan which is adaptable to express what all this information means is "Use it or lose it" (which originally was developed to describe the sexual capacities of the elderly). When we have not perverted Nature, we have not taken advantage of what Nature has made available in the development of young children in significant sections of our populations both in the way our cities are structured and what goes on in them in early child rearing. In each city and each country, this is true to varying extents. In the United States, it is estimated that three to five per cent of the population is retarded, $3/4$ of which is due to inappropriate or deficient experience in the first years of life. In some cities more than others over the world, the poor are in a sense being trained in early childhood to think and function in limited ways.

Both before and after the birth of individuals who are Nature's experiments, we are more and more knowledgeable about keeping them alive and functioning. For example, more and more children are born with what is called (for lack of a better name) the minimal brain syndrome. These children are often awkward and poorly coordinated, have perceptual difficulties, such as difficulty in judging distances, shapes, and sizes, and have too little or too much energy, or special sensitivities. We know a considerable amount about how to overcome these handicaps. In our cities, if we have people who cannot move around too well themselves, we have means to move them around. Most importantly, we must help them with their mental development, and not only help their intact brothers and sisters. Most of these handicapped individuals will not be able to earn their living with their physical apparatus. We must therefore help them achieve optimal use of their mental potentials. I have four such youngsters as patients, given up as hopeless in early childhood, who have recently graduated from college. It can, and is, being done. It is even being presented to the public in the U.S. as a concept. Today on American T.V. there are heroes who include a blind detective and one in a wheelchair. It is estimated that 300,000 specially trained teachers will be needed in the U.S. to help with 7,000,000 handicapped children. Teachers and special schools are not enough. The house, the neighborhood, and the playground must be planned not only to enhance the development of undamaged young children, but also with the more or less damaged child in mind.

What Doxiadis has defined is an ambitious and creative approach to matching the knowledge about human development with what the city needs and does not have to enhance it. I am confident, from what we know of human capacity to survive, that we could eventually have people who have adapted to living with smog, polluted water, ugliness of buildings, very close living conditions and eating what are now toxic contaminants of food. My point is that we do not have to do this if we put our knowledge about development to work in structuring our cities and what goes on in them. Thus we will need partnerships between the planners and the child development experts as well as the social services, infant educators and the politicans. In other words we need ekisticians to provide the cement that can hold them all together.

In terms of putting to work what we know about early child development in designing the house and the neighborhood, let us look at a few examples. In the newborn infant the senses are all present, but in roughed-in-form, and they are not coordinated with each other. Making the connections between them is an important developmental task. Should we then design the house so that the baby can be in the kitchen when its mother is there, so that it can make connections between smell, taste and the looks of food? Can there be a place in the kitchen to hang a bassinet (as they do in airplanes), and later to have the playpen so that the infant has its mother's moves and activities imprinted — a sort of "sound and light" program for the baby? He can then learn quite early how to communicate, even when to curse, such as when a pot falls and spills. Also, the attachment process can be enhanced, as well as the knowledge that mothering is available on shorter notice than when the infant is off in a bedroom. The freedom to participate in the kitchen when the child is ambulatory can help it to learn how to postpone or avoid the then inappropriate or forbidden.

Inexpensive playground materials have been developed in forms that allow for both learning and corrective experiences with the body in space. There should be the opportunity to learn basic facts such as the "feel" of earth. The child must learn for example, that plants are untouchables in the house, but touchable outside, thus enhancing flexibility and the ability to adjust to more than one standard, which is very necessary in this life. Creativity and fantasy can be encouraged or discouraged in the earliest years of life, by either the opportunity for freedom of the toddler to experiment safely, or the need for severe restrictions dictated by safety. As the child enlarges its horizons from a short distance from its doorstep to the corner, there might well be a store or a kiosk or a stand, where it can be introduced to the world of commerce. It needs to be able to learn how to communicate with other children as well as animals, worms, etc.: i.e., the basic ingredients of a world in microcosm.

Very importantly the very young child must have the opportunity to deal with its normal fears, so that they do not become exaggerated or perpetuated. In the high-rise apartment house, there is a hazard in the resolution of the fear of separation and loss when parent figures are five or more stories above the playground and a real or imagined danger comes along. In the problems of developing the ability to have body control, impulse control and to overcome fears of body damage, the mothering people should be a short distance away, and not multiple stories away from the play area. In the Pruitt-Igoe housing project in St. Louis, it was reported that the urine smell and blood stains in the elevators came mostly from young children who could not make it to their home toilets in time, or to their source of bandages. Can we not expect a lack of confidence in the body controls and integrity to be a consequence?

There should be built into each residential area centralized services. These should include universally available infant and preschool day care, and super-markets for human services. These all call for sharing of information about how they should be structured and what they should contain if they are to serve the objective of helping each individual and his family to achieve his potential in the humanistic city.

From the viewpoint of the developmentalist, cities too have developmental stages. It used to be that the end result of this developmental process was that Nature killed the cities. However, now we can keep the cities alive. We even venerate the aged parts of them. Sometimes the only thing to venerate in these old components is their age, since they were quite uncomfortable to live in by modern standards. Should we look at the components of our cities as experiments of Man and think in terms of survival of the fittest? What is fittest should be measured in terms of its usefulness in enhancing, certainly not retarding, human development. We are on the leading edge here of an exciting and meaningful dimension and mission for our cities. Let us widen that edge so that it dominates the future.

# 18. "Thoughts on the City for Human Development"

## Erik H. Erikson

The life-cycle is a dominant theme in Doxiadis' work that has not been taken up in the discussion so far. Two of Doxiadis' statements circumscribe our theme. He says: "Man's relationship to the whole system must be examined by the phases of his life, as in this respect we do witness similar phenomena all over the world." And he concludes: "We are beginning to see that the city should provide opportunities for a gradual increase of freedom, and challenge for each person as it changes in size, structure, and quality, so that these gradual changes will enable the population to gain the maximum benefit by their gradual exposure to more challenging environments, with the greater freedoms and greater potential dangers that these environments present."

But first it is necessary to overcome a certain fixation which all of us share, namely, the vision of Shakespeare's seven ages of Man. I speak with feeling, because not so long ago, an inaugural lecturer in an English University managed to make fun of my own "seven stages" without having noticed that in my book there are eight. Doxiadis fits my eight stages into his twelve without doing violence to them: he merely sub-divides some of his to be host to mine. (I object only to his calling 40-60 "real" adulthood. In the world of the future, 20-40 had better be "real" too). But, in the middle of Doxiadis' discourse on the city it is somewhat surprising for the reader to encounter such references as: "This is the phase when 'basic trust versus basic mistrust' develops," or:

"This is the phase Erikson says, of 'autonomy versus shame, doubt.'" To those not acquainted with my stages of life (Fig. 143) the sudden introduction of emotional and partly unconscious matters may seem somewhat forced.

These stages were originally so named to derive, from the psychoanalytic knowledge of the lasting vulnerabilities inherent in each stage, some indication of the lasting strength potentially provided by each. Applied to our theme, this means to demonstrate the vulnerabilities which the spatial arrangement in which people live (the use they make of space, and the meaning they give to it), can aggravate in persons of a given age-group, and the strengths which the right environment may help to foster. We must visualize, then, not only how each individual passes through his life-cycles, but also how a succession of generations unfold within the confines of a city.

If the infant's relation to his maternal caretakers must establish a certain ratio of trust over mistrust, then a mother's mistrust of her own environment and her disgust with her own placement within the spatial scheme, obviously will curtail her capacity to convey trust. Where this is the rule in a whole neighborhood or type of city, not only individuals but also communities will suffer some lasting

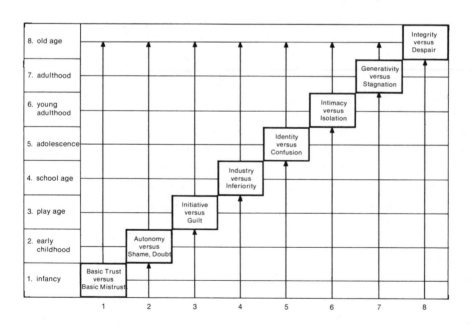

143.    psychosocial crises in the life cycle.

consequences. Correspondingly, if, in the "initiative versus guilt" stage, a child is habitually made to feel that he is a *bad* child because he uses space in a playful and exploratory way and ignores warnings he has not understood, this represents a particular environmental reinforcement of the way in which parents establish inhibitory guilt in the child, instead of making the world — as far as they can — both safe and explainable. Thus, with each stage, some aspect of the architectural environment is "built into" the next generation; becomes part of its tensions and conflicts, and contributes to the disturbances to which individuals and groups are prone. All this can lead to a fatal combination of "forbidding" circumstances and oppressive "bad" conscience, which, perversely, may appear in the form of carelessness or criminality. On the other hand, it must be said that such dichotomies in our inner nature as my formulations reflect, are part of our evolutionary heritage. Nobody should assume that we could build such a foolproof environment that Man, once and for all, would be free of mistrust, shame or guilt.

What excites me about this whole discussion is the possibility of planning for Man, instead of a "forbidding" urban environment, a facilitating one; that is one which supports Man's developmental and creative potentials, and permits him to feel central rather than shunted to the periphery, active rather than inactivated, challenged to participation rather than isolated, enhanced in awareness, rather than manipulated by blind forces, etc. For, to feel central, active and aware is necessary for the ethical affirmation which induces Man to participate in the creation of his environment instead of being caught in the vicious circle of paralysis and excess, of self-hate and the suspicious mistrust of his neighbors. It, therefore, makes sense to me if Doxiadis translates such a vast predicament into the immediacy of architectural space, as when he exclaims: "when we advise that the mother should not always say 'NO', why do we allow the city to tell us 'NO' in two-thirds of the cases when we reach intersections? (Red and orange lights take two-thirds of our adult walking time). Are we sure that this is not one cause of the nervous strains that we create?"

Such an attitude would have to be supported, throughout the life-cycle, by a rethinking of the way by which an individual, at a given stage, can govern himself, be given choices he can understand, and not be treated (beyond a reasonable point) as being dangerous to himself or others by the same token, city planning must somehow make it possible for older children to support and guard younger ones. It is only with such considerations in mind that a *dynapolis* can also reflect the productive side of Man's "inner dynamics".

Doxiadis' four principles, then, can be translated into the terms of each stage of life. There should be:

1. A maximum availability of human contacts that can be utilized and of objects that can be "grasped";
2. A certain parsimony of learnable techniques, and a minimization of repetitive failures;
3. An optimum of needed protection built into the spatial arrangements without restricting playful effort;
4. An optimization of inter-relationships which I would call "mutual actualization".

This brings us to the human bubble. In the developmental sense, each person at each stage lives in an overall bubble, which consists of a variety of sub-bubbles, marking the extent of this mobility, the horizon of his perception, the field of his choices, and the arena of his interactions. But a bubble really is not a convenient metaphor since it does not have that active center which makes a person; nor does a bubble permit interaction with other bubbles without undue consequences.

I have therefore introduced the German word *Spielraum*, literally playspace, but meaning a sphere of active leeway and of scope for interaction. Of course, when I use the word here, I do not mean the pretense and the unreality often associated with the word, but rather a maximum of freedom within an optimum of limits, which Man needs at all ages. Such leeway, I should add, includes a knowledge of the *factual*; that is, the sum of countable, measurable, and nameable facts which must be respected and, if necessary, avoided. Such a body of known facts, at any given stage, feels varyingly real to the person; that is, they are more or less meaningfully experienced and interacted with. I would then speak of the *actual* as the sphere of interaction with others, whom one actualizes and by whom one is actualized. A child feels active when he is both acted upon and invited to interplay; and what we, in psychoanalysis, call ego is an ordering process by which the person not only organizes his inner world, but, together with others, restores that shared sense of centrality and activation without which we wilt.

Where such a sense of awareness, of centrality and mutuality, are denied to Man at any stage, a sense of deadness and depression is apt to ensue; and people who habitually suffer such denial in a society in which some others do have a certain freedom of choice and scope within the major social and economic forces, must come to hate others and do violence — to somebody. This has vast consequences, aggravated by the fact that in some parts of our world, wars may cease to serve the cathartic purpose they may once have had.

Dr. Dubos' remark about the city as a stage makes additional sense if one considers the importance of vision as an early integrator of all sensory and social experiences — that is, what Man's visual experience can help him see in the factual sense: what he can visualize as vivid reality, and what he envisages as the horizon of a new or renewed order.  For this he has always employed, as Huizinga has pointed out, not only the sphere of play in childhood, but also the arenas in which games take place, as well as those courts and holy places on which various realities and actualities fuse ceremonially.  In this sense, no doubt, a city is not only an area to exist in, but also (as in the City with a capital C) a stage on which Man sees himself build the proper setting for a new cast of men.  So you will not mind (knowing of my intensive studies of human play) if I see an important connection between what children visualize when they build with blocks in a given play space, and Doxiadis' proud claim of being a brick layer who plans and executes a *dynapolis* for the new Man.

Now, all of us (I assume) enthusiastically approve of some of Doxiadis' detailed suggestions;  from the pedestrian home-street (rows of homes of distinct identity) to the dwelling group system;  from the playing squares and shopping streets to the machine streets underground;  from the system of transparent gates (which permit the visual anticipation of space to be mastered later) to the network of youth stations in and way beyond the city.  But some of us non-architects, when looking at an architect's drawings, always come to wonder what kind of men are visualized as living in the completed buildings.  One wonders what kind of historical coincidence of political and architectural vision (in the widest sense) produced the classical cities of the past?

Does not all city planning visualize a *Homo novus*, and is not every *Homo novus* to some extent the reintegration of some traditional Man?  This may be the reason that in Doxiadis' drawings of the future, one detects the latent presence of ancient images: atrium, agora, and Athens — all, of course, adapted to modern materials and needs.  By now, there must be a wealth of data on the motivation of different people in different ages concerning the cities they want to live in or will tolerate living in.  Maybe wherever something creative is done in building, it first appeals to a new type, maybe a new elite of some kind, who finds reciprocity between their personality type and the new vistas.  At any rate, a new sense of perfectability, new tangible techniques of living and new education goals are always implicit in a system of planned dwellings.  One has to know (or study) then, what factual aspects of life a given population wants to materialize, what declining reality they want to hold on to, and what joint vision they want to actualize;  and then, what they (for whatever reason) do *not* want.

There is a Jewish story, according to which a man who was wrecked on a lonely island, was found after many years.  He had built himself a very nice little house.  A few feet away was a more imposing shell.  He explained that it was the synagogue where he prayed. But over the hill there was another shell and they asked him what he built that for? His answer was: "That's the other synagogue which I wouldn't be caught dead in". What I mean to illustrate is that whatever one's vision of a simple or ideal city is, people bring with them dependencies on old forms, ambivalent feelings toward new ones, and (overt or covert) superstitions in regard to what a city must or must not include in order to make life "safe" and "happy" — whatever *their* connotations of these two little words are. Here, incidentally, I would like to know: what were Aristotle's exact terms for "happy" and "safe", and what were their meanings?

Every one of us of course, has some kind of a vision that will give different connotations to the two words "safe" and "happy". To me, as I said, happiness has a lot to do with scope and leeway, whatever the techniques by which we make use of that scope. As for safety, I don't think anybody can feel safe who doesn't feel that the world he lives in gives him a kind of inner coherence. I would in fact, relate those two things to what Dr. Dubos said yesterday about the inner shelter and the horizon. We need not only to have an inner shelter around and within ourselves; we need also to recapture the horizons that we have visualized. Architecture must help us in this.

Yet, as we look at the terrible city districts in the United States, we realize that they, too, were originally built and populated by people with a new vision, for the sake of which they were ready to adapt to the nearly unbearable, to accept hardships and challenges so that their children could become self-made men. In fact, as a friend of mine, Richard Sennett, has suggested, there originally was something of a creative disorder which many productive people would hate to do without. An all too obvious order allows for few idiosyncracies and no hiding places.

As I enjoy Doxiadis' sketches, the artist in me argues with the Montessori teacher in me, and they banter with each other (and with Doxiadis) on some details. Especially charming is the breast dependent baby (Fig. 84). Far from critically viewing his room, he is rightly depicted as looking straight at the architect, wondering what *he* is wondering about. And, indeed, soon he will be hungry and sleepy; that is, interested primarily in the bubble formed by the warm arms that are holding him; by the meeting of his eyes with those of the mother; and his facial contact with the breast; then in the bubble provided by the covers of his crib and his closed eyes, and in his sense of being withdrawn to some inner world. If the question is, "How do we stimulate the infant at this stage?" this can only mean that we must surround him with items which he can grasp in every sense of the word, exercising what is ready in him, and when. In the meantime, the varying limits of his readiness also protect him against over-exposure; and we should discuss carefully whether, and to what extent, he needs a special room (shell) in which he (and his mother) can be encapsulated, but may soon feel imprisoned. Here I only wish Signora Dottora Montessori were still with us. But surely, there are any number of women and men, parents and teachers, alive and ready to help us define such fundamental spatial problems!

Does Fig. 90 really show "the room as the infant sees it"? I think that the room as seen by an actual infant in it would take many different forms depending on his selective attention to things and people that suit his always changing mood and quest for expansion at one time, and contraction at another — for plenty of company at one moment and solitary play at another — etc. What one should strive for, then, are built-in choices, not static prescriptions as architectural expressions of his "stage". It seems important, in addition to showing the optimum private world for each stage, to indicate the maximum interplay between (say) toddlers, striders, and players. For each stage must be seen in all its interdependencies, and this is true for all stages. But it is clear that we will not be able to discuss the details step for step through the whole life-cycle to the end.

Fig. 130 for example suggests an arrangement for old people which, to the taste of some, may represent more an anticipated mausoleum than a place to keep one's waning senses alert. Maybe, some old people would prefer a safe niche, close to a doorway from which the changing world of children, of youth, and (yes) of motor cars could be watched.

Finally, I will "stick my neck out", and say that my vision of the future city could include in selected areas an imaginative use of (moderately) high-rise buildings. Obviously, for what Aristotle called "partnership", the differing "identities" of circumscribed towns within the megalopolis are as essential as are the identities of neighborhoods. If one asks what gave the "romantic" cities of the past their out-spoken identities, one remembers not only cathedrals and castles, but also hills and valleys. A well integrated block of multi-story buildings of different heights, where the roofs of the lower buildings serve as outdoors for the higher ones (and are connected with them not only with elevators — manageable for older children — but also with sweeps of ramps and stairs) could be a rather exciting environment. Playgrounds as well as small parks for the aged; small sport fields; communal swimming pools and selected stores could serve not only the spatial expansion but also the visual enhancement of upper stories. Such city blocks, furthermore, could serve the different needs of single and married persons of childless households and groups of families with children. They could have their own communal and ceremonial centers: kindergartens and pediatric clinics, communal centers for improvised as well as planned contacts between the young, and places for meditation and arts and crafts. Such planning may also help to rephase and reconsider the community of men and women, for surely Doxiadis' frequent references to women's need for "gossip" must give way to a consideration of the communal function gossip served in the cities and villages of the past, and the technological means which can now serve the purposes of rapid and farflung intercommunication. In fact, women so far, seem to be under-represented in Doxiadis' city.

And so is worship! For the future community not only needs a minimization of the spatial pressures which would aggravate timidity and guilt as inner guardians of safety; it also needs esthetic and ceremonial assurances which represent a sensory affirmation of communal values. This, in the end, is what makes a City. If Doxiadis concludes that at age 100: "God, in several forms, may need to enter by now," he must mean that such (old and new) forms must have entered at every step of life; not only as a kind of death insurance at the end. (In this sense I certainly agree with the suggestion that burying places somehow be made a part of city planning so that they may not be experienced by the young as some kind of pious garbage disposal on the outskirts.)

Come to think of it, work (as well as women and worship) is under-represented in the discussion so far. I assume this consideration is reserved for the question where all those underground cars are going in the morning, and where they come back from at night — although it may well be considered right now that day and night will not be as differentiated in the well-lit future as they are now. But no doubt, also small factories will remain in, or move back into, neighborhoods. The neighborhoods, such as I have described here, will employ a workforce close to the homes in activities visible and comprehensible to children. All this will make a rapprochement of work and home life possible, creating new roles for women and men and thus a new communal spirit.

To conclude with the beginning, this whole consideration of the intermeshing of the city and the life-cycle somehow implies an assumption that the rounding out of the full cycle of life becomes itself a focus of future visions, and a matter of universal interest.

# 19. "Individuality, nutrition and mental development

## Spyros A. Doxiadis

My comments are related to hypothesis eleven of the report by C.A. Doxiadis on "City for Human Development". This hypothesis states that human development must have as a goal:

1. to help the average person develop to the maximum of his potential, and
2. to gradually increase the level of this potential to its maximum in order to help humanity develop to its utmost.

As a pediatrician talking to a predominantly non-medical audience, I would like to stress the multiplicity of causes, factors and mechanisms implicated in the attainment of the goal of hypothesis eleven, i.e. development for each person to the maximum of his potential. Thus, on the one hand, I shall bring to your notice some recent advances in our understanding of human development and, on the cooperation of many sciences and disciplines, a policy which has been emphasized in all the Delos symposia and related activities of the Athens Center of Ekistics.

In my brief presentation I have chosen examples from three fields. These were selected because of their inherent value, their illustrative potential and my own familiarity, interest and work on them. I shall try to link the data from each field to the interests of city planners.

## Individuality

There is no need for our purpose to define individuality in a way acceptable to all. Everyone has his own conception of it, but also we agree that there are differences in development, in behavior, and in style of performance which distinguish one person from the other.

As always, poetry has been in advance of science. We cannot form our children in our own likeness, and I find this best expressed in "The Prophet" by Khalil Gibran:

> "Your children are not your children.
> They are the sons and daughters of Life's longing for itself
> They came through you but not from you
> And although they are with you, they belong not to you.
> You may give them your love but not your thoughts,
> For they have their own thoughts.
> You may have their bodies, but not their souls,
> For their souls dwell in the house of tomorrow
> Which you cannot visit, not even in your dreams,
> You may strive to be like them
> But seek not to make them like you.
> For life goes not backward nor taries with yesterday."[118]

Whether it is desirable during development to promote individuality, i.e. to cultivate individual differences, is a value judgement since there are not scientifically ascertained facts to indicate if groups in which individuality is enhanced eventually become happier than groups in which individuality is stifled. However, individuals who have acquired a group identity are more likely to fall victims of a totalitarian regime while, when we promote the identity of the individual, we give a better chance for the development of a democratic society.

We have now various methods to describe individual differences even from the first days of life. One such method distinguished nine separate items which can be studied in very young infants. We have used such a scale in our studies of infants living in an institution as compared to infants living in normal families. Differences between the two groups appear as early as the second trimester of life. For example institutionalized infants become more withdrawn than family infants. They develop a more negative mood than the controls. They have more regular rhythms than babies reared in families.

It is likely that other environments, and not only residential nurseries or orphanages, emphasize conformity of behavior and stifle individuality. These could be the family, the school or the community. Clinical experience provides many examples of disturbed behavior or nonachievement of potential by disregard of individual differences. We, the students of human beings, are responsible for this disregard because we made statistics our master and not our servant. By using means, averages, standard deviations and groups we tend to forget that, useful as these concepts are, they are only abstractions, arrived at by depriving the individual of exactly those qualities which make him an individual.

From what we know, individuality and the sense of identity are enhanced when the environment responds to each infant in a way most appropriate to his own temperament. The response to all infants in the same way, as happens in an impersonal institution, tends to minimize individual differences in style of performance and in behavior.

## Questions

What is the importance of this for planning our physical environment?

The developing organism needs variety in space, so that every infant and child is exposed to many types of stimulations, allowing each individual, according to his temperament, to get more from the one and less from the other; to approach more closely to one set of stimuli and withdraw from others.

The individual also needs variety over time; change in the environment from day to day, from one period of the year to another: not a desert nor an evergreen woodland. He should be exposed to physically harmless but unexpected incidents, such as may happen in any community; not overprotection which leads to monotony.

How do we achieve this?

## Nutrition, growth and learning

There are differences in height from one individual to the other and from one race to the other which are genetically determined. However, we come to realize more and more that a large part of these differences are caused by different environmental conditions, mainly nutrition. For example there are differences in the heights of various races and nationalities which are not only genetically determined. If you take the Japanese race you find there is a great difference in the average height of a native born Japanese in 1900 and fifty years later (Fig. 144)[119]. American born Japanese are even taller, not because they have been mixed with the white race, but because of better environmental conditions, nutrition, etc.

In England, there is an enormous difference in average height between public school boys of 13 and 14 and council school boys over thirty years ago (Fig. 145)[120]. These are not genetically determined differences, but environmentally determined differences.

We can see this even more dramatically in animal experiments. If you divide the same group of newborn rats and, for the first three weeks of their life, keep half of them undernourished and the other adequately nourished, and then (after the third week) you allow both groups to eat as much as they like of the same food, you will find that the difference in development of the two groups persists even after 100 weeks. This means that undernourishment during the critical period of development has made them dwarfs for the rest of their lives.

Up to about 20 years ago, we believed that adverse nutritional circumstances, although affecting the body, spared the brain as the most noble organ. But we know that inadequate nutrition may affect the development of the brain. Furthermore, we know that this type of influence on the development of the brain may also affect the learning abilities of an individual.

The earlier the nutritional insult, the more far reaching its effects. There is a very definite relationship, repeatedly shown, not only in cases of overt malnutrition but also in hidden malnutrition, between weight at birth and subsequent learning ability. In other words if the small size of an individual, especially in the early stages of his development, is not genetically determined, it is an indication of a handicap which may extend to the development of his mental abilities.

Malnutrition of the individual during intrauterine life (and this may not be caused only by bad nutrition of the mother but also by other factors such as smoking) makes it less likely that this individual will attain his full potential.

## Questions

Since such an effect on the development of the human brain may be irreversible after the first year of life, what should our policy be for protection of the future mental abilities of the unborn children?

Should the priority be better education for expectant mothers? Better nutrition? Less work (at home and outside it)? Special provisions for the education of teenage girls?

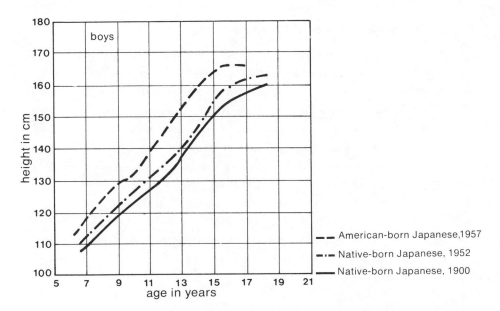

144.　average standing height of American-born Japanese boys compared with that of boys in Japan, 1900 and 1952

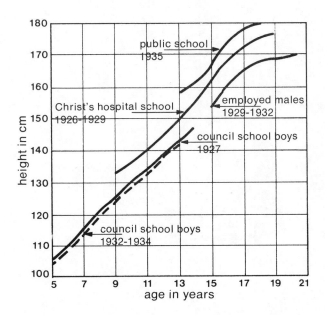

145.　height of boys and young men by social groups, 1926-1935

# Environment and mental development

It is well known that there is a definite relationship between mental ability and social class. This is not due to inherent, genetically determined hereditary factors. Environment consists of many things and even in the absence of an obviously depriving environment (as it exists in impersonal institutions) there may be less obvious factors, important for mental development. These can be detected by a study of large groups. Such factors may have to do with the social class of the mother's family, with family size, with the presence of preschool children in the family and many other causes. These early environmental influences are only reversible by better environment later, such as school. Since complete reversibility is impossible, early depriving environments lead to nonattainment of full potential; therefore to creation for the next generation again of a depriving environment and these social factors become in the end a "hereditary" disease.

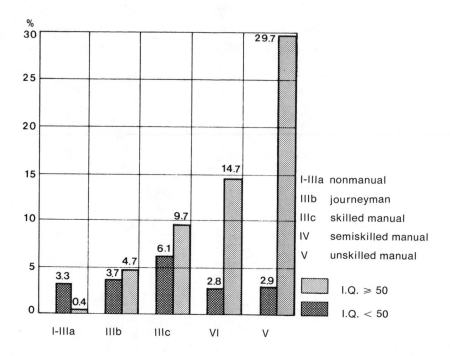

146. prevalence by social class of severe (I.Q. < 50) and less severe mental subnormality (I.Q. ≥ 50) for children aged 8 to 10 years in Aberdeen, Scotland

Studies were made of the percentage of Aberdeen schoolchildren scoring in the highest quartile. It was found that 43% of the children from the professional classes had high performance, but this proportion dropped in the skilled manual and the semi-skilled manual classes. One might consider that this difference was not environmentally produced because the lower social classes have more prenatal complications. But Fig. 146[121] shows that this is not entirely so. The severe degrees of mental deficiency are very much the same in all social classes. But in the milder degrees of mental deficiency (which we know are much more likely to be environmentally produced) we find that the unskilled manual workers of the lower social class have definitely a much higher incidence of mild mental subnormality than the higher social classes.

If we go one step further back, to the previous generation, we can see a continuing effect. All the children represented in Fig. 147[122] were raised in social class three (skilled manual workers), but their mothers came from different social groups. Some mothers came from the professional, technical and managerial classes, others belonged to the same social class, others to the unskilled manual workers. The children, I repeat, were raised in the same social class, but their performance at the ages of seven, nine and eight to twelve had a definite relation, not to the social class in which they were raised, but to the family background from which the mother had come.

Our own studies regarding school failure in a moderately isolated Greek community have shown the greater importance of the environment over hereditary factors; although we had expected the latter to be present because of a high incidence of inbreeding in this community. This study was made on the island of Furnis near Ikaria, a very typical, nice, small island. It is fairly well off, because they have a lot of fishing and quite a few people go into the merchant marine or dive for sponges. However, we were told from the Minister of Education that very few of the children qualify for high school. A team of us went there to investigate whether the high school failures were due to inbreeding — because, until recently, this has been an isolated community — or to social factors. We could find no relation at all between inbreeding and failure at school. But we found, first, that there was a much lower ratio of retardation in the ages zero to six than in the ages six to 13; second, that, if we rated family conditions, the better family conditions (taking the father's occupation and everything else into account) showed a much lower degree of retardation than the poorer family conditions.

Now we come to the most important question: Are these early influences reversible or not? This has been studied by Douglas in an excellent survey in the north of England, in which he followed 4,500 children from birth until the age of 25. He found that better school conditions might eliminate some of the earlier family disadvantages. If you have, for example, poor family conditions, a good school may help to improve the child's performance, but it can never bring it up to what it would be if the child had started with good family conditions.

Whether we take my second heading, where bad nutrition caused decreased learning ability, or my third heading, the influence of the environment on mental

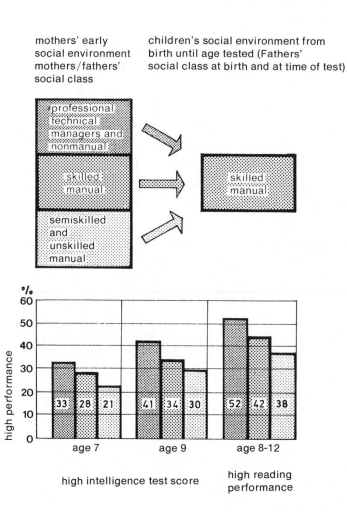

147.    relation of Wechsler-Bellevue intelligence test grades to interclass movement at marriage

ability, we come to the same conclusion: poverty and failure is a hereditary disease (Fig. 148)[123]. This means that if you come from such a family you enter into life, not with a pack of 52 cards in your hand, but with 48, 49, 47. No matter how much you are helped later, you still go through life pitted against other people who play their games with 52 cards, and you play yours with 49 or 48.

## Questions

How do we break this vicious circle of the "hereditary" disease of poverty? Better schools for children, or better training for adults? Better homes or better communication with the outside world for small communities?

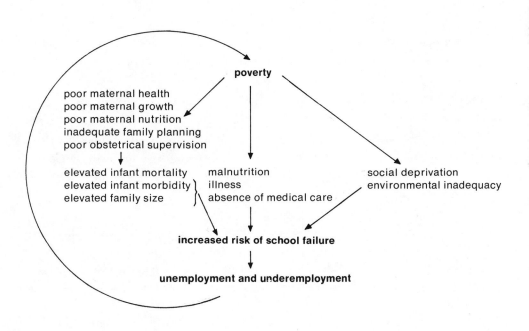

148.    environmental relationships between poverty and educational failure

# 20.  Discussions

The participants decided to concentrate their discussion on the following points:
1.  definition of what Man needs from the city (biologically, psychologically)
2.  muscular development
3.  crime and the city
4.  variety and diversity
5.  future evolution of Man and relation to the evolution of the city.

**Mead:** I first want to ask the members of our panel, as this is the very last session, if there is anything that they want to say in general.  It need not be immediately reactive to our speakers this morning, but if there may be something that they would like to say now to get it on the record.  I am going to start with Dr. Gabor who's been incredibly silent since the first day, so I am going to make him the first speaker.

**Gabor:** I want to say a few things about how both science and technology are likely to influence the things we are talking about.  Science is ready for a good many problems which we do not solve, because we are up against various deadlocks, some economic which only political decisions can bring and others due to tradition, etc.

We have heard about defective children who are born with extra chromosomes or have chromosomal defects.  Actually, there is today no need for any child to be born with chromosomal defects because a technique exists to take a small sample of the placental fluid, check the chromosomes and, if there is any defect, to abort the child.  But at this moment we come up against the taboos. I don't have to say anything more about that deadlock.

In building cities, we find another sort of deadlock. I am talking only of developed countries, in particular of the United States. There the builders are pricing themselves out of business. Unemployment in the builders' unions is about twice that in other trades, but they don't care so long as they are highly paid. The technological fix to solve the problem is modular housing which will make the cities even more hideous than they already are.

As regards other possibilities of building, tunneling for instance will become much cheaper. The price of moving earth above the surface has come along very strongly, and the price of tunneling is to decrease very steeply, so this tunneling traffic which is the only solution in big cities is likely to become much stronger.

Now, other technological influences: what goes into the houses? And there of course the most important thing is conveyance of information and its emotional impact — television being, of course, the most important. The American child at any rate spends far more time (even before he goes to school) before the T.V. sets, than he spends with any living person, let alone with his parents. So television is an enormous educational influence and up to now it was chiefly used to educate consumer trainees, i.e. people who will become good consumers. Here an important change is coming: it is cassette television — the possibility of choosing your own program.

This is a very interesting case of how a new invention can be handicapped simply by there being eight different solutions for it. For the time being not one of those systems can go on, because there are so many competitors; but sooner or later it will come into everyones homes and then there will be of course the possibility for the parents to educate their children by choosing such programs. It has not yet come, but it will do so in ten or twenty years from now. For the moment it exists of course as a possibility if the parents want to educate the children by tape. Tape machines are cheap and a number of programs are available.

I must say that physicists and technologists have got a very strong revulsion against children being educated by machines. But I must say I may have to change my mind because the children take it wonderfully as soon as it is an interactive device, nothing else but pushing a few buttons. I have seen such a new panel: they call it the plasma panel in action. You can program a good many things (and cheaply) and what's coming out is your own interaction. You just can't take children away from it, from the age of six they simply love it. As regards the possibility of increasing the amount of perceived material, there is hardly any technological limit to it.

Finally I want to mention something which is very important in my mind. I always think that it is better to go against the worst evils instead of going for the greatest good, which is very difficult to determine. One of these evils is, of course, safety against crime and terrorism and drugs. In this field, I must confess, technology cannot help very much. The suggestion to supervise streets, car parks, etc. with video cameras is certainly not a final solution. It is a frightfully expensive thing and crime would simply go into the houses. Here, I must say, that I think the solution is up to the city builder. Crime flourishes in the slums. The crime-infested regions always correspond to the poor regions and there is no other method than to break up the slums. You can hardly break up the slums in the large cities but you can build new cities which are not slums and this is why I repeatedly ask: "Is the small city really hopeless and must we put up with megalopolis?" I hope we shall not have to do it.

**Dubos:** Fortunately I can organize my remarks around some of the statements made by the pediatrician member of the Doxiadis family and then also continue with what Dr. Gabor has just said. While Spyros Doxiadis was speaking this morning, there was in my mind all the time a book, or rather an essay, which a former colleague of mine used to quote as we were editing the journal of EXPERIMENTAL MEDICINE. It is an English essay. I have forgotten the author's name. The essay is on the advantages of being rather small. This is not a trivial remark. If there were time I would like you to answer this question, but I am not going to ask you to answer it today. Do you (Spyros Doxiadis) believe that the present and the next generation of Japanese, who are so much taller than their parents were one generation ago, are going to be more intelligent, more creative, more artistic and contribute more to history than if they were shorter? Do you believe that the present generation of Jews, taller and so vigorous in the kibbutz are going to be more creative than their parents coming from the ghettos of central Europe? If I mention this, it is not to question, of course, all the well-documented facts that you have offered to demonstrate the relation between nutrition, body size and even brain size, but I just suggest that we really don't know enough at this stage to even claim that size can be an index of how well-civilized human beings we are going to be.

Now, what's the relation of this to the design of human settlements? First let me for a minute ask Dr. Gabor, and question one of his statements, perhaps two of them. He stated that there is more crime in the slums. Well I don't think there is any evidence of that. Obviously if you live in the slums of New York City and commit a crime the police will get you. But if you live in Scarsdale or on Park Avenue and use drugs your name will appear in the newspapers. There is no evidence that I know that the slums bring more crimes than do the very wealthy suburbs of our cities. Then you stated also that television in more sophisticated forms can be a very strong educational force. Well I think television unquestionably brings information, but I am not sure if I do believe that exposure to information is a very effective educational method. I believe that offering information is not very useful unless you provide at the same time an environment in which one can act on the information and convert the visual or auditory information into some kind of activity. You can look at the box all you want, but if you don't exercize your own muscles you will not develop and the same with regard to mental activity.

I have all this in mind because after writing so many times on the effects of the environment on Man, I have been compelled to recognize that in New York City the environment which has produced the richest number of creative people was the Lower East Side around the turn of the century and certainly the Lower East Side was very deficient in all the physical qualities of which we speak. Another environment which has been immensely creative in the United States has been of course the small family farm, and I am sure that what I say here applies to any other country. So there are two very different kinds of environment that have made many people able to be creative in all aspects of life. It is a fact that if you were a child on the Lower East Side in New York, you were not only exposed to the immense variety of cultures and activities brought in by the immigrants, but you also had a chance, were required even as a child to function, to do something: to be involved in the making or selling of things. I remember so well an American physicist telling me, "Really my education has been in the streets of the Lower East Side where, from the beginning, and when I was very young at the age of three or four, I had to do so many different things". Now what is there in common between the Lower East Side and the American family farm? Or any other family farm? Is it not that both situations provide a wide range of experiences but also demand the child acts and functions and does something that he could see the results and the consequences of? So if I were to try to suggest that we convert this idea into some kind of planning in the design of human settlements, this means that the human settlements must provide enough variety of situations in which the child can act. In other words, the concept of the adventure playground (which has first grown I believe, in Sweden, then in Great Britain and which we are trying to apply in New York City) must be enlarged very much so that the whole city can be an adventure playground in which one is not only a witness but an actor.

**Waddington:** I only want to make a short comment really to put this discussion into a broader framework. We have been concentrating on formulating ideals for a city suitable for human development and I think it is quite legitimate to confine our discussions to this for a time; but I think one should recognize that nothing will be done about this, and that doing anything about this is essentially a political matter.

I think we have to look forward to a world in which in order to help, a political economic system is going to be radically changed, partly by technology and partly by telecommunications, automation, use of computers, different sorts of transport and so on. But also partly by a change in people's attitudes, their basic political attitude: just what they want from life. I believe that people who say they can't go on much longer have as their main ideal material growth measured as GNP; and I don't think any of these things we are talking about for the cities will actually get done until we do come quite a long distance away from that old idea of growth and GNP.

If we are going to have anything like the restructuring of the cities we are talking about, there will have to be a totally different sort of political economic will behind it. We certainly don't have time to discuss this, but I think one should mention this as a broader background against which you've got to see this discussion of the specialized problem: what kind of cities would we want to get if we had a method of doing so. I think this is the only point I haven't made before and I'd like to make.

**Lourie:** If I might be permitted perhaps a little personal touch — this panel is in one sense a kind of dedication of this hall in the name of Evanthia and Apostolos Doxiadis. And I have the feeling that there was a memory trace that produced Evanthia here and I can better understand those eyes of the baby; but also we have the influence of Apostolos Doxiadis, the pediatrician who was very wisely involved with the problems of people and I think we have, maybe, one of the answers to one of the problems we were talking about in terms of appropriate stimulation.

**S.A.Doxiadis:** I have been asked questions and yet not asked as you heard Dr. Dubos say. I think that Dr. Dubos really knows the answer, but I think I'd better say a few words for those of the audience who may not be from the biological fields. When we are talking about development, we have to realize that there are a multitude of factors and influences. Nutrition is only one of them. By improving nutrition we eliminate one inhibiting factor: we do not add positive factors. Therefore, if all things are considered, the new race of Japanese may turn out to be less good than the old; but that does not mean that we should not eliminate the negative factors of the past, one of which is inadequate nutrition. This is one of the questions I have been asked. Regarding anything more, always, during these discussions, and generally speaking, I am preoccupied by the question of the vicious circle, and which is the weakest part of the vicious circle we can attack and break. By vicious circle I mean the repetition from generation to generation of mental illness or if you like of poverty, or inadequacy, or school failure. Where do you attack? I would like to know, Dr. Mead, whether there will be time for the audience to contribute, especially the young people to tell us what is their feeling about education of teenagers in matters of mental health. If there is time. If not my question will remain for another time.

**T.A. Doxiadis:** In 1948 I had an invitation to lecture to the Medical Association of Basel, and they left the topic open for me. As we were then rather isolated after the War, I had no idea at first what I should speak about to the Swiss doctors. But suddenly I knew I could speak on something about which they had no idea. I would speak about hunger in terms of my clinical experience.

Greece has always been a country very short of food, so in the occupation, when the Germans and Italians started confiscating all the food they could find, hunger started. We were obliged to change our food habits, eliminating the more valuable foods from our diet and eating more green herbs, etc. I remember how I started waking at two or three in the morning with a very disagreeable feeling in the stomach. As a clinician, I thought I had some kind of ulcer of the duodenum, but a few days later I diagnosed that it was simply hunger. This situation lasted a whole winter with tremendous effects on the population: 60,000 or more people died from hunger. I will never forget making my afternoon rounds in the hospital and finding all the beds taken by the people who had been brought in there that morning. I knew that the next day they would all be dead and I was unable to do anything. I must add that I admired these candidates for death. One would imagine that death from hunger would be something terrible, but these people were looking at me, perhaps smiling, knowing they were beyond my reach; and the next day they were dead.

In the spring the Allies decided to break the blockade and sent in food supplies. Conditions improved immediately. But as the conditions improved there came a real explosion of a vitamin deficiency—pellagra—which lasted all summer and disappeared in the fall. Astonished, we saw that we had before us clinical pictures of conditions which had been in Greece for a long time, but we had not known they were due to malnutrition and malabsorption. The Greek population had been surviving for centuries with hidden rickets — hidden pellagra — and God knows what other deficiences. As I have said, Greece has always been very short of nourishing food, and I wonder if the miracle of ancient Greece—this explosion in some decades of poetry, philosophy, athletics, and so on — happened in an undernourished population or not? Or perhaps there were not too many infections, then, I mean malaria and tuberculosis and so these were eventually the leading factors? During the occupation we saw different diseases disappearing, among them diabetes. Today, with all the insuline naturally and with all the other tablets we see the diabetic patients increasing in every population. If we continue in this way, there will come a day when all humans will be diabetic. Should we continue so or not? I think this is a very difficult question. Anyway during the occupation and our starvation, natural selection took over in Greece, because naturally the starvation took away first of all the T.B. patients (so the sources of infection eventually disappeared) and then all the mentally ill patients, and this was perhaps another selection. I can't wish a population to suffer such a hunger or a third world war: but just to finish with these patients. Thank you.

**Mead:** Now, we have on the board the neglected points, that came up today, yesterday and the day before yesterday and have not been completely dealt with. Do you want to introduce the first one Dinos?

**C.A. Doxiadis:** On the first one, I really have to pose my strongest question (being only a bricklayer) and turn to all of you and ask: How do we now define what Man needs? Because although we have specifications for cars, and we have movements of people insisting that the car be made more safe by the industries, we cannot find specifications for Man.

**Lourie:** I think we have learned that you cannot use just one pattern, but Man needs a kind of flexible city that allows for a range of different kinds of people and a range of different kinds of cultural phenomena. We need to consider how we can structure a city to maintain such flexibility. That is not very specific, but it's a part of the biologists' and the behaviorists' challenge to the planner.

**C.A. Doxiadis:** Well, we begin to understand and to respect these general principles, but a bricklayer who designs every night and builds in the morning contributes to crimes if he makes mistakes, so I have to be more specific. Let's turn to point two, which is a partial expression of one: muscular development. I made a strong statement that Man, when he is no longer training his muscles by going up and down, is turning into the first animal that may become two-dimensional only. Could we take a strong position on this?

336

**Waddington:** I would like to make a remark on the first point, Dinos. And I could put this by saying. I think you should be more modest. I think, as a builder, you should not ask yourself: What does Man need? Or what can I do for him? I think you should say: What harm could I be doing Man? I do not think it is possible to formulate what Man needs. In the near future his needs may change. For instance, we may have personal video telephone communication in a few years' time. But you cannot state for sure whether Man really needs it or not. On the other hand, what you can state is that Man is harmed by undernutrition, by various sorts of stress, and this includes not giving him a way of life which naturally exercises his muscles. And this is not just going up and down after the bisons in the midwest plains of America, or in the African savannah (where they hardly go up and down, the land is practically flat but they do run a lot, and so it is not just reducing exercise to going up and down).

Man is always tempted to be a lazy sort of devil. If he is given an opportunity to go up in an elevator (or lift) he will do so; if he is given the opportunity not to walk but go by car, he will take his car to go a distance of a couple of hundred yards. I think that builders could do something to fix the city in such a way that it would more naturally call upon Man to take some muscular exercise.

**Mead:** Can I go back to this question of need or harm? It seems to me that, when we are dealing with human beings' absolutely basic needs (nutrition, protection against the weather, amounts of rest) we have one kind of imperative. The city must not be constructed so that some people in it cannot have anything to eat. A city must not be constructed so that people can get no rest (and in some city centers today that is almost impossible). In these respects, I agree that the builders should ask: what harm do I do? But I think it is also fair to ask: what good can I do? We must first put down a floor, beneath which people must not be allowed to fall and die. But then you have the ceiling, and I think we have no idea how far up or out people can go.

When Dr. Thomas Doxiadis was talking about hunger in Greece — I think it is very necessary to realize that half the world is hungry. As Professor Waddington says, there has to be an enormous economic/political change. This has to occur, I think, not in terms of utopian visions but in terms of the constraints of hunger, suffering, poverty and injustice all over the world. C.A. Doxiadis has spoken of what the poor suffer in a badly constructed city, and it is terribly important that we begin to attack these basic points as quickly as possible. Only if we can keep them constantly in mind will we have the kind of goals that will make the economic/political change possible.

One of the curious problems of the human race has been that we have always been very good at picturing hell, and very poor at picturing heaven. Every heaven that anybody has ever conceived has been dull. Another thing that we have experienced, particularly in America, is that reward is not the alternative to punishment. If you stop whipping a child and give him little gold stars you don't get good results. Punishment produced a kind of result that the little gold stars never do. Maybe the constraints put upon us today by the hunger and suffering and the needless destruction that is going on, will force us into the kind of open-ended construction of cities which is the closest thing we can come to a utopia.

The only utopia we can really build is the utopia we can't imagine. The minute we imagine it, it gets dull, and the risk and the challenge of the variety tend to disappear. C.A. Doxiadis talks about providing people with the basic structure, which includes their basic human needs for fresh water and transport, etc., and then letting the people build part of the city themselves. This is really talking about letting the people create their own utopia and not producing a blueprint ourselves. Now Dr. Spyros Doxiadis asked that he wanted to hear something from the young, something about the handling of teenagers, but I think you had better ask the question yourself, and then I'll ask anybody who classifies himself as strictly young to answer.

**S.A. Doxiadis:** We tend to believe that early experiences are terribly important for intellectual and emotional development and in most cases the early environment is provided by the young parents. If these young parents are inadequate themselves they perpetuate intellectual poverty and emotional problems, and the vicious circle goes on from one generation to the other. Is it possible to start breaking this vicious circle by introducing, at the teenage period, much more education in matters of mental health and infant rearing?

**Mead:** All right, now are there any members of the younger generation who would like to reply to that challenge?

**An Architect from Bombay, India:** I would like to tell you something from my personal experience. I do not know how far it will be universally applicable. I was put in a hostel in our village which was about 70 miles from Bombay. It was run by a group of nationalists who were our educationalists. The advantage of this place was that we were close to Nature, away from our parents and we did everything by ourselves, of course not the cooking, but we served food in turns, we managed our own affairs, we washed our own clothes, etc. which gave us the sense of responsibility at an early age. I am talking about the age from eight until sixteen, before we went to the universities. It also gave us a sense of national spirit and some of us did participate in the national movement. And apart from merely participating in the national movement, the example that was set to us by our teachers led us, many of us I should say, to do something for our community and while we were earning our own livelihood we were also in one way or another trying to do something for our fellow beings who were less fortunate than us. Of course in certain respects being away from our parents we had certain disadvantages, but there were many more advantages and we have seen that children who did not take their studies, could not study well, do well, those were physically deficient. On the whole I think if you compare the advantages and the disadvantages there were many more advantages and of course so far as parental care was concerned whenever they went back to their houses during holidays, they were with their parents so they were not completely away from their parents.

**Mead:** You are interpreting Dr. Spyros Doxiadis' question as introducing a break. Do you need to introduce a break in tradition in order to give young people a different kind of training? I don't think that's quite what you meant. Was it? What you meant was you take them where they are, you're stuck with them during teenage or adolescence. You concentrate a great deal more on giving young people the insights that we now have about bringing up children, that's what you meant, wasn't it? The question is: where do you break any tradition that is going badly? Are you going to repeat the errors of the past? What do you do with the school or educational system? Where do you break it?

**D. Kennedy** (U.S. Architect and Planner): I would like to suggest that maybe we should go back to the discussion on communes yesterday. There might be a form of commune which is beginning to be realized by some young couples, whether married or not married, especially the young couples who are having less children and who are trying out the system of living together in a sort of cooperative dwelling type of thing and thereby having more contacts for these singular children; and on top of that let us say the cross fertilization of ideas of how children should be handled in younger ages is very important to break down this vicious circle that we are talking about.

**Anthy Tripp:** I dare respond to Spyros because he has something to do with my mothering. A vicious circle, it seems to me, had some good reason for being a vicious circle, and if we break it, for one thing it will stop being a circle. For another thing I don't think it can be broken if we believe in some ways that unconsciously we bring up our children — we mother our children — the way we, ourselves, were mothered. I think no matter how much information one gives teenagers, they still will mother their children the way their mothers mothered them. By this I don't mean to suggest that we should not educate teenagers, but maybe we should think about moulding the vicious circle gradually to where we want it and not breaking it.

**Ruairi Quinn** (Irish Architect): To be specific to what was a very specific question from Doxiadis. In our education system, particularly with groups which are mostly disadvantaged people, it has been shown that access to education on a free basis has not been the great equalizer that the previous generation thought it would be. In education we are not educated to be parents. I, in my stupidity, argue with my wife over young children and I am wrong 200% on everything. She has read and she has educated herself, and the sort of things that Doxiadis was talking about and that Erik Erikson said are things that should be incorporated: boys should be trained in home economics, and home economics should incorporate bringing up children. You now have the facts on the effects of either mobiles or malnutrition. The husband in a poor family must be shown how important it is that his pregnant wife gets the right food: before, he never knew this. So if you want to attack what I think is one of the weak links in the system you should train males and females, teenagers, how to be parents because I think they don't get the information. I certainly did not get it.

**Mead:** Well, let's go back to answering questions about how we build a city or town plan. If we had three generations together I would say you should start educating them all at once. The only really successful transformation I have ever seen was when they took the grandmothers along too, and then you can re-educate mothers and grandmothers together. It is when you take one age-group out that you are likely to find they will revert. We found this for the American adolescents: we teach them new food habits in college, for instance: they go all the way through college and when they get married they revert and cook the food that their mother cooked and which she was still cooking. Now if she'd stop cooking it, they'd still very likely cook the food their mother cooked, but there would also be new food.

**Erikson:** I am trying to say that we have not had time to go through what is in this book. I have a feeling the city plan which is suggested here would really permit life-long education as you suggest. There are two big breaks now which have to do with the enormous expansion of information that is now possible.

One is that there is possible a kind of "informed ethics" where one learns to discuss why something should be, is necessary and should or should not be done because one begins to realize what the consequences would be. I have the feeling we are talking about too many parts of crime, I remember that Dr. Gabor mentioned in one breath homosexuality, drug addiction, drug pushing, and criminality. These four crimes would form very deformed aspects, but what is very difficult today and I think the present generation of young people are just recovering from, is a period of anti-morality that was based on an excess of moral pressure that existed before. Margaret Mead has written about that in her book on the generations. Now, there is quite a lot of this (which I wish we had time to discuss) among what are probably the later teenagers which are closer to young adulthood: namely the necessity for them to learn to know the world. Doxiadis, you speak of conquering the world and remind us of Alexander the Great — of course that was a rather different setting. But we have something here about (I think you call it) hospitality centers. Margaret has described them thus. We also mentioned something very important, namely the Networks of communication and preambulation which we have discussed very little. So, namely, how should it be possible in the kind of city that you propose that the teenagers could have a free access to the means of transportation and would pay very little or nothing to be able to travel, and that there would be all over the world places where teenagers or young adults could go and stay for a while and look around.

Now, why does this seem to be so important from the point of view of identity? It is that obviously what we are all struggling for at the moment is the "all-human" identity; is the identity of a human species. Before this we have had what I call "pseudo-species", namely a lot of groups of people, nations, tribes, religions, acting as if they were the elected species and everybody else might have to be tolerated but also ought to be fought at intervals to support their sense of election. Now I think that the problem at the moment is that young people all over the earth are losing this sense of pseudo-species, this identification with any group of people who can say that they are the elect as against all the others. The young people are also objecting to what they call the super-ego pressure and the constant emphasis on being good on the basis of what is forbidden.

One very interesting thing in your report, for example, is the meaning of red lights. I don't mean the other kind of red lights, I mean now the red light of traffic lights. What does it do to us on the street when primarily what we must do or must not do is ordained by signals which say STOP! NO! and so on, rather than by a pre-arranged planned traffic in which it would be very difficult to make a mistake. And this is a kind of architectural idea which to my mind would facilitate a sense of information, affirmation, confirmation of what seems reasonable and right. But one of the important ideas would be transportation, because the future identity would be a combination, or actually a reinforcement of one's place in such a city scheme — an affirmation because one has seen others and because one has experienced variety and diversity. I think, for example, when it comes to child training, it would be very important for young people to learn in how many different ways children have been brought up in different parts of the world and why in certain places they were brought up in a certain way and in another in another. Then we can come to a reasoned, thoughtful conclusion as to why it should be like this in our community.

**Mead:** Let's go back to the question about communes which we really did not do anything with and to the point where you have a small number of children mothered by and fathered by a large or a larger number of young adults. We should go back to the fact that people should not have to learn how to hold a baby by bearing one; never having seen a baby until they do. I mean in ordinary human societies people hold babies when they are young. In most primitive societies both boys and girls have a lot of experience with babies, just as they have a lot of experience with death, before they have to face the death of their own parents, for instance. Now these young communes, where they just have one or two babies and everybody has access to the baby, are I think an accentuation or sort of prefiguring of what we need today. We should have neighborhoods in which everyone has access to children whether they have children or not, and where they all learn about children.

My New Guinea Stone Age people, when they transformed their society under their own steam, sat down and wrote out a new set of ways in which their children were to be brought up. They made up a whole manual of child-rearing and brought it to me and asked me what I thought of it. Some of the ideas were good and some were not good, but they had grasped the idea that when you change your society you must look at the way in which you bring up children and ask: Are we bringing up our children in the way we want our society to be?

**Lourie:** There is some practical experience along these lines. The colleges of home economics used to have groups of babies and they tried to teach how babies should be taken care of, but it did not work. However, one of the most effective ways that I have seen is to bring junior high school children (male and female) into Head Start programs with three-, four-, and five-year-old children. The teenagers of 12-14 are in a developmental stage where they are exploring old answers and matching them up with the new ones that they will need to have. It is one of the most effective times at which you can have an impact in changing some of the distortions persisting from the past.

Of course the most logical and the most effective time for such intervention is in early parenthood, because parenthood itself is a developmental stage and there is an opportunity for appropriate interventions in those areas where they are feeling helpless; where they are saying: "I'm telling my child what my mother said to me; and I know how I hated it when she said it, but I cannot help it." A situation when there is anxiety — when there is a crisis — is an opportunity to introduce change: hopefully, change for the better.

**C.A. Doxiadis:** On crime. We have at this moment about 200 clients in more than 15 countries including the U.S.A., France, Spain, Africa, Asia. Every time I am asked to advise on a city and we talk about the problems and they mention crime, I insist that they take me immediately to the neighborhood or area with the highest percentage of crime. I can assure you it is not related to poverty, but it is always related to a very bad quality of neighborhood.

Then, I go to see other neighborhoods and forgetting about crime, I say to myself, if I have to settle here for a month which neighborhood would I select? And I always select the one where we have no crime. Now, this does not speak of some recent aspects of crime related to drugs. I am speaking of crime in the streets: raping, killing, attacking. Every time I find an area which I would perhaps not call beautiful but which I would call balanced, I see people walking in the streets, going to their shops, and talking to each other, etc., and I also find the lowest percentage of crime.

**Mead:** How are you going to answer the question that the people who become criminals or have been criminals since childhood go into particular neighborhoods which are disorganized — for instance a lot of things that are broken, houses are deteriorated and dilapidated. Now where would you break that particular circle with your design?

**C.A. Doxiadis:** I don't know. I know one thing. We had in the past only one area, within the Athens region of 2,500,000 people, where we had a really higher percentage of crime. This was in Drapetsona, in Piraeus, near the port. It was the worst neighborhood to see and walk through, even for policemen during the day, regardless of crime. Now this has been eliminated and we have no crime there; the quality is much better.

**Mead:** Where do the criminals live?

**C.A. Doxiadis:** They are spread all over the city in an equal way.

**Erikson:** I would like simply to ask Dr. Dubos one question about when he says that it is not true that most crime is in the ghetto. Well, in the ghetto there is relatively little you can steal, but isn't it still true that many criminals come from the ghetto, although their crimes are committed somewhere else?

**Dubos:** First, let me restate. I don't think one knows the real facts, because if you peddle drugs in New York City and you live on Park Avenue, you are not arrested. Anybody knows that who lives in New York, whereas if you peddle drugs and you live in any one of the slums the police will get you.

**Mead:** No, René, they share the loot. They don't get you. There is no protection in the ghetto provided by the police for anybody against anything. That's the reason it's a dangerous place. They only arrest a few people once in a while.

**Dubos:** We happen to live in a house near Garrison, New York, which is about fifty miles away from New York City. One can see by reading the newspapers (and by the way, there are very few black people, very few poor people) that it is one of those communities which is no longer a community, which has lost its sense as a community, and the incidence of drug peddling and drug addiction is high, and everybody in the community knows it. Now I am not going to give you a percentage because it could not be meaningful, because one does not know what the percentage is in other areas. I think the difference of recognition of crime from one social group to the other is so conditioned by our social prejudices that we just don't have the facts.

Last week, during the discussion about whether the death penalty should be abolished in the United States, I was very much impressed by the statement of one of the former members of the cabinet. He said "Look, who is suffering really the death penalty?" And he made a list covering the past twenty years and some of the most famous crimes where one knows who the persons were, but because they came from a wealthy family they never suffered the death penalty. The death penalty is for the boy who cannot hire a good lawyer.

So I really want to stand against the view that crimes come from poverty, or even come from the slums and maintain that crime exists as much on Park Avenue or in Scarsdale and Riverdale. I don't know how to define it, but it depends upon the kind of social structure of the neighborhood.

**C.A. Doxiadis:** I agree.

**Gabor:** As a scientist I never disagree about facts. But here there is a simple fact taken from Ramsey Clark, the former attorney general of the United States, who says that if you make a map of crimes it exactly coincides with the slums. Now if you take drugs, that of course is a different business. Erikson has pointed out that crime and assassinations are different and that of course the drug addicts have to commit crimes just to keep themselves in drugs. So there is a very strong correlation there too.

**Mead:** I think that we are mixing up what happens to people. A slum is not only poverty, that is really your point, isn't it Dinos? A slum is a terribly disorganized place and a lot of people who live there are not necessarily poor. But a slum is a place certainly in New York City where you are likely to be robbed of everything you possess any minute. In Harlem today you are likely to be knocked down and mugged at any minute, which is a different point. It is a point that the way we construct our cities we make concentration points of victims (if you prefer to talk about the victims instead of the perpetrators). But the victimization in the slums is terrible and nobody feels safe for a single minute. I think the point of poverty is important, but the point that Dinos is making is the way you build your city and you let this kind of disorganization spread that produces these concentrations of victimization. But you don't think that there is any doubt, Dinos, that a real slum has an association with crime if you define your slum as something more than poverty?

**C.A. Doxiadis:** Yes, definitely so.

**Lourie:** I think we are dealing with two sets of truths. I think there are some basic fundamental ones which may be best illustrated by the story of the boy who disappeared from his house one day and his parents were ready to call the police after a few hours, when he suddenly reappeared and they asked him, "Where have you been?" "I have been in the attic," he said. "How could you be in the attic and not be heard for so long?" He answered, "I found a wonderful book!" They said, "We don't have any books up there that would keep you so occupied." And he answered, "Oh, yes, and it's all about rape and love and murder and revenge and war." "My God!" They said, "We have not got a book like that in this house?" "Oh yes, and on the cover it said *Holy Bible.*"

In other words we are dealing with a pervasive phenomenon in terms of crime and human relationships with each other, but there is no question that in the slums there is an exaggeration of this pattern, partly because we are bringing up individuals with very limited choices available to them. And the choice that they can make so easily surrounded by the amount of crime we see in the police reports, is the kind of model that provides the key points in a child's life. An opportunity is given to go in one direction or another and only too often the most successful man a child sees available on his block, the best dressed and driving a Cadillac in the inner city is the criminal.

**Mead:** Now, I am going to ask Doxiadis to summarize or pull together this discussion as some of our audience have indicated that they would like it pulled together for them.

# 21.    Concluding statements

**C.A. Doxiadis:** Thank you Margaret. Now I think I cannot really summarize such an important discussion. Perhaps, though, I can bring up three points which have been very useful for me because they have convinced me either that we know something and that we are moving in some right direction or that we don't know and we must learn.

The first is that we should not see the city as a plan but as Man sees it. If we live in a two-story building or on the lower floors (Fig. 56) we see the city as a jungle from down below. If we live high up on a tower (Fig. 57) we see it as a bird flying over it. Man, home have disappeared and all that we see transmits the message that there is no order in our life system. One of the ways we can face such situations is to define landownership and properties on the understanding that the air cannot belong to the owners of the land. If we start this way the community can create the utilities and can then build the home system by creating a structure covering the low level street. The community owns the street but there are garages for every house. The next idea is to create a housing system by building long concrete walls to keep us apart; but the open fronts are wide enough to allow the individual dwellings to express great diversity. This system enables us to have separate homes, kept sufficiently apart not to harm each other, and yet leave everyone free to express himself. Some people can have a garden in front and the house behind (the car is underneath). Others can have a terrace and swimming pool and a house in front.

We can also gradually change the present picture, which is dominated by machines, where we have lost the human scale and where we tend to have uniformity and no diversity. First, we need to close the street to the car; then to cover the cars, facing the houses to the other side so that the people will feel free to remodel their dwellings as they wish. Somebody coming from the Mediterranean can add terraces and the Bavarian or Scandinavian people can express their own style.

This is a simplified answer as to how we can reorganize our society to give ourselves the maximum of community life and the maximum of diversity.

As my second point, I would like to transmit several lessons that I learnt from our discussions:

1.  We recognized that the previous human systems of towns and cities are being replaced by commercial forms of energy and we have the obligation to insist that all our cities must be human, although the communications Networks will be technological.

2.  The second lesson, confirmed by our discussions, is that we should not think of our systems of life as a number of separated functions, with the city totally separated from Nature. But we must understand the need of the infiltration of Nature down to the small city garden.

3.  The present tendency is to segregate everything: industry, commerce, offices, etc. Here again we need the same type of infiltration. We need both commercial centers distributing everything, and also need commerce inside our neighborhoods. The same with education: we need a big university but we also need education to infiltrate into the system of our daily lives.

4.  We spoke a lot about the diversity of local cultures and expressions. I have tried to transmit this as a great obligation to achieve two things. First, to organize the best technological Networks — all types of Networks — to create a unifying language. Next, but at the same time, to respect everything local. The big task is to avoid the invasion of the technological forces into the human sphere and to achieve a balance.

5.  We also spoke of human contacts and how we need a system where we can isolate ourselves (or isolate our family) yet make contact with friends and the local community and have access to the broad social system that we need. In this connection I would like to comment on satisfaction and safety. Man's desire for close contacts — higher density — declines with increasing space, and over time and increases with satisfaction. Man's desire for safety increases over time: the safer the place the longer we stay. We jump from a rock to swim: it is dangerous, but it is a matter of a second. We act dangerously but for short periods. This has led me, as a builder, to a simple formula when we have to take decisions on action: time multiplied by satisfaction and safety is equivalent to happiness. When the question

of happiness is brought up I can only paraphrase Aristotle's *Politics:* "The city-state has at last attained the limit of virtually complete self-sufficiency and thus while it came into existence for the sake of life, jobs, security, health services, it exists for the good life, happiness. As a natural system, it attracts us for the safer life and then exists for the good life."

6. I would like to emphasize one other lesson: the big mistake in the term "developed nation". We have no developed nations in this world. They are all very underdeveloped. Because a nation has a high income and technology the people should not believe they have a culture. Every nation is developing, and we have to see within each nation what is missing, and try to supply it, but not try to impose western standards on the whole world because we assert that high income western nations are developed.

I now come to my last point. The Ekistic Anthropocosmos Model tries to give an image of what the city is. The total system of our life consists of five elements in the following order of their creation: Nature, Man, the individual (the forgotten element in our generation), Society, which is more important in some political systems than the individual, and lastly Shells and Networks.

*Nature* consists of climate, land, water, air, flora and fauna. Each has different aspects. (Thus climate depends on temperature, humidity, rain, wind, etc.). Nature can be represented by about 32 components.

*Man* can be seen in as many ways as there are individuals, but in a systematic approach he has to be seen in the basic phases of his life, which in spatial terms are 12. But he also consists of body, five senses, mind and soul. Therefore every individual can be seen in eight different ways. This means that the individual can be presented by 96 components. What a baby sees, what an adolescent hears and what an old man needs to move in space are all very different.

*Society* can be seen in two basic ways: first in terms of dimensions, that is the number of its members. Society is very different if we are dealing with a neighborhood group of some hundreds or with a metropolis of millions. To evaluate Society we can use the ekistic classification of 15 units ranging from the individual to the total population of Ecumenopolis. Next, as we did for the individual, we must differentiate between primitive and developing societies. This can be seen in six developmental phases. Thus we reach 90 components: 15 social units in six phases.

*Shells,* which are all sorts of buildings, can be classified from the most indispensable ones, houses, to the most symbolic ones, like temples, or the most technologically developed ones, like power stations or modern factories. Practice shows that Shells can usefully be classified in about 20 categories.

*Networks* range from pedestrian paths to roads and highways, sea and air routes, water supply and sewerage or drainage systems, gas and electricity conduits and all telecommunication networks. These can be classified in about 20 categories.

The relationship between these 258 components can only be complete if we include all possible combinations of them, such as how the invasion of babies in a road can change its character, how a factory can cause changes in air temperature and therefore, affect the climate. This means that we now have to multiply 258 by 258 components which equals about 66,600 relationships, some of which may be causal ones (like the ones mentioned above), some non-causal (we do not know whether a certain type of plant may influence a certain building although we could say that it does create esthetic effects).

Next we must differentiate between 15 units of space. A factory has a different impact on a small town than on a continent. Any phenomenon can be understood only if we look at it in its appropriate space unit from the smallest one of the individual with his body, clothing, furniture to the next unit, the room, to the house then to the city and finally to the whole earth and beyond.

Then comes the time scale divided into 10 units, from one second to 1000 years. Any evaluation of components and relationships must also be looked at in the proper time scale from seconds (for noise which may be endurable for only such a time unit) to thousands of years (for ocean pollution which may leave eternal signs). This means that we have to deal with 150 units of space-time. Action in a metropolis may have to result tomorrow morning but it can have a very different effect in a single home.

We now come to the evaluation of quality. For any understanding of the meaning of the components and their relationships with Man and his values, we have to look at them through the basic sectors of Man's concern: economic, social, political or administrative, technological or functional, cultural or esthetic.

Finally there is what I call the reality-criterion of desirability and feasibility. We may dream of the monumental garden or city, but we have to recognize that they are not feasible and may never be.

This is how we can establish order out of chaotic situations and great confusion. We have 258 basic components in the system of our life which have 66,600 relationships which can be understood and evaluated in a system of 1500 units. Our total concept model, which can illuminate all aspects of Anthropocosmos as a developing system, has 100 million parts. This is a frightening figure unless we see the whole as a model which allows us to understand everything existing or happening in an organized way (Figs. 149 to 158).

As the outcome of my 40 years of working and writing I could cover only the

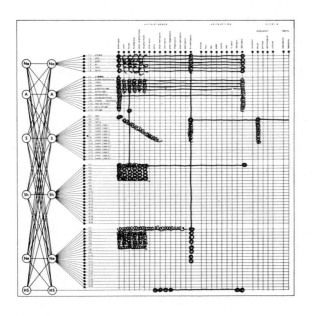

149.    fields covered by C.A. Doxiadis

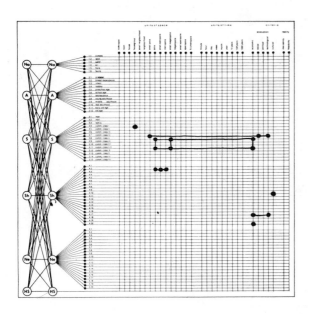

150.    fields covered by Dennis Gabor

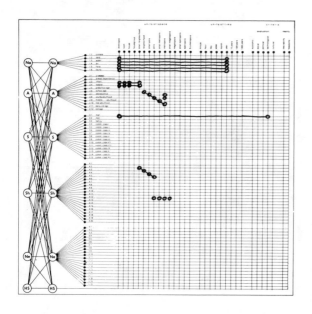

151.    fields covered by C.H. Waddington

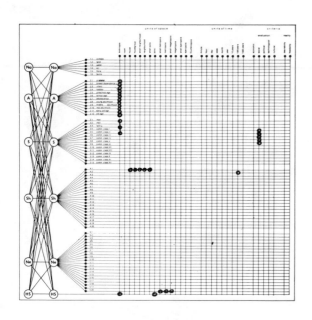

152.    fields covered by René Dubos

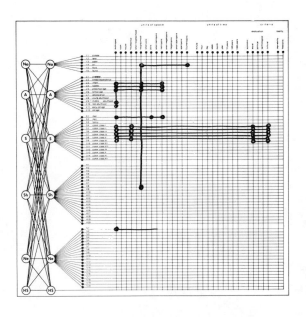

153.    fields covered by Margaret Mead

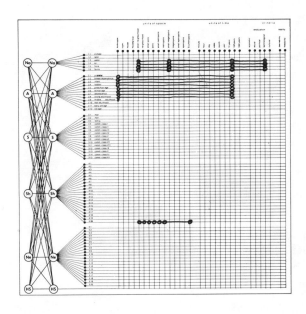

154.    fields covered by Thomas A. Doxiadis

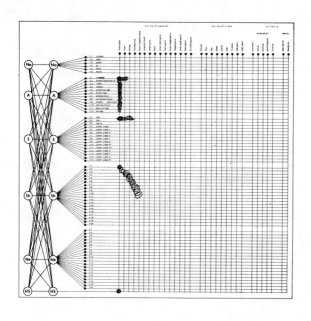

155.    fields covered by Erik H. Erikson

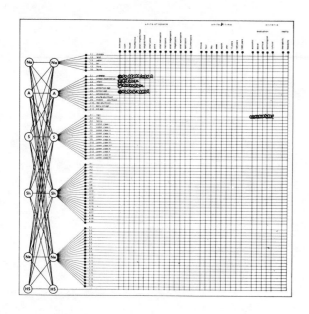

156.    fields covered by Reginald S. Lourie

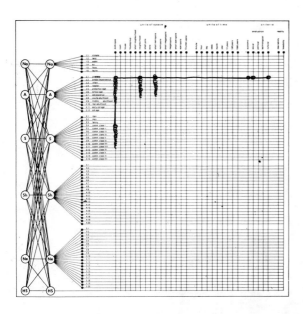

157.　fields covered by Spyros A. Doxiadis

area of the model shown in Fig. 149.　Dr. Gabor, speaking about the multi-generation house, the campus, small and big towns, covered the aspects shown in Fig. 150.　Professor Waddington spoke about the infant who should see things grow, specialized areas and biological needs (Fig. 151).　The less he covered, the deeper he went.　Dr. Dubos spoke about undefined human needs, social separation, contacts between people, protective enclosures, ancient buildings, longevity, happiness, etc. (Fig. 152).　He was followed by Margaret Mead speaking about giving a sense of the shared sky, children exposed to adults, preparing children for the city, Man moving to the town, and real community formation (Fig. 153).　Thomas Doxiadis spoke about pollution and how Man fought it, changes in conditions of human health and unified Networks connecting small with big systems (Fig. 154).　Erik Erikson concentrated on the stages of human development; he spoke about bubbles, and the need for a stage for our expression of happiness (Fig. 155).　Reginald Lourie spoke of the prenatal phase, of changing situations and consequent priorities, and he brought up the problem of the partnership between basic disciplines (Fig. 156).　Spyros Doxiadis spoke about the child's development related to the small island and to big cities, and he touched on the aspects of poverty and economics (Fig. 157). Finally, Fig. 158 shows what we all said. Out of about three thousand points on Fig. 158 (representing one hundred million points in the complete model) illustrating what the city is, we covered about four hundred. This is the problem of ekistics. Everybody speaks in his own way about the most difficult and complex system of life.

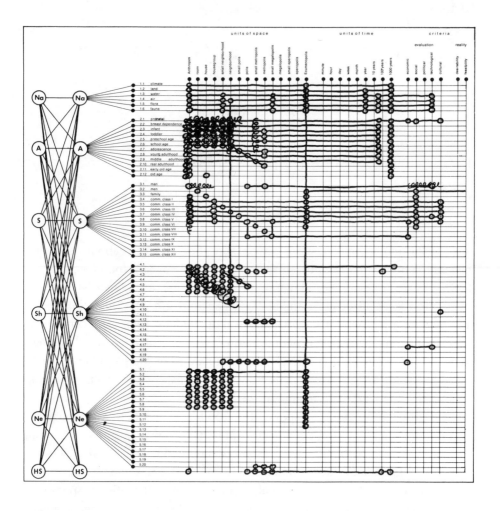

## 158.    fields covered by all the participants

**Erik H. Erikson:** Judging from these charts it looks to me as though I should say a little more. I would like to say a few words primarily because I would like to go through the life-cycle and come to an old age which Doxiadis ends by saying "the hundredth year of life, Man has normally retreated to the smallest unit which is often covered with flowers".

I bring this up because I think that the last remark in this symposion should be devoted to Apostolos Doxiadis and Evanthia Doxiadis; because isn't it true that Apostolos now would be almost one hundred? And undoubtedly his grave is covered with flowers. I would like to say that there is much more to the life and the death of a man like that and a woman like that.

I wonder whether what has been mentioned here is not, if you don't mind the word, what I would call a religious devotion to the City of Man. Most of us have a feeling that anybody living in the city which has just been shown to us would be able to develop his own symbols. Yet we know somehow that esthetic and ceremonial occasions are terribly important to experience a unity in that living. So the new city which Doxiadis is planning in a changed world still has to become a city of generations who find ways of handing on to each other certain values. He has suggested elsewhere that maybe one should have small cemeteries in the neighborhoods where the children can see who were their ancestors. With the population change that is going on in the world, one wonders how many people will be able to be buried close to where they lived. But there is no reason why a new generation should not have new ways of remembering people as part of the generational process.

Let me just repeat what Doxiadis says in the epilogue to his book:

The oracle of Delphi will function again, not to make forecasts about the future but to guide the human spirit when in doubt. Then Man will not elect his leaders only for their administrative ability as he now does, but will select those leaders dedicated to new creative action for the benefit of Man, that is his demiurges. And for this I think that the brothers Doxiadis have given us the perfect example.

# Appendix 1:

# Observations
# on visual information
# in Hydra

## C.A. DOXIADIS

In order to gain some insight into the question of the amount of optical information that we get from a variety of different subjects and our reactions to them
(an insight that I learned early in my life that we badly need[124]); I conducted an
experiment in the small town of Hydra on its own island in the Aegean Sea and
the specific area that I chose to view was the eastern part of the town. I sat
and worked in the upper floor of one of the old, traditional houses on the western
side of the harbor for many days. For many hours I looked towards the shorter
wall of the big old room and I had no problem when I wanted to think. It was
an old and beautiful stone wall; I liked it but it did not disturb me at all. I
could work for hours and concentrate on my subject by looking at the desk, or
at the wall without any problem at all; I could always decide what to think and
what to do.

I then changed my orientation by 90⁰ and turned to the East, facing the balcony door which was open.  As it was already afternoon, the sun was illuminating (it was August) the opposite part of the town (Fig. 159).  This balcony door was the frame of the picture which I could see.  It was vertical and oblong and it was really shaping my field of vision, changing it from a horizontal oblong — which it usually is for everybody — to a vertical one.  I could see the hard rock of the island against the sky, a good portion of the old ruins at the top and old houses at a lower level.

The sight was beautiful but it did not disrupt my concentration on my manuscript.  I worked for many hours and always had the pleasure of looking out in order to relax.  I then measured the angle: My field of vision encompassed no more than 30⁰ and the town was coming into my room, through my eyes to my brain, in a sector of less than 15⁰.  We were in a very good balance: I did not suffer at all nor did the town lose its attraction for me — on the contrary I had optical relaxation when I needed it.

I then changed my position again;  shifting from my original orientation in order to get a broader exposure to the town.  I moved closer to the balcony door in a way that brought my total view into a sector of 60⁰ (Fig. 160) instead of the 30⁰ which was the sector that had been feeding me with information before.  With this move I ran into trouble.  The town, which covered about 36⁰ of the total sector of 60⁰ that I was viewing (that is double the previous sector) now became the main subject of my interest.  I could not work as before because I was attracted by it too much, for two possible reasons.

The first reason was definitely the increase of the sector that I could see covered by the town: from less than 15⁰ (probably 12⁰) it had grown to 36⁰.  This is comparable to the Ionian concept in ancient Greece of the sector to be covered by an important building which is viewed by the visitor from 36⁰ to 72⁰ but in any case no less than 36⁰ versus the Doric concept of 30⁰, which are really very close to each other and change only the amount of the view[125].  The second reason was probably that by coming closer to the balcony I could see small boats moving in and out of the harbor; I was now exposed to life versus my previous static exposure to a picturesque part of the town.

I then selected my fourth location;  with the same orientation, but so close to the balcony that the sector I could see of the city was 90⁰ or possibly a bit more since I could not keep my head straight in the same position exactly like a statue.  When the distance from the opening is longer, a small shift of the head does not matter, but now that I moved closer to it, it did.  At this location my picture changed completely in shape (Fig. 161):  from a vertical oblong it turned into a horizontal one as now the balcony door could not really be seen;

159.　a view of Hydra:　second position

160.     a view of Hydra:  third position

161.    a view of Hydra:  fourth position

only its vertical sides could be felt as a frame of my picture;  I had to move my head much more in order to see the lower part of this frame, even more for the upper part.

Thus situated, my work was very difficult as both previous factors were intensified:  the angle was too great and my whole field of vision was encompassed by the town and the town was alive.  Concentration at my desk was very difficult indeed — it required a big effort as there was now too much information.

Taking my fifth location, I went out on the balcony and tried to concentrate on my work, but it was impossible. I was really overexposed to a huge optical panorama and, as I knew it, I tried to concentrate on the central view, the one I was used to from my earlier exposures, but it was not possible. Although I was attracted by the old buildings, the ruins of the war in the upper part of the town as well as the huge rock — controlling this whole section like a huge statue of a God — my eye or my mind was attracted to the left.

When I tried to find the reasons for this, I realized that they could be psychological — with the eye acting as an agent who had to achieve an attraction. I always turned my head to the left where the sea and the mountains beyond it would allow me to concentrate neither on my desk nor ahead of me. There could be other reasons as well, but I could not be sure. Two probable ones are: the wider horizon to the left and the movement of the waves, sailing boats and ships. I cannot say that I am sure these distracted me because I viewed it again when the darkness did not allow me to recognize the distant horizon or the movement and the effect was the same. But I did not stick to this attraction, as something was pulling me from the back of my head compelling me to turn to the right.

Here the situation was different: I could see a whole town and not the sea, great nearby rocks and distant mountains; but the force of attraction was as great as before. I could not easily abandon this view and turn back to the middle and to the left. But I had to, as new forces were pulling my head; it was then that I understood that three shifts did not satisfy me completely, although theoretically I could cover the entire 180° of my balcony with three 60° views. This is quite valid when you have to see only one subject like the ancient Greek temple of Aphaia in Aigina[126] but not when you see such a view which consists of so many parts. To be satisfied I had to shift my head to at least six sectors of 30° and I felt the need to concentrate on smaller angles, both horizontally and vertically; I wanted to see both the monastery on one hillside and the boats in the port. This process of left-right, up and down was endless. I was a prisoner of the open, uncontrolled view. All these experiments were made during the same hours between 4 p.m. and 8 p.m. so that I, myself would be in the same mood and the town in the same conditions. I was gradually induced by the balcony itself and it was here that I could no longer work as the view was too overwhelming. The open sector was so big that I could not catch it as a whole so I was moving my head first to the left and then to the right: how can you accept seeing only a part of the Hermes of Praxiteles if you have come too close to admire its skin? You will move your head up and down or you will step back to admire it totally. I could not step back in my case so I was constantly moving my head to catch the whole subject and my work could not continue any more; it was the end.

The question thus raised was very important: Was the exposure to a very wide angle or the motion of the lively city and its harbor the cause of my confusion? Was the photograph responsible or the movie? It was here that I began to get the direction for an answer when I tried to analyze the cause; I found that it was not the life and movement in the port but the overall picture which attracted my attention most of the time. This perhaps could have been different if a child were in my position — he probably would have been attracted more by the boats moving in the harbor since children like movement. It is also possible that an old lady, if she still could see well at a distance, would select the view of the water-front because the life in the coffee houses of the port could have been an excellent subject for gossip. But such cases should not bother us anyway, no matter what happens, as they are related to the individual observer and I can only speak for my reaction as one example of the impact that optical information can have on our life.

In any case, I thought, I have an opportunity to check both factors separately and this is what I did. I first tried to work on the balcony after dinner. It was late August and the new moon had not yet come up, so the town was dark with the exception of a few lights here and there, and the port was lighted as everyone was coming to it for dinner or for a walk. I had no difficulty working. The lively port covered a small sector of my field of vision and the activity in it was not enough to distract me from my desk. At times I could look down and enjoy the picture, but this was not enough to stop my work as had happened before sunset.

To check the other factor I woke up early in the morning so that I could start working before the sun rose. Now I could see the whole panorama again, but there was no life in the port with the exception of the occasional departure of a small boat. I then had confirmation of my hypothesis. It was the very wide sector of my sight which was giving me so much information that I could not work. It was really impossible.

If there is any question that this whole experience was not only due to the function of the eye but also of the ear, I must state that so as to be sure about this I blocked my ears when trying my fifth location and so it is quite certain that the eye was the only factor in this game. To transmit the proper picture of these last views I have also sketched some of them separately as pieces of the continuum of 180°, since the reader would look at the whole without understanding that no human eye can catch it in its entirety: the whole of Nature consists of separate parts for Anthropos (Man) when he sees and does not think.

## My conclusions

1. It is said that noise is too much information.
2. I agree — but sometimes it is not necessarily noise — it can be beautiful music as in Hydra —- but good music will not allow you to work unless it is low or you are used to it.
3. If the information is not noise or good music but bad music — an industrial area for instance with pollution in the air — then you are not esthetically attracted, you will become angry.
4. No matter what the subject is — too much exposure makes concentration impossible.
5. If our vista is only the sea or the desert, then it will be too vast an area which transmits too little information (unless there are waves which give a sight and sound experience).
6. Final point: Should we avoid views like the ones I have mentioned? No! On the contrary: we should have as many as possible, *but* we must also have the opportunity to control the view when we do not want to be exposed to it.

   — This means that the traditional heavy wall with deep windows or balcony doors had its values.

   — If we open the whole wall (which also has its value) we must be prepared to close it — to control the view for our several kinds of action.

# Appendix 2:

# Thoughts
# on the City for Human Development

## Gordon Tripp

Apart from the symposion members, a certain number of collaborators received the *City for Human Development* document a month before the discussion. **Dr. Gordon Tripp**'s response presents one view that has not been discussed, but is of interest for those who deal with Anthropopolis, and here we present it.

I think that a document of this kind shows at least one danger in terms of a focus for discussion: mainly, where does one begin? It seems like such a comprehensive kind of document and the tendency might be to accept it as gospel rather than take the time to try to sort it out, or respond to particular segments. The other danger would be nitpicking; in other words, arguing or discussing, demonstrating erudition in some particular small segment. Now, both of these could be useful if not over done, but I would guess that the discussion would have to be tightly controlled in order to get the best of both worlds; that is, cogent, concise responses to the document as a whole as well as filling in specific gaps that might relate to the particular areas of expertise of the people involved.

One approach to this document reflects some of my ideas about a way of viewing human beings and, by extension, cities and human settlements. That is to think of a city not only in evolutionary terms, but in philogenetic terms as well, as an extension and manifestation of historical trends occurring in human beings themselves. In other words, does the city historically have a life cycle that is in any way comparable to what we can observe in a generation of men? Now, there has been some discussion relating to Man's evolutionary history as manifested in a capsule form in the development of a particular individual; that is, as prenatal Man recapitulates evolution in its embryological development, perhaps the history of mankind is recapitulated in the postnatal development of a particular individual. As I know you are well aware, this is an extremely fuzzy and unclear speculative area. I felt that some of my thoughts and comments of a speculative nature, although not directly responding to the monograph in a specific or organized way, might be useful to you in some of what I have felt have been your most recent thoughts about cities.

I guess I hesitated somewhat before beginning this because I have the suspicion that you undoubtedly anticipated, perhaps rejected, perhaps incorporated, just such kind of philosophical speculation. On the other hand, sometimes it's useful to hear one's own thoughts expressed by someone else.

We know that Man is born, develops, and dies, that this life cycle is repetitive, constant, universal. It is conservative, that is, it tends to resist change; it tends to set time back in a way, that is, like an instinct, it represents an encapsulated piece of time, an earlier state. How the life cycle is divided depends on who is doing the dividing and for what purposes. I think some of the schema outlined in the monograph represent a good cross section. Psychiatrists, one way, sociologists another, theologians a third, and architects, perhaps a fourth or a synthesis of others. The actual divisions are less important than an agreement upon them so that a systematic approach at least can be begun. When I think of Man, it is in terms of cycles, repetitions, unfoldings of development. There is a very preordained quality about a good deal of what Man does. I suppose in one way this is understandable since only a very small percentage of Man's mental activity is known to him at any one particular time or even in the course of his lifetime, something like ten per cent or less. The great bulk of his mental activity is actually unconscious and what I as a psychiatrist am interested in in a developmental way. Most people are unaware of and do *not* refer to the unconscious when they speak of themselves. They usually mean their conscious perceptions, memories, etc. Since most mental activity is unconscious, is not known, perhaps is not knowable the fact that it functions autonomously, perhaps automatically, is not surprising. The knowable part of Man which, let us say, constitutes less than ten per cent of his mental functioning (by the way, here I am not referring to neurological activity really, but to a more metaphysical concept of mind or person, something like that) is in itself also probably to a large extent automatic, predetermined or programmed. So, when we think of that part of a person that is educable, changeable by direct means, we are actually dealing with a very small percentage of what goes on inside a particular person's head. Now we know that Man's physical development is to a large extent programmed and will unfold reasonably automatically in what is called an average expectable environment. We assume that most of Man's mental activity is also automatic, pre-programmed, certainly extremely sensitive to responding to the external environment, but by definition, probably with limited responses. That is the repertoire is probably limited, at least less than infinite. With most of Man's physical and mental activity and development pre-programmed or repetitive, one could make the assumption that the behavior that Man demonstrates in regard to his environment probably also in most ways is repetitive and programmed, i.e. unconscious. We know that in the functioning of his personality he tends to re-experience himself at earlier times over and over again, and by extension to shape other people or his perception of other people into familiar, archaic molds. We could assume then that he would probably also do this with his institutions, e.g., technology, which is simply an extension of perception and motility; the assumption that he would build his cities in a similar kind of way, I think is probably a valid one.

You've certainly graphically shown that his dwelling, his room, has evolved over time in harmony with his physical capabilities. Can we assume that his larger institutions are also similarly shaped? One could postulate a good many variations, trials and errors, discarded modes that have affected Man's institutions as they have affected Man. Evolution is obviously extremely inefficient, but over a period of time, it is absolutely efficient, so that the evolutionary forces can afford to be patient. As numerous variations of Man's physical form have been tried and discarded or adapted or found to be useful from a survival point of view, I am sure that his institutions also have. The city is one of these.

Since Man tends to recapitulate and re-experience his own development, his species development to a particular point in the individual development of a single man, again what about the institutions? Do the cities show evolutionary development; do we have ways of studying these, of understanding them, speculating about them? Where in the evolutionary scale, that is, in terms of a cyclical development, are Man's cities today? In fact, for that matter, where is Man? Is mankind still in infancy, latency, adolescence, maturity, old age? I am sure again that one can get a variety of viewpoints depending upon who one talks to and how pessimistic or optimistic he might be. Perhaps the easy conceit is that wherever the present is, is adulthood, maturity, although I am not sure that this is indeed the case. The history of mankind is repetitive in that most of pre-history, at least, until Man assumed the upright posture, and had developed a cranial capacity that definitely made him classifiable as *Homo sapiens* could be assumed to be prenatal, and that history up until, say, the birth of Christ was infancy, followed by a long and somewhat turbulent latent period up until the end of the Renaissance when adolescence began. It is in adolescence where we still find ourselves as a species. Now, this is an interesting theory. How verifiable, I am not sure I know. Now, it is certainly true that adolescence can have a multiplicity of faces, but at least from a psychiatric point of view, most psychiatrists feel that there are three or four main tasks of adolescence that everyone can agree upon. The first described perhaps as the drive toward in-dependence, that is, the breaking of old relationships, in most cases, with parents, and the search for new ones. Secondly, a progression towards a mature, sexual identity, and thirdly, reaching some decisions in regard to vocation, education, etc. How one applies them directly to the study of mankind, I am not sure. What are the correlates; what are the similarities-differences, and I suppose basically is there any particular purpose served in viewing mankind and again, by extension, his institutions, does it serve any particularly useful purpose? I am not sure I know. It is interesting though to use this as a somewhat unclear and shaky framework for viewing the behavior of Man in groups, mankind in general, certainly cities as an extension of Man.

The one very clear similarity between an adolescent and the city is that they are both in crisis, and they are both in crisis most of the time. They are also given to easy and somewhat tenuous identifications with attractive personal-ities, simplistic all-or-none, black and white answers and a desire to conform to the prevailing peer pressure. The analogy, of course, becomes difficult because in order to carry it out, certain anthropormorphicizing (!) of cities is required. Obviously, this is fraught with difficulty. The question of value in this perspective might be that it gives us at least grounds for a certain kind of optimism.

The resolution of adolescence can be diffusion, a disaster, but it can also be progression, maturity, and stability. Obviously, the outcome of both mankind and his institutions is at this point in doubt. If one takes a different point of view that, no indeed, Man is a declining species, in other words, we are entering senescence or old age, there is not much ground for optimism and this point of view would say, "oh no, the decay, confusion, and chaos in our cities is only a reflection of that stage in the historical life cycle." I obviously take a different point of view.

Is there other additional evidence that might be marshalled to support an argument that Man's institutions, that is, cities as well as mankind follow definitive developmental patterns, patterns that are laid down in an evolutionary manner over time? It does seem to me apparent that evolution, that is, development over time flows throughout whatever Man has studied. Atoms and molecules evolved, developed in fractions of seconds. Galaxies, universes over immensities of time. The earth itself develops, stars have a life cycle, animals, men. That this is a universal phenomenon probably is generally agreed on, and I think I mean more here than just the passage of time or development per se, but a directed change over time shaped by incredible complexities to no particular end.

The two extremes of this phenomenon, that is, say, a species evolution or the evolution of a solar system have an infinite vagueness to them, that is, they seem to be not knowable and moving toward ends that are certainly unknown. An individual, on the other hand, who represents an encapsulated moment of evolution is extremely determined and consequently predictable. We have a hard time understanding, following, knowing vicissitudes of an individual man, which becomes more difficult when we think of mankind and even more difficult when we think of Man's institutions in developmental evolutionary models. Again, where are we on the time scale? How do we determine this? How do we draw the correlates?

My own particular bias is that the closest we will come to the answer to this question will be in the study of Man. Initially, Man the individual in the present and by extension groups of men, Man over time and then his institutions which I have a feeling reflect quite accurately the particular stages of the development of mankind. To know something about the individual, and his own particular life cycle will allow perhaps tenuous hypotheses to be drawn concerning mankind and Man's institutions.

In reflecting back on what I've said, I am wondering if perhaps I haven't sounded a somewhat subtle, pessimistic note throughout this. That is, if indeed Man is unconsciously motivated, unconsciously repetitive, conservative in the changeability of his cycles, of what use, then indeed, is planning, studying, classifying, attempting to change and order the future? Why not sit back and watch nature take its course? That might be an easy way.

I'm inclined to think another given for Man is his need for action, his need to try and shape, even his need to try and change in the face of a very small part that he can effect. It's what I said earlier about the unconscious motivations and actions of Man; obviously, it would also apply to what's happening with the cities. We might even be left with, say, only five per cent of the factors affecting cities knowable or affectable. That, to my mind, is not grounds for discouragement, but a challenge for action.

I'm sure you've found all this disconnected and disjointed, speculative, hopefully entertaining, and perhaps even useful. But it in itself is a testimony to the monograph, *City for Human Development* in that it has stimulated and awakened in me a whole host of theories, questions, ideas, that I am sure was at least part of your purpose in writing it.

# Glossary

*Anthropos:* For years I thought that "Anthropos" (the ancient Greek word for human) would be better than the English word "Man" to describe human beings or mankind, because the word "Man" is confused also with the masculine gender. Now the American Anthropological Association has passed a resolution (November 1973) and has taken the following decision: "In view of the fact that the founders of the discipline of anthropology were men socialized in a male-dominated society which systematically excluded women from the professions and thereby prevented their participation in the formation of our discipline, including its terminology; and being trained as anthropologists to understand that language reinforces and perpetuates the prevailing values and socio-economic patterns that contribute to the oppression of women.

We move that the American Anthropological Association:

a. urge anthropologists to become aware in their writing and teaching that their wide use of the term "man" as generic for the species is conceptually confusing (since "man" is also the term for the male) and that it be replaced by more comprehensive terms such as "people" and "human beings" which include both sexes;

b. further urge that members of the Association select textbooks that have eliminated this form of sexism which has become increasingly offensive to more and more women both within and outside the disciplines."

I agree with this basic goal and I change the word Man to Anthropos, meaning all humans no matter what their sex, age, etc. which I prefer in some cases in relation to the words "human", "human beings", "mankind", etc. as it is more symbolic like Nature and Society.

*Dynapolis:* The dynamically growing city or "polis", in contrast to the traditional static city of the past; completely unknown before the 18th century.

*Ecumenopolis:* The coming city that will, together with the corresponding open land which is indispensable for Anthropos (Man), cover the entire earth as a continuous network of urbanized areas forming a universal settlement.

*Ekistic elements:* The five elements which compose the human settlements: Nature, Anthropos (Man), Society, Shells and Networks.

*Ekistic Logarithmic Scale (ELS):* A classification of settlements according to their size, presented on the basis of a logarithmic scale, running from Anthropos (Man) (unit 1) as the smallest unit of measurement to the whole earth (unit 15). The ekistic logarithmic scale can be presented graphically, showing area or number of people corresponding to each unit, etc., so that it can be used as a basis for the measurement and classification of many dimensions in human settlements.

*Ekistics:* The science of human settlements. It conceives the human settlement as a living organism having its own laws and, through the study of the evolution of human settlements from their most primitive phase to megalopolis and Ecumenopolis, develops the interdisciplinary approach necessary to solve its problems.

*Ekistic Unit:* A classification of parts or whole human settlements, starting from unit 1 corresponding to Anthropos (Man) and ending with unit 15 corresponding to Ecumenopolis. From unit 4 which corresponds to community class I to unit 15 which corresponds to community class XII, the ekistic units coincide with the classification of human communities expressed in the ekistic logarithmic scale (ELS).

*Eperopolis:* Corresponding to ekistic unit 14 and community class XI, with a population of five thousand million, eperopolis replaces the old term "urbanized continent". It is derived from the Greek words "Ηπειρος meaning continent and πόλις meaning city.

*Great Lakes Megalopolis (GLM):* The megalopolitan formation which is emerging around the Great Lakes of North America involving parts of the States of Wisconsin, Illinois, Indiana, Michigan, Ohio, Pennsylvania and New York and a strip of the provinces of Ontario contiguous with the Great Lakes and the St. Lawrence Seaway. This main part of GLM had in 1960 a population of 36 million, within an area of about 89.2 thousand square miles. It is encompassed by a secondary and outer zone, with about 36 million inhabitants within an area of 457.6 thousand square miles, extending into the states of Minnesota, Iowa, Missouri, Kentucky, West Virginia and Vermont, in addition to covering more area of the states and provinces mentioned above.

*House, and housegroup:* These terms replace "dwelling" and "dwelling group", corresponding to ekistic units 3 and 4, with a population of four and 40 people respectively. Housegroup corresponds to community class I.

*Isolation of Dimensions and Elimination of Alternatives method (IDEA):* The gradual isolation of dimensions and the selection, by elimination, of the alternatives, conceived along the isolated dimensions, that satisfy certain ekistic criteria. It is an attempt to eliminate the arbitrariness in the search of the many-dimensional parameter space of the urban system for the optimum alternative.

*Kinetic field:* The distance Anthropos (Man) can move within a certain period by walking, by using animals or by using vehicles.

*Megalopolis:* A greater urbanized area resulting from the merging of metropolises and cities into one urban system. Its population is calculated in tens of millions. It is distinct from the metropolis, either because its population exceeds ten million, in which case it also covers a vast surface area, or because it has incorporated more than one metropolis. Term used since ancient Greece when the small city of Megalopolis was created in Arcadia. Jean Gottmann gave a special meaning to this ancient term in 1961 in his book *Megalopolis, the Urbanized North-eastern Seaboard of the United States*, a 20th Century Fund Study, the M.I.T. Press, Massachusetts Institute of Technology, Cambridge, Mass., 1961.

*Metropolis:* A major, multi-center urban area with more than 50,000 people incorporating other small settlements both urban and rural, growing dynamically to sizes as high as ten million people. The average population of such settlements between 50,000 and ten million inhabitants is of the order of 2.5 million, while about one half of these settlements have a population varying between 50,000 and 100,000.

*Nature:* The natural environment of Anthropos (Man) as it exists before he

374

starts remodelling it by cultivation and construction. It provides the foundation upon which the settlement is created and the frame within which it can function.

*Networks:* Anthropos- (Man-) made systems which facilitate the functioning of the settlements, such as roads, water supply, electricity.

*Shells:* All types of structures within which Anthropos (Man) lives and carries out his various functions.

*Sidewalk:* We must eliminate this word from our vocabularies, because if we keep using it we will have to recognize that Anthropos (Man) is a slave who has to be put on the side.

*Society:* Human society with all its characteristics, needs and problems, where every individual is examined only as one unit of it.

*Strider:* Development phase five extending from 2.5 to 5 years. This is also called the Play-Age Phase. The strider increases his contacts beyond the small neighborhood, though he now moves freely within his neighborhood, and joins a playgroup.

*Toddler:* Development phase four extending from 16 to 30 months. At this time the toddler moves within the house in a natural independent way, and beyond the house in a natural dependent way.

*Ekistic Logarithmic Scale (ELS)*

Throughout this book I use the ekistic logarithmic scale which is the foundation for classification of all human settlements on the basis of their population. More information on the ekistic logarithmic scale can be found in my book *Ekistics, an Introduction to the Science of Human Settlements*, p. 29, Fig. 22, p. 31.

Throughout the long years during which this scale was used I have been working on nomenclature and finally have concluded that the most proper names are:

1. Anthropos — instead of Man (as explained in the Glossary)
2. room
3. house — instead of dwelling
4. housegroup — instead of dwelling group
5. small neighborhood
6. neighborhood
7. small polis — instead of small town
8. polis — instead of town
9. small metropolis — instead of large city
10. metropolis
11. small megalopolis — instead of conurbation
12. megalopolis
13. small eperopolis — instead of urbanized region
14. eperopolis — instead of urbanized continent
15. Ecumenopolis

# Bibliography

**Aldridge, John W.,** *In the Country of the Young*, Harper's Magazine Press, New York, 1970.

**Calhoun, John B.,** "Environmental Control Over Four Major Paths of Mammalian Evolution", in *Genetic and Environmental Influences on Behaviour*, Oliver & Boyd, Edinburgh, 1968, pp. 65-93.

**Calhoun, John B.,** "Population Density and Social Pathology", in SCIENTIFIC AMERICAN, February 1962, pp. 139-146.

**Calhoun, John B.,** "Space and Scale: Insights from Animal Studies Relating to the Architecture and Contents of Housing for the Aged", in *Spatial Behavior of Older People*, Ann Arbor, Institute of Gerontology, University of Michigan, 1970, pp. 182-193.

**Calhoun, John B.,** "Space and the Strategy of Life", Moving Frontiers of Science Lecture No. 3. Annual Meeting of the American Association for the Advancement of Science, Dallas, Texas, 1968. Published in *Behavior and Environment: the Use of Space by Animals and Men*, Plenum, New York, 1971. Abridged version published in EKISTICS, June 1970, pp. 425-437.

**Doxiadis, C.A.,** *Architecture in Transition*, Oxford University Press, New York, 1963.

**Doxiadis, C.A.,** *Urban Renewal and the Future of the American City*, prepared for the National Association of Housing and Redevelopment Officials, Public Administration Service, Chicago, Illinois, 1966.

**Doxiadis, C.A.,** *Between Dystopia and Utopia*, Trinity College Press, Hartford, Conn., 1966 (out of print).

**Doxiadis, C.A.,** *Ekistics, an Introduction to the Science of Human Settlements*, Oxford University Press, New York, 1968.

**Doxiadis, C.A.,** *Emergence and Growth of an Urban Region, the Developing*

*Urban Detroit Area*, Vol. 1, 1966; Vol. 2, 1967; Vol. 3, 1970. A project of the Detroit Edison Company, Wayne State University and Doxiadis Associates under the chairmanship of W.L. Cisler, Chairman of the Board, The Detroit Edison Company, directed by C.A. Doxiadis, and published by the Detroit Edison Company, Detroit, Michigan.

**Doxiadis, C.A.,** *Architectural Space in Ancient Greece*, trans. by Jaqueline Tyrwhitt from the German original *Raumordnung im griechischen Städtebau*, M.I.T. Press, Cambridge, Mass., 1972.

**Doxiadis, C.A.,** *The Two-Headed Eagle*, Lycabettus Press, Athens, 1972.

**Doxiadis, C.A.,** *The Great Urban Crimes We Permit by Law*, Lycabettus Press, Athens, 1973.

**Dubos, R.,** *Mirage of Health: Utopias, Progress and Biological Change*, Harper and Bros., New York, 1959.

**Dubos, R.,** *Only One Earth*, Penguin Books, Harmondsworth, Middlesex, 1972.

**Dubos, R.,** "Science and Man's Nature", DAEDALUS, Winter 1965, pp. 223-244.

**Dubos, R.,** *So Human an Animal*, Scribners, New York, 1968.

**Dubos, R.,** *A God Within*, Scribners, New York, 1972.

**Dubos, R.,** *Man Adapting*, Yale University Press, New Haven, Conn., 1965.

**Dubos, R.,** *Man, Medicine and Environment*, Praeger, New York, 1968.

**Erikson, E.H.,** *Childhood and Society*, Norton, New York, 1960.

**Erikson, E.H.,** "Ego Development and Historical Change", *Psychoanalytic Study of the Child*, International University Press, 1959, Vol. 2, pp. 359-396.

**Erikson, E.H.,** *Identity, Youth and Crisis*, Norton, New York, 1968.

**Erikson, E.H.,** (ed.) *Youth, Change and Challenge*, Basic Books, New York, 1963.

**Erikson, E.H.,** *Identity and the Life Cycle*, International University Press, New York, 1967.

**Erikson, E.H.,** *Insight and Responsibility*, Norton, New York, 1964.

**Gabor, D.,** *Innovations: Scientific, Technological and Social*, Oxford University Press, London, 1970.

**Gabor, D.,** *Inventing the Future*, Secker & Warburg, London, 1963.

**Hall, Edward T.,** *The Silent Language*, Doubleday Co. Inc, New York, 1959.

**Hall, Edward T.,** *The Hidden Dimension*, Doubleday & Co. Inc., New York, 1966.

**Holden, Constance,** "Le Vaudreuil: French Experiment in Urbanism Without Tears", SCIENCE, Vol. 174, No. 4004, October 1, 1971, pp. 39-42.

**Huizinga, Johan,** *Homo Ludens: a Study of the Play Element in Culture*, Beacon Press, Boston, Mass., 1955.

**Lorenz, Konrad,** *Evolution and Modification of Behavior*, University of Chicago Press, Chicago, Illinois, 1965.

**Lorenz, Konrad,** *King Solomon's Ring,* Methuen, London, 1964.

**Lorenz, Konrad,** *On Aggression,* Methuen, London, 1966.

**Lorenz, Konrad,** *Studies in Animal and Human Behaviour,* 2 volumes, Methuen, London, 1970-71.

**Lourie, R.S., et al.,** *Early Child Care; the New Perspective,* Atherton, New York, 1968.

**Lourie, R.S., et al.** "The First Three Years of Life: an Overview of a New Frontier of Psychiatry", AMERICAN JOURNAL OF PSYCHIATRY, May 1971, pp. 33-39.

**Mead, M.,** "Anthropology and Ekistics" and "Neighborhood and Human Needs", EKISTICS, February 1966, pp. 88-94, pp. 124-126.

**Mead, M.,** *Coming of Age in Samoa,* The New American Library, New York, 1958.

**Mead, M.,** *Culture and Commitment,* Natural History Press, Garden City, N.Y., 1970.

**Mead, M.,** "Research with Human Beings", EKISTICS, July 1969, pp. 4-9.

**Toynbee, Arnold,** *A Study of History,* Oxford University Press, London, 1935-1961, 12 volumes.

**Waddington, C.H.,** "The Basic Ideas of Biology", *Towards a Theoretical Biology-Vol. 1, Prolegomena,* Edinburgh University Press, Edinburgh, 1968.

**Waddington, C.H.,** "Progressive Self-stabilizing Systems in Biology and Social Affairs", EKISTICS, December 1966, pp. 402-406.

**Waddington, C.H.,** "Biology and Human Environment", EKISTICS, February 1966, pp. 90-95.

**Waddington, C.H.,** (panelist) *Biology and the History of the Future,* IUBS/UNESCO Symposium, Edinburgh University Press, Edinburgh, 1972.

**Waddington, C.H.,** *Biology for the Modern World,* Barnes & Noble, New York, 1962.

**Waddington, C.H.,** *The Ethical Animal,* Atheneum, New York, 1961.

**Waddington, C.H.,** *How Animals Develop,* Harper, New York, 1962.

**Waddington, C.H.,** "The Importance of Biological Ways of Thought", *The Place of Value in a World of Facts: Nobel Symposium 14,* Wiley, New York, 1970, pp. 95-104.

**Waddington, C.H.,** *The Nature of Life,* Allen & Unwin, London, 1963.

# Notes

For years I thought that "Anthropos" (the ancient Greek word for human) would be better than the English word "Man" to describe human beings or mankind, because the word "Man" is also confused with the masculine gender. Now the American Anthropological Association has passed a resolution (November 1973) and has taken the following decision: "In view of the fact that the founders of the discipline of anthropology were men socialized in a male-dominated society which systematically excluded women from the professions and thereby prevented their participation in the formation of our discipline, including its terminology; and being trained as anthropologists to understand that language reinforces and perpetuates the prevailing values and socio-economic patterns that contribute to the oppression of women.

We move that the American Anthropological Association:
a. urge anthropologists to become aware in their writing and teaching that their wide use of the term "man" as generic for the species is conceptually confusing (since "man" is also the term for the male) and that it be replaced by more comprehensive terms such as "people" and "human beings" which include both sexes;
b. further urge that members of the Association select textbooks that have eliminated this form of sexism which has become increasingly offensive to more and more women both within and outside the disciplines."
I agree with this basic goal and I change the word Man to Anthropos, meaning all humans no matter what their sex, age, etc. which I prefer in some cases in relation to the words "human", "human beings", "mankind" etc. as it is more symbolic, like Nature and Society.

| No. | Page | |
|-----|------|---|
| 2 | 4 | Jacques Monod, *Le Hasard et la Nécessité*, Le Seuil, Paris, 1970. |
| 3 | 5 | C.A. Doxiadis, "Confessions of a Criminal", EKISTICS, Vol. 32, No. 191, October 1971, pp. 249-254.<br>C.A. Doxiadis, *The Great Urban Crimes We Permit by Law*, Lycabettus Press, Athens, 1973. |
| 4 | 6 | C.A. Doxiadis, *Ekistics, an Introduction to the Science of Human Settlements*, Oxford University Press, New York, 1968, pp. 212-213, 364-371, 467-479. |
| 5 | 6 | Werner Jager, *Paideia*, Oxford University Press, New York, 1963-1965. |
| 6 | 7 | C.A. Doxiadis, *The Two-Headed Eagle*, Lycabettus Press, Athens, 1972.<br>See also EKISTICS, Vol. 33, No. 198, May 1972, pp. 406-420. |
| 7 | 7 | These are projects of Doxiadis Associates International, a company of Consultants on Development and Ekistics created in 1951 and operating in 40 countries. |
| 8 | 9 | The application of such ideas started with the post-war reconstruction of Greece (1945-1951) and then in the development efforts of several countries (1951-1972).<br>In a specific way and under this title, the idea of a city for human development was presented to medical, technical and other groups of a broader range on many occasions, some of which are mentioned herebelow:<br>Hillcrest School, Washington D.C., February 29, 1968.<br>University of Washington, Seattle, Washington, March 20, 1968.<br>International Congress of Pediatrics, Mexico D.F., December 2, 1968.<br>American Council on Education, Denver, Colorado, October 10, 1968.<br>"A City for Human Development", a symposion at the State University of New York, April 28-29, 1970. |

| No. | Page | |
|-----|------|---|

This idea has been presented in the seminars of the Athens Center of Ekistics during the academic years 1965-1966 and 1966-1967, and during the Athens Ekistics Month in 1967. EKISTICS, Vol. 25, No. 151, June 1968, pp. 374-394.

9    11    Alexis Carrel, *Man the Unknown*, Hamish Hamilton, London, 1961, pp. 15-39.

10    12    C.A. Doxiadis, *Architecture in Transition*, Oxford University Press, New York, 1963.
C.A. Doxiadis, *Ekistics, an Introduction to the Science of Human Settlements*, 1968.

11    12    C.A. Doxiadis, *Ekistics, an Introduction to the Science of Human Settlements*, pp. 21, 34-35.

12    20    C.A. Doxiadis, "Ekistics: an Attempt for a Scientific Approach to the Problems of Human Settlements", *Science & Technology and the Cities*, a Compilation of Papers Prepared for the Tenth Meeting of the Panel on Science and Technology, U.S. House of Representatives, U.S. Government Printing Office, Washington D.C., February 1969, pp. 9-32.

13    20    Jean Gottmann, *Megalopolis, the Urbanized North-eastern Seaboard of the United States*, M.I.T. Press, Cambridge, Mass., 1961.
John Papaioannou, *Megalopolises: a First Definition*, Athens Center of Ekistics Research Report No. 2, 1967.

14    21    G. Clarke and S. Piggott, *Prehistoric Societies*, Hutchinson, London, 1965, p. 75.

15    21    L. van der Post, *The Lost World of the Kalahari*, Penguin Books, Baltimore, Md., 1962, p. 25 (a paraphrase).

16    24    C.A. Doxiadis, "Ekistics, the Science of Human Settlements", SCIENCE, Vol. 170, October 23, 1970, p. 402. Copyright 1970 by the American Association for the Advancement of Science.

No.    Page

See also EKISTICS, Vol. 33, No. 196, March 1972, where the whole question of the formation of the room is handled.
See also EKISTICS, Vol. 36, No. 215, October 1973, pp. 277-281.

17    25    C.A. Doxiadis, *The Two-Headed Eagle*, pp. 26-29.

18    25    C.A. Doxiadis, *Ekistics, an Introduction to the Science of Human Settlements*, pp. 190, 193-199.

19    28    Aristotle, *Politics*, 1252b, trans., H. Rackham, I. i. 8, Loeb Classical Library, William Heinemann Ltd., London, 1959, p.9.

20    32    C.A. Doxiadis, *Ecumenopolis, the Settlement of the Future*, Athens Center of Ekistics Research Report No. 1, 1967.
John Papaioannou, *Megalopolises: a First Definition*, Athens Center of Ekistics Research Report No. 2, 1967.

21    40    *Dwarfs:* The dwarfs, or gnomes (Kabouters in Dutch) are one of 28 political parties which contested the April 28, 1971 general elections in the Netherlands. Though they failed to win any seats, they are interesting for being a "protest" movement, limited almost entirely to young people, and opposed to such features of contemporary society as environmental pollution, strangulation of cities by the motor car and high-rise housing. See *Keesing's Contemporary Archives*, Keesing's Publications Ltd. (of London), Bristol, May 29 - June 5, 1971, p. 24633.

22    42    C.P. Cavafy, "The City", Edmund Keeley and Philip Sherrard trans., *Collected Poems of C.P. Cavafy*, Hogarth Press, Ltd., London, 1970.

23    47    See note 9, p. 204.

24    47    Ibid, p. 214.

25    47    C.A. Doxiadis, "Ancient Greek Settlements", EKISTICS, Vol. 31, No. 182, January 1971, pp. 4-21, EKISTICS, Vol. 33, No. 195, February 1972, pp. 76-89, EKISTICS, Vol. 35, No. 206, January

No.    Page

1973, pp. 7-16.

C.A. Doxiadis, *Architectural Space in Ancient Greece*, trans. Jaqueline Tyrwhitt from the German original *Raumordnung im griechischen Städtebau*, M.I.T. Press, Cambridge, Mass., 1972.

26    48    Burrhus F. Skinner, *Walden Two*, Macmillan Co., New York, 1969, and *Beyond Freedom and Dignity*, Alfred A. Knopf, New York, 1971. Copyright 1971 by B.F. Skinner.

27    49    Quote from Teilhard de Chardin in Theodosius Dobzhansky, *Mankind Evolving: the Evolution of the Human Species*, Yale University Press, New Haven, Conn., 1962, p. 348.

28    51    Edward T. Hall, *The Silent Language*, Doubleday, New York, 1959 and *The Hidden Dimension*, Doubleday, New York, 1966.

29    51    C.A. Doxiadis, *Ekistics, an Introduction to the Science of Human Settlements*, pp. 300-302.

30    51    Claude Cuénot, *Teilhard de Chardin*, Collection Microcosme, Le Seuil, Paris, 1962, p. 91.

31    52    C.H. Waddington, "Space for Development", EKISTICS, Vol. 32, No. 191, October 1971, p. 268.

32    52    Quote by Margaret Mead at the Symposion on the "City for Human Development", Athens 1972.

33    52    Erik H. Erikson, "Notes on the Life Cycle", EKISTICS, Vol. 32, No. 191, October 1971, p. 260.

34    53    C.A. Doxiadis, *The Two-Headed Eagle*, 1972.

35    54    Presented by Robert Aldrich, International Seminar on Ekistics, the 1971 Athens Ekistics Month, July 19, 1971.

36    56    The poem "Confucius" from *The Analects of Confucius* was

No.　Page

translated by Arthur Waley and copyrighted in 1939. It is reprinted by permission of the Macmillan Company and Allen Unwin Ltd. of London. "Song of a Life" is from the *Penguin Book of Chinese Verse* and is reprinted by permission of Penguin Books, Ltd., Harmondsworth, Middlesex, England.

37　56　"Human Development and Public Health", World Health Organization Technical Report Series, No. 485, Geneva, WHO, 1972, p. 8.
Jerome Hellmuth, ed., *Exceptional Infant*, Vol. 1, *The Normal Infant*, "Manual for COLR Research Form of Bayley's Scales of Motor Development", PS-2, Rev. 1-61, pp. 44-50.
Laura L. Dittmann, ed., *Early Child Care: the New Perspectives*, Caroline A. Chandler, Reginald S. Lourie, Anne DeHuff Peters, conts., "Appendix B", Atherton Press, New York, 1968, pp. 374-377.
L.J. Stone and J. Church, *Childhood and Adolescent*, 2nd ed., Random House, New York, 1968.

38　56　C.R. Markham, *The Incas of Peru*, London, 1910, pp. 161-162.

39　56　"As You Like It", from *The Complete Works of Shakespeare*, II:vii 127-176, Odhams Press Ltd., Basil Blackwell, England, 1947, p. 622.

40　62　C.A. Doxiadis, "Man's Movement and His City", SCIENCE, Vol. 162, October 18, 1968, pp. 326-334. Copyright 1968 by the American Association for the Advancement of Science.

41　62　"Little Houdini", Associated Press, INTERNATIONAL HERALD TRIBUNE, August 21-22, 1971.

42　62　C.A. Doxiadis, "Man's Movement and His City", pp. 326-334.

43　62　See note 25.

44　63　Testimony of C.A. Doxiadis before the Committee on Com-

| No. | Page | |
|-----|------|---|
| | | merce, U.S. Senate, *National Transportation Act*, S.924 and S.2425 "To Develop a Comprehensive National Transportation System", U.S. Government Printing Office, Washington D.C., 1970, pp. 153-161. |
| 45 | 67 | "Busing: an American Dilemma", NEWSWEEK, March 13, 1972, pp. 20-21. |
| 46 | 69 | Pablo Neruda, "To the Foot from its Child", *A New Decade (Poems: 1958-1967)*, Ben Belitt and Alastair Reid, trans., Grove Press, Inc., New York, 1969. |
| 47 | 69 | Quote by Erik H. Erikson at the International Seminar on Ekistics, the 1971 Athens Ekistics Month, July 1971, Athens, Greece. |
| 48 | 70 | Photograph by Jean Amoyet. |
| 49 | 73 | Reginald S. Lourie, "The First Three Years of Life: An Overview of a New Frontier of Psychiatry", AMERICAN JOURNAL OF PSYCHIATRY, 127:11, May 1971, p. 1457-1463. Copyright 1971 the American Psychiatric Association. |
| 50 | 78 | Erik H. Erikson, 1971 Athens Ekistics Month. |
| 51 | 78 | Edward T. Hall, "Architectural Implications of the Thermal Qualities of the Human Skin", EKISTICS, Vol. 33, No. 198, May 1972, pp. 352-354. <br> R. Bowling Barnes, "Thermography of the Human Body", SCIENCE, Vol. 140, May 24, 1963. <br> Richard L. Currier, *Sentic Communication in a Greek Island Culture.* Paper presented in December 1971 at the Annual Meeting of the American Association for the Advancement of Science as part of the AAAS Symposium: *Sentics, Brain Function, and Sources of Human Values.* |
| 52 | 79 | "Europe Today: a Survey of European Opinion Leaders", Section 2, the Environment Table, THE TIMES, January 14, 1972. Reproduced from The Times by permission. |

386

| No. | Page | |
|-----|------|---|
| 53 | 84 | Drawing by Anna Karydaki, 14 years old, reproduced in EPI-KAIRA, Athens, Greece, No. 284, January 11, 1974, p. 52. |
| 54 | 85 | Carl H. Kraeling and Robert M. Adams eds., *The City Invincible*, University of Chicago Press, Chicago, 1960, p. 93. |
| 55 | 87 | "Looking Backward", TIME, January 24, 1972, p. 48. |
| 56 | 87 | Jean D'Ormesson, "C'est toujours dans l'enfance de l'artiste qu'il faut chercher le secret de son oeuvre", PARIS MATCH, 1973 |
| 57 | 92 | "Psychologists' Report Finds New Town in West Germany Boring to Children", THE NEW YORK TIMES, May 9, 1971. ©1971 by the New York Times Company. Reprinted by permission. |
| 58 | 92 | Duncan Spencer, "Defiant Children of Divis Flats", THE WASHINGTON SUNDAY STAR (evening ed.), February 6, 1972. |
| 59 | 96 | Ben A. Franklin, "Vista Work Said to Turn Youths to the Left", INTERNATIONAL HERALD TRIBUNE, May 25, 1971. |
| 60 | 103 | C.A. Doxiadis, *Ekistics, an Introduction to the Science of Human Settlements*, pp. 27-34. |
| 61 | 111 | Henri Mondor, *Vie de Mallarmé*, Gallimard, Paris, 1941, pp. 684. |
| 62 | 115 | See note 3. |
| 63 | 116 | Nigel Calder, *The Mind of Man*, Viking Press, New York, 1970, p. 35. Copyright © 1970 by Nigel Calder. Reprinted by permission of The Viking Press, Inc. |
| 64 | 117 | See note 37, WHO, p. 124. |
| 65 | 117 | Erik H. Erikson, "Notes on the Life Cycle", p. 261. |
| 66 | 117 | See note 49. |

| No. | Page | |
|-----|------|---|
| 67 | 117 | Quote by Reginald S. Lourie at the International Seminar on Ekistics, the 1971 Athens Ekistics Month, July 19, 1971. |
| 68 | 117 | Betty Werther, "The Czechs' Answer to Dr. Spock", INTERNATIONAL HERALD TRIBUNE, December 19, 1973. |
| 69 | 120 | Lee Salk, *What Every Child Would Like His Parents to Know*, David McKay Co., Inc., New York, 1972, pp. 8-9. |
| 70 | 120 | "Blue is Beautiful", TIME, September 17, 1973, pp. 44-45. |
| 71 | 120 | B.E. McKenzie, R.H. Day, "Object Distance as a Determinant of Visual Fixation in Early Infancy", SCIENCE, Vol. 178, December 8, 1972, pp. 1108-1110. |
| 72 | 120 | Edward M. Swartz, *Toys That Don't Care*, Gambit, Boston, 1971. |
| 73 | 120 | Erik H. Erikson, "Notes on the Life Cycle", pp. 260-265. |
| 74 | 122 | Robert Escarpit, "Ecologie", LE MONDE, Paris, December 28, 1971. |
| 75 | 129 | Erik H. Erikson, 1971 Athens Ekistics Month. |
| 76 | 131 | Nigel Calder, *The Mind of Man*, pp. 33-34 and diagram by Donald Hebb. |
| 77 | 135 | Photograph by Alain Le Boulch. |
| 78 | 140 | The International Seminar on Ekistics, the 1971 Athens Ekistics Month, July 19, 1971. |
| 79 | 140 | C.A. Doxiadis, *The Great Urban Crimes We Permit by Law*, 1973. |
| 80 | 140 | Erik H. Erikson, "Notes on the Life Cycle", p. 263. |

| No. | Page | |
|-----|------|---|
| 81 | 145 | Quote by a member of the Advisory Council on Human Settlements of Doxiadis Associates, Inc., Washington D.C., June 1970. |
| 82 | 149 | Erik H. Erikson, "Notes on the Life Cycle", p. 263. |
| 83 | 151 | Michael Grant, *Cities of Vesuvius*, Macmillan, New York, 1971, p. 60. |
| 84 | 153 | Photograph by Albert Declerck. |
| 85 | 157 | Erik H. Erikson, *Childhood and Society*, rev. ed., Norton C. Norton, New York, 1964. C.A. Doxiadis, "The Formation of the Human Room", EKISTICS, Vol. 33, No. 196, March 1972, pp. 218-229. |
| 86 | 159 | See note 16, pp. 393-404. |
| 87 | 159 | "Citizens and City Centers", THE OBSERVER, London, November 13, 1971. |
| 88 | 159 | C.A. Doxiadis, *Urban Renewal and the Future of the American City*, prepared for the National Association of Housing and Redevelopment Officials, Public Administration Service, Chicago, 1966. |
| 89 | 163 | Quote by Margaret Mead from the International Seminar on Ekistics, the 1971 Athens Ekistics Month. |
| 90 | 163 | Erik H. Erikson, "Notes on the Life Cycle", p. 264. |
| 91 | 165 | C.A. Doxiadis, "Cities in Crisis and the University", *The Future Academic Community*, ed. by John Caffrey, American Council on Education, Washington D.C., 1969, pp. 305-327. |
| 92 | 167 | *Campus Planning in an Urban Area: a Master Plan for Rensselaer Polytechnic Institute*, prepared by Doxiadis Associates, Inc., Praeger Publishers, Inc., New York, 1971. |

| No. | Page | |
|-----|------|---|
| 93 | 167 | Margaret Mead, "Cross Cultural Significances of Space", EKISTICS, Vol. 32, No. 191, October 1971, pp. 271-272. |
| 94 | 167 | See note 12. |
| 95 | 167 | C.A. Doxiadis, *Urban America and the Role of Industry*, report for the National Association of Manufacturers, January 1971, p. 47. |
| 96 | 167 | C.A. Doxiadis, *Emergence and Growth of an Urban Region, the Developing Urban Detroit Area*, Vol. 1, 1966; Vol. 2, 1967; Vol. 3, 1970. A project of the Detroit Edison Company, Wayne State University and Doxiadis Associates under the chairmanship of W.L. Cisler, Chairman of the Board, the Detroit Edison Company, directed by C.A. Doxiadis, and published by the Detroit Edison Company, Detroit, Michigan. |
| 97 | 167 | C.A. Doxiadis, "The Future of Human Settlements", Nobel Symposium 14, *The Place of Value in a World of Facts*, Arne Tiselius and Sam Nilsson eds., John Wiley & Sons, Inc., New York, 1970, pp. 326-327. |
| 98 | 167 | Margaret Mead, "Cross Cultural Significances of Space", pp. 271-272. |
| 99 | 169 | Erik H. Erikson, "Notes on the Life Cycle", p. 265. |
| 100 | 171 | C.A. Doxiadis, "Confessions of a Criminal", EKISTICS, Vol. 32, No. 191, October 1971, pp. 249-254. |
| 101 | 171 | Ibid, and, C.A. Doxiadis, *The Great Urban Crimes We Permit by Law*, 1973. |
| 102 | 175 | See note 96, Vols. 2 and 3. |
| 103 | 175 | See note 25. |

| No. | Page | |
|---|---|---|
| 104 | 175 | Quote by René Dubos from the California Institute of Technology Conference, Pasadena, California, October 20, 1970. |
| 105 | 191 | C.A. Doxiadis, "The Need for Courage and Order", lecture delivered to the International Council for Philosophy and Humanistic Studies, Salzburg, Austria, September 23, 1971. |
| 106 | 192 | C.A. Doxiadis, *The Two-Headed Eagle*, 1972. |
| 107 | 192 | "A City for Human Development", a Symposion at the State University of New York, April 28-29, 1970. |
| 108 | 192 | C.A. Doxiadis, "Ekistic Synthesis of Structure and Form", EKISTICS, Vol. 26, No. 155, October 1968, pp. 395-415. C.A. Doxiadis, "Social Synthesis in Human Settlements", EKISTICS, Vol. 28, No. 167, October 1969, pp. 236-240. C.A. Doxiadis, "A Methodological Approach to Networks", EKISTICS, Vol. 30, No. 179, October 1970, pp. 331-336. See also note 12. |
| 109 | 194 | C.A. Doxiadis, *The Two-Headed Eagle*, 1972. |
| 110 | 199 | Kathleen Kenyon, *Archaeology in the Holy Land*, Praeger Publishers, New York, 1960. |
| 111 | 199 | George Mylonas, "A Common Form of Settlement in Mycenean Times", EKISTICS, Vol. 33, No. 195, February 1972, pp. 97-98. |
| 112 | 199 | See note 96. |
| 113 | 201 | Igor Stravinsky, *Poetics of Music in the Form of Six Lessons*, Harvard University Press, Cambridge, Mass., 1970, p. 89. |
| 114 | 204 | C.A. Doxiadis, *The Great Urban Crimes We Permit by Law*, pp. 25-30. |
| 115 | 205 | C.A. Doxiadis, *Urban Renewal and the Future of the American City*, p. 15. |

| No. | Page | |
|-----|------|---|
| 116 | 206 | N. Kondoleon, "Apollo and the Sanctuary at Delphi" (in Greek), *Proceedings of the First International Humanistic Symposium at Delphi,* September 25 - October 4, 1969, First Volume, Athens, 1970, p. 98. |
| 117 | 206 | Real-Encyclopedie, IV, 1901, 2856-1862 under DEMIOURGOI and Webster's Seventh New Collegiate Dictionary under DE-MIURGE. |
| 118 | 322 | Khalil Gibran, *The Prophet,* William Heinemann, Ltd., London, 1926. |
| 119 | 324 | W.W. Greulich, "Growth of Children of the Same Race under Different Environmental Conditions", SCIENCE, Vol. 127, 7 March 1958, p. 515, fig. 1. |
| 120 | 324 | J.B. Orr, *Food, Health and Income,* Report on a Survey of Adequacy of Diet in Relation to Income, Macmillan and Co., London, 1936, p. 40. |
| 121 | 327 | Stephen A. Richardson, "The Influence of Social-Environmental and Nutritional Factors on Mental Ability" in *Malnutrition, Learning and Behaviour,* edited by N.S. Scrimshaw and J.E. Gordon, MIT Press, Cambridge, Mass., 1968, p. 350, fig. 3. |
| 122 | 327 | E.M. Scott, R. Illsley and A.M. Thomson, "A Psychological Investigation of Primigravidae", Part II, JOURNAL OF OBSTETRICS AND GYNAECOLOGY, No. 63, 1956, p. 340, fig. 1. |
| 123 | 329 | H.G. Birch and J.D. Gussow, *Disadvantaged Children,* Grune & Stratton, New York, 1970, p. 268, fig. 11.1 |
| 124 | 358 | C.A. Doxiadis, *Architectural Space in Ancient Greece,* 1972. |
| 125 | 359 | Ibid. |
| 126 | 363 | Ibid. |

# Index